Migrant Imaginaries

NYU Press gratefully acknowledges the Frederick W. Hilles Publication Fund of Yale University for assisting in the publication of this work.

NATION OF NEWCOMERS

Immigrant History as American History

Matthew Jacobson and Werner Sollors
GENERAL EDITORS

Beyond the Shadow of Camptown: Korean Military Brides in America
Ji-Yeon Yuh

Feeling Italian: The Art of Ethnicity in America
Thomas J. Ferraro

*Constructing Black Selves: Caribbean American Narratives and the
Second Generation*
Lisa D. McGill

Transnational Adoption: A Cultural Economy of Race, Gender, and Kinship
Sara K. Dorow

Immigration and American Popular Culture: An Introduction
Jeffrey Melnick and Rachel Rubin

From Arrival to Incorporation: Migrants to the U.S. in a Global Era
Edited by Elliott R. Barkan, Hasia Diner, and Alan M. Kraut

Migrant Imaginaries: Latino Cultural Politics in the U.S.-Mexico Borderlands
Alicia Schmidt Camacho

ALICIA SCHMIDT CAMACHO

Migrant Imaginaries

Latino Cultural Politics in the
U.S.-Mexico Borderlands

NEW YORK UNIVERSITY PRESS
New York and London

NEW YORK UNIVERSITY PRESS
New York and London
www.nyupress.org

Library of Congress Cataloging-in-Publication Data
Schmidt Camacho, Alicia R.
Migrant imaginaries : Latino cultural politics in the U.S.-Mexico borderlands /
Alicia Schmidt Camacho.
p.   cm. — (Nation of newcomers)
Includes bibliographical references and index.
ISBN-13: 978-0-8147-1648-9 (cl : alk. paper)
ISBN-10: 0-8147-1648-2 (cl : alk. paper)
ISBN-13: 978-0-8147-1649-6 (pb : alk. paper)
ISBN-10: 0-8147-1649-0 (pb : alk. paper)
1. Mexican-American Border Region—Emigration and immigration—History—
20th century. 2. Mexican Americans—Mexican-American Border Region—
Politics and government—20th century. 3. Mexicans—Mexican-American
Border Region—Politics and government—20th century.   I. Title.
F787.S36 2008
304.8'7210730904—dc22   2008009852

New York University Press books are printed on acid-free paper, and their
binding materials are chosen for strength and durability. We strive to use
environmentally responsible suppliers and materials to the greatest extent
possible in publishing our books.

Manufactured in the United States of America

c 10 9 8 7 6 5 4 3 2 1
p 10 9 8 7 6 5 4 3 2 1

En unión con mi familia, dedico este libro a la lucha inmigrante con ganas de alcanzar una nueva realidad transfronteriza de paz y justicia.

CONTENTS

ACKNOWLEDGMENTS

Many people helped write this book. I am indebted to the migrants and activists who partnered my projects while they also redefined the border crossing in ardent struggle. I thank members of Justicia Para Nuestras Hijas, Nuestras Hijas de Regreso a Casa, Casa Amiga, and Las Hormigas de Anapra, in Ciudad Juárez; La Red de Solidaridad con México/Mexico Solidarity Network in Chicago and Washington, DC; El Sindicato de Trabajadores de la Industria y Comércio 6 de Octubre in Tijuana and the Support Committee for Maquiladora Workers in San Diego; and Unidad Latina en Acción and Junta for Progressive Action in New Haven. *Les deseo un futuro de justicia y paz en una nueva realidad transfronteriza.*

I am grateful to Eric Zinner and Emily Park at New York University Press for their invaluable oversight of my work. The insightful commentaries of my three anonymous readers made this a much richer project. Anyone who reads this book should be grateful to David Lobenstine for his brilliance as an editor. I thank David for all the lessons he imparted with such care as we worked together. Despina Papazoglou Gimbel, Andrew Katz, and Ciara McLaughlin also kindly lent their expertise to the publication process. Not only is Matthew Frye Jacobson a favorite guide to the migrant imaginaries that remade American Studies during the years that I worked on this book; he is also the most generous. He is the *richtiker chaifetz*, the true *haimisher mensch.*

I received generous support for my studies and scholarship from the Ford Foundation, Mellon Foundation, Wenner-Gren Foundation, and from the Stanford University Irvine Fellowship. At Yale University, I received faculty research grants from the MacMillan Center for International and Area Studies, which were administered through the Council for Latin American and Iberian Studies and Ethnicity, Race, and Migration. The Frederick W. Hilles Publication Fund was also vital to the book's completion. Charles Long and the Office of the Provost also provided resources and guidance vital to the completion of work. I thank the Ribicoff family for the teaching award named in their beloved daughter's memory.

I am grateful for the sustaining spirit of friends, staff, and faculty who contributed so much to this project. I thank Paulla Ebron, Akhil Gupta, Mary Louise Pratt, and Ramón Saldívar for their exemplary scholarship and teaching. They have been extremely generous with their support and interest in my career. I owe special thanks to Monica Moore for her tireless encouragement and assistance. Al Camarillo was a wonderful mentor through the Irvine Program. I thank him and his family for their warm friendship. Charlene Aguilar and Luis Fraga helped launch my work at the Stanford Center for Chicano Research. Lora Romero nourished my thinking from a first breakfast at Tom's Diner in New York—this work reflects her vibrant teaching. Yvonne Yarbro-Bejarano was an inspiring presence throughout this work. Donald Moore read drafts of this work and helped me reconceptualize the border space. I also thank the mad chicks: Victoria Bomberry, Daniel Contreras, Sung-hee Kim, Renya Ramirez, and Ardel Thomas.

I hold a singular debt to four people who made the final completion of this work possible just when it seemed most impossible: Christopher Geissler, Sara Hudson, and Victorine Shepard, who is a constant friend. Ravit Avni-Singer knows just how much this work owes to her generosity of spirit.

Working at Yale University and living in New Haven have enriched the book immeasurably. I thank my colleagues with special mention to Jean-Christophe Agnew, Jasmina Besirevic-Regan, Jon Butler, Hazel Carby, George Chauncey, Jean Cherniavsky, Brenda Crocker, Elizabeth Dillon, Wai Chee Dimock, Kathryn Dudley, John Mack Faragher, Seth Fein, Matthew Frye Jacobson, Rosalinda García, Paul Gilroy, Ron Gregg, Zareena Grewal, Jonathan Holloway, Gil Joseph, Alice Kustenbauder, Mary Ting Yi Lui, Sanda Lwin, Enrique Mayer, Hope Metcalf, Joanne Meyerowitz, Cheryl Morrison, Alyssa Mt. Pleasant, Alexander Nemerov, Diana Paulin, Patricia Pessar, Nancy Phillips, Matthew Regan, Vicki Schultz, James Scott, Kathy Sulkes, Alexandra Vásquez, Vron Ware, Laura Wexler, Michael Wishnie, Bryan Wolf, and Karianne Yokota. Michael Denning read the manuscript at various stages and gave invaluable guidance in my revisions. For their inspired interventions and thinking I thank the members of my writing group: Elizabeth Alexander, Kellie Jones, and Alondra Nelson. I also thank my colleagues and friends at Trumbull College for their support over the years of this work: Jan Foery, Victor Henrich, Curtis Lee, Peggy Lee, Edd

Ley, Peter Novak, Mary Beth Radigan, and Debbie Rueb. I thank Janet Henrich for her mentorship.

My thanks to the members of the 2005 reading course in Latin American Cultural Studies, black-belt border feminists all three: Gloria Melissa García, Kaysha Corinealdi, and Juan Orrantia. Melissa García enlivened my work by assisting me with a study of human rights and gender in Latin America. The most extraordinary students contributed to this project, including Gloria Alday, Mike Amezcua, Geraldo Cadava, Cecilia Cárdenas-Navia, Eunice Hyunhye Cho, Alexandra Cox, Ana de Santiago Ayón, Noah Dobin-Bernstein, Amina El-Annan, Sushma Gandhi, Adriana García, Paul Grant-Costa, Laura Grappo, Josh Jelly-Shapiro, Priscilla Leiva, Marisol León, Monica Martínez, Angela Naomi Paik, Sandy Placido, Elizabeth Son, Teresa Tapia, Sarahi Uribe, Lee Wang, and Julie Weise.

My work benefits from the exemplary work and collaboration of many friends and scholars at other institutions: Mary Pat Brady, Macrina Cárdenas, Debra Castillo, Ernesto Chávez, Vilashini Cooppan, María Cotera, Ana Dopíco, Jorge Durand, Dionne Espinoza, Rosa Linda Fregoso, David G. Gutiérrez, Michelle Habell-Pallán, Guillermo Irizarry, David Kazanjian, Anne Lambright, Devon Peña, Ana Rosas, María Josefina Saldaña Portillo, Rosaura Sánchez, Blanca Silvestrini, Raúl Villa, and Melissa W. Wright. I owe special thanks to María Soccorro Tabuenca Córdoba and Julia Monárrez for their invitation to be part of the Primer Encuentro de Estudios de la Mujer en la Región El Paso del Norte in 2003. Vicki Ruiz has been a vital champion of the migrant imaginary. Jonathan Fox has been a constant source of vital research materials and conversation. Jill Lane opened new possibilities for pursuing my scholarship in the terrain of performance and human rights. Lisa Lowe is a guiding presence in my work. Fina and David were wonderful interlocutors since our days on York Street. I have never forgotten Marcellus Blount's teaching on poetry, or on *The Odyssey*, for that matter. Finally, I hope that Jean Franco will find a trace of her world-making imagination in this project.

I am very grateful to ASU archivist Christine Marin for her engagement with this project, and to the filmmakers Vicky Funari and Sergio de la Torre for use of the image from Maquilapolis. My thanks to Alma Lopez for the luminous Santa Niña de Mochis who graces the cover of this book.

I offer special thanks to compañeras and compañeros at Junta for Progressive Action, especially Sarahí Almonte, Ana de Santiago, Brett Dignam,

Norma Franceschi, Laura Huizar, and Kica Matos, and Sandra Treviño. Antonio Cid, Olga Emma Cid, John Jairo Lugo, Raúl Rivera, and Fatima Rojas provided important lessons in *otro modo de hacer política*.

I have enjoyed vital friendships with compañeras/os who accompanied me in this work: Graham Boyd, Vilashini Cooppan, Kabir and Rohan; Guillermo Irizarry, Anne Lambright, Corazón, Isis, Paloma, Mobey, and Maya; David Kazanjian and María Josefina Saldaña Portillo; Mary Ting Yi Lui, Vincent Balbarin, Mateo and Octavio; Michael Lynch, Diana Paulin, Michaela and Dominic; Yasmin Haque, Ray Pagliaro-Haque, and Eduardo; Kenyatta Monroe-Sinkler and Rob Sinkler; and Susannah Eldridge.

My parents, María Aurora Camacho de Schmidt and Arthur Schmidt Jr., first schooled me in the migrant imaginary; I write for them. My sister Genevieve has been my *compañera de peregrinaje*. I thank Genevieve and her family, Thomas Quinn and Nayeli and Elena Paz, for finding our own corner of the transnational circuit and for furnishing it so beautifully. Edith and Joseph Pitti made my years of writing much richer and far more meaningful. Gina Marie, Michael, Araceli, and Amalia Friedman Pitti, Catherine, Christian, and Benjamin Esquivel also left their loving imprint on this project. The ethical imaginations of Ana and Joseph Pitti, of Rita and Arthur Schmidt, and of Aurora Elena Gutiérrez de Camacho and José Luis Camacho animated my education and made all things possible.

Stephen Joseph Pitti and I first plotted our future together while staring out at the Pacific Ocean from a beach in Davenport, California. These pages are just one part of all we have lived since then. *Hay tantos caminos por andar.* The dedication of this book is a small gesture before his generosity; I cannot give him what is already his. With Steve, I offer this book with love to our children, Antonio Malik and Thalia María, and to the familia nómada that holds us close even as it moves and grows.

A NOTE ON LANGUAGE

This study engages Spanish- and English-language sources and texts. Its bilingualism reflects the mobility among languages and dialects common to migrants and Latina/o communities in the United States. Non-English words appear without italics or quotation marks—this will allow the two codes to work together, without making Spanish the lesser language in the book.

I have struggled to find terms to describe a changing, transnational population over the course of its tangled history. Terminology reflects the disposition of nation-states toward migrants and other vulnerable social groups. For the purposes of this study, "migrant" refers to those with Mexican citizenship who cross the international boundary into the United States. "Mexican American" indicates people of Mexican descent born in the United States, who have U.S. citizenship. In keeping with current feminist scholarship, I have adopted the combined masculine and feminine ending ("a/o") for Spanish terms. I use "Chicana/o" for Mexican Americans active in the civil-rights movement of 1965–1975, in order to reference their political claims as a racial minority of the United States. The broader population of Latin American origin and descent in the United States are called "Latinas/os." The adjectives "undocumented" and "unauthorized" describe those migrants who lack legal status as immigrants in the United States. Of course, most of the time, the communities I discuss in this work include people from each of these groups.

Introduction

> For all their permeability, the borders
> snaking across the world have never
> been of greater importance. This is the
> dance of history in our age: slow, slow,
> quick, quick, slow, back and forth and
> from side to side, we step across these
> fixed and shifting lines.
> —Salman Rushdie, *Step across*
> *This Line* (2002)[1]

This is a book shaped by struggle, by the efforts of migrant people to assert their full humanity in border crossings that confer on them the status of the alien, the illegal, the refuse of nations. The women, men, and children who traverse the boundary between Mexico and the United States have rarely conformed to the usual trajectory of immigration, of leaving behind one national polity to assume a settled existence as citizens of another. "Nos ha tocado ser gente que no es de aquí ni de allá" [It has been our lot to be people who are neither from here nor from there], lamented Guadalupe Gómez in 2006, expressing the dilemma that has confronted the millions of Mexican migrants since the establishment of modern forms of border policing in 1924.[2] Gómez participated in the massive, immigrant-led protests that swept the country after the House of Representatives passed HR 4437, the Border Protection, Anti-Terrorism, and Illegal Immigration Control Act, in December 2005. Opposing anti-immigrant reforms that would have made even humanitarian assistance to undocumented people a felony, Gómez uttered the common wish of Mexican migrants to defend their autonomy of movement and their bonds of kinship and community across national boundaries: "Ahora

1

seremos gente tanto de aquí como de allá, las dos cosas al mismo tiempo"
[Now we will be people from here and there, both at the same time].[3] Her
assertion defied the unitary logic of citizenship and the state imperative to
police its territory.

At the Mexico-U.S. frontier, the fiction of a regulated border has long
sanctioned the violent conversion of poor, working-class, and exiled peoples into persons without a place. And yet the border is, as Salman Rushdie would have it, both a fixed and shifting line, one that paces the dance,
back and forth, among the undocumented, the refugee, the labor contractor, and the police. "Somos los que venimos a dejar nuestro sudor" [We are
the ones who come to leave our sweat], states Timoteo from Jalisco, describing a political regime that has rendered Latina/o migrants ineligible
for membership to the nation, even as it has accepted their labor.[4] The
criminalization of the migrant has occurred since the nineteenth century
alongside the development of a capitalist economy that actively recruited
laborers from Mexico and Latin America. State officials and labor contractors have long colluded to produce the ideal migrant, the temporary
worker stripped of labor rights and the entitlements of citizenship.

The condition of being "illegal" has meant much more than the lack of
formal rights before the U.S. state, however. Migrants have also contested
their deliberate subjection to forms of racism and class domination that facilitated their removal from the protected spheres of communal belonging
and social life. "These people are not aliens," argued the Guatemalan-born
organizer Luisa Moreno in the 1930s and 1940s, whose denunciation of the
mass deportations of Mexicans, both citizens and noncitizens, rested on
those residents' longstanding claims to the lands of the Southwest. As we
shall see, Moreno and others did more than demand the protection of racialized noncitizens; they have also called for the recognition of the transborder polity that linked Latinas/os in the United States to a broader field
of social, economic, and political affiliations. To deny these relationships
in favor of a limited path to naturalization, Moreno and others warned,
would not only reduce Latinas/os to a laboring caste within the United
States; it would also deform American democracy at its source, its definition of "the people."

Migrants have not only sought incorporation into their places of labor
and settlement in the United States; they also worked to transform their

Freight train departing from the southern border town of Tapachula, Mexico, one of the principal crossing points for Central and South American emigrants heading north to the United States. Photograph by Jerome Sessini, taken August 2005. (Corbis)

countries of origin. While defending their own mobility, they demanded "el derecho de no migrar" [the right not to migrate], issuing indictments of the conditions and policies in Latin America that mandated their departures north. For the leading scholar of Mexican immigration in the 1950s, labor organizer Ernesto Galarza, "migration was a failure of roots."[5] Galarza, like many of his generation, viewed the binational labor loan, the Bracero Program of 1942 to 1964, as a contract-labor system that allowed the state to rank the imperatives of capital accumulation above its obligation to its citizens. Migrants not only troubled the republican ideals of a bounded, regulated population in the United States, Galarza knew; they also threatened to expose the failures of development policies that shaped transborder terrains. Migrants' refusals to conform to the assimilative structures of the nation-state have provoked hostilities in Mexico and the United States over the past hundred years, inciting not only state repression but also vigilante violence and racial terror.

And yet migrants have often espoused a flexible nationalism in their travels that has made them custodians of their hometowns and allowed the Mexican state to retain a claim on their earnings. As for roots, this study contends that most Mexican migrants experience displacements from home, kin, language, and labor long before undertaking the border crossing. Their mobility across the national boundary has often corresponded to an itinerant existence through places of work and residency in Mexico that preceded their arrival in the North. But migrants have been equally capable of a rooted existence, and their lack of legal status in the United States has not necessarily corresponded to a lack of social integration. Mexican migrants have long sustained transnational households while also pursuing education, religion, and political organization—in short, all the markers of civic life—in the United States.

Against the charge of criminal trespass, migrants have been impatient to show their full integration into the fabric of U.S. national life, not only in the spheres of labor and economics but also in the terrain of culture. *Migrant Imaginaries* traces the historical forms of migrant expression and cultural politics in the transnational labor circuit linking Mexico and the United States. My study highlights the complex and often conflicted relationships between Mexican migrants and Mexican Americans as they pursued civil rights and cultural autonomy in the United States, documenting the cultural and social practices that sustained labor and social movements over the twentieth century. This interdisciplinary work delineates the fragile agency of migrants and the racialized ethnic community, whose mobility and cultural formation cannot conform to the trajectory of immigration. Transborder communities of Mexican nationals, migrants, and Mexican Americans have continually exposed the limits of state formation for both the United States and Mexico. Their provocation of national sovereignty provides a different departure point for social theory, one that addresses the entwined processes of racial, gender, and class subjection, territorial displacement, and agency from the vantage point of the displaced, rather than that of the rights-bearing citizen. Bearing their distinctive historical formation as a group for whom the journey north is both a journey away from national belonging and a recovery of lost Mexican territories, Mexican border crossers have long been, in the words of Arturo Islas, "migrant, not immigrant souls."[6]

Migrant Imaginaries

I use the term *migrant imaginaries* to encompass the world-making aspirations of Mexican border crossers, whose mobility changed the character of both U.S. and Mexican national life over the twentieth century. The migrant in this study not only connotes one who moves within and across national boundaries; it also references a subordinate position with respect to that of the citizen. The transnational refers to the space in which distinct national localities are linked together by migratory flows, and the diaspora formed by this migration. The transnational may also stand in opposition to the bounded community of the nation-state. As migrants narrate a condition of alterity to, or exclusion from, the nation, they also enunciate a collective desire for a different order of space and belonging across the boundary. Their narratives imaginatively produce forms of communal life and political organization in keeping with their fragile agency as mobile people. Migrant social movements define justice in terms that surpass the sovereignty of nations or the logic of capital accumulation, just as their struggles revive the repudiated body of the migrant as the agent of ethical survival.

My inquiry into the imaginative life of Mexican migrants derives in part from the work of Cornelius Castoriadis, who introduced the concept of the social imaginary into political philosophy as a corrective to the economic determinism of Marxist thought.[7] The imaginary represents a symbolic field in which people come to understand and describe their social being.[8] Castoriadis argued that social relations must first be imagined by subjects in order to be comprehended and acted on. This means that the repertory of symbolic representation and practices that constitute cultural life may exert material force in the everyday existence of a people. Thus, for Dilip Parameshwar Gaonkar, social imaginaries are "ways of understanding the social that become social entities themselves, mediating collective life."[9] Cultural forms are not a reflection of the social, or merely a detached "set of ideas," but rather the means by which subjects work through their connections to a larger totality and communicate a sense of relatedness to a particular time, place, and condition.[10]

In most social theory, the nation offers the preeminent example of the "imagined community," representing the foremost expression of peoplehood.[11] Modern concepts of political rights, ethnicity, and governance all reinforce the primacy of nationality in the social realm.[12] And yet the worldwide movement of populations—as refugees, immigrants, and guest workers—continued to rise in the later decades of the twentieth century, with no sign of abating. Responding to conditions of voluntary or coerced departure, migrants create new imaginative worlds out of their trajectories of loss and displacement. These social imaginaries traverse geopolitical space with little regard for national authority over territory or culture —even as the precarious status of migrants also renders their claims to place and rights invisible or, worse, vulnerable to violent repression in the polities where they settle. Despite the increasing integration of national economies, culture industries, and communications media, human rights —and in particular, the entitlement of movement—remain firmly embedded within the purview of nation-states. Migrant imaginaries, as articulated by subaltern groups, rarely break into the closed domain of national sovereignty. The noncitizen may not vote, own property, or determine the political status of his or her children. In this way, the nation-state most often segregates migrant imaginaries from those of the nation—hence the symbolic and material importance of English-only initiatives in the United States, to maintain an absolute divide between the noncitizen alien in the realm of culture, as in the realm of political rights.

The experience of displacement intensifies migrant desire and exaggerates the demands of memory. The traumatic separation from home makes narrative a vital instrument for staving off further loss. Chicana/o literature has been an imaginative space for reckoning with the wounding divisions that the geopolitical border imposed on transborder communities. The plurality of languages and forms that distinguishes Chicana/o narrative from Mexican and U.S. national literatures reflects the complex interactions among the distinct imaginaries of Mexican migrants and ethnic Mexicans in the United States. Chicana/o narratives challenge the official imaginary of the nation, because the experience of displacement and exploitation have often endowed transborder communities with vernaculars, ideologies, and values that set them in a category apart from sedentary communities of citizens. Tomás Rivera's celebrated novel *Y no se lo tragó la tierra* [And the Earth Did Not Swallow Him] (1971) renders the collective desire of migrant farmworkers in a South Texas town for relief from the burdens of poverty and social isolation during the late 1940s and early

1950s.[13] Rivera relates a young boy's growing awareness of his people's condition in a series of vignettes voiced by unnamed interlocutors who interrupt the protagonist's stream-of-consciousness narrative. The orality of the text is meant to reveal how the migrants come to understand and act on their situation. The brilliance of the novel comes in its faithful depiction of the imaginative process itself and the importance of that process to the boy's survival as an ethical agent. In this way, *Tierra* introduces one central thesis of *Migrant Imaginaries*—that the migrant presence would indelibly mark ethnic Mexicans in opposition to the ideal citizen-subject of the U.S. nation.

Tomás Rivera recounted writing *Tierra* as a "document" of the farmworker struggle of the 1940s, "but giving it some kind of spiritual strength, or spiritual history."[14] Rivera's poetic, multivoiced text recalls Antonio Gramsci's dictum that subaltern history is necessarily "fragmentary and episodic" in form.[15] Interspersed within the story of the boy's lost year are moments when the Mexican American migrants refuse, or fail, to incorporate themselves into the settled order of national life. A young mother afflicted with agoraphobia is arrested for shoplifting when overcome by terror at the local chain store; farmworkers are unsure of their route to harvesting jobs in unknown corners of the United States; and the boy himself lacks "a sense of his geographical space or real time" in his ruminations over deprivations suffered in the fields.[16] In one scene, farmworkers hire the local priest to bless their cars before their departure for the seasonal harvest to the north:

Antes de que la gente se fuera para el norte, el cura les bendecía los carros y las trocas a cinco dólares el mueble. Una vez hizo lo suficiente para ir a visitar a sus padres y a sus amigos a Barcelona en España. Le trajo a la gente el agradecimiento de su familia y unas tarjetas de una iglesia muy moderna. Estas loas puso al entrar a la iglesia para que vieran y anhelaran una iglesia así. Al poco tiempo empezaron a aparecer palabras en las tarjetas, luego cruces, rayas y con safos así como había pasado con las bancas nuevas. El cura nunca pudo comprender el sacrilegio.

[Before people left for up north the priest would bless their cars and trucks at five dollars each. One time he made enough money to take a trip to Barcelona, in Spain, to visit his parents and friends. He brought

back words of gratitude from his family and some postcards of a very
modern church. These he placed by the entrance of the church for the
people to see, that they may desire a church such as that one. It wasn't
long before words began to appear on the cards, then crosses, lines, and
con safos symbols, just as had happened to the new church pews. The
priest was never able to understand such sacrilege.][17]

The blessing of the cars only anticipates the hardship that awaits them at
the migrant camps, where Mexicans were commonly treated as disposable
workers. The farmworkers show no interest in the church building but,
rather, desire the more intimate blessing of their travels. The farmworkers, after all, cannot easily accumulate goods, since their very movement
disrupts the logic of their possession. The "spiritual strength" that Rivera
records in the minute articles affixed to the postcards and church pews
are not simply articulations of faith but enunciations of presence against
erasure. Their small statements of self-possession, "con safos," resist the
dehumanizing effects of their labor.

The Spanish priest's bewilderment at his flock's lack of respect for the
church reflects how migrant imaginaries may deviate from those of sedentary citizens. He represents a benevolent authority who can only conceive
of the improvement of migrants' condition by conversion, that is, in the replacement of their most intimate wishes—the milagritos—with the appropriate object of worship, the shining church structure.[18] The verb "anhelar"
of the original Spanish text combines a sense of desire and lack together:
the priest admonishes his parishioners "para que vieran y anhelaran una
iglesia así" [so they would see and desire a church such as that one]. That
is, his postcards represent an effort to impose on the migrants a sense of
their own deprivation and need for reform. Hence the priest's anger at his
parishioners' faith practices.

Rather than conceive of the migrants' refusal of conversion as a failure,
as the priest does, Rivera's novel invites us to identify with their subversion. Out of these reassertions of folk culture, other more explicitly political
acts of insubordination may emerge. The quiet insistence with which the
migrants in *Tierra* refuse the priest's censure against marking the church
thus becomes meaningful as an expression of what James Scott has called
"the work of negation," the ways that the powerless find to contest their
domination.[19] Scott's phrase is particularly apt, since it combines both a

sense of the condensation of oppositional energies contained in the migrants' articulations of stubborn faith and their conscious labors of survival within the narrow spaces of action available to them.

In depicting the social worlds of migrants, Rivera and the other protagonists of this study compel us to ask what forms of political subjectivity resist subordination to the nation-state. Mexican and Mexican American cultural politics have emerged from imaginaries shaped by the experience of laboring for the nation without the promise of inclusion into its community as the bearers of rights. *Migrant Imaginaries* argues that the particular formation of Mexicans as a transborder laboring class forced migrants to articulate expansive definitions of civic life and community that defied conventions of national citizenship in both Mexico and the United States. By narrating the histories of conquest, labor exploitation, and racial terror, migrant social movements have sought to secure a precarious space of collective agency autonomous from either nation-state. In turn, they have enlarged the field of political opposition and cultural expression for the ethnic Mexican communities with which they shared bonds of kinship, language, and cultural affinity.

The discourses of transborder social movements anticipate the problem posed by Etienne Balibar: "for whom does the nation-state fail in its promise as the 'ultimate form' of political institution?"[20] The historical racialization of Mexican migrants as temporary workers ineligible for naturalization determined their efforts to acquire rights and complicated Mexican American pursuits of substantive citizenship in the United States. The fortunes of social movements for civil and labor rights rose and fell according to the capacity of leaders to address the migrant presence within their communities. This was not a matter of declaring cross-border unity, *sin fronteras*, but of recognizing the costs that the border inflicts on the full plurality of migrants and fronterizas/os subjected to its regulatory force.

Taking on the Nation Form

As migrant workers and as a racialized ethnic group, Mexican migrants have played a constitutive role in processes of national formation for both Mexico and the United States. They have often found that state institutions were inadequate to the task of recognizing and protecting their rights in either country. As the geopolitical border separated kin, class, and ethnic communities, Mexican migrants and Mexican Americans confronted state boundaries that defined peoplehood and communal rights. Official nationalisms depicted Mexican migrants and Mexican Americans as failed national subjects or belated arrivals to the nation. In Mexico, emigrants represented a troubling reminder of the country's dependency on its powerful neighbor and therefore posed a threat to U.S. national sovereignty. During and after the Mexican Revolution of 1910, as leaders in the country articulated nationalist visions that linked tradition and modernity, emigration created forms of transnational traffic that threatened that very nationalism. While some Mexicans justified temporary emigration as an act of nation-building, many officials in the United States emphasized that differences in language, culture, and ethnicity made Mexicans a threat to national unity. Mexicans, according to U.S. national lore, had lost the Southwestern territories in 1848 because of their innate inferiority to Anglo-American society.

For their part, migrant Mexicans arrived in the U.S. territory that had once been Mexico with few protections from the national institutions of either country. Migrant efforts at self-defense exposed the incompleteness and inherent limitations of national formation at the Mexico-U.S. border. When they emphasized transborder solidarity, Mexican migrants and Mexican Americans refuted the supremacy of national sovereignty over nonstate claims to rights. Their demands reflected a political vision formed from a belated relationship to nationalization. Many migrants knew intuitively what historian Adolfo Gilly has argued, that "the development of capitalism lost Mexico half its territory" and that this loss produced a subaltern laboring class with little purchase on citizenship.[21]

This study contends that for much of the twentieth century, Mexican migrants exposed the limits of the nation form—meaning its instruments of governance and its structures of legitimation. Transnational economic and political integration has placed the border region in a tense relationship to the nation-state. The transborder region is best understood as a social form distinct from that of the nation, a form that is alternately a place of exception from the nation and subject to its domination. While their projects of financial investment, commerce, and political partnership traversed the national boundary, the two countries rarely acknowledged the consequences of binational integration for migrants and ethnic Mexicans in the United States. The particular nature of capitalist development at the U.S.-Mexican border worked against the full nationalization of the poorest laboring classes in the region.

In the United States, employers and government officials have been quick to capitalize on the weak nationalization of the Mexican working classes. Historian David G. Gutiérrez quotes Colorado congressman Ralph Taylor in 1930:

> It is not at all like we were importing inhabitants of a foreign country. We understood each other. They have no influence whatever on our habits of life or form of civilization. They simply want to work. . . . Generally speaking they are not immigrants at all. They do not try to buy or colonize our land, and they hope some day to own a piece of land in their home country.[22]

The western congressman depicted Mexicans as neither fully alien nor prone to settle in the United States, as people whose desire to work separated them from both U.S. citizens and other immigrants. His remarks echoed the Supreme Court's findings in the Insular Cases of the early 1900s, when the justices deemed the native populations of "unincorporated territories" like Puerto Rico and the Philippines "foreign in a domestic sense."[23] These racialized populations were under the sway of U.S. hegemony, but the imperial state granted them provisional U.S. nationality without the full rights of citizenship. Taylor's remarks invoked, perhaps unconsciously, the neocolonial formation of the southwestern United States that made it reflexive for him to imagine that Mexicans held no hopes of permanent settlement in lands that merely decades before had belonged to their home country. Taylor's remarks illustrate the disqualification of ethnic Mexicans and Mexican migrants as either citizens or immigrants: Taylor and his associates never imagined their workers as members of their own national community. Mexicans could not be "immigrants" because the immigrant is on a path to citizenship, and for Taylor and his colleagues, the utility of Mexican laborers derived from their exclusion from naturalization.

Mexicans were, nevertheless, members of southwestern society—as the House Committee on Immigration recognized in 1930, the U.S. economy could not subsist without their abundant presence in the labor force. Their exclusion from the spheres of citizenship and national belonging, then, was a constitutive fiction of U.S. national formation, a fiction that revealed the constructed nature of the nation-state itself. The congressional debates in the 1920s and '30s over the Mexican presence thus helped produce U.S. national society in its imperial cast, as the white landowning class laid claim to Mexican labor through the apparatus of restrictive immigration law and the civil apparatus of legal and de facto segregation. Even so, Taylor and his confederates were perhaps correct in one sense, that proletarian Mexicans did not easily identify themselves as part of the "people" that U.S. nationalism produced. Its state was not their own.

In the parlance of the nation-state, migrants are either failed citizens or belated arrivals to the national community, no matter what causes their mobility across national boundaries. Etienne Balibar takes up the concept of belatedness to ask, "*For whom today is it too late?* In other words, which are the social formations which . . . can no longer completely affect their transformation into nations, except in the purely juridical sense and at the cost of interminable conflicts that produce no decisive result?"[24] Migrants and other border Mexicans have in fact resisted and exploited their interpellation as nonnational subjects. At times they refused the state's monopoly on subject formation, remaining loyal to the other social formations that contravened against their nationalization as proper citizens.

For migrants, the defense of rights has entailed a renewed search for form—for a politics that might carry forward their desires for justice and preserve the integrity of their communities across the border. The demand for a different framework of governance doubles as a search for political and aesthetic forms that can perform the work of representation in all its senses. This study examines the cultural productions that emerged from the transborder migratory circuit, to see how their enunciations of the distinct historical consciousness of migrant subjects opposed or modified the assimilative narratives of Mexican and U.S. nationalism. The migrant imaginaries encoded in song, manifestoes, poetry, novels, and testimonials preserve both a repertory of practices for collective action and a social map of the vast terrain covered by border crossers. This is hardly a coherent or unified field of representation; rather, the often discordant modes of representation covered in this book suggest that the migrant most often embodies a melancholic condition, rather than one of simple autonomy from the strictures of national citizenship.

El Norte es como el mar

Because of that melancholic condition, it is only fitting to begin my account of the migrant experience with the testimony of one who failed in the border crossing. By his own account to Mexican immigration scholars in 1992, Aurelio, a native of Ameca, Jalisco, made the attempt to cross the border dozens of times, only to be stranded by smugglers, detained by border police, deported, and left with insufficient resources to complete the trip:

> El Norte es como el mar. Prefiero pensar que nunca fuí a Estados Unidos, y cuando escucho hablar de aquel país, muy pronto me acuerdo del mar; he ido al mar, pero nunca me han dado ganas de bañarme, ni de comer ahí siquiera, por eso pienso cuando uno va de ilegal, pues va de cola o basura, yo me imaginé como el mar que toda la basura la arroja afuera, dije, a lo major aquí también estoy en el mar y entonces me está arrojando pa'fuera cada rato.

> [The North is like the sea. I prefer to think that I never went to the United States, and when I hear people speak of that country, I remember the ocean; I have been to the sea, but I have never wanted to bathe, or even eat there, so that's why I think that when one goes as an illegal, one goes as the tail or the garbage, I imagined that it was like the ocean, which throws the trash out, I told myself, maybe here is also like the sea, and it is tossing me out every now and then.][25]

The incompleteness of Aurelio's journey makes him no less a part of what I am calling the migrant imaginary; his humiliations grant him a privileged vantage point from which to judge the cruelty of the passage. "El Norte es como el mar" [The North is like the sea], he tells us, conjuring the expansive divide that the territorial boundary inscribes between the wealth of the United States, its promise of opportunity, and the life of itinerant labor he knows in rural Jalisco. Aurelio refuses to incorporate his failed crossings into his narrative of self: "prefiero pensar que nunca fuí a Estados Unidos" [I prefer to think that I never went to the United States]. And yet the North looms large in his self-definition as a wage earner and as a man. If, as Jorge Durand writes, the migrant sojourn has been a rite of passage for men in villages like Ameca for generations, then Aurelio's repeated expulsions mark a failed interpellation in either polity.[26] Even so, Aurelio uses the experience to chart a different sense of his self-worth, as he asserts that he will not live the life of the illegal in the United States.

The ocean that could figure freedom and adventure serves Aurelio as a metaphor for an overpowering force that threatens the migrant with the annihilation of his personal agency. Aurelio depicts the undocumented alternately as the tail end of an animal or as refuse, images that conjure the loss of motive will and self-mastery in the border crossing. His narrative neatly inverts the common depiction of Mexican migration as a unidirectional wave or as an unwelcome deluge of the border boundary. The would-be migrant experiences his failure as rejection, of having been treated like garbage by the northern society that would not admit him. His testimony reflects the interpellating force of the migratory circuit even for those who remain behind. Aurelio reconciles himself in terms that repudiate the seductions of dollar wages and U.S. cultural dominance:

> Todas las frustraciones y fracasos me hicieron arraigarme más en mi tierra, me hicieron reflexionar que aquí nunca me ha faltado el trabajo, y que no soy el único al que no le alcanza para comer ni para vestir, entonces que ando haciendo por allá . . .

> [All these frustrations and failure made me more rooted in my homeland, they made me reflect that here I have never lacked work, and that I am not the only one who doesn't earn enough to feed or clothe myself, so what would I be doing over there . . .][27]

Aurelio recovers a sense of place and his own masculine agency by differentiating himself from the migrant stream. His narration marks a fixed divide between North and South, as the oceanic expanse of the United States becomes "that country" in an act of symbolic reduction that contains its dominating presence. Along with his recovery of "roots," Aurelio must also reckon with losing the means to satisfy his material hungers. But by understanding that he is "not the only one," he opens the space for a new collective struggle for better living conditions. By mastering his hunger, he regains his sense of self, which he imagines he would have lost in the migrant passage. He can do without the food or clothes that dollars would buy him: "nunca me han dado ganas de bañarme, ni comer ahí siquiera" [I have never wanted to bathe, or even eat there].

Aurelio's narrative enacts the struggle to retain a sense of social agency amid the oceanic forces that uproot migrants and place them at the mercy of the transborder labor market and its racial caste system. If Aurelio defends his right against his conversion into "basura" by remaining in Mexico, he nevertheless remains connected to the migratory circuit as a member of a village completely embedded within the seasonal demands for Mexican workers. His narrative is instructive for the ways it plots the quotidian struggles over the place and status of Mexicans in the transborder economy, both as laboring bodies and as subjects of rights.

Like other displaced peoples, Mexican migrants like Aurelio occupy a space between rights and rightlessness, between belonging and alienation, as they work and move through the transnational circuit. The Mexican migrants described in this book continually invented forms of agency from within this space of opposition and displacement.

My account of the migrant presence in the United States speaks of social imaginaries in the plural, since there has been no single framework for contending with the diversity of Mexican border crossings. *Migrant Imaginaries* casts a wide net, examining a range of oral, literary, and visual texts, as it traces Mexican migrant and Mexican American pursuits of cultural autonomy and political rights during the twentieth century. This inquiry is decidedly historical, looking at the different transitional moments in the forms of labor, migration, and subject formation that determined the Mexican presence in the United States since 1910. The textual analysis addresses how artists, political figures, laborers, and writers engaged with the problem of representing the subjectivity of the noncitizen.

The first part of the book, "Border Crossers in Mexican American Cultural Politics," assesses how noncitizens and transborder mobility have figured in the divergent imaginaries of Mexican migrants and ethnic Mexicans in the United States. These five chapters discuss the writings of Lorna Dee Cervantes, Ernesto Galarza, Luisa Moreno, Américo Paredes, and Richard Rodriguez, among others, in relation to a range of musical, visual, and political texts. Here I examine how advocates for Latina/o civil and labor rights have had to contend with the particular status of migrants as a criminalized and racialized class within the nation. Divisions that the border imposed on transborder communities also appear in the literary and political forms of expression linked to Mexican American mobilizations for civil rights. This part offers new approaches to a range of literary texts and historical struggles, highlighting how migrant and gender difference both disrupted and sometimes expanded the field of Mexican American cultural politics.

The second part, "Border Crossings: Frontiers of New Social Conflict," examines the vast transformations in the border region and the transnational migratory circuit during the last decades of the twentieth century. These chapters depart from the thematic concerns of the first part, looking at Mexican migrants, and especially Mexican women, from a more global perspective. The unprecedented mobility of money, goods, and people made the Mexico-U.S. border a paradigmatic site of new forms of governance linked to global capitalist integration. Chapter 6 examines the recruitment and promotion of third-world women as the ideal labor force for the new international division of labor that emerged in the 1970s. My analysis draws on the testimonial literature of women workers in border factories, theoretical works by Chicana feminists, and women's border writings to discuss women's agency in relation to transnational capitalism. The final chapter attends to an emergent narrative of migrant sorrows, at the onset of a new century, one that expresses the melancholic condition linked to the devastating effects of neoliberal policies and border militarization on the migrant communities that span both countries.

Migrant testimonials belong to a submerged history of migrant struggle, one that has yet to dispel the primacy of the nation over other forms of political community. Raymond Ileto has written in the context of the Philippines—another country bound to the United States by emigration— that new histories must emerge to contest the ideologies of development and nationhood that currently legitimate the power of nation-states. "This history," Ileto argues, "should throw into focus a whole range of phenomena that has been discredited or denied. . . . it should give equal status to interruptions, repetitions, and reversals, uncovering the subjugations, confrontations, power struggles and resistances that linear history tends to conceal."[28] The migrant cartography that we have come to call the transnational is a directive to consider distinct narratives of social being otherwise obscured by national histories. These narratives only rarely puncture dominant discourses of national progress. When they do, migrant narratives speak for a new order of citizenship and shared interest, an order that follows from the struggles of people who move. It is their world-making imaginaries that animate this book.

PART I

Border Crossers in Mexican American Cultural Politics

Detention center in Tapachula, Mexico. A ten-year-old Guatemalan boy awaits his deportation hearing in a cell with other minors. Photograph by Jerome Sessini, 2005. (Corbis)

CHAPTER 1

These People Are Not Aliens

Transborder Solidarity in the Shadow of Deportation

> In desperation, we moved to Fort Worth, Texas. There my father worked as a laborer for the Atchison, Topeka and Santa Fe Railroad Company. Discontented, we continued to migrate as enganchados [hooked ones][1] contracted as stoop-laborers. We traveled north by train and were fed balogna sandwiches on the entire trip. We worked in the sugar beet fields of Augusta, Minnesota. Accidentally, my sister slit her thumb with a machete used to cut the green tops from the beets. The children suffered and felt adverse to change.
>
> —Juanita Vásquez, "Kidnapped" (1987)[2]

By the time Juanita Vásquez and her family boarded the train to begin their movement north as itinerant workers in the 1920s, the migratory circuit linking Mexico and the United States was well entrenched. Both countries relied on the transnational movement of Mexican workers, contracted into a labor force composed of both Mexican Americans and Mexican nationals. Emigration reached a new peak during the Mexican Revolution (1910–1920), but thousands of migrants had established patterns of seasonal and long-term settlements across the southwestern United States from the 1890s onward. Historians estimate that 1.5 million Mexicans entered the United States during the four decades leading up to the Great Depression, drawn to employment in agriculture, mining, railroads, and domestic work.[3] The Mexicans who laid track, harvested sugar beets, and stoked furnaces in midwestern steel mills followed the rails to a variety of industrial, craft, and agricultural occupations. Although U.S. employers tended to depict Mexicans as unskilled workers, new to capitalist routines, most migrants who arrived in the United States had already weathered the profound upheavals of the capitalist expansion in their native country.[4] By 1910, notes historian Devra Weber, "over nine and a half million people, 96 percent of Mexican families, were landless," having been displaced from traditional trades and subsistence farming under the dictatorship of Porfirio Díaz (1876–1910).[5] A decade later, their migrations north more than doubled the size of the Mexican-born population in the United States, which numbered nearly half a million people in the 1920s.[6]

Extreme economic hardship and political turmoil exposed migrants to a fleeting existence of arrivals and departures, in which illness, injury, and broken contracts commonly dictated survival. Juanita Vásquez recalled with a child's memory the rhythms of the train that schooled her in the tedium of hunger (bologna sandwiches) and nomadism (Michoacán, Texas, Minnesota, Illinois). Despite her age, her earning capacity proved critical. For migrants, the family wage system played a prominent part in shaping community life and political organization in these years.[7] Vásquez worked alongside tens of thousands of other Mexican men, women, and children who traded their strength and creativity for meager wages. These laborers created political and cultural ties that sustained communities across the international boundary; they struggled to preserve communal and familial bonds through their everyday acts of endurance and their vernacular expression.

Migrant testimonials and songs expressed the indelible experience of converting one's body into a salable resource and the social estrangement wrought by the arduous journey north. In 1926, the Mexican anthropologist Manuel Gamio recorded the migrant corrido [ballad] "El Ferrocarril" at one of the migrant labor camps he visited while studying Mexican emigration to the United States. The song resonated with the communal loss of able-bodied workers to the migrant labor circuit:

La máquina pasajera	[The departing engine
no puede hacer cosa buena	can't do any good
porque oscurece en su casa	because at dusk it is at home
y amanece en tierra ajena	and awakes at dawn in a strange country

Oigan y oigan	Listen, listen
el ferrocarril bramar	to the train bellow
es que lleva a los hombres	it carries men away
y nunca los vuelva a traer.	And never brings them back.][8]

Migrant corridos evoked the relentless cadence of the rumbling engine as a metaphor for the rapacious demands of capitalist industries; like the train, endless work consumed Mexican bodies, with little promise for their return. Just as the train removed them from the national body, migrants experienced the material deprivations and rigor of work as an evacuation or destruction of their own bodily agency.

Racial terror was also a prominent feature of the migrant labor circuit. In 1916, Arnulfo Vásquez sent for his family from Cleburne, Texas, in the hopes of escaping the tumult of the Revolution in their native Parucho, Michoacán. His daughter formed her first childhood memories in the sun-blistered cotton fields of Venus, where she helped her parents and brothers fill countless white canvas sacks for meager wages. In her oral history, "Kidnapped," delivered in 1987, Juanita Vásquez vividly recalled the events that pushed her family north from its relatively settled life in the cotton fields of Venus, Texas:

The entire family worked picking cotton. The kind owner of the farm, Mr. John C. Kimble, made my father the paymaster, for he noticed that my dad was quick with figures and was very trust worthy. Eventually, the owner appointed him foreman of the entire farm. All the children happily attended Hines School. Enviously, the biased Anglo workers and near-by farmers protested and asked my father to leave, but he ignored the warning. Several days later he was kidnapped by a group of men led by a gasoline station owner. At dusk, my mother was frantic, and she hid all her children in different places of the house. I was tiny and could fit almost anywhere, so she pushed me under the sewing machine. Soon, the pedals started swaying back and forth . . . and out I rolled. I was not far from the front door. I heard loud shouts, and one man angrily shouted, "Next time it will be your children!" I saw the men toss a white heavy sack out of the car. Shots followed aimed at the front screened door. My mother screamed and ran to my father in the sack. She saw he was horribly beaten. The car took off with great speed. This was an intimidating reason to leave.[9]

Her father's punishment for transgressing the racial division of labor was to be beaten and disposed of in the same cotton sack that he labored to fill. The message was clear: Mexicans had no social value beyond their productive capacity in the racialized economy of stoop labor. The vigilante threat to seize the children expressed the lengths that white society would take to restrict the boundaries of national community in the border region, by denying Mexican migrants any future in the towns where they labored. Having enjoyed a brief respite from the rigors of itinerant labor ("All the children happily attended Hines School"), the Vásquez family returned to the migratory circuit. Their expulsion from settled life (stable work, home, school) marked the Vásquez family as a different order of immigrant, racially barred from naturalization as U.S. citizens. The racial barrier imposed a punishing routine of arrivals and departures that kept the children out of that primary institution of citizenship, the public school: "The children suffered and felt adverse to change." Mexicans like the Vásquezes crossed the border as migrants and not as immigrants—a difference that defined their claims for civil and labor rights in the United States thereafter.

This chapter examines the contradictory ways that Mexicans and Mexican Americans contested their exploitation in the transborder labor circuit of the 1920s and '30s. If their subordinated class, immigration, and racial status rendered Mexicans vulnerable to exploitation, it often made them willing to fight back. Migrants and Mexican Americans struggled against the miseries of crowded, unsanitary labor camps, they organized against police abuses, and they struck against wage differentials that favored whites. Whether they acted out of indignation, desperation, or in accordance with ideological commitments, Mexicans retained the lessons of survival and self-defense acquired in their native country. Migrants established social networks and mutual-aid organizations that allowed them to adapt to the migratory circuit but that also formed the basis for collective organizing and opposition. Given their isolation, migrants had few political resources or claims to state protection in either country, but their particular status as a transborder proletariat led them to devise new ways of exercising rights within the racial and class structure of the migrant labor stream. During the Great Depression, Mexicans and Mexican Americans sought a political framework for exercising rights within the border region as they responded to the mass deportations, racial hostilities, and brutal labor repression that established patterns for Mexican migration and U.S. responses for decades to come.[10]

This chapter argues that, in the spheres of culture, as in the domain of politics, the migrant presence forced the Mexican population as a whole to confront its subordination in the United States. Throughout the 1930s, Mexican migrants engaged in dramatic conflicts over labor exploitation and civil-rights abuses in ways that elided the limits of national citizenship and state sovereignty. The diverse strikes, political campaigns, and civil-rights movements redefined what it meant to be Mexican in the United States. So, too, the growing presence of proletarian migrants remade the Mexican American barrios of the border, leading to conflicts between citizens and noncitizens but also to new aspirations to greater cultural integrity and advancement as a single México sin fronteras. The migrant presence, for better and for worse, impelled Mexican Americans to demand their citizenship rights and social inclusion in the United States, just as it gave rise to new articulations of a cross-border nationalism, if not always class based, then certainly rooted in the culture of laboring.

By the 1930s, I argue, in the wake of new immigration policing and the mass deportations that followed, a new generation of Mexican American and immigrant activists and writers questioned the primacy of national sovereignty over the historical claims of Mexican people to the border territories. Out of their histories of border insurrection and racial terror, these intellectuals elaborated visions of a "Greater Mexico" that superseded the national boundary.[11] Their aspirations, recorded in various literary and performance texts, help us to determine how Mexicans contended with their uneasy juridical status as migrants or descendants of the original settlers of territories ceded to the United States in the U.S.-Mexican War. Many migrants and Mexican Americans saw the history of Mexican border communities as markedly distinct from—indeed, antagonistic to—the sovereignty of the U.S. government. The various critiques of official nationalism voiced in song and in oral and literary culture pointed to the insurgent potential contained in the Mexican and Mexican American working class. Radical unionists and civil-rights advocates hoped that the force of this insurgency might surpass the political divide that the U.S.-Mexican border imposed on Mexican communities.

My discussion of this period examines how migrants and Mexican Americans opposed official U.S. and Mexican nationalisms in the terrain of expressive culture and political discourse. I begin this interdisciplinary inquiry with migrant songs from the 1920s to show how the laboring population experienced and contested the forms of class racism that shaped the transborder market in Mexican bodies. Migrant aspirations achieved radical expression in cross-border campaigns against mass deportation. Luisa Moreno's address before the American Committee for the Protection of the Foreign Born in 1940 stands as the most expansive vision for migrant and labor rights in any period of Latina/o militancy before or since. I conclude by discussing Américo Paredes's 1935 poem "The Mexico-Texan" in relation to Emma Tenayuca and Homer Brooks's revision of communist theories of nationalism and colonialism.

As artists and activists sought to push beyond the limits of the nation form, their struggles gave rise to a ferment of aesthetic and cultural innovation. By retrieving the suppressed histories of border peoples, Mexican and Mexican American authors revealed that the nation is itself a kind of narrative. As a *narrative*, the story of the nation could be changed so that new subjects could enter the terrain of politics and culture as historical agents.

The Migratory Circuit

Beginning in the 1890s, masses of Mexican migrants joined Filipinas/os, African Americans, Latinas/os, and poor whites in the mobile labor stream that serviced the rapacious growth of the U.S. economy. These Mexican laborers filled a void left by the prohibition on Asian immigration to the United States; labor contractors sought an abundant supply of low-wage workers to feed the demand of large-scale industry and agriculture.[12] The growing numbers of Mexicans—combined with their vulnerable position in the United States—made them ideal for employers seeking a tractable workforce that could be recruited for employment and disposed of when no longer useful. Labor contractors saw the proximity of Mexico as a means to regulate the labor supply, and the racial perception of Mexicans as foreigners made it easy for employers to treat them as a temporary workforce, whatever their actual claim to residency in the United States. Employers created a labor surplus to undercut workers' capacity to organize, using the threat of deportation as an instrument of labor discipline.

The migratory circuit linked new migrants with Mexican Americans, who experienced the rigors of legal and de facto segregation as a devalued caste with little claim to rights as members of the U.S. polity. "Mexican" became a racial term that addressed citizen and foreign-born people alike, connoting a class of persons with little social value beyond their laboring capacity. White supremacy and U.S. nativism made Mexicans, in Carlos Vélez-Ibañez's memorable phrase, "not only strangers in their own lands, but strangers to themselves."[13]

The racialized "peons" of southwestern industries and agriculture posed significant challenges to liberal discourses of nation at a time when nationality meant residence in one place, fluency in the official language, and membership to an ethnically defined people. Neither the postrevolutionary Mexican government nor the architects of the U.S. New Deal adequately addressed the disfranchisement of Mexican migrants. The continued instability of the Mexican state and its failed land-reform policies left the government relatively indifferent to the fortunes of el México de afuera [Mexico abroad]. Because of the country's reliance on foreign investment and migrant earnings, Mexican consuls and State Department officials often colluded with U.S. employers and government officials in repressing migrant revolt. As the U.S. government instituted new forms of border policing in the mid-1920s, migrants found themselves caught between capitalists' demands for their labor, on the one hand, and the nation's refusal to grant them membership and rights, on the other.

The presence of a mobile Mexican proletariat troubled the institutions of racial governance in the southwestern United States, where Jim Crow

Mexicans entering the United States. U.S. immigration station,
El Paso, Texas. Photograph taken by Dorothea Lange for the Farm
Security Administration in June of 1938. (Library of Congress, Farm
Security Administration Office of War Information Collection,
LC-DIG-fsa-8b32436)

segregation extended to practices for monitoring the national boundary
between the two countries. In this period, U.S. nationhood and white supremacy reinforced each other, so that immigration policy served political leaders as an instrument for fixing the figurative and material limits
of the national body. The narrow frame of "Americanization" could never
assimilate Mexicans as full national citizens: by their language, their ethnic particularity, and their perceived racial difference, working-class Mexicans remained indelibly alien. Indeed, those who debated in the 1920s over
the Mexican presence remained intransigent before Mexican American
demands for social equality. Neither immigration advocates nor restric-
tionists of the period could conceive of Mexicans moving beyond the segregated spaces of southwestern barrios or migrant camps. Debates over
Mexican labor and migration in the 1920s only extended so far as determining whether Mexican labor value could offset the possible danger of
creating a subordinate caste of racialized workers.

The passage of the Johnson-Reed Act in 1924 radically altered the character of transborder Mexican communities. Following intense debates over the threat of foreigners to U.S. national identity, Congress passed reforms that set national quotas for immigrants from outside the Western Hemisphere, in the service of an explicitly defined project of racial exclusion. Although Mexicans were not included in the quota system, new mechanisms for border policing curtailed the longstanding mobility of people across the southern U.S. border. With the establishment of the U.S. Border Patrol in that same year, Mexicans and Mexican Americans were forced to address the new category of the "illegal alien," as the criminalization of Mexican migration marked Mexican Americans and migrants, lawful and undocumented alike, as trespassers in the United States.

This comprehensive, racially encoded, immigration policy gave the U.S. government new mechanisms for the restriction and removal of populations, as immigration agents could now track, detain, and deport aliens according to politically defined interests. The federal government deemed these functions critical to the defense of national sovereignty and the protection of a political boundary on rights, freedom, and membership within the nation. Historian Mae M. Ngai argues that these immigration restrictions "produced the illegal alien as a new legal and political subject, whose inclusion within the nation was simultaneously a social reality and a legal impossibility—a subject barred from citizenship and without rights."[14]

Mexicans, who constituted the majority of the illegal-alien population in the 1920s, experienced the new regime of border law enforcement and immigration regulation as a profound assault on the integrity of their communities and as an abridgement of their historical claims to the U.S. southwest. New legal requirements for visas and national documents disrupted the daily traffic of workers across border bridges, just as they also reconfigured families that spanned the international boundary. Zaragoza Vargas relates how the onset of the Great Depression gave new purchase to popular conceptions of Mexican criminality: "It was at this time that the notion of the illegal alien gained notoriety, transforming Mexican workers into potential fugitives of the law unless they procured proper documentation."[15]

The practice of law enforcement did not distinguish between the rights of lawful citizens and undocumented migrants within the same racialized community: during the economic recessions following World War I and the collapse of the U.S. economy in 1929, local and federal authorities deported Mexican Americans along with Mexicans as a means to deny them access to federal relief benefits. Half of the estimated four hundred thousand Mexicans forcibly repatriated during the Great Depression were U.S. citizens; one-quarter of the deportations took place in Texas, where the historical primacy of tejana/o settlements did nothing to dissuade local authorities from uprooting long-term residents and neighbors.

The mass repatriations were only the most overt expressions of authorities' willingness to use race to limit Mexican and Mexican American claims to equality and civil rights. The condition of being "undocumented" did not simply imply a lack of legal protection or status but rather entailed the active conversion of Mexicans in the border region into a new category of people who were effectively removed from the national sphere of rights. This peculiar form of statelessness emerged with the contradiction between market demands for mobile labor and consumable goods and the immobility of civil rights beyond the bounds of the nation-state. Like other displaced peoples, Mexican migrants continually invented new forms of collective agency within that space of opposition. It was a melancholy task. Against crushing odds, Mexicans and Mexican Americans drew on their intimate knowledge of the transnational circuits of global capitalism to stage new claims to rights and belonging in a deliberately nonnational framework of humanist, ethnic, and class solidarity.

Migrant Imaginaries: From "El Lavaplatos" (1926) to "El Deportado" (1930)

Migrants contested their marginality in the vernacular of the Mexican proletariat, introducing their distinct cultures of laboring in the song forms they carried north. In 1926, Los Hermanos Bañuelos released the corrido "El Lavaplatos" [The Dishwasher], the first known commercial recording by Mexican artists in the United States.[16] The Mexican brothers David N. Bañuelos and Luis M. Bañuelos pioneered the corrido form in Los Angeles; they are also credited with introducing steel guitar to the song performance. "El Lavaplatos," which features the brothers' vocal duet with a simple guitar accompaniment, formed part of what Manuel Peña describes as the "watershed moment" of Texas-Mexican musical development.[17] Commercial linkages between Monterrey and southern Texas gave rise to a vibrant trade in Mexican music that spanned the border, recording the folk traditions of working-class peoples and initiating new experimentation in orchestral and dancehall music.

The border ballad became an ideal form for encoding the life worlds of Mexican migrants in the transborder labor circuit. "El Lavaplatos" adopts the voice of a disillusioned migrant who narrates his experience of backbreaking work with weary irony. Having hoped for success in the glamorous industries of Hollywood, he ends up an itinerant laborer. What begins as adventure concludes in the punishment of stoop labor:

Un día muy desesperado	[One day very desperate,
por tanta revolución	because of so much revolution,
Me pasé para este lado	I came over to this side of the border
Sin pagar la inmigración	without paying the immigration
Qué vacilada,	Oh, what a fast one,
qué vacilada,	Oh what a fast one,
me pasé sin pagar nada	I crossed without paying anything
Al llegar a la estación	On arriving at the station,
me tropecé con un cuate	I ran into a friend,
que me hizo la invitación	who gave me an invitation
de trabajar en el traque	to work on el traque
Yo el traque me suponía	I supposed el traque
que sería algún almacén	would be some kind of warehouse,
y era componer la vía	but it was to repair the track
por donde camina el tren	where the train ran
Ay qué mi cuate	Oh what a friend,
ay, qué mi cuate,	Oh what a friend,
cómo me llevó pa'l traque	how he took me to the track
Cuando me enfadé del traque	When I got sick and tired of the train
me volvió a invitar aquél	he invited me again,
a la pisca del tomate	to pick tomatoes
y a deshojar betabel	and thin beets

Y allí me gané indulgencias	And there I earned indulgences
caminando de rodillas	walking on my knees;
como cuatro o cinco millas	about four or five miles
me dieron de penitencia	they gave me for penance.][18]

The Catholic rites of supplication provide a metaphor for the migrant's submission to the punitive discipline of field work. A few decades later, the United Farm Workers elevated this association of brute labor with penitence to the status of a political rite in the Peregrinación of 1966, when unionists marched from Delano to the California state capitol to demand the right to organize. For the new farmworker movement, the act of atonement intended to redeem workers tied to a corrupt labor system that robbed them of dignity and humanity. For the migrants of the 1920s, tending rows of beets on their knees was a reminder of their abject status in the United States. U.S. growers used stoop labor both as an efficient means to extract profit and as a system of labor control.

However much commercial agriculture mimicked the coercive discipline of colonial plantations, the capitalist wage system allowed growers to depict the contract as an equitable arrangement, as the song says, by "invitation," rather than by force. This construction of wage work as an entirely free labor system masked the persistence of unfree, captive labor built in the migrant labor economy. The narrative tension of the corrido derives from the protagonist's keen awareness that he himself has facilitated his own capture into a brutal labor system. His experiences lead him to regret his abandonment of his status as ciudadano [citizen] for a position entirely defined by his labor function, "El Lavaplatos." "Oh what a friend," sings the migrant in comic lamentation, regretting his association with the labor contractor who played on his desire. The friend personifies the capitalist labor market that induced migrants to cross the border for false promises of economic mobility. He embodies the same trickster figure that historian Stephen Pitti has located in the ideologies of labor and race that bedeviled Mexican communities in Northern California or that anthropologist José Limón chronicled in his studies of South Texas.[19]

This "Devil of discrimination" constructed Mexican migrants as the ideal workforce for the racialized hierarchies of labor in the southwestern United States.[20] Throughout the 1920s, the agricultural lobby cannily promoted U.S. growers' fantasies of a tractable, pliant labor force through the figure of the Mexican migrant. In their accounts, Mexican men were biologically suited to stoop labor because of their shorter stature and a capacity for endurance that distinguished them from white workers. Farmers depicted Mexicans as lacking in ambition and imbued with racial traits that prevented them from progressing beyond unskilled occupations. The proximity of Mexico, they argued, meant that U.S. society would not have the burden of integrating Mexicans into the mainstream. In this way, agriculturalists and their associates in Congress envisioned Mexicans as a temporary workforce that could be made to appear and disappear at their convenience. In the words of historian Mark Reisler, congressional debates of the 1920s fixed Mexican migrants in the status of temporary workers ineligible for U.S. citizenship: "To most Anglos, the immigrant from south of the border was always the peon laborer and never the potential citizen."[21] The longstanding claims of Mexican Americans to the Southwest did nothing to alter this view. Instead, the racial discourse applied to migrants had a corrosive effect on Mexican American citizenship, weakening the Mexican population's fragile claims to state protections and services and exacerbating its racial and class marginality in the United States.

Of course, the "migratory character" of the Mexican laborer was not an inherent trait of Mexican culture or of mestizo [mixed-race] ancestry but, rather, the intended outcome of systematic U.S. policies of segregation, discrimination, and ethnic removal. On December 23, 1930, the Hermanos Bañuelos returned to the Los Angeles studio to record their most famous corrido, "El Deportado" [The Deportee].[22] The song's sixteen stanzas trace the fateful trajectory of a migrant's departure from his homeland for the border crossing in Ciudad Juárez, his deception in the renganche [contract], and his ultimate roundup for deportation. The song lacks the knowing humor of the brothers' first release, as "El Deportado" substitutes melancholic refrains for the wry self-mockery of their earlier recording. If the protagonist of "El Lavaplatos" entered the migratory stream with illusions of adventure, here "El Deportado" cherishes no such dream. His sojourn is one long itinerary of loss:

Voy a cantarles señores	[I'm going to sing to you, gentlemen,
todo lo que yo sufrí,	about all that I suffered
Desde que dejé mi patria	Since I left my country
por venir a este país.	to come to this nation.

Serían las diez de la noche	It must have been about ten at night
comenzó un tren a silbar.	the train began to whistle.
Oí que dijo mi madre,	I heard my mother say,
"Ahí viene ese tren ingrato	"There comes that ungrateful train
que a mi hijo se va a llevar."	that is going to take my son."
Adiós mi madre querida	"Goodbye my beloved mother
écheme su benedición.	give me your blessing.
Yo me voy al extranjero	I am going abroad
donde no hay revolución."	where there is no revolution."
Corre, corre maquinita	Run, run little train
vámonos de la estación.	let's leave the station.
No quiero ver a mi madre	I don't want to see my mother
llorar por su hijo querido,	cry for her beloved son,
por su hijo del corazón.	for the son of her heart.
Al fin sonó la campana	Finally the bell rang
dos silbidos pegó el tren	the train whistled twice.
"No lloren mis compañeros	"Don't cry, my companions,
que me hacen llorar también."	for you'll make me cry as well."][23]

The song begins with the formal address of the corrido form, signaling the veracity of the narrative and its connection to actual lived experience. The song inscribes the migrant imaginary as exclusively the domain of men, in which the singers, their audience, and their subjects constitute a homosocial world of male mobility and performance. The exchange between the mother and son is an allegory for the national trauma of emigration, in which kinship ties must extend beyond the nation-space in order for the family to remain intact. Although the song articulates a sense of national identity, the lyrics themselves offer no strong evocation of patriotic feeling beyond the anxiety of leaving what is familiar. The Revolution represents chaos that impinges on personal survival, rather than a political contest in which the protagonist has a stake.

The shrill whistle of the train initiates the migrant's subjection within the transborder labor economy, performing the hailing function that Marxist theoretician Louis Althusser used to describe the process of interpellation.[24] In order to accept his new status as a migrant, the song's protagonist must reject his mother's sorrow and suppress his own feeling. He warns his companions not to provoke him, as if admitting his distress would imperil his capacity to accept his subjection. As the train lurches into motion, its passage through the Mexican countryside remakes the Mexican national as the "migrant character" so desired by U.S. agriculturalists, a process that reaches its conclusion in the U.S. border checkpoint:

Cuando Chihuahua pasamos	[When we passed Chihuahua
se notó gran confusión,	There was great confusion,
Los empleados de la aduana	the employees from the customhouse
que pasaban revisión.	were checking things out.
Llegamos por fin a Juárez	We arrived at Juarez at last
Allí fué mi apuración.	there I ran into trouble.
"Que 'ónde vas que de 'ónde	"Where are you going, where do
vienes?"	you come from?"
Que cuanto dinero tienes	How much money do you have
para entrar a esta nación?"	to enter this nation?"
"Señores traigo dinero	"Gentlemen, I have money
para poder emigrar."	so that I can emigrate."
"Tu dinero nada vale	"Your money isn't worth anything
te tenemos que bañar."	we have to bathe you."
Ay, mis paisanos queridos	Oh, my beloved countrymen,
yo les platico no más.	I'll tell you no more.
Que me estaban dando ganas	I was beginning to feel
de volverme para atrás.	like turning right back.]

The passage through the border checkpoint demonstrates how U.S. capitalists used the state apparatus to procure their idealized labor force. The border police inspect and disinfect the bodies of the migrants, a scene of abjection that almost leads the protagonist to refuse his interpellation as a migrant worker. The proximity of the lines "tu dinero nada vale" and "te tenemos que bañar" speaks to the ways the migrant worker's body was itself a kind of currency, an object of exchange between the two countries. The absence of any official voice for Mexico, however, reminds us of its lack of power in the transaction: Mexican money is worth nothing to the mocking border guards.

The song conveys the injury that the border crossing could inflict. The migrant's reticence speaks to the power of the state to impose a commodity value on braceros that violated the sense of their own human worth and rights as working people and ethnic Mexicans:

Crucé por fin la frontera	[At last I crossed the border
y en un renganche salí.	and left in a contracted group.
Ay mis queridos paisanos	Oh, my beloved countrymen,
fué mucho lo que sufrí.	I suffered so much.
Los güeros son muy malores	The Anglos are very wicked
se valen de la ocasión.	they take advantage of the occasion.
y a todos los mexicanos	They treat all Mexicans
los tratan sin compasión.	without pity.]

Rather than narrate the repatriations as an incident of national humiliation, however, the song dramatizes its effects on the migrant population as a racialized class: the protagonist bids farewell to compatriots in the United States, alternately addressing them as "compañeros," "paisanos queridos," and "cuates queridos."

The song concludes with the acute awareness that Mexicans are merely the convenient scapegoats for U.S. economic misfortunes. The dust storms of the Great Depression evoke the wave of popular resentments that led relief agencies, police officials, and state governments to coordinate the mass repatriations of the 1930s:

Hoy traen la gran polvadera	[Today comes a large cloud of dust
y sin consideración	and with no consideration,
mujeres, niños y ancianos	women, children, and elders
los llevan a la frontera.	are being driven to the border.
Nos echan de esta nación.	We are being kicked out of this country.
Adiós paisanos queridos	Goodbye, beloved countrymen
ya nos van a deportar.	they are going to deport us.
Pero no somos bandidos	But we are not bandits
venimos a camellar.	we came to work hard.]

The refrain "no somos bandidos / venimos a camellar" resounded from the 1930s onward as a statement of self-defense against the criminalization of economic migrants. As it addresses the repatriations directly, the song extends its account of migrant hardships to the "women, children, and elders" swept up in the campaign of ethnic removal. The song treats this group as mere dependents of the male wage earner and citizen; few corridos gave voice to women's particular testimony as migrants. It is worth noting too how little emphasis these two corridos gave to Mexican claims to southwestern territories: migrant songs commonly staged their demands for rights and fair treatment in the discourse of ethnic and class struggle, not national conflict. In this domain Mexicans refused their racial and class subjection by reminding U.S. society of its own dependence on migrant labor. The term "camellar" accepts the assignation to brute work but invests Mexican labor with dignity beyond its denigrated status.

The corrido concludes with the migrant's hopes for his successful reintegration within his home country, as he exhorts his compatriots to leave with him:

Los espero allá en mi tierra [I will wait for you in my homeland
ya no hay más revolución. there is no more revolution.
Vámonos cuates queridos, Let's leave, my dear friends,
seremos bien recibidos we will be welcomed
por nuestra bella nación. by our beautiful nation.][25]

These People Are Not Aliens

Few people—least of all the authorities—contested the repatriations of the 1930s. Mexican consuls, nationalists, and migrants alike saw the repatriations as a means to resolve the problems of emigration. On the U.S. side, labor leaders and civil-rights activists also hoped that the repatriations would diminish the competition between migrants and U.S.-born Mexicans for scarce jobs and relief services. Only a small minority of activists and intellectuals on either the U.S. or Mexican left could imagine the resolution of migrant sorrows in ways that did not divide citizens from noncitizens.

One such figure was the leftist civil-rights leader Luisa Moreno. In her 1940 address to the Fourth Annual Conference of the American Committee for Protection of the Foreign Born, Moreno proposed an alternate vision of inter-American unity centered on the concerns of the migrant proletariat. Decrying the forced repatriations, which she termed "Caravans of Sorrow," Moreno attacked the class and racial apparatus that denied Spanish-speaking immigrants the rights of citizens and made Mexican Americans a subordinated caste:

> These people are not aliens. They have contributed their endurance, sacrifices, youth, and labor to the Southwest. Indirectly they have paid more taxes than all the stockholders of California's industrialized agriculture, the sugar beet companies, and the large cotton interests that operate or have operated with the labor of Mexican workers.[26]

Moreno, a prominent figure in women's labor movements in the prewar period, spoke out as a member of El Congreso de Pueblos que Hablan Español [Congress of Spanish-Speaking Peoples], a civil-rights organization that refused to draw distinctions between U.S. citizens and foreign-born members of the Latino population. The Congreso held affiliations with U.S. and Mexican labor unions, leftist groups, and the Communist Party. Its positions diverged from the more segregated politics of other civil-rights organizations, most notably the League of United Latin American Citizens (LULAC). Established in 1929, LULAC restricted its membership to U.S. citizens and advocated a closed border. Its leaders could not conceive of how Mexican Americans could achieve full rights as U.S. citizens if unauthorized immigration continued to provoke racial resentments against the Mexican population as a whole.

For Moreno, herself a Guatemalan immigrant and a seasoned leader for the United Cannery, Agricultural, Packing and Allied Workers of America (UCAPAWA), racialized Latinas/os in the United States shared substantial class and ethnic concerns with new Latin American migrants. Members of the Congreso had extensive experience of cross-border political campaigns that originated in Latin American anarchism and socialism; these experiences led its Mexican American leaders, Bert Corona and Josefina Fierro among them, to look beyond citizenship as a vehicle for rights. The Congreso rejected LULAC's premises for "Americanization" because its members viewed the discourse of assimilation as a divisive tactic that merely reinforced white supremacy in the domestic United States and furthered U.S. political hegemony throughout the Americas. With her simple phrase "these people are not aliens," Moreno broadened the debate on immigration by questioning the primacy of the nation's interests over labor and human rights.

In 1940, anticipating her audience's concerns about the European war against fascism, Moreno addressed the contradiction between U.S. postures of inter-American unity and its undemocratic treatment of "Non-Citizen Americans of the South West." Rather than accept the construction of undocumented migrants as "illegal aliens" or failed nationals, she placed the blame for migrants' lack of incorporation into the nation squarely on the U.S. government and U.S. employers. Reviewing the structural reasons why Mexicans commonly did not naturalize, Moreno concluded,

> Arriving at logical conclusions, the Latin American non-citizens, rooted in this country, are increasingly seeing the importance and need for naturalization. But, how will the thousands of migrants establish residence? What possibility have these people had, segregated in "Little Mexicos," to learn English and meet educational requirements? How can they, receiving hunger wages while enriching the stockholders of the Great Western Sugar Company, the Bank of America and other large interests, pay high naturalization fees? A Mexican family living on relief in Colorado would have to stop eating for two months and a half to pay for the citizenship papers of one member of the family. Is this humanly possible?

Moreno continued to condemn the repatriation drives as symptoms of an undemocratic government that withheld citizenship from deserving workers while using the state apparatus to deliver profits to the capitalist classes. Asking her audience what would become of the "1,400,000 men, women, and children" of Mexican descent should the practice of repatriation extend as far as the "anti-Semitic persecutions in Europe," Moreno warned,

> A people who have lived twenty or thirty years in this country, tied up by family relations with the early settlers, with American-born children, cannot be uprooted without the complete destruction of the

faintest resemblance of democracy and human liberties for the whole population.

The specter of European fascism added gravity to Moreno's interpretation of the repatriation drives as a danger to U.S. democracy. In conclusion, Moreno offered her audience a simple answer to the immigration problem, well within the boundaries of state power and sovereignty: the United States should pass legislation to encourage all migrants from the Western Hemisphere to naturalize as citizens.

But in her larger indictment of "anti-alien" legislation and anti-Mexican sentiment, Moreno also questioned U.S. liberal democracy and the limits of liberal nationalism itself. She cautioned that the very forces that removed Mexicans and other migrants from the spheres of rights also corrupted normative citizenship and threatened the state's function as guarantor of rights. Her remarks spoke to the contradictions between capitalist expansion and state sovereignty that erupted once more during debates over the North American Free Trade Agreement in the 1990s. Her vision for noncitizens in the Southwest could not overcome the resurgent nationalism of World War II. Moreno's demand for a hemispheric unity that could support the rights of all workers, regardless of national status, remained unanswered.

Moreno's activism resonated beyond the sphere of immigration legislation, taking root in the domain of border vernacular culture. The corrido form embodied popular aspirations to a different order of rights and communal belonging in the border space. Its refrains conjured an inherently unstable ethnic and class solidarity that refused to conform to the codes for assimilation within the nation-state. Border songs became the template for tejana/o literary creation, especially in the works of their preeminent interpreter, Don Américo Paredes.

Américo Paredes and the Border Vernacular

If, as Etienne Balibar writes, "*Every social community produced by the functioning of institutions is imaginary*," then the political status of Mexican migrants posed a troubling problem for Mexican American intellectuals.[27]

In the 1930s, in the midst of repatriation, artists and activists sought new means to mobilize border communities. Dominant narratives of U.S. nationalism negated border Mexicans' own self-concepts as "a people"; similarly, U.S. institutions divided Mexican American families along the lines of citizenship status and access to civil rights. The bilingual vernacular of migrant communities fell far outside the lettered domain of "high culture," just as the orality of the laboring classes meant that their expressive productions were ephemeral and episodic. As a result, the search for the proper political form for contending with the fragile agency of migrant people doubled as a search for the aesthetic forms that could register their cultural value—beyond the simplistic and ruthless economic codes of their commodified labor.

Throughout his extraordinary career as a performer, writer, and folklorist, Américo Paredes offered a stunning indictment of the racial suppression of Mexican communities in the border region. More important, his studies of folklore demonstrated the desire of subalterns to refashion the repressive geographies of modernity and remake the geopolitical border according to their own interests. His account of border vernacular culture evoked the restless subjectivity that emerged from Mexicans' lived experience of imperial dispossession and exploitation as captive labor for capitalist expansion. Paredes's sense of the insurgent possibilities latent in the vernacular derived from his own experience growing up in Brownsville, Texas, in close proximity to the Mexican Revolution, and hearing fabled accounts of Mexican resistance to Anglo hegemony. In both his own life and his writings, the traditional ballads of border conflict and revolutionary heroism merged with migrant stories of labor and travel, all manifesting the vibrant cultural memory of Mexican workers. Communal memories of displacement animated Paredes's foundational work to recast the divided border region as "Greater Mexico," a federation of pueblos that would form, in Ramón Saldívar's words, "communities of fate."[28]

This lifelong scholar of border folk understood culture as an arena of social conflict, of popular opposition to domination.[29] Américo Paredes Manzano was born in Brownsville on September 3, 1915, the year of the anarchist revolt in San Diego, Texas, when seditionists called for a multiethnic uprising against U.S. imperial control of formerly Mexican lands.[30] The Mexican Revolution was transforming northern hacienda society and creating new bases of opposition to the racial terror that Rangers and other

Anglo authorities imposed on the Mexican communities of South Texas.[31] Paredes's family belonged to the educated, landed class of Mexican ranching society; he could trace his family ancestry to the original Hispanic colonists who established the province of Nuevo Santander in 1748. But his writings brought him far from the provincialism of border elites.

Paredes began his writing career as a reporter in the Japanese theater of World War II. While in Tokyo, he married Amelia Shidzu Nagamine, a Japanese-Uruguayan woman educated in both Mexico City and Tokyo. The two returned to the Texas-Mexican border in 1948, where he returned to his studies. While in school, the young author wrote a collection of short stories, *Border Country* (1952), and the novel *The Shadow* (1955), which earned him five hundred dollars in a writing contest. Paredes became the first Mexican American to earn a Ph.D. at the University of Texas, where he also taught English and Folklore from 1958 until his retirement in 1984. His doctoral work on South Texas vernacular culture became the basis for an incendiary assault on the ideologies of racial supremacy embedded in the Anglo-Texan academic establishment at the time. Paredes's 1958 study of the corrido, *With His Pistol in His Hand: A Border Ballad and Its Hero*, is justly celebrated as "a masterful work of intellectual intervention," in part because its experimental form laid a foundation for the oppositional practice of Chicano Studies.[32] His scholarship in defense of Mexican civil rights earned him recognition in both Mexico and the United States. In 1991, Mexico awarded Paredes its highest national honor, El Orden del Águila Azteca, a prize also given to César Chávez and Julian Zamora.

With the mobilizations of ethnic communities during the Chicana/o civil-rights movement in the 1960s, Paredes found a new audience for his early works of fiction and poetry. The decades following El Movimiento saw him publish myriad works of folklore and song, most notably *A Texas-Mexican Cancionero* (1976) and the essays on border identity and social conflict collected in the 1993 volume *Folklore and Culture on the Texas-Mexican Border*. After his retirement, Paredes was able to revise his earliest creative works for publication. The appearance of the novel *George Washington Gómez* (1990), the volume of poems *Between Two Worlds* (1991), and the collection *The Hammon and the Beans and Other Stories* (1994) had the astonishing effect of retroactively transforming the formation of a Chicana/o literary canon. These works demonstrate a versatility of form and imagination and articulate with subtle authority a "border-defying" vision of cultural possibility.[33]

Periodizing Paredes's literary works thus presents an intriguing challenge for his critics, not only because of the gap between their first conception in the 1930s and 1940s and their ultimate dates of publication but also because they voice an awareness of the historical contingency of social identity which we have come to define as singularly "postmodern." In his introduction to *Between Two Worlds*, Paredes wryly noted the peculiar predicament of making public the poems of a "'proto-Chicano' of a half-century ago."[34] But it was precisely his ability to speak out of time that permitted Paredes to articulate the presence of the past in cultural politics, to speculate on a possible future despite the narrowness of the present. Don Américo died on May 5, 1999, in the midst of another great migration of Mexicans to the United States, a subject that engaged him right up until his death. Throughout his life, Paredes remained concerned by the violence present in every phase of the cultural and political evolution of the Mexico-U.S. border—a violence visited on the border peoples who were the subject of his life's work.

Paredes's earliest writing revealed his abiding concern not only "with the existence of political boundaries, but the circumstances of their creation [in] cultural conflict."[35] His skepticism toward the hegemonic narratives of national development led him to develop a concept of communal power that was markedly distinct from citizenship or national belonging. This model of border subjectivity also prefigured a postmodern preoccupation with the limits of the nation as a stable container for lived social processes. José David Saldívar, among many others, celebrates the author's "*cartographic* . . . poetry of decolonization."[36] What concerns me here is the *substance* of the agency that Paredes, and others of his generation, ascribed to Mexicans, as they—like Luisa Moreno—sought to displace the national as the primary and singular repository of modern social identity. Delineating that fragile force became the life work of this novelist and poet, folklorist and essayist, trickster and singer.

The history of Américo Paredes's earliest poem, "The Mexico-Texan," offers a marvelous example of how the author's desire to capture the contours of border subjectivity intersected with the Mexican American struggle for identity during the 1930s:

The Mexico-Texan he's one fonny man
Who leeves in the region that's north of the Gran',
Of Mexican father he born in these part,
And sometimes he rues it dip down in he's heart.

For the Mexico-Texan he no gotta lan'[37]

In the spring of 1934, when Américo Paredes first composed "The Mexico-Texan" as a high-school senior, labor unrest inflamed the fields of California and Texas. Mexican and Mexican American farm laborers, tenant farmers, and cannery workers participated in mass organizing drives to address oppressive conditions, poor wages, and racial discrimination. The year 1933 alone witnessed thirty-seven major agricultural strikes in California, in areas where ethnic Mexicans made up an estimated 95 percent of the rank and file. Similarly, in Texas the early 1930s saw ethnic Mexicans, blacks, and poor whites join together in opposition to the grinding poverty and racial inequality that the sharecropping economy had generated.

Coming of age amid the social ferment, Paredes drafted the first version of the poem that came to represent the political uncertainties of the period. For many critics, the work demonstrates the first positive statement of a distinctly *bordered* Mexican American identity in letters. In the notes to his 1991 collection of poetry, *Between Two Worlds*, Américo Paredes recalls composing "The Mexico-Texan" "while walking the 21 blocks home from school one afternoon."[38] The poem retained the spontaneous quality of its creation in its emphatic use of rhythm and repetition. The young poet transcribed and revised his composition, which then circulated widely in manuscript form among various political campaigns in South Texas. The piece took on a life quite apart from its author, appearing in the July 1937 edition of *LULAC News* without Paredes's knowledge.[39] After being "reprinted a few times as anonymous," Paredes states, "'The Mexico-Texan' . . . entered oral tradition locally."[40] The status of the work as "folk poetry" was vividly demonstrated in the 1960s, when the student of one of Paredes's colleagues at the University of Texas, Roger D. Abrahams, heard it on a trip to Brownsville. The most famous of Paredes's poems, "The Mexico-Texan" has lent its historic voice to numerous studies of Chicano history, serving as a departure point for conceptualizing Mexican American cultural studies as a field of postcolonial inquiry.

The unstable relation of the verses' "popular oral" and "literary written" elements makes "The Mexico-Texan" a profound artifact of Mexican Americans' desire for social justice in the 1930s.[41] In its formal construction, the poem articulates the inherent difficulty of confronting the contradictory discourses of eugenics, agribusiness, and citizenship, each of which determined the racial and class status of Mexicans in the border region. Paredes's title functions as a statement of that problem. By addressing its subject in the singular, "*the* Mexico-Texan," the title parodies the objectifying tendency of official discourse. But its very personal investigation occurs within a surprisingly strict form. The text uses a third person, omniscient narrative, creating a critical distance from its subject, and its six stanzas are divided into lines of eleven syllables, which follow a strict pattern of AA/BB end-rhymes.

This regularity of meter and rhyme operates in profound tension with the voice of the poem, which speaks in a crude approximation of the marked speech of a migrant Mexican laborer. This tension speaks to the impossibility of recovering intact the Mexican migrant from the objectifying desires of capitalism; this problem is the unstated thematic concern of the poem. But its use of exaggeratedly "broken" English poses yet another problem: why does the composition speak in a decidedly *anglocentric* rendering of Texas-Mexican speech? Why does Paredes ignore the code switching, the jumping between English and Spanish so characteristic of the border vernacular?

In *Between Two Worlds*, Paredes admits revising the 1934 version of "The Mexico-Texan" after critic Hart Stilwell argued that its language sounded "too much like the stage 'Italian' dialect of the time."[42] Still, the revised poem retains its monolingual character as the narrator laments,

For the Mexico-Texan he no gotta lan',
He stomped on the neck both sides of the Gran',
The dam gringo lingo he no cannot spik,
It twisters the tong and it makes you fill sick.[43]

In contrast, in the 1936 composition "Tres faces del pocho," Paredes's comedic monologue on mestizaje [racial mixture] alternates between rhythmic, bilingual slang and rigorously crafted Spanish verse. Describing an imagined tableau in which the "Passionate Spaniard" recovers from a tourist adventure in Mexico City, Paredes writes, "After a weekend of tacos, whores, and mariachis, we find him enthroned on the crapper, spilling out his guts and suffering the torments not of the damned but of the *gademes*. He has been called a *pocho*, and has paid out three or four *mordidas*, and finally had his wallet stolen."[44] Following this scene, which stages a symbolic annihilation of the speaker's Spanish ancestry, Paredes moves with irony into the lyric mode, in Spanish:

> Raza gloriosa y real de mis   [Glorious race and royalty of
>   abuelos!   my grandfathers!
> ¡O, mi raza giganta!   Oh my great race
> que aplastaste en el polvo   you crushed in the dust under
>   con tu planta!   your heel
> ¡cuánto guerrero altivo!   how many proud warriors!]

The striking diversity of poetic language in Paredes's early verse speaks to the larger project to determine the form in which to articulate the complex historical consciousness of the border subject. Still, Paredes's poems ultimately choose one language over the other; English and Spanish remained marked off from each other in the poems by stanza breaks. It was decades before the practice of code switching within phrases came to dominate Chicano/Chicana verse as an expression of ethnic difference. Even as Paredes's inventive forms prefigure post-Movimiento literature, they remain faithful to the historical standards of their moment of conception. The omission of Spanish from "The Mexico-Texan" reflects the historical pressures delimiting the poet's invention of a vernacular aesthetic. In other words, the deficiency of Paredes's rendition of subaltern Mexican speech is not a failing of the poem but of its political context. The problem of attaining a "true" vernacular, for Paredes and for so many after him, is a symptom of the inherently contradictory nature of identity for Mexicans residing at the border of two, dissonant nations.

Paredes used the unstable form of the border vernacular to signal a greater instability latent in border subjectivity. In his study of the folk elements of African American literature, Houston Baker situates the vernacular "at the crossroads" of the emergence of the "peculiar subjectivity" of racialized African Americans within a modern order not of their own making. Baker signals the double meaning of the term "vernacular" as it informs the creation of African American expressive culture. The "vernacular" signifies not only an art "native or peculiar to a particular country or locality," but it is also an adjective for a "slave . . . born on his master's estate."[45] The term gains its aesthetic connotation of the "native" through the juridical status of the slave as property, drawing an implicit contrast between the "home-born" and the imported captive. In this way, "vernacular" doubles as a description of both the nature of the art *and* the particular subjectivity of its producer.

For our purposes, it is important to note that the vernacular arts originate in a condition of dispossession. Having been "born on the master's estate" describes a state of homelessness originating in the separation of the subjects from homelands, language, labor, and selfhood. In the context of the Mexican American border, we can see how the vernacular of Paredes's poem takes its form from the historical displacement of Mexicans from their lands, during imperial conquest and the expansion of capitalist agriculture. With "The Mexico-Texan" Paredes voices a state of total self-alienation:

> Except for a few with their cunning and craft
> He count just as much as a nought to the laft,
> And they say everywhere, "He's a burden and drag,"
> He no gotta country, he no gotta flag."
> He no gotta voice, all he got is the han'
> To work like the burro; he no gotta lan'.[46]

The labor economy commodifies the state of dispossession, so that the Mexico-Texan registers his value as a "nought to the laft" on a bank ledger. The only affirmative statement in the poem, "all he got is the han'," comes as an expression of the subject's labor value, "to work like the burro." All other descriptions of the Mexico-Texan are conjugated in the negative, "he no gotta lan'"—a basic condition of the vernacular.

The vernacular subject of "The Mexico-Texan" lacks agency because "he no gotta lan'," a refrain that links property rights metonymically with the rights of the citizen. In her reading of Marx's "On the Jewish Question," Lisa Lowe has demonstrated how this relation between rights of property and rights of citizenship operates to deny racialized immigrants full incorporation into the nation-state. Immigrants who have served as a surplus labor force experience state repression as a function of the state's obligation to act as the "guarantor of capitalist relations of exploitation" that support the property rights of the governing classes. The "abstraction of the *citizen*," Lisa Lowe writes, "is always in distinction to the particularity of *man's* condition."[47] In this sense, relations of production deny the racialized migrant entry into the political spheres of civil society and capitalist relations; for us, then, the vernacular describes a condition of self-alienation as property, as labor value for others.

Ultimately, the poem describes a subject completely at the mercy of external forces, who can only achieve the "imagined community" of national membership in fantasy, when "He can get him so drank that he think he will fly / Both September the Sixteen and Fourth of July."[48] Paredes's use of the vernacular thus enacts a complex critique of the juridical and economic discourses that structured the interaction of the Mexican American population and the nation-state during the 1930s. The condition of total self-alienation expressed in "The Mexico-Texan" speaks to the irresolvable tension that the criminalization of undocumented migration had created for border Mexicans. Popular anxieties about "illegal aliens" made all Mexicans suspect, thus putting Mexican Americans in an impossible bind. The economic demands placed on Mexican workers precluded the resolution of the political status: they were more valuable to the nation as surplus labor than as citizens. As we have seen, the agricultural lobby demanded that Mexicans be imported as workers, not as citizens. The prevailing system of labor and immigration regulation during the 1930s canceled migrants' national status by constructing Mexican subjects within the logic of property relations. The awkward, omniscient narration that Paredes adopts in "The Mexico-Texan" is an appropriation of capitalist discourse, which the author uses to reveal its dehumanizing effects. The force of Paredes's poem thus derives from his strategic use of the vernacular to interrogate the nation form. The poem subverts the metaphors of disease and contamination operative in U.S. immigration debates of the period.

For Paredes to have composed "The Mexico-Texan" in bilingual verse would have limited, ultimately, his questioning of national sovereignty. By placing Spanish under erasure, the poem captures the alienation of the border Mexican. A bilingual vernacular, by contrast, would connote the capacity to move comfortably between and among nations, and in the 1930s the combined force of Jim Crow segregation, border surveillance, and deportation drives precluded any such freedom of movement for Mexicans —like the Vásquez family or the singer of "El Lavaplatos"—in the United States. The true language of Paredes's subject speaks a language unintelligible within the grammar of Mexican and U.S. nationalisms, precisely because his is a nationality that cannot be voiced or embodied.

As Américo Paredes searched for the appropriate poetic form for articulating Mexican American identity, he embraced the contemporary social movements that sought to protect the uniqueness of Mexican communities at the border. His poem should be read as a dialogue with contemporary social movements that used the border as a site of contestation to state power and control. Paredes's cultural aspirations for Greater Mexico found their echo in the political aspirations of his compatriota Emma Tenayuca.

La Pasionaria: Emma Tenayuca and the Mexican Question

Like Américo Paredes, Emma Tenayuca was born into a tejana/o family whose residence in South Texas predated both Mexican independence and the Mexico-U.S. War. Her family belonged to the poor working class of San Antonio, and Tenayuca began her political education in the West Side barrio, which, at the time of her birth in 1917, was home to one hundred thousand tejanas/os living in conditions of desperate poverty.[49] Rates of infant mortality, malnutrition, and diseases like tuberculosis in the West Side community were among the highest in the country. One of eleven children, Emma Tenayuca spent much of her childhood in the care of her maternal grandparents, who taught her the violent histories of Klan terror and of armed Mexican resistance to Anglo dominance in Texas. Growing up in the aftermath of the Mexican Revolution, Tenayuca saw her San Antonio community expand with the arrival of new migrants, who brought their own dire economic need and histories of militant struggle to the barrio. The native tejana forged her career as an immigrant organizer, one whose politics encompassed new migrants and Mexican Americans alike in a shared vision of social justice.

Emma Tenayuca attributed her radical politics to her mestiza identity, identifying strongly with the historical resistance of indigenous people to

colonial rule. Tenayuca shared with Paredes a fascination with the social
ferment of the Mexican Revolution and border conflict that enlivened political discussions within her family circle and in communal gatherings
in San Antonio's Plaza del Zacate. But these lessons about ideology came
freighted with other kinds of schooling in the forms of political corruption sustaining the racialized caste system of South Texas. In her 1984 address to the National Association of Chicana/Chicano Studies (NACCS),
Tenayuca related an incident that recalls the electoral fraud that Paredes
described in "The Mexico-Texan":

> I remember as a youngster attending a political rally with my father.
> Sandwiches were distributed and inside the sandwich was a five-dollar
> bill. . . . Let me give you an idea of what it meant to be a Mexican in
> San Antonio. There were no bus drivers that were Mexican when I was
> growing up. The only Mexican workers employed by the City Public Ser-
> vice and the Water Board were laborers, ditch diggers. . . . I came into
> contact with many, many families who had grievances, who had not
> been paid.[50]

Tenayuca's observation of how state agencies denied Mexican workers access to well-paid, higher-status jobs reveals her incipient critique of how
the nation-state operated as an instrument of capitalist domination. According to historian Zaragoza Vargas, the young Tenayuca identified with
radical social thought from adolescence, when she began reading the
novels of Emile Zola, alongside socialist histories of the British working
class.[51] Her interest in historical materialism also led her to a critique of
patriarchal power; her first political actions involved campaigns on behalf
of female garment workers. Tenayuca began labor organizing when she
joined the picket line, at the age of sixteen, in defense of female employees of the Finck Cigar Company in 1934. The young tejana experienced her
first arrest and began to articulate a gendered critique of the social relations of production.

Tenayuca forged her public image as a principal organizer in the 1938
pecan shellers' strike, when ten thousand Spanish-speaking residents of
San Antonio walked out of the Southern Pecan Company for thirty-seven
days. The company kept production costs low by relying on handwork,

rather than machines, for shelling the nuts. The workforce was predominantly Mexican and female, many of them new migrants, with whole families engaged in piecework for wages averaging two dollars a week. The company steadfastly ignored New Deal provisions for higher wages, and during the Depression, wages went still lower, to mere pennies for the day's work. The 1938 strikes began as a spontaneous uprising against wage cuts and poor working conditions and quickly expanded to full-scale revolt against economic and racial discrimination.

The workers selected Emma Tenayuca as their chair for the strike committee. The pecan shellers respected Tenayuca for her steadfast solidarity as an organizer for the Workers' Alliance, under whose auspices she had campaigned against labor-rights violations, housing problems, and racial discrimination on behalf of West Side residents. The strike drew from a number of political traditions, incorporating border anarchists, communist organizers, mutual-aid organizations, and Mexican unionists. Ultimately, the strikers sought representation from the new Congress of Industrial Organizations, which had formed in 1935 as a vehicle for rank-and-file organizing in industries with workers deemed "unorganizable."

Police repression was swift and severe, as local officials feared the escalation of class revolt in the city. Officers used tear gas, water hoses, and batons to put down strikers and their supporters. The police chief, Owen Kilday, made a particular target of Tenayuca, naming her as a "Communistic leader"; Kilday called the strike action illegal and began a systematic campaign of harassment against picketers, while issuing explicit threats of physical reprisal against the militants. Although the Catholic Church, a dominant social force in tejano communities, supported the strikers, it also cautioned against incitements to class warfare. The Catholic newspaper *La Voz* echoed the extreme hostility of the English-language press toward the strikers, accusing the jailed Tenayuca of being a traitor to her people: "If she were a Mexican she would not be doing this kind of work."[52] As Irene Ledesma documented, the Spanish-language press was more sympathetic to the strikers than were the *San Antonio Express* or *San Antonio Light*, but it still sought to distance Mexican Americans from Tenayuca and the "red" union UCAPAWA (United Cannery, Agricultural, Packing, and Allied Workers of America).[53] The negative press response expressed social discomfort with women's visibility in the labor movement, as the predominantly female workforce occupied center stage in the strike. Tenayuca became a lightning rod in the conflict as every side defended its position in relation to the outspoken activist. Her advocacy on issues of race troubled the city's leadership, just as her communism made her a liability for the labor movement.

Tenayuca earned the title "La Pasionaria" [The Passion Flower] during the 1938 strike, for her defiance of police intimidation and her forceful speech, which reminded San Antonio unionists of Dolores Ibárruri Gómez, a famous resistance leader in the Spanish Civil War. During the 1936 Battle of Madrid, the communist journalist had incited support for the Republican cause over radio broadcasts with the slogan "¡No pasarán!" [They shall not pass].[54] In her exhortations to the San Antonio strikers, Tenayuca also used the metaphor of civil war to draw connections between the local labor movement and a broader, international justice movement: "They can stand me up against a wall and fill my body with bullets," she declared, invoking the image of fascist executions, but social justice would prevail. For Tenayuca, the "leading role" in the inevitable liberation struggle would belong to the Mexican American proletariat.[55] It was this conviction that had led Tenayuca to join the Communist Party in 1937, because she recognized an insurgent possibility in the transborder communities of the Mexican and Mexican American working class.

During the 1930s, the Communist Party in the United States (CPUSA) established local parties throughout the South and Southwest in order to draw its laboring classes into Party institutions. Tejanas/os brought their own political culture to the Communist Party in Texas, investing their own traditions of collective action and radicalism in the revolutionary unionism of the moment. In addition to the CPUSA, the Communist Party of Mexico was also operating in Texas, training Mexican Americans in labor organizing alongside the Congreso de Trabajadores Mexicanos [CTM, Congress of Mexican Workers]. In 1936, Emma Tenayuca and Manuela Solís Sager were among several tejanas who received instruction from the CTM at the El Colegio de Obreros [Workers' College] in Mexico City. Mexican Americans used CTM resources to advance civil- and labor-rights campaigns throughout the Southwest and as far north as Chicago, which the Mexican union promoted as its CTM del Norte.

For Emma Tenayuca, like other Mexican Americans of her generation, the intellectual culture of Marxist-Leninism offered a useful framework for contending with the South Texan climate of racial and class repression. Mexican Americans were determined to reform U.S. society, inspired in part by the sentiment of the New Deal, but the ever-present "Mexican Problem" set a political boundary on their integration. Militant migrants were an important base for labor- and civil-rights struggles, but unionists and civil-rights leaders generally excluded migrants from political campaigns. In a situation in which Mexican Americans occupied the lowest rungs of labor, few organizations extended membership to noncitizen migrants. By contrast, the CPUSA spoke boldly on issues of racism and class oppression and offered a dynamic international framework, whereas middle-class, nation-centered civil-rights organizations remained silent. Throughout the 1930s, union drives by Mexican Americans, many of them assisted by Communists, animated the social movements of the Southwest.

By the time Tenayuca was elected chairperson for the Texas State Committee of the Communist Party, a position she held between 1938 and 1941, she had begun to formulate a study of Mexican border communities and the thorny issue of nationalism. During the 1938 strike, she and her husband, Homer Brooks—a communist organizer sent to Texas for the southern recruitment effort—wrote "The Mexican Question in the Southwest," hoping to draw the attention of national Communist Party leadership to the struggles of Mexican communities in the border region. First published in the CPUSA journal of political theory, *The Communist*, the article constituted a ground-breaking effort to bring Marxist principles to bear on the situation of Mexicans in the southwestern United States. Tenayuca drafted the piece while imprisoned with fellow pecan strikers in San Antonio. The authors elaborated their program for social redress in the language of the U.S. Popular Front, a coalition of groups that encompassed a spectrum of socialist, communist, and working-class ideologies aligned with the international movement against fascism. The struggles of Mexican peoples against class and racial oppression, they argued, would form a vital part of the worldwide fight against fascist forces. Even decades later, the article remains a remarkable document. Zaragoza Vargas writes, "Not since 1915, when the irridentist program, El Plan de San Diego, was drawn up, had a member of the Spanish-speaking community of the Southwest raised the issue of nationhood in a radical form."[56]

The authors begin with Stalin's definition of a nation: "a historically evolved, stable community of language, territory, economic life, and psy-

chological make-up manifested in a community of culture."[57] Tenayuca
and Brooks then argue that Mexicans in the United States claimed neither
territorial nor economic community:

> Should the conclusion, therefore be drawn that the Mexican people in
> the Southwest constitute a nation—or that they form a segment of the
> Mexican nation (South of the Rio Grande)? Our view is no. Historically
> the Mexican people in the Southwest have evolved in a series of border-
> ing, though separated communities, their economic life inextricably con-
> necting them, not only with one another, but with the Anglo-American
> population in each of these separated Mexican communities. Therefore,
> their economic (and hence, their political) interests are welded to those
> of the Anglo-American people of the Southwest.[58]

In rejecting Stalin's formulation of the national question, Tenayuca and
Brooks showed that the racial formation of Mexican peoples as a disfranchised minority followed a different trajectory from that of national domination. Mexican communities at the border had never achieved full incorporation into the Mexican nation following its independence from Spain
in 1821. Like Paredes, Tenayuca understood that postrevolutionary Mexico
offered little to emigrants and Mexican Americans. Simultaneously, Mexicans and Mexican Americans were not fully nationalized as U.S. citizens
because of their continued treatment as "a conquered people." By demon-
strating the incomplete nationalization of "bordering communities," Tenayuca and Brooks called attention to the distinctive political agency of
border Mexicans and argued that the transborder division of labor made
Mexican American subjectivity incommensurate with that of the citizen.

In critiquing the nation form, Tenayuca and Brooks depicted Mexican American citizenship in terms that departed entirely from LULAC's
integrationist strategy for fighting racial discrimination during the 1930s.
Their demand for incorporation into the Popular Front was not only an
expression of political solidarity but also an appeal for federal action to
protect poor Mexican communities from police repression and racial hostilities. Writing from prison, Emma Tenayuca had personally experienced
constant harassment from local Texas authorities acting on behalf of police chief Owen Kilday. As a tejana, Tenayuca knew intimately the vigilante traditions within Texas law enforcement, a tradition in which police

violence functioned as a form of labor discipline. Within this context, the Communists found it necessary to use federal power as a wedge between local state authorities and employers.

"The Mexican Question" argued that the state owed all workers equal protection, whatever their immigration status, because their labor enriched the national economy. Rather than view Mexican nationals as a threat to Mexican American citizenship, they opposed the mass-deportation drives and decried the actions of the Mexican government to suppress migrant organizing efforts. Tenayuca and Brooks's proposals for ameliorating Mexican poverty and racial discrimination sought to expand New Deal programs beyond their function to stabilize the national crisis. Their proposed platform of redistributive reforms would appropriate the nation-state apparatus for radical social change.

Tenayuca and Brooks cited the "desire of the Mexican people for unification" as the basis for their plans for economic and social redress. While demanding the full recognition of Mexican American citizenship in the United States, they never recognized the sovereign boundaries of the nation-state. In language that anticipated later designations of "cultural rights," their platform required that the state make full accommodation of Mexican cultural difference. Demanding "educational and cultural equality," they argued "for the granting of equal status to the Spanish language." In demanding culturally relevant curriculum and desegregated schools for the Mexican American population, Tenayuca and Brooks sought to interrupt the perpetuation of Mexican stoop labor, social marginality, and electoral discrimination.

Tenayuca and Brooks's appeal to the federal government was not without its own internal contradictions, however. Even as they demanded the removal of racial barriers to Mexican American occupational mobility and political participation, they were unable to fully answer the constant demand of capitalism for cheap, racialized labor. The nation-state could only extend its protection to Mexican workers by making them U.S. citizens. Still, the liberal state required high levels of production as a basis for economic growth. Entrenched inequalities between the Mexican and U.S. economies would continue to draw Mexican workers north, and conditions of deprivation would make them vulnerable to exploitation.

Neither communist nor liberal thinkers of the time could imagine the movement of oppressed peoples toward self-determination apart from the teleological framework of development ideology. For subordinated populations to become fully *national*, they would also have to become *modern* and abandon indigenous cultural practices and social forms. (For this reason, as we will see in the next chapter, Paredes critiqued the eradication of the ejido and indigenous beliefs in the border region as he repudiated binational schemes for border development.) Even as Tenayuca and Brooks affirmed the autonomy of Mexican culture within the nation form, they remained ambivalent about the relationship of Mexican identity to the culture of laboring—which was precisely what distinguished border peoples and migrants from the more settled and economically secure Mexican American communities. In keeping with the Marxist conception of working-class emancipation, the two authors required the "cultural development of the Mexican people, which would help eliminate the conditions for their status as unskilled workers." Their treatise could not resolve the problem that Américo Paredes posed in "The Mexico-Texan": here landless Mexican laborers remained a problem for the two communists because of their purported resistance to modernization.[59] For border Mexicans to achieve self-determination as full citizens, they would have to become a different order of subjects.

Thus, the contradiction between the inclusive potential of liberal nationalism and the abusive realities of capitalist expansion would continue to bedevil Mexicans in the United States. Tenayuca and Brooks clearly anticipated this problem when they argued that civil rights should accrue equally to noncitizen and citizen workers alike. But their demand exceeded the capacity of the liberal state to intervene in the forms of capitalist development. In this sense, Tenayuca and Brooks's assertion that "the Spanish-speaking population of the Southwest, both the American-born and the foreign-born are one people" constituted an implicit recognition of the limits of the nation-state as a guarantor of rights. The fortunes of Greater Mexico would continue to depend on the ephemeral movements of migrant subaltern classes, which, as Antonio Gramsci argued in 1934, were "necessarily fragmented and episodic."[60] Not surprisingly, the aspirations of border Mexicans could only find expression in migrant cultural forms that lay outside national histories.

Despite her contributions as a labor leader and intellectual, Emma Tenayuca lost her position at the front of the union struggle in San Antonio.

Toward the end of the strike, UCAPAWA president Donald Henderson removed her from the strike negotiating committee, fearing that her reputation as a subversive endangered the union's objectives. For Tenayuca, this
was a terrible betrayal. It also meant that CIO directors privileged national
leadership over developing local organizing capacity. Although the CIO
managed to obtain small wage increases for the pecan shellers, the industry returned to mechanized processing shortly afterward, a move that
cost close to ten thousand jobs. As historian Gabriela González notes, the
strike ultimately had far greater significance as a social movement than
as a successful bid for better wages: "The role that Tenayuca played . . . as
a Mexican American woman taking to the streets and demanding radical
reforms, represented an attack on the racial, class, and gendered caste system holding up the edifice of San Antonio's political machine."[61]

Soon after, Tenayuca was forced into hiding. In August 1939, the mayor
of San Antonio, Maury Maverick, granted the Communist Party use of
the city's Municipal Ballroom for a meeting. An angry mob of five thousand stormed the auditorium, destroying the building and threatening the
safety of the mayor and the Communist leaders. In early 1940, Tenayuca
fled the city under death threats. In 1941 she divorced Brooks, having lived
apart from him for much of their marriage. She moved to Houston, took
the name Emma B. Giraud, and earned her living doing office work.

According to Zaragoza Vargas, Tenayuca felt disillusioned with the
party structure, finding its adherence to Marxist principles in conflict with
the task of building the mass movement for radical reform in the United
States. With the announcement of the Soviet-German nonaggression pact
in 1939, the communist movement lost many of its adherents in the United
States because they could not abide Stalin's accommodation of Nazi Germany. These included the disheartened Tenayuca. Shut out of the U.S. war
effort, Tenayuca eventually moved to Los Angeles and then San Francisco
and obtained her bachelor's degree from San Francisco State University in
the late 1940s. She formally resigned her party membership in 1946, after a
long struggle with tuberculosis made it difficult to continue in a position
of leadership. She eventually returned to San Antonio to pursue a master's
degree and worked as a school teacher until 1982.

The emergence of Chicana/o and feminist studies brought Tenayuca's
work back into circulation during the 1980s, when she participated in

various gatherings of the National Association of Chicana and Chicano tudies and of the organization Mujeres Activas en Letras y Cambio Social. Emma Tenayuca died in her native San Antonio on July 23, 1999, having inspired new generations of Chicana/o scholars and activists with her life history of tireless advocacy on behalf of the voiceless of Greater Mexico and beyond.

Mourning at the Limits of Nation

By way of conclusion, I wish to linger on the communal aspirations that Luisa Moreno, Emma Tenayuca, migrant singers, and Américo Paredes helped to articulate—especially their vision of the border as a single, linked cultural entity apart from the nation-state. The ferment of transborder culture in the 1930s suggests another reading of Paredes's "The Mexico-Texan." There remains a paradoxical relationship between the poem's *construction* —as a rendition of complete and total abjection—and the poem's *reception* as the foundational statement of border Mexican identity. For the communities that circulated the poem as an oral artifact, "The Mexico-Texan" embodied their collective, oppositional political will. As it entered the oral tradition in South Texas, through gatherings of tejanas/os organizing in the defense of civil rights, the poem came to effect the transformation of collective consciousness, as part of a "working-through" of the conditions of subjugation. The poem gains its power as a powerful invocation of historical trauma; the performative aspect of its stilted vernacular enacts a form of *racial mourning*. Racial mourning describes a reckoning with the forces of racial subjection so that new possibilities for emancipation might emerge for the powerless.

Within the bounds of the poem, the Mexico-Texan does not possess speech; his identity is completely defined by the discourse of others. In this way, the poem describes what Michel Foucault called "disciplinary subjection" in his analysis of subjectivation within the relations of domination structuring the modern prison.[62] Following Foucault, scholars have demonstrated how the state's power to produce subjects is double-edged. The state possesses the power of dominance over the citizen-subject, but by recognizing the subject, the state also grants its political and social being.

For Judith Butler, the process of *activation* permits the subject to contest or redirect the repressive force of the state.[63] State domination thus works to delimit or restrict the kind of subjects that may exist as different orders of citizenship.

For Mexican migrants and Mexican Americans, subjection to U.S. legal authority entailed exposure to state-sanctioned racial violence, exclusion from the national community, and their racial construction as "peons" and stoop labor. Border ranchers exacted extreme deference from Mexican workers as a means of labor control, acting with the tacit or explicit cooperation of local officials. In 1920, the Texan farmer A. P. Thames shot and killed Ramón Ramírez in a wage dispute. When a grand jury ruled that Thames acted in "self-defense," the county attorney argued, "From my personal knowledge of Thames' crop this year, I can say that he is the greater loser by the Mexican's death and the departure of other Mexicans from the premises. Instead of there being a good crop, there is almost a failure due to its not being worked."[64] With this ruling, the voice of the state reaffirmed property rights over Mexican human rights, following a precedent that continues to define class relations in the transnational labor circuit.

"The Mexico-Texan" can thus be read as an expression of the Mexico-Texan's melancholia, if the condition of melancholia is understood as a psychic response to the extreme sense of loss and the violent theft of social power that accompanies racial subjection. Melancholia, a state of distress, denotes incapacity to comprehend the loss and to recover motive will and the integrity of personal identity. The loss comes to be constitutive of subjectivity itself. But if the loss of agency in melancholia is total, it is not a sign of its complete or permanent absence. In his 1917 essay "Mourning and Melancholia," Freud describes melancholia as a state of rage against the other who has abandoned or injured the self, an inarticulate rage that cannot be directed against its proper object. Melancholia is thus a state not of passivity but of thwarted rebellion.

Paredes's task in the poem was to locate the trace of insurrectional energy residing in the Mexico-Texan's consciousness. It is precisely the Mexico-Texan's nonconformity to, or incapacity to perform within, the strictures of national belonging and citizenship that emerge in Paredes's poem as the potential for rebellion. Having rejected the liberal project of Americanization, Paredes took the charge of failed citizenship leveled at Mexican migrants and inverted it as a weapon against racial governance.

Performances of the poem moved the expression of Mexico-Texan identity beyond the stasis of melancholia into the realm of mourning, the more
dynamic work of reckoning with loss. With its enunciation, the poem created the conditions for imagining a Mexican community that would circumvent state sovereignty and the transborder division of labor. In their
collective voicing of historical memory and loss, Mexican migrants and
Mexican Americans refused the abject position that the state and employers imposed on them with such violence and indifference. In the migrant
vernacular, Paredes located an insurrectionary desire that might not simply oppose discrimination but release Mexican subalterns from state repression and the limited forms of subjectivity that the state could authorize. Through the protection of migrant difference, a more expansive order
of citizenship becomes imaginable.

The migrant culture that we now term "transnational" emerged with the
volatile social movements of laborers within and across national boundaries following the expansion of capitalist agriculture and the Mexican
Revolution. Mexican migrants opened up new challenges and horizons
of possibility for Mexican American social movements in the 1930s. Luisa
Moreno, Emma Tenayuca, Américo Paredes, and others used the construct
of the transborder community, what Paredes called "Greater Mexico," as
an expression of social relations that found no accommodation within the
nation-state. As they fought to give meanings to rights and cultural forms
within the interstitial border space, they reckoned with the fundamental conflict between the lives of border peoples and the interests of the
modern nation. Moreno's argument on behalf of "Non-citizen Americans"
defends the intransigence of border peoples before the assimilative narratives of nation and development underwriting the nation form as a form
of melancholic dissidence. The Bracero Program made this melancholic
formation into a national condition, as Mexico and the United States brokered a labor contract in 1942 that ultimately transformed the boundaries of Greater Mexico—and the laboring Mexican subject—with profound
consequences for both countries.

The next chapter examines the Bracero Program and the collapse of the
Mexican Revolutionary project of land reform through the lens of Américo
Paredes's 1955 novel, *The Shadow*. Paredes recalled being unable to find a
publisher: "Nobody was interested in it," he remembered. "They wanted
me to make different changes to give it more local color."[65] Local color

is, of course, one expression of the vernacular, perhaps its more palatable aspect. Paredes refused the prevailing codes of offering Mexicans as "local color" in the service of Anglo-Texan mythology. His rendering of the border vernacular reminds readers of the codes of property relations and racial terror underwriting national development. His historical and imaginative works of the 1950s, *With His Pistol in His Hand* and *The Shadow*, depicted border crossers as new political actors, moving the border out of its peripheral status at the margins of the nation. Paredes used the codes of communal memory, of relatedness to the past, to address the future. His vernacular made room for what did not yet exist.

CHAPTER *2*

Migrant Modernisms

Racialized Development
under the Bracero Program

> Is this indentured alien—an almost
> perfect model of the economic man,
> an "input factor" stripped of the
> political and social attributes that
> liberal democracy likes to ascribe to
> all human beings ideally—is this
> bracero the prototype of the produc-
> tion man of the future?
> —Ernesto Galarza, *Merchants
> of Labor* (1964)[1]

> The fact that here are body-men means
> that there are *men without bodies*.
> —Etienne Balibar,
> "Class Racism" (1991)[2]

The advent of World War II intensi-
fied and transformed the longstanding economic and social ties between
the United States and Mexico. The migratory circuit between the two
countries gained new prominence in the wartime economy of the United
States. This chapter examines the cultural politics of the Bracero Program, a joint venture of the U.S. and Mexican governments, which sought
to bring the vast transnational labor market under full state regulation.
This labor loan spanned the years 1942 to 1964 and brought hundreds

of thousands of Mexican contract workers to over two dozen states for seasonal jobs in agriculture and the railway industry. An estimated five million men participated in the program over its two decades, with many thousands more coming as undocumented migrants. State representatives for Mexico and the United States sought to use the contract system to control the massive migration flow between the two countries. In practice, however, this regulation merely sanctioned the capitalist demand for a flexible workforce made up of laborers stripped of effective civil and labor rights. The Bracero Program ultimately cemented the vision of Mexican migrants as temporary workers in the United States, to the detriment of both migrants' labor autonomy and Mexican American civil rights.

By the 1940s, migrant Mexicans, alternately vilified and valued, were the embodiment of tractable labor, fulfilling a capitalist fantasy of endless productivity. The imported stoop laborers of cotton and food cultivation became, in Etienne Balibar's phrase, the "body-men" of the wartime economy, workers whose entire existence could be appropriated for generating profit. The term "bracero" derived from the Spanish word brazos [arms], a designation that captured the limited terms of the men's recruitment. Carted to and from the border, they were valued as laboring bodies, mere arms detached from intellect or political will. Braceros were designated not by name but by a serial number on their contracts. As the United States and its Latin American allies assembled the necessary labor and natural resources for combating fascism in Europe and the Pacific, the war provided a new cast to modernization discourse. The bracero, shuttling between a developing nation and the advanced industrial power of the United States, served not as a soldier of national combat but as a soldier of labor.

Even as the war revitalized a militant nationalism that made Mexicans and Mexican Americans vulnerable to racial terror and exclusion, the war against fascism also provided a new language of citizenship and democracy for border communities, and for migrant workers who aspired to greater gains from their mobility and labor power. The discourse of development would not simply belong to the nation-state and its corporate interests, but would find expression in the border communities' campaigns for social justice. Whether the emergent ideology of reform and revolution would accommodate the migrant presence remained a troubling question for transborder communities during the Cold War and the civil-rights period.

The leading Mexican American scholar of migration and labor in the postwar years, Ernesto Galarza—himself an immigrant from the Mexican state of Nayarit—rightly questioned the creation of a floating army of workers. For Galarza, the bracero was neither a guest, in the sense of being a voluntary migrant, nor a temporary worker, in the sense of operating as a free agent, but was, rather, a category apart—a captive worker uprooted from home, unable to integrate into U.S. society. Galarza viewed braceros as a threat to the livelihood of U.S.-born farmworkers. Claims for inter-American friendship and national progress, he knew, acted as a powerful sanction for racial and class discrimination against both migrants and U.S.-born Mexicans. The importation of "indentured aliens" as farmworkers was less a resolution to the problems of unequal development in the Mexico-U.S. borderlands than an expansion of a neocolonial caste system within the globalizing agricultural economy. As such, the presence of thousands of imported workers in labor camps, or encamped outside Mexican recruitment centers, recalled the longer history of racialized class struggle both within Mexico and in the agricultural labor market.

The specter of hundreds of thousands of these "production men"—mere arms detached from the enfranchised body of the citizen—crossing into the United States revealed the lineaments of class racism in the transborder society. For Mexican Americans, the Bracero Program forced a reckoning with far more than their economic vulnerability in the United States: it revealed, once again, their own alienated status within the nation. The mass arrival of braceros increased Mexican American ambivalence toward the migrant newcomers, with whom they shared ethnic ties, class identity, and a history of racial discrimination. While intellectuals like Galarza exposed capitalist modernization as a racializing project, Mexican Americans contested the conversion of their vibrant laboring culture into nothing more than an "input factor."

For Galarza, as for many of his generation, migration was "the failure of roots."[3] In the aftermath of World War II, the predicament of stateless people cast emigration in a new light, making visible the meager protections for emigrants and refugees. The postwar discourse of human rights placed new obligations on nation-states to track and protect their subjects;

internal displacement and transnational emigration raised the specter of the state's failure to act as guarantor of rights.

This chapter examines the years of the Bracero Program through the lens of print culture, in the photojournalism of the Hermanos Mayo in Mexico City, and by way of the writings of Ernesto Galarza and Américo Paredes, whose documentary and fictional work indicted the national failures that created a permanent market in migrant people. The Hermanos Mayo [Mayo Brothers] were five Spanish émigrés who developed new aesthetics for photojournalism as they documented the mass labor exodus from their adoptive Mexico. As refugees from the Spanish Civil War, the photographers observed the mass mobilization of Mexican workers through the lens of their own history of displacement and leftist struggle. The dignity of their portraits contrasted strongly with the prevailing attitudes of Mexican nationalists, who used the figure of the bracero to indict the failures of the postrevolutionary government. The Hermanos' pictorial record mirrors the writings of Ernesto Galarza, whose studies of Mexican laborers in the 1950s established new transnational frameworks for viewing class and civil-rights struggles in the Americas.

A committed trade unionist, Ernesto Galarza navigated the precarious straits between naming the costs of institutionalized contract labor and blaming the migrants themselves, whose mobility frustrated organized labor and civil-rights leadership (just as it posed a problem for state authorities). Américo Paredes, writing without the strictures of making policy, used the imaginative space of the novel to explore the contradictions within national ideals of progress and order. For Paredes, the taint of colonialism, and in particular its racial ideology, was at the very core of the transnational labor economy. His novel *The Shadow* explores the postrevolutionary crisis in Mexico, in which the failure of roots derived from the collapse of the ejido system; but the slim text also attends to the ways economic development doubles as a project in subject formation.

Both Ernesto Galarza and Américo Paredes were ultimately less concerned with the economic or class features of capitalist domination of Mexican and Mexican American communities than they were interested in how postwar developments functioned as a new regime of subjection for the discriminated and displaced communities of the Mexican border-lands. Through the figure of the immigrant—for Paredes, the peon, and for Galarza, the bracero—the two intellectuals explored the uncertain sub-jective worlds of laboring Mexicans, citizen and noncitizens, whose mar-ginality and mobility precluded their access to rights or the goods of the modern order that their labor helped produce.

The Bracero Program, which represented the largest historical transfer in contract workers in the Western Hemisphere, could only be sanctioned through an enormous expenditure of resources. Historians have shown that the wartime claim to a labor shortage was a convenient fiction for growers accustomed to using labor surpluses to control both foreign and U.S. workers. The ideologies that defined and legitimated the temporary-worker program deserve attention beyond the question of its economic or political impact for domestic workers. Mae Ngai terms the contract-labor system a mechanism of "imported colonialism" for the way the delivery of temporary workers mimicked colonial labor systems abroad. As Cindy Hahamovitch has shown, the guest worker has been a global feature of capitalist development dating to its initial emergence in colonial planta-tions and slavery.[4] It is distinguished from slavery because it is a voluntary rather than involuntary labor transaction; nonetheless, the contract most often stipulates the isolation of the imported workforce from integration into the national society. That is, the guest worker is a temporary alien presence, rather than a candidate for naturalization. State controls over the movement of workers, and their ultimate repatriation, give powers to employers that mirror the unfree economies of indentured labor and slav-ery. Workers do not determine the sale of their labor but are subject to the brokerage of the state and employers' agents, and they are thus given lim-ited enjoyment of their "legal" status in the labor market and host society. Inequality and opportunity for exploitation, then, are inherent in guest-worker contracts.[5]

Advocates for agricultural workers in the United States uniformly op-posed the Bracero Program. No unionist could abide giving employers the power to repatriate workers. Braceros who protested their dissatisfaction with their contracts in the United States were often summarily deported. But Mexican American labor leaders in the bracero period also contended with nativism within the labor movement that left all Mexicans, citizen and noncitizen, and especially farmworkers, without access to collective bargaining and effective representation. The bracero posed a threat not only because imported labor undercut the bargaining power of U.S. workers; their presence intensified the racialization of Mexican people as a subordinated class in the United States. The Bracero Program stipulated that Mexican laborers were a temporary or reserve labor force, a fiction that had a corrosive effect on Mexican American efforts to move beyond their identification with stoop labor. Ernesto Galarza was above all painfully aware of the demands that this labor relation imposed on his people: it deformed kinship and communal bonds, and it deprived Mexicans of full cultural expression.

While the Bracero Program enabled a tactical negotiation at the level of the state between capitalist demands and anti-immigrant forces, it left the fundamental problems of racial and class domination intact. The Bracero Program design of the ideal immigrant worker threatened to coopt all of Mexican labor, under the ideological projection of the "production man." The managed labor migration reinforced the historical pattern of treating Mexican migrants as "always the laborer, never the citizen."[6] If employers valued Mexicans' supposedly unique predisposition to stoop labor, this designation worked against their social integration, since their very suitability for degraded work indicated their disqualification from full citizenship in the United States. The expansion of the contract-labor system further imperiled historical claims of Mexican peoples to the Southwest as a rooted community, integral to both national landscapes.

Emigrants Made to Order

As the United States emerged from the Depression in the late 1930s, U.S. growers and railroad industrialists raised complaints about labor shortages, seeking permission to import Mexican workers for the harvest and building season. Unionists and civil-rights leaders protested that employers were simply using foreign workers to create a labor surplus and keep wages artificially low for the U.S. labor force. Even before the United States entered World War II, California agriculturalists had initiated procedures for bringing Mexican workers into fields and railyards as a protective measure against shortages caused by the draft. Following the bombing of Pearl Harbor, the labor concerns of growers became a matter of national security.

On August 4, 1942, Mexico and the United States implemented the first of several historic agreements for the large-scale transfer of Mexican workers from Mexico to the United States. The "Mexican-United States Program of the Loan of Laborers," known informally as the Bracero Program, lasted until 1964 and oversaw the emigration of five million Mexican citizens to U.S. soil for temporary, unskilled work. The two governments sought to protect their own interests through the labor loan. Both hoped that state regulation would control the informal traffic in migrant labor. For Mexican leaders, the Bracero Program offered a solution to mass unemployment and unrestricted emigration. The bracero was to act as a modernizing agent, by sending needed revenue in the form of wages and by resettling in Mexico with knowledge of industrial agriculture and having discarded provincial customs. U.S. legislators envisioned the program as a means to curtail illegal immigration while also obtaining a low-cost source of stoop labor, without the costs of providing for their social welfare.

Despite concerns about the notorious mistreatment of Mexican migrants in the enganche [subcontract, literally "hook"], Mexican policymakers in the Comisión Inter-Secretarial responded positively to the U.S. solicitations. Mexican officials demanded strict quotas and contract regulation in order to protect the rights of nationals and to offset potential negative effects on domestic agriculture. Most pressing was the question of how to prevent a mass exodus of Mexican laborers, given the profound disparities in wages and job opportunities between the two countries. Officials outlined ways to track the movement of workers and retrieve them when necessary, with the hopes of deterring the out-migration of skilled nationals and securing the return of the emigrant labor force.

The legal documents that governed the contracts were a study in bureaucratic fantasies of total control: the contracts, in both English and Spanish, bore the signatures of U.S. and Mexican officials who pledged to keep bracero work free and secure and to guard against coercion and exploitation. The contract guaranteed that braceros would obtain, at minimum, a wage of thirty cents an hour and would receive medical benefits, insurance policies, the right to refuse unwanted work and the right to unionize, and access to consular services while abroad. Employers could subcontract their imported workers, but braceros could not move from their jobs to new sites of employment. These provisions allowed both governments to represent the labor loan as a patriotic sacrifice to the war effort and as a symbol of cooperation between the two countries.

In practice, these standards were never secured. Employers resisted the authority of the federal oversight and hired masses of unauthorized workers. Mexican laborers arrived to filthy work camps, encountering poor food, minimal care, and a hostile work environment. Their wages routinely fell well below the required minimum and consular officials did little to intervene on behalf of injured or discriminated nationals. Emigrants often could not read their contracts, and many did not even know their ultimate destination. The design of the program gave employers a variety of means to control their labor force, such as deciding who could use services like mailing wages to Mexico and who had access to leisure time beyond the work camp. Often the threat of deportation was enough to confine workers to miserable quarters or force them to accept additional jobs beyond the stipulation of their contract.

But Mexican braceros often refused to perform as a tractable labor force or as tradable commodities for the state. Their movements defied the authorities that brokered the loan of their laboring bodies. The number of men (and sometimes women) who sought entry into the program quickly overwhelmed the bureaucratic apparatus at the offices of the Secretariat of Labor in Mexico City, forcing a move to the Estadio Nacional [National Stadium]. These aspirantes [aspiring candidates], including the employed and unemployed, the skilled and unskilled workers, the rural and urban residents, belonged to what the state termed the "población económicamente activa" [economically active population], who lacked sufficient opportunities for good employment in their home communities. The rising cost of living, coupled with insufficient job growth, meant that the offer of work abroad was a matter of survival for many who gathered in the national capital. By the end of 1942, the city had to accommodate a floating population of candidates camped out around the processing center.

Throughout the 1940s, aspirantes staged protests against bureaucratic delays and manipulation of the quotas. The banner for one march appealed to President Miguel Alemán (1946–1952) to intervene on their behalf: "Reintegramos Nuestra Petición de Emigrar Como Braceros" [We reiterate our petition to emigrate as braceros]. Their marches drew police repression, with firefighters aiming water hoses at the crowds. Many of the aspirantes were unwilling to accept their exclusion from the program and entered the migratory circuit as unauthorized workers. The mobile crowds signaled a crisis for the newly renamed ruling party, the Partido de la Revolución Institucionalizada [Institutional Revolutionary Party or PRI]: the spectacle of idle able-bodied men showed the incapacity of the state to generate revenue through the working classes, except by converting them into commodities. Ciudadanos [citizens] became brazos [arms], mere economic men, just as Mexico sought to promote its own national strength and development.

If the 1940s ushered in a "golden age" of Mexican development, for aspirantes, its wealth and promise were another country. In 1947, the intellectual Daniel Cosío Villegas published the controversial essay "Mexico's Crisis," stating that "the goals of the Revolution have been exhausted, to such a degree that the term revolution has lost its meaning."[7] Lamenting the failures of Mexican postrevolutionary leadership, the national critic argued that the poor implementation of agrarian reform had cost Mexico needed resources for a coherent process of modernization. For Cosío Villegas, the failures of democratic reform to offset oligarchic power left campesinos [peasants] in a precarious situation, ill suited to play the historic role of revolutionary proletariat. The crisis, he concluded, necessitated "a reaffirmation of principles and a purification of men."[8] For the subaltern classes, such declarations were familiar gestures of bourgeois paternalism: the call for "purification" reiterated the demand that to become agents of progress, the poor, the campesino, the indigenous, would have to become *modern* —an amorphous quality that could change according to the imperatives of the moment.

Development, then, was a discourse that allowed nationalists simultaneously to advocate on behalf of marginalized groups as categories of need and to deny them self-determination as equal stakeholders in designing Mexican modernity. Nationalists like Cosío Villegas understood the need for workers to emigrate to obtain a living as the absolute negation of revolutionary principles and as a loss of national character. The overwhelming dominance of U.S. economic power and culture, Cosío Villegas warned, would lead to "the sacrifice of our nationality. . . . then there will be no autoregeneration in Mexico; and consequently, regeneration will come from the outside."[9]

By definition, Mexican legislators had hoped to use the Bracero Program to permit economic and social "regeneration from the outside." But by the mid-1950s, the Bracero Program was a source of concern for Mexican nationalists: beyond the income generated by remittances, few of its promises had materialized. Echoing Ernesto Galarza's statement that "migration is a failure of roots," Mexican nationalists depicted emigration as a matter of national disgrace. For Senator Pedro de Alba, the emigration of thousands indicated a failure of postrevolutionary development:

Quizás no exista problema más trágico para nosotros que el que se refiere a los trabajadores emigrantes de México, a los que se ha dado en llamar "braceros." No se trata del proletariado o del gañán en nuestro ambiente, sino del hombre que trabaja con sus manos y que busca el sustento en tierras lejanas. Es ésta una falla de nuestra organización social y política que tiene largas y profundas raigambres y que se necesita remediar a toda costa. Van de por medio el decoro y la dignidad de nuestro país y el prestigio de la Revolución Mexicana. La inestabilidad y las inquietudes económicas se compendian y agudizan en esa ola móvil de trabajadores desarraigados que parecen no encontrar ni la substencia ni la tranquilidad en su propio país.

[Perhaps there exists no more tragic problem for us than the one of emigrant workers from Mexico, those customarily referred to as "braceros." This does not pertain to the proletariat nor the wage earner in our midst, but an issue of the man who works with his hands and who seeks his livelihood in distant lands. This is a failure of our social and political structure that has long and deep roots and that needs to be remedied at all costs. The decorum and dignity of our country and the prestige of the Mexican Revolution depend upon it. Economic instability and shocks add to and increase that mobile wave of uprooted workers who appear to find neither subsistence nor tranquility in their own country.][10]

De Alba served two terms for the state of Aguascalientes in the Senate, where he headed the Comisión de Relaciones Exteriores del Senado (Senate Commission for Foreign Relations). From 1936 to 1947, he was the subdirector for the Pan American Union, where he may well have encountered Ernesto Galarza, who visited Mexico City throughout his years of employment with the U.S. offices of the Union. Like Galarza, the senator took a hemispheric view of the tasks of social reform and development in the Americas, and he also valued higher education as a vehicle for democratization and progress. Trained as a medical doctor, he wrote numerous homenajes to the great men of American history, among them de Las Casas, Bolívar, and Martí, as well as the memoir *El Roosevelt que yo conocí* [The Roosevelt I Knew].

Writing on the various historical factors that made emigration a matter of survival for many of the landless in Mexico, Senator Pedro de Alba understood emigration as an expression of social inequalities left unresolved within the revolutionary project. Unlike Galarza, however, his concern for workers was merely in the service of national interest. He concluded with a fatalistic summation that blamed state failure on the Mexican character: "Somos un pueblo andariego" [We are a wandering people]. However acute the problems of hunger and malnutrition, "En el caso de los braceros, además de los factores económicos, figura el afán de aventura; los mexicanos somos inclinados a conocer tierras lejanas y a explorar caminos peligrosos" [In the case of braceros, in addition to economic factors, the eagerness for adventure is notable; we Mexicans are inclined to get to know distant lands and explore dangerous paths].[11] For Ernesto Galarza, the failure of roots lay with the state's incapacity to provide for its citizens; for de Alba, the rootless emigrant threatened the primary claims of the nation-state over its people—that is, the capacity of the emigrant to act as an independent agent in the sale of his or her labor contravened against state authority.

Few Mexican officials publicly addressed the weakness of state formation as an outcome of the particular history of Mexico's path to capitalist development; the faith in modernization displaced a critique of capitalism and liberal nationalism in favor of culture-based explanations for the belatedness of national development. Within the bracero debate, the unauthorized emigrant emerged as a figure of opposition to state authority, a wandering, rather than rooted, national subject. The term "andariego" places an implicit value on the mobility of the migrant: he is aimless wanderer, rather than the focused, entrepreneurial "merchant of labor" that Galarza described. Senator de Alba could not account for why braceros might choose to remain in the United States:

> Lo que parece inexplicable es que a pesar de las horas amargas de soledad y abandono, de las fatigas y sufrimientos físicos y morales que pasaron en esas experiencias, hayan quedado muchos braceros con el vehemente deseo de regresar a los Estados Unidos.

> [What appears inexplicable is that despite the hours of loneliness and abandonment, of fatigue and physical and moral suffering passed in the experience [of contract labor], so many braceros retain the vehement desire to return to the United States.][12]

Absent from this discourse was an actual accounting of the political and social geographies linking Mexican communities with the United States, or a historical memory of the migrations that began well before the Mexico-U.S. War. Nor did the senator acknowledge the role of government officials in encouraging and managing that historic migration. Mexican nationalists omitted to mention the Mexican American communities that sustained emigrants in ways that would have complicated their narrative of "rootlessness." The repeated phrase "distant lands" for the southwestern United States obscured the relative proximity of border communities for many braceros from communities already integrated into the transborder labor circuit; for many emigrants, socialization into southwestern society complemented or replaced their "proper" attachment to the Mexican patria [fatherland]. Although the anthropologist Manuel Gamio observed in the 1920s that nationalism among Mexican emigrants took on an "almost religious quality," their attachment remained unacknowledged by their compatriots in Mexico.[13] Despite apparent sympathies for migrant suffering, the voice of the state retained the charge of failed citizenship.

Many defenders of the Bracero Program in Mexico saw the labor loan as a lesser evil to unregulated emigration. The Mexican scholar José Lázaro Salinas, writing in 1955, voiced open frustration with the government's incapacity to block emigrants at the northern border:

Por su parte México no contaba con ningún recurso eficaz para con-
tener la emigración de sus hombres que atraídos por el señuelo del
dolar dejan el país sin llevarse ninguna documentación que siquiera los
identificara, ya no digamos que los protegiera allende el Bravo.

[For its part, Mexico could not count on any resource for containing
the emigration of its men, who attracted by the siren call of the dollar,
leave the country without taking any documentation that could identify
them, let alone protect them on the other side of the Bravo.][14]

For Salinas, the Bracero Program represented the state's best effort to protect the rights of nationals working in the North; for Mexico, as for the
United States, the migrant without documents posed a problem for the
government. Although Salinas blamed the United States for luring workers
away from their home country (and undermining Mexican sovereignty in
the negotiation over the labor contract), he also condemned the braceros
for their willful refusal to recognize the authority of the Mexican state.

For Salinas, as for de Alba, the plight of braceros derived at least in
part from their willingness to accept mistreatment, to trade their labor
for "the siren call of the dollar." This notion of "migrant adventurers" made
discrimination less a matter of rights violations than of national humiliation. The redress for discrimination would require state advocacy on behalf of nationals, which would only entail greater state control of migrants
themselves. Despite their declared interest in protecting nationals abroad,
Mexican officials consistently subordinated the labor and citizen rights
of braceros to state interests. For this reason, it was perfectly logical for
Mexican consuls to devote more attention to regulating out-migration
and repatriating workers than to attending to braceros' complaints about
contract violations in the labor camps. The disdain of Mexican officials for
unions reflected the principle that labor and civil rights could only derive
from the state. Apart from the state, those rights lost their meaning. As a
field representative for the Joint United States–Mexico Trade Union Committee, Ernesto Galarza continually militated for the rights of braceros to
seek union representation in the United States. His efforts met with firm
refusal from Mexican consuls, who saw union organizers as competition
for control over the Mexican nationals, rather than as partners in the defense of their rights under contract.

Emigrants Looking at Emigrants

In the mid-1940s, as the Bracero Program was irrevocably altering their country, Mexicans were given a pictorial view of bracerismo, one that marked a radical departure from the perspectives of nationalists and government officials. The Hermanos Mayo published images of braceros that privileged class solidarity and labor power above national brotherhood. The collective of Spanish photojournalists operated out of Mexico City, having arrived as refugees from the Spanish Civil War. Outside the repository of identification photographs in state archives, these photographers created the most extensive visual record of the bracero mobilization, documenting the situation of aspirantes for Mexican newspapers.[15] Their photographs—of candidates who congregated outside recruitment centers and of physical exams, interviews, and contracts—showed a keen eye for the dynamic relationship between the mass event and the individual drama.

As refugees themselves, the Hermanos Mayo were emigrants looking at emigrants—exiles depicting Mexican nationals who could find no subsistence within their home country. They created images that ignored nationalist claims about braceros and instead attended to mobility itself. The pictures explore the implications of moving masses of men through the recruitment centers, to railroad cars, and across disparate terrains. Their cameras lingered on bracero bodies: under scrutiny, in motion, under contract, at rest, and in revolt. They scrutinized the upheaval with an interest in the hidden war behind the economic migration, a war all the more repressive for going unacknowledged as the outcome of national and class conflict.

The two sets of brothers—Francisco (Paco) Souza Fernández, Cándido Souza Fernández, and Julio Souza Fernández; Faustino del Castillo Cubillo and Pablo del Castillo Cubillo—were adherents to the Republican cause. In Spain, they had published with mainstream liberal papers and socialist periodicals of the more radical left. They took their name from the event that launched their careers: in the early 1930s, Paco and Faustino had recorded an assault by the Guardia Civil on a May Day labor march in Madrid that left several workers wounded and dead.[16] The images circulated as "las fotos mayo" [the May photographs], and the young photographers became the Hermanos Mayo. Later, the pseudonym became a means to protect the families of the photographers, whose identification with radical causes brought reprisals on the men's parents and siblings. (Paco was an associate of Dolores Ibarrurí, the original Pasionaria, for whom Emma Tenayuca was named during the pecan shellers' strikes of 1938.)

All five men enlisted with the onset of the Spanish Civil War in 1936, working as soldiers and as photographers. Franco's defeat of Republican forces in 1939 forced them to seek protection abroad. Faustino and Cándido spent time in French-run concentration camps for the captured International Brigades, until Paco secured their release with the assistance of Mexican diplomats. Under President Lázaro Cardenas, Mexico supported the Republican cause and began accepting refugees once it became apparent that the fascists would triumph. Three of the men, Paco, Faustino, and Cándido, arrived in Veracruz in June 1939, disembarking to the sounds of a Mexican military band playing the socialist anthem "The Internationale."

After forming their company, "Foto Hermanos Mayo," the trio established a high profile for their photojournalism in Mexican newspapers and periodicals. They furthered a collective tradition of leftist documentary work that had, in the assessment of critic John Mraz, a "'democratizing'" effect in Mexico, "a country where mass publications have generally been under government control."[17] The remaining Hermanos emigrated later, Julio in 1947 and Pablo in 1952. Scholars credit the Hermanos with introducing numerous innovations into Mexican documentary photography, beginning with the use of the lightweight German Leica camera that made photographers more mobile and unobtrusive in the midst of unfolding events.[18]

Mraz argues that the Hermanos' aesthetic established close proximity to the photographic subject and refused the fiction of an objective lens in favor of partiality and closeness. The brothers brought the public into the clamor of political marches with closeup images of the faces of striking workers, emphasizing the expressive features of the people immersed in struggle. Although the images of the Hermanos Mayo studio demonstrate impressive command of the formal qualities of the genre, the brothers were commercial, not artistic photographers. They did not choose their assignments, and they had to produce images at high volume for sale to Mexican publications. Some papers gave the photographers more control over the final images than others, but for the most part employers treated the Hermanos as reporters, rather than as crafters of the visual record of events.

The bracero movement provided a vital human drama for the Hermanos Mayo and an opportunity to merge their work obligations with their political commitments toward the largest labor and migratory movement in the hemisphere. The four hundred negatives devoted to the contract-labor program make up a minute percentage of the five million images contained in the Hermanos' total archive.[19] Still, these images have come to define the collective memory of the state-sponsored exodus in Mexico. In recent years, the photographs have appeared in major exhibitions at the Museo Nacional de Arte and other national museums, as well as in Madrid at the Institut Valencià d' Art Modern. In May 2003, the Mexican periodical *Ojarasca* introduced the Mayo collection to readers with the statement, "Su archivo es parte del patrimonio de la memoria nacional" [Their archive is a part of the patrimony of national memory].[20] Their role in the national memory was to record the people invisible to history, "los olvidados" and "los de abajo" [the forgotten and the underdogs]. The braceros are among the subaltern groups who have figured most prominently in the postrevolutionary imaginary as a source of spectacle and anxiety. Now relegated to history, these men and women represented Mexico in the full promise of modernization, though they are now viewed most often through a lens of national disillusionment.

The Mayo images are marvelous portraits. Their braceros appear in street clothes, milling around plazas, awaiting their interviews, or gathering in line to meet the health inspectors. The braceros smoke and swagger, they nap, they stare confrontationally at the camera or look away, and they jostle against the policemen that stand guard at the recruitment centers. The cameras capture the watchful glances of men reviewing their contracts, the inward gestures of self-defense during the medical exam, and the tension and excitement in crowds of young men. The plurality of the images is astonishing when measured against Mexico's prevailing discourse, which viewed the bracero as a single, simplistic figure. Instead, these men are beautifully complex—young and old, campesinos and urbanites, hopeful and resigned, both interacting with one another and contemplating their individual futures.

Through these photographs, each stage of the bracero movement assumes both historical and personal import. An image from 1950 shows a worker changing money at a bank in Ciudad Juárez. The shot records the

Bracero changing money at a bank in Ciudad Juárez. Photograph from the Fondo
Hermanos Mayo Collection, taken in 1950. ("Photo 41," reprinted with the generous permission from the publisher of *Uprooted: Braceros in the Hermanos Mayo's
Lens* by John Mraz and Jaime Vélez-Storey, © 1996 Arte Público Press—University
of Houston)

transaction through the glass of the bank teller's station, with a closeup on
the worker's face as he carefully places the bills on the counter. The teller,
located outside the frame, and the photographer are both slightly above
the worker; he has to reach up to make the exchange. The photograph dis-
tills the complex process of subjection confronting Mexican nationals in
the labor circuit. The money in the man's hand becomes an extension of
himself—it is all he holds in his line of sight. His modest clothes imply
that the bracero has gone into debt for this contract. The glass dividing
him from the banker reminds us that he is not working for himself but
in connection with the large state and financial apparatus controlling his
movements. In preparation for the border crossing, the worker changes
not only his money but also himself into a different currency. The reflections of other men crowd the glass, and the abacus on the teller's counter invokes the serialization of the mass human traffic, the conversion of

thousands of men into numbers to be recorded in corporate ledgers (or what Galarza called the "input factors" of agribusiness).

The camera nevertheless shows restraint in this image—it would have been easy to make moralistic claims through the spectacle of Mexican nationals selling themselves for dollars.[21] Instead, the photographer lingers on the graceful lines of the man's face, neck, and arms, providing an almost sculptural rendition and portraying him as a figure of profound dignity. A single gold chain draws the eye of the viewer, a personal detail that conveys the singular identity of the person under the photographic lens, and implies an interior self that lies beyond the camera's access.

In this and many other images, the Hermanos Mayo suggest that they are telling the bracero story in partnership with their subjects. Though perhaps a fabrication of the photographers, the impression of a relationship is a marked departure from the objectifying lens of the photojournalism of the period. In the Bracero Program the brothers found numerous scenes that resonated with their recollections of civil war: the men in the plaza with their few possessions must have been reminiscent of the refugees of their own struggle. The images of departing braceros on trains resemble the military transports used for departing soldiers, and indeed, the larger movement of the emigrant workforce mimicked the martial project of national defense. They were economic agents, not soldiers of war, enlisted in a campaign of nation-building through foreign labor. But like soldiers, they gave their bodies to the effort.

The Hermanos Mayo lens replaced the nationalist frame with one of class, depicting the braceros as a laboring caste. The portraits juxtaposed the physicality of the candidates' bodies with the apparatus that transformed them into nameless contract workers. The aesthetic reflected an ideological commitment to socialism, and many images adopted the visual codes of socialist realism, rendering the braceros as an uprooted proletariat. But the images also convey the photographers' concern for the ways nations could unloose their laboring classes from the contract of citizenship. In an interview with John Mraz, Julio recalled the brothers' profound identification with the emigrating workers:

We were emigrants for political reasons, and they were emigrants because of hunger. We had no problem earning our living in Spain; the problem was that we would have been killed if we stayed. But we did feel badly for those poor devils who had to leave their families and homes just to be able to earn a living. They should have been able to do that in Mexico.[22]

Here again braceros are an "uprooted" people, improperly cared for by the state. Unlike the Mexican legislators, however, Julio does not dictate that Mexican nationals should remain in Mexico—his own experience as a political refugee provided a different understanding of human mobility. Julio was less concerned with the bracero's national status than his ability to make good wages.

Nor did the Hermanos treat aspirantes and braceros as the isolated, "orphaned" subjects of nationalist discourses. From the plazas to the railway stations, the Hermanos' photographs show them accompanied by those who remained behind. The Hermanos placed women in the frame of the bracero story—as vendedoras selling food and drink to the men in line, as secretaries at the registration desks, and as girlfriends, mothers, and children at the railway departure. By including families, the images recorded the bracero movement as a project of entire kinship groups and villages, rather than that of a single, enterprising male agent.

One image in particular offers a revealing glimpse into the masked familial and gender dynamics that supported the labor contract. The photograph, taken in 1945 at the Buenavista railway station in Mexico City, captures the rituals of parting for one bracero family. A father leans far out of the train window to grasp his toddler son in a farewell embrace. The child's mother stands on the platform, one arm clutching the suspended toddler and the other nestling an infant. The four figures form a single uninterrupted chain, with the toddler in midair providing the link between the mother and father, and the second child tied to the mother in a rebozo [shawl]. Though the human chain is striking, the image resists a sentimental reading of family unity. Despite their connection, the four figures are looking in different directions. The father gazes down at the top of the boy's head; the toddler looks out at the camera in an expression of trepidation; the mother stares away at a point beyond the picture frame; and the infant glances up at his father. The man and woman do not appear to be communicating at all even as they hoist the child between them, and the woman's distant gaze suggests her distraction from the scene of departure.

Family of a bracero saying farewell at the train depot,
Mexico City. Photograph from the Fondo Hermanos
Mayo collection, taken in 1945. ("Photo 44," reprinted
with the generous permission from the publisher of
Uprooted: Braceros in the Hermanos Mayo's Lens by John
Mraz and Jaime Vélez-Storey, © 1996 Arte Público Press
—University of Houston)

By contrast, the man, who appears slightly older than the woman, is focused entirely on the son in his arms. The woman is in fact slightly outside
the line linking the father and the two boys in the frame of the picture.

There are numerous possible interpretations of this family assemblage.
The father appears alongside another emigrant, and each man is contained
within the frame of a train window; the squares seem to create individual

cells confining the men within the railcar. The two men wear fedoras and collared shirts, dress that links them to the urban emigrants, not the landless campesinos that the program had targeted.

The woman's posture and her apparent disengagement suggest that she is not fully part of this goodbye scene; she is perhaps simply the conduit for the communication among the children and their father. In this role, she manifests the subordination of women to the male citizen and wage earner—women did not become fully enfranchised citizens of the republic until 1953. Within the national discourse framing Mexican development, women served as bearers of citizens, not national subjects in their own right. Women derived their status from their relationship to men, to fathers, husbands, and sons. As Jean Franco reminds us, "Women's attempts to plot themselves as protagonists . . . became a recognition that they are not in the plot at all but definitely somewhere else."[23] The distracted gaze of the young mother conjures the difficulties that Mexican women faced as they attempted to make themselves into national actors in the midst of the Bracero Program and other struggles.

The success of the labor loan depended on women's capacities to maintain their households and complete the subsistence work abandoned by emigrating family members. Nonetheless, these labors remained outside the calculated costs of the program and largely invisible to history. In her brilliant study of families within the bracero migration, historian Ana Rosas has uncovered evidence of women's complex negotiations with the demands of the contract-labor system.[24] Women entered recruitment centers and migrant labor camps as vendors, domestic workers, and sex workers, in addition to the many thousands of women who joined male family members in the migratory circuit as undocumented workers. Their labors formed part of the complex and hidden negotiation over the price and arrangement of Mexican farm labor; their burdens, voluntary and involuntary, followed from the conversion of their countrymen into brazos. Though the spectacle of indentured labor sparked concern about the class racism confronting Mexican migrants, the hidden gender contract that sustained the labor system did not.

But perhaps the photograph also records more of the woman's will than a first glance might suggest. As the body of the son joins the father to the mother, it also serves as an object of negotiation between the two adults.

The father could be trying to take the son on board, and the mother is thus either handing the son over or pulling him back. The uncertainty in the image allows us to see the woman's active role in scripting this scene of departure. Although we know that the son will undoubtedly remain with his mother, the scene suggests another hidden aspect of the Bracero Program: once a family entered into the migratory stream, its members often remained within it. The father might have promised to return, but the seasonal migration led many braceros to a circular pattern of movement, rather than the temporary contracts that the two governments stipulated. So, too, the suspension of the son between the two parents, between home and departure, suggests how the child is himself forcibly inducted into the migratory circuit. The father's embrace doubles as a conferral of his own migratory status onto his heir. In this way, the chain of familial connection is also a binding contract and an intergenerational obligation that is structured by, but also makes possible, the transnational labor program. Within this system, the mother (who embodies the home country) yields her own reproductive labors to replenish the labor supply. Through the lens of the family portrait, then, the Hermanos Mayo convey the complex relationship between the waged and unwaged, voluntary and involuntary, and gendered burdens awaiting the migrant men and women who partook of the international trade in manual labor.

A keen awareness of how transnational migration disrupted Mexican family life also drove Ernesto Galarza, whose public criticisms of the Bracero Program derived from his close connections with the emigrants themselves.

The Journey He Remembered: Ernesto Galarza among the Braceros

I take good care of my documents. I have the contract, the passport, the blue card that gives the name of the contractor. The blue card is only in English. I don't know what's the advantage of these documents except in case we get lost. It seems we are lost even when we are right in camp.
—bracero, interview by Ernesto Galarza, *Strangers in Our Fields*[25]

> This was the journey he remembered. The actual journey may have been
> quite different. . . . The memory was all that mattered.
>   —Ernesto Galarza, *Barrio Boy*[26]

By the time Ernesto Galarza got around to writing his memoirs in 1970, he had already published definitive studies of Mexican migration and agribusiness in the United States, including *Merchants of Labor: The Mexican Bracero Story* (1964), *Mexican-Americans in the Southwest* (1970), and *Spiders in the House and Workers in the Field* (1970). The story of his coming of age as a Mexican immigrant during the 1910s and '20s, *Barrio Boy*, appeared in 1971. Galarza's own biography was embedded in the narratives of the migrant workers who formed the subject of his life's work as a scholar, policy researcher, and labor organizer.[27] Like many of the braceros he interviewed, Galarza had known the rigors of "peregrinations," of extended itinerancy brought on by civil war and hunger.

Born in the "hideaway" village of Jalcocotán, Nayarit, on August 15, 1905, Ernesto Galarza left the shelter of the Sierra Madre with his mother, aunt, and uncles amid the upheaval of the revolutionary conflict. The group made its way north through Mazatlán, Nogales, and Tucson, Arizona, before arriving permanently in Sacramento, California. While in school, the young Galarza worked the harvest seasons and participated in the labor movement. In the fields his facility with English made him an advocate for Mexican workers, who asked him to translate their petitions to employers for better living conditions in the farm labor camps. Galarza won a scholarship to attend Occidental College in Los Angeles, where he wrote (and eventually published) a senior thesis on the role of the Catholic Church in Mexican politics.[28] He pursued advanced studies in the social sciences, first at Stanford and then at Columbia University. Galarza married Mae Taylor in 1929, and the two entered careers in secondary education while Galarza continued his doctoral work in New York. In 1947, Galarza obtained his doctorate in economics with a dissertation on the Mexican electrical industry.[29]

Beginning in 1940, Galarza took a research position on education and labor concerns for the Pan American Union, a policy institution devoted to promoting trade and diplomatic relations among the countries of the Americas, which later became part of the Organization of American States. Acting as chief for the Division of Labor and Social Information, Galarza

wrote controversial reports on Bolivian tin workers and Mexican farm labor. His disillusionment with the actions of the U.S. State Department in
Latin America put him at odds with standard practice of inter-American
cooperation and the United States' Good Neighbor policy. Throughout the
1940s, Galarza argued that these agencies failed to promote the advancement of social welfare in the hemisphere and were actually instruments of
U.S. companies and U.S. imperial interests. His disillusionment led him to
abandon Washington, DC, for San José, California, where he took a position with the National Farm Labor Union (NFLU), which represented field
workers in Arizona, California, Florida, Louisiana, and Texas.

With his work for NFLU, Galarza moved from high-level operations in
the realm of policy to grassroots organizing, and from this ground-level position, he gained a profound sense of the complex economic and political
systems of labor. His work on behalf of strikers in the early 1950s brought
him face to face with the problems wrought by the Bracero Program's contract-labor system. No union effort, he soon realized, could compete with
the steady presence of imported field workers, from Caribbean cane cutters
to Mexican harvesters, whose contracts denied them access to union representation. As a critic of the imported-labor program, however, Galarza
was cautious not to take the nativist position common to the U.S. labor
movement. His defense of labor interests against the power of U.S. agribusiness was equally concerned with the status of Jamaican immigrants
and Mexican braceros. He saw all itinerant laborers as vital participants
in the integrated system of food and agricultural production in the hemisphere. As Stephen Pitti has shown, Galarza's position required a delicate
balancing act: he sought to oppose contract labor and defend the rights of
U.S. field workers without participating in the popular discourse that de-
monized braceros and "wetbacks." "Unlike other crusading reformers who
set their sights on California agriculture," Pitti writes, "Galarza knew that
at least two governments—of both the United States and Mexico—had
helped to reshape that region since the early 1940s."[30] As such, the strong
ties of migrant people to the southwestern United States deserved recognition alongside any consideration of the international dimensions of agricultural production. Mere opposition to immigration, Galarza knew, could
not resolve the needs of the laboring population, citizen or noncitizen.
During his years with the NFLU, Galarza worked exclusively in Mexico to
address the concerns of landless migrants, taking a binational approach to

labor organizing. His strategies to contest transnational capitalism were far more farsighted than those devised by the United Farm Workers Union in 1965 or by the cross-border labor campaigns that followed the enactment of the North American Free Trade Agreement of 1994.

Galarza's perspective developed in response to his experiences in the field. In the early 1940s, he had initially shared the common perspective of liberal policymakers, that a government-sponsored program for importing field laborers would offset the routine abuses of migrant laborers and provide an answer to the problem of undocumented migration. The contractual promise of government oversight and the protections for the wages and working conditions of braceros suggested that the bilateral agreement might even elevate the status of other field laborers and migrants in the United States. A decade later, Galarza's incendiary report, *Strangers in Our Fields*, ruefully recounted the failed promise of the bilateral contract:

> Thus, the legal situation in which the migrant finds himself is probably unique among agricultural workers in this hemisphere. In theory, the civil liberties recognized by the Constitution of the United States, the specific economic rights guaranteed by the International Agreement and the work contract, the provisions of hard-won progressive state laws and the immediate obligations of private companies to attend him in sickness and disability form a wide and solid base for personal security and individual dignity. If this were actually in place, it would be impressive.[31]

The answer to this "if" was, for Galarza, decidedly in the negative: "Serious violations of the rights of Mexican nationals were found to be the normal pattern rather than the exception," he concluded.[32] While still at the Pan American Union, Galarza visited over twenty labor camps across the West, where he found the lack of program oversight pervasive and noncompliance with basic labor protections depressingly routine. As the outrages of the contract system mounted, Galarza took his concerns to the Pan American Union and the presidential offices of both countries in 1944.[33] The disinterest of officials on both sides of the border led Galarza to reject the rhetoric of binational cooperation as a mere cover for the damaging influence of probusiness interests in national government.

As Galarza reported the roundups and deportations of braceros who militated for better conditions, he emerged as a leading critic of state repression. From 1944 through the '50s, he was the singular advocate for transnational unionism within the U.S. labor movement. While the postwar labor movement adopted a posture of economic nationalism—aligned with U.S. hegemony and anticommunist crusades—Galarza rejected such tactics in favor of a hemispheric solidarity among working people. Through his campaigns to educate organized labor about conditions in Latin America, Galarza countered the class racism endemic to both rank-and-file and high-level union representatives. For him there could be no distinction between dignifying the labor struggles of Latin American miners and peasants and promoting the racial integration of the union movement throughout the western United States. At a moment when U.S. unions and agribusiness colluded in treating undocumented migrants as unorganizable people—indeed, even as potential communist subversives—Galarza demanded that "Mexican immigrants be allowed to join U.S. unions without fear of deportation."[34]

In the early 1950s, Galarza joined the NFLU with the independent organization Mexican Alianza de Braceros Nacionales de México; the merger brought together the most vulnerable sectors of both Mexican and U.S. labor movements. Their fledgling union was an effort to contest racism and corruption in U.S. unions, as well as government cooptation of the national unions in Mexico. While migration continued unabated, Galarza charted plans for cultivating and celebrating what Stephen Pitti describes as "a new social movement that would capture the 'spirit' of an inclusive and antistatist Mexican cultural nationalism."[35] His vision, although unfulfilled in his career with the NFLU, found expression in his masterworks on Mexican labor. This scholarship documents the rapaciousness of capital and the "unorganized drift" of migrant labor, while also tantalizing readers as a proletarian literature of the highest order. "As readable as a Steinbeck novel," judged the Alaskan senator Ernest Greuning in his preface to *Merchants of Labor*, hinting that the power of Galarza's writing derived not only from the scholar's capacity for social documentation but also from his imaginative re-creation of the worlds in which migrants traveled and made their chanza.[36]

With his associates in the National Farm Labor Union, Ernesto Galarza contested the Mexican government's "comercio en carne morena"—literally, the trade in brown flesh—that united the Mexican and U.S. economies in the Southwest.[37] The modernizing project masked a more sinister discourse of racialization embedded within it: "it cast the whole enterprise as a massive educational enterprise by industrial managers who, besides profiting . . . would also gladly teach."[38] Such industrial pedagogy interpellated *all* migrants as the ideal farmworkers of agribusiness—flexible, transferable, and disposable—under the dictates of managed migration. The denial of collective-bargaining rights to contract workers made the Bracero Program, for Galarza, "a working model of totalized, though not yet totalitarian, labor merchandizing."[39] The threat for Latina/o unionists was clear: that, left unchecked, agribusiness could dominate all Mexican (not to mention Caribbean and Asian) migrants, by forcing them to accept the disposable-labor ideal, at grave cost to their communal health and rights.

Far more than fair wages and worker safety were at stake; such a power gave the state and its business partners an unreasonable purchase on the social and cultural life of the subaltern population. A passage from Tomás Rivera's *Y no se lo tragó la tierra*, a fictional chronicle of Mexican migrant existence during the 1950s, conveys the disciplinary force of the seasonal labor circuit:

— ¿Para qué van tanto a la escuela?

— El jefito dice que para prepararnos. Si algún día hay una oportunidad, dice que a lo mejor nos la dan a nosotros.

— N'ombre. Yo que ustedes ni me preocupara por eso. Que al cabo de jodido no pasa uno.[40] Ya no puede uno estar más jodido, así que ni me preocupo. Los que sí tienen que jugársela chango son los que están arriba y tienen algo que perder. Pueden bajar a donde estamos nosotros. ¿Nosotros qué?

[— Why do you all go to school so much?

— My father says we need to prepare ourselves. If some day there's an opportunity, maybe they'll give it to us.

— No way. If I were you I wouldn't bother about that. Anyway, the wretched can't get any more wretched. We couldn't be any more fucked than we are already, so I don't worry anymore. The people who have to play the game like monkeys are the ones who are better than us and have something to lose. They could lower themselves to where we are. What do we have to lose?][41]

This exchange among youths in a migrant labor camp punctures any pretense of pedagogical value in farm work touted by the Bracero Program. The second voice warns the children that their studies will not provide the social mobility that their father desires for them, since their caste is by definition excluded from the realm of opportunity.

Though the public school system was intended to reward those deemed eligible for effective citizenship, Rivera shows that most migrants in the 1950s labored without that possibility. (Rivera and Galarza were among the very few of the migrant class to obtain formal education, let alone the status of ilustrados, as authors and educators. Galarza published *Barrio Boy* in the same year that Rivera completed *Tierra*.) *Tierra* narrates the painful processes by which Mexicans internalized their subordinate status. In a reversal of expected roles, the elder speaker admonishes the children for their aspirations. The speaker uses "jodido," the adjectival form of "joder" [fuck up], to convey the hopelessness of being the lowest of the low, a condition arising from profound violation. The migrant vernacular thus encodes an acute sense of poverty as an unnatural condition, of suffering made all the more terrible for being the deliberate outcome of the labor system. The speaker's expression is one of barely controlled anger, but an anger all the more potent for lacking direction. The violence of the verb "joder" captures the violence of subjection, of being forced to accept one's poverty and marginality as an irredeemable situation. In its multivocal treatment of the migrant farmworker community, *Tierra* mirrors the spirit of Galarza's writings on the bracero labor camps. Both are vivid reckonings with the negative aspect of the migrant imaginary.

In 1956, Ernesto Galarza published his report on contractual abuses in the bracero system, *Strangers in Our Fields*, for the Joint United States–Mexico Trade Union Committee. The pamphlet exposed the dehumanizing effects of the temporary-worker ideal:

> The braceros work in a foreign land, surrounded by strangers whose language they do not understand. They are totally unorganized—or more accurately, almost totally *dis*organized. The National may have grounds for complaint but he is accustomed to look around and measure the distance between him and the help he would need if his claim is denied and resented. (75)

Galarza used the dominant terminology of the era, calling braceros "strangers" and depicting the Southwest as foreign territory to Mexican nationals. But in his account these terms are not a description of Mexican foreignness; they are an invocation of the Mexican nationals' alienation. Galarza accentuates the deliberate political estrangement of Mexican nationals in the migrant labor force, rather than their inherent lack of belonging. Galarza took pains to show that the apparent distance between Mexican nationals and their U.S. surroundings was a matter of political disorganization, rather than of incommensurable differences of culture and society. The apparent passivity of the braceros, Galarza knew, was actually an expression of cold calculation on their part, absent viable partners in their efforts at self-defense. Throughout the report, Galarza enumerates incidents of repatriations, in which employers effectively disappeared potential organizers within the camps.

The confinements of the labor camps stood out against the postwar declarations of universal human rights: the privations of the migrant camps were a crisis of inhumanity operating within the triumphal liberalism of the postwar United States. The camps were, with Jim Crow policies, the classist and racist engine of the labor economy that drove U.S. economic expansion and pretensions to global hegemony. Galarza cited a banner headline from a Los Angeles paper, *El Angelino*: "Esclavos Modernos: En pleno siglo de libertades los Braceros mexicanos son objetos de las más inhumanas explotaciones" [Modern Slaves: In the Age of Liberty Mexican Braceros Are Subject to the Most Inhuman Exploitation].[42] The very edifices of the migrant-labor circuit originated in policies of ethnic removals during World War II. Alongside converted chicken coops and warehouses, the state approved the use of former Japanese internment camps for housing Mexican nationals—their isolation from cities appealed to employers who sought to control the movements of their labor force. The camps were only the outward sign of the ideological continuity linking the formation of a subordinated caste of foreign workers and the denial of citizenship to people of Asian and Latin American origins.

The British sociologist Paul Gilroy has called the camp the emblematic architecture of racialized modernity: it embodies the contradiction of postwar ideology, between liberal conceptions of universal human freedom, on the one hand, and the need to cordon off problem populations from the spheres of rights, on the other.[43] To the concentration camp and the bantustans we should add the migrant labor camp to the architecture of unfreedom in the age of development. The bracero contract system was one expression of what Gilroy delineates as the "camp mentalities constituted by appeals to 'race,' nation, and ethnic difference, by the lore of blood, bodies and fantasies of absolute cultural identity."[44] The camp mentality of postwar nationalism required the suppression and containment of human mobility beyond the sanctioned boundaries of the nation-state, so that the state itself functioned as a carceral space for racialized migrants who were denied full membership to the spheres of rights.

As workers were confined to fields and dormitories, the imprisonment of the camp became anything but metaphorical. In *Strangers in Our Fields,* Galarza relayed a particularly vivid exchange with a bracero about the peculiar status of contract labor:

"It is not a matter of a strike," one man told me. "It is a matter of discussion, but everything looks like a strike to the Association. When the men stop work owing to the circumstances that problems are not resolved, you cannot call it a strike. It is a stoppage. How can you strike when you are already in jail?" (69)

The bracero interview exposed the consequences of the denial of bargaining rights to braceros in the fields. As temporary foreign workers, braceros inhabited an irregular juridical status in which the contract bound them to employers (who themselves formed collectives called "Associations"), without autonomy of movement or the exercise of collective labor power. By design, their enforced social isolation made the contract system one of indenture, rather than of free labor. Their subjection under the contract made Mexican nationals into captive workers: a work stoppage could not attain the status of a strike, the bracero explained, because it took place within the carceral regime of the labor camp. As Galarza showed, it was impossible to enforce the labor protections built into the bracero contract, because the state and employers retained control over workers' representation and also over their mobility.

The contract became a prison sentence, rather than an enfranchising document for the worker. The very documents that designated nationals as citizens and bearers of rights—passport, contract, blue card—functioned to curtail the exercise of those entitlements.[45] Because Mexican consuls and U.S. labor authorities never inspected the camps and routinely ignored bracero complaints, the paperwork merely tied the braceros to places of exploitation. "I don't know what's the advantage of these documents except in case we get lost," one national told Galarza. "It seems we are lost even when we are right in camp." The best solution for many was to "skip" the contract altogether and take on the status of undocumented migrant. "The Wetbacks are more free" was the consensus of many.[46] When the contract failed as an instrument of labor protection, it also inverted the compact between the state and the expatriated citizen. So even though becoming a "wetback" threatened braceros with the loss of status entailed in canceling the documents binding them to the state, it also enabled them to recover their fuller humanity beyond the restrictions of the contract.

If, as Etienne Balibar suggests, the modern capitalist regime of subjection finds its ultimate expression in the production of "body-men"—mere laboring bodies—then the presence of these "production men" necessarily provokes a crisis for the societies in which they labor. Any labor system must contend with the humanity of its workers. In fact, all labor relations depend on this humanity, even as masters or employers seek to extract a maximum profit from the laboring population. This has been the historical dilemma for any system of unfree work: how to manage the very human qualities that undercut the fantasy of total labor control? As the Bracero Program evolved, employers themselves resisted the contract system and began to hire more and more undocumented workers. This was not done out of respect for the autonomy of the migrants but because, as Galarza put it, Mexican labor was "no longer considered supplemental, it [was] the labor supply."[47] The growers' inordinate investment in Mexican nationals as an ideal labor force contradicted the public fiction of a *temporary* labor loan; this inconsistency, however small, suggests that braceros and undocumented migrants frustrated the totalizing narrative of labor control and rationality. Despite the public clamor for immigration restrictions, agribusiness made its demand for imported Mexican fieldhands a matter of permanent emergency. Not only employers but migrants themselves created a political economy that could not function without the productivity and cheap labor of Mexican emigrants; in America's postwar economy, Galarza noted, "crisis has become a permanent condition."[48]

The "crisis" was ultimately a problem for the state, as it sanctioned the importation of braceros even as it criminalized "wetbacks" for responding to the very same lure of the market. The oppositional forces of importation and expulsion were reconciled in the official attitude toward the migrant pool, of identifying which migrants fulfilled the United States' criteria for determining the legitimate migrant. In the Cold War years, aspirantes passed through a sorting process under the close watch of the police state, which sought to ensure no communist subversives entered in the floating labor pool. In her oral history, *The Bracero Experience*, María Herrera-Sobek recounts the infamous hand inspection that accompanied the physical examination of candidates: to be considered eligible, workers had to have the calloused, hardened hands of seasoned farmworkers.[49] Candidates with scars were commonly rejected as likely "troublemakers." In this undeclared contest over mastery of the Mexican body, candidates and state officials negotiated a process of "reading" the racialized body in a scene reminiscent of colonial practices of labor extraction. However unequal the encounter, migrants devised ways to subvert the process and retain a sense of dignity. In order to meet the state criteria, men would deliberately raise blisters on their hands and perform according to the expectations of the inspectors.

Even as Ernesto Galarza sought to convey the unfree terms of the binational labor contract, he took pains to communicate its dehumanizing effects without reducing the humanity of the migrant laborers themselves. His writings earned him a nomination for the Nobel Prize in Literature for 1976. Galarza wrote with an ear for the migrant vernacular, for the wry humor that encoded the necessity of hard labor but also an appreciation for migrants' capacity for survival.

That wry humor also animated the scholar's own writings—it is the resonant voice in his memoir, *Barrio Boy*, which he subtitled "The Story of a Boy's Acculturation." The elusive process of his subjection as a Mexican American immigrant during the era of the Mexican Revolution took place between the migrant camps of his seasonal labor and the relative comforts of settlement in the barrio. Galarza's narrative continually reminds us that "the Americanization of Mexican me was no easy matter," in part because the author refused the imperatives of nationalization altogether, neither adopting a posture of cultural nationalism nor making his story one of

assimilation to the liberal ideal of citizenship. Camp life featured prominently in the formation of his binational identity. Galarza concludes *Barrio
Boy* with his first strike, in which he acted as a translator for the migrant
community: "In a camp near Folsom during hop picking," he writes, "it was
not wages but death that pulled the people together."[50] After a child died
from diarrhea, the women of the camp determined that the cause was
contaminated drinking water. The camp committee sent Galarza to obtain
the assistance of some "Autoridad" [authority] to bring an inspector to the
camp. The journey from the camp to downtown Sacramento foreshad-
owed what was to be his longer career in struggle. The designated authority, Simon Lubin, instructed the young man "to tell the people in the camp
to organize." Rather than stage this scene as the confirmation of his illus-
trious future, however, Galarza subverted the developmental frame of the
autobiographical genre. His personal destiny, like that of his community,
remained uncertain:

> I reported the interview with Mr. Lubin to the camp. The part about
> the inspector they understood and it was voted not to go to work until
> he came. The part about organizing was received in silence and I knew
> they understood it as little as I did. Remembering Duran in that camp
> meeting, I made my first organizing speech.[51]

The journey into public life did not begin auspiciously: Galarza reports that
he was fired shortly after the water inspector came and that he "finished
that summer nailing boxes on a grape ranch near Florin."[52] The wages of
hunger denied the young striker the chance to observe the power of collective action, and of speech. The narrative ends with a bicycle ride through
the dirt roads back to Sacramento, where the young Galarza begins to
consider his entry into high school, hinting at what might lay ahead. The
narrative ties his imaginings (joining the debating team) to the physical
action of powering the bicycle, as he traverses the social distance between
the subaltern rural community and the state capital. If the author could
not find a conclusion to the "boy's story of acculturation," he nonetheless
conveys that his future was ineluctably linked to the conditioning of the
migrant labor camp. The exercise of his own migrant imaginary would depend on where his laboring could take him.

Laboring under Development: Américo Paredes's
The Shadow

> In the distance, the men still worked, and Cuitla peered at them through
> the glare with half-shut eyes. He saw them and he did not, for as he
> looked he did not see skinny little men in cotton drawers, sun-shriveled
> men sweating their lives into the sun-baked land. He saw green, waving
> fields, networks of canals, white-washed houses, trim fences and flower-
> bordered lanes. And moving about them a brown and happy race: har-
> vesting, feasting, playing. And in the foreground, looking straight at
> him with confidence in his eyes stood a brawny farmer, his child on his
> shoulder, his young wife by the hand, and all three smiling at him with
> strong, white teeth, smiles of contentment and cleanliness and health.
> And it was all in several colors, as he had seen it many years ago on the
> cover of an educational magazine.
>
> —Américo Paredes, *The Shadow*[53]

Ernesto Galarza developed his own migrant imaginary as a member of
the mass exodus wrought by the Mexican Revolution. For him, the civil
war meant displacement from the sierras of Nayarit and the conversion
of his family into racialized itinerants. The political turmoil of Mexico led
directly to the camps and to the confinements of the segregated barrio
in the United States. For Américo Paredes, the Revolution not only signified the same unresolved class and ethnic strife that troubled Galarza,
but its ideological tenets also formed a resource for contesting the liberal
racism that he saw in his native Texas. The border conflicts that drew in
his uncles also provided the scenes of insurrection against white primacy
and Anglo dominance in the Southwest. Both Galarza and Paredes participated in, and studied, postrevolutionary Mexican society as a means
to understand the racial logic of development that so dominated the lives
of Mexicans in the transborder region. Galarza's indictment of the Bracero
Program was a prominent force in the debates over migration and farm
labor in the postwar period; Paredes's own contributions to the literature
of migration are less well known. His novel *The Shadow* came into print
four decades after it first composition in 1955, but its critique of Mexican developmentalism demonstrates how the tejano scholar was deeply

engaged in debates over the ways modernization functioned as a racial-izing project at the border.

Paredes is best known for his studies of U.S. racism and Mexican life north of the Rio Grande, but the author was also a keen observer of post-revolutionary society in Mexico. He wrote his first novel, *The Shadow*, in 1955, amid broad debates among Mexican Americans about the combined impact on their citizenship rights of the Bracero Program and unauthor-ized migration. His novel was among the first Mexican American writings about the emergent Mexican social order. With its critical assessment of the failure of Mexican land reform, Paredes anticipated the similar con-cerns of scholar and farm-labor activist Ernesto Galarza, who published *Strangers in Our Fields* in the following year. Like Galarza, Paredes sought to understand how the "revolución interrumpida" [interrupted revolution] converted the landless soldiers of the Mexican civil war into economic migrants and émigrés, with little protection from their national govern-ment.[54] Paredes's interest in unresolved class and racial fractures within the postrevolutionary nation offers a new departure point for examining representations of Mexican American identity in his other works, as I dis-cussed in chapter 1. Paredes's novel is a study in revolutionary subjectivity; his revision of the early manuscript during the 1990s provided him with an occasion for revisiting the heroic mode of cultural resistance that he had depicted in *With His Pistol in His Hand*.[55]

In Américo Paredes's work, the border marks a space of contestation to the controlling narrative of Western modernity, that of the nation. In his slim novel *The Shadow*, Paredes addresses the revolutionary Mexican state-in-the-making. The text is thus of vital importance for understanding his efforts to delineate a bordered historical consciousness. Paredes first drafted the book for submission to a literary competition in the early 1950s, while looking for ways to supplement his income as a graduate student.[56] Although Paredes won the contest, the novel lay untouched until the early 1990s, when the success of his novel *George Washington Gómez* sparked an excavation of his unpublished fiction. *The Shadow* was finally published in 1998, following his revision of the forty-year-old text. With this book, he once again touched on the decline of northern Mexican ranching society, a theme he first explored in *With His Pistol in His Hand*.

The Shadow is set in Mexico in the late 1930s, during the reconsolidation of bourgeois and capitalist power. It offers a fascinating lens on Mexico during the first decades after the revolutionary conflict of 1910–1920. In this phase of economic nationalism, the government broke with its commitment to land redistribution, subverting the ejido system of small, collective landholdings in favor of large-scale commercial agriculture. The revolutionary Constitution of 1917 hailed the peones of Mexico's historical division of labor as citizens and patriots, and it made land reform a reward for their sacrifices in battle to the modern nation. Despite its promise, however, the revolutionary state quickly reverted to the rigid hierarchies of the prior regime, even as it pursued the rapid modernization of public institutions, finances, communications, and industry.

The ejido system conflicted with the imperatives of capitalist development, since the shared tenancy of lands in small communities deprived the national economy of the surpluses necessary for the accumulation of profit. By 1940, land redistribution had stalled, leaving the mass of landless workers without a stake in the national economy. The wartime labor shortages in the United States gave Mexico a front for addressing rural discontent while masking the class interests of the ruling party. Mexican legislators seized on the binational labor contract as a means to gain control over the entrenched problem of emigration. By representing the Bracero Program as a vehicle for economic advancement, the Mexican government cloaked its internal class fractures in the rhetoric of nation-building.

For Paredes, the trade in brazos resonated with his abiding suspicions of both nationalism and capitalist development. After all, the rhetoric of nation-building projects in the 1940s repeated much of the same ethnic and class chauvinism espoused in defense of the Anglo takeover of tejano lands in the nineteenth century. Like the braceros, ethnic Mexicans in the United States had lost property and cherished communal traditions to capitalist development in the Southwest. In the fictional world of *The Shadow* lies Paredes's most trenchant critique of the ideology of development. With its focus on the failure of revolutionary land reform, the novel exposes the lived contradictions of nationhood and migration, as experienced by Mexicans whose citizenship remained indeterminate in the border economies of labor. The ejidatarios of *The Shadow* are not so much new national subjects as future emigrants, captured in the moment of their final dislocation from the revolutionary project.

Américo Paredes came from a family intimately connected to the political intrigue of the northern theater of the Mexican Revolution. Paredes credited his maternal uncle with the inspiration for the novel, which concerns a local conflict over land appropriations in the border state of Tamaulipas. According to his uncle, the president of an ejido had complained of having contracted susto, or "fright sickness." The man believed that he had encountered the departing ghost of an agrarista [a government agent of agrarian reform], who had been killed during his inspection of the community. On his deathbed, the man was convinced that he was ill from susto; he died locked in a conflict between his traditional ways of thinking and his "rationality, which told him that dead men's spirits don't walk the earth."[57] For the novelist, of course, dead men *may* walk and demand a hearing. Paredes made this story the basis for his study of postrevolutionary Mexico; here, the specter of death forecasts the collapse of the national ideal. The shadow embodies all that resists incorporation into the modernizing project.

The Shadow tells the story of a revolutionary commander, Antonio Cuitla, frustrated in his efforts to secure plans for the development of the agrarian community of Los Claveles. Cuitla is president of the ejido because of his leadership of the local squadron of soldiers in the northern theater of the Revolutionary War. Anxious to shore up his status, the commander determines to reach an understanding with the former hacendado [hacienda owner] and to stave off his rival leader, Jacinto Del Toro. Del Toro threatens the uneasy peace of Los Claveles by calling for the further seizure of private lands, refusing to conform to the administrative processes established by the regional government of Morelos. As Cuitla finds himself trapped between the old, traditional order and the national faith in progress, the ejido president becomes embroiled in political intrigues involving Del Toro and the Don José María Jiménez, the local hacendado. Jiménez has retained the most arable lands, whereas the farm is located well away from the more fertile banks of the river. Unwilling to concede the best of his ancestral lands to the new ejido, Jiménez tries to protect his interests in commercial agriculture by orchestrating the murder of Del Toro. Cuitla forms an uneasy alliance with Jiménez, unaware that the former oligarch is merely using him to his own ends. When Cuitla kills Jiménez's hired assassin, Gerardo Salinas, he has a fateful encounter with a dark mass he believes is the man's departing spirit. Soon after, he succumbs to fright and dies.

The novel is embedded in the transnational circuits of the agricultural economy. Cuitla and Del Toro were once workers in the cotton fields of Texas, and Salinas dies on his way north to Texas from Monterrey. So, too, the class struggle involving the oligarchy, the new business elites, and field workers takes place in a transnational field—Cuitla and Del Toro recall their political awakening in Texas labor insurrections. Throughout, Paredes delineates the pressures of U.S. capital on the Mexican political economy, as a defining force in the transboundary formation of Greater Mexico.

The Shadow opens with the hot stillness of midday in northern Tamaulipas:

> The noon was a glaring quietness. There was no breeze, no movement. People were indoors, waiting for the fury of the sun to pass; outside, dogs and chickens panted in the shade-speckled dust. In the chaparral, life was also still. It had sought the cool, dark places and lay hidden from sight. There was a heavy loneliness in the hour, as if the whole world were dead.[58]

Like the ghostly village of Juan Rulfo's 1955 novel, *Pedro Páramo*, the rural colonia of Los Claveles first appears suspended in time, all signs of human activity hidden from view.[59] Paredes describes a society governed by the rhythms of traditional village life, its sense of time resistant to modern imperative of productivity. Only the men working the communal farm violate the stillness by plowing the unyielding soil "against time" under the watchful eyes of Antonio Cuitla, president of the ejido (1). The "glaring quietness" masks a state of conflict and turmoil, as *The Shadow* evokes the friction between the modern and the traditional in the postrevolutionary nation (1). Rather than stasis, the stillness describes a climate of reaction to the imperatives of modernization. The "men in sandals and white cotton drawers," Paredes writes, labor "against time—time lost," to create a new agricultural economy that will secure Mexico's economic advancement (1). The liminality of the noon hour marks a moment of reckoning in the progress of social reform, when the forces of bourgeois reaction against the capture of private lands appropriate the instrument of the new state to discipline campesino militants. The ejido, prized object of revolutionary desire, now becomes a means for the state to maintain its dominance, by dictating the commercial, rather than communal, exploitation of the farm.

Cuitla tries to instill the appropriate national values in his men, to transform them into citizen-workers and agents of modernization. Under Cuitla's modernizing gaze, the new state authority coopts the men's labors, as subsistence production gives way to the production of commodities. Cuitla, the former commander of the men laboring in the fields, invests the ejido with his conception of linear progress. Looking into the future, El Presidente observes the land not as it is but as what it must become: the unfenced chaparral gives way to a vision of "green waving fields, networks of canals, white-washed houses, trim fences, and flower-bordered lanes," images that bind social reform to economic prosperity. Into this fantasy intrudes the unavoidable influence of U.S. capitalism, as the imagined scene centers on the smiling farmer, the robust property owner, the citizen, and patriarch. Only the farmer's brown complexion distinguishes him from the idealized white subjects of commercial agriculture to the north of the border. The educational magazine from which Cuitla takes his reverie could either come from his years picking Texas cotton or from the propagandistic literature of Mexican agricultural agencies. Despite Mexico's economic nationalism in the 1930s, the state remained dependent on U.S. and European finance and technology. As he gazes out onto the imagined landscape, the commander embodies the ambivalence of postrevolutionary Mexican nationalism.

The vision of a "brown and happy race" engaged in the productive enjoyment of the land represents a critical moment in Mexico's postrevolutionary process of state-formation, when the ejido system had to provide both social reform and agricultural modernization (1). These two contradictory poles of the government seek their resolution in the figure of the indigenous campesino laborer. In the narrative of nation-formation, the men in white cotton are either the new racial agency of the mestizo nation or the backward figure who resists the progressive development of the modern state. Paredes wrote his indictment of the Mexican government as a witness to the failures of the Bracero Program; he looked at the campesinos as future braceros. His concern remained with these workers, whose labor facilitated the integration of the two national economies, even as the public postures of U.S.-Mexican cooperation masked the exploitation endemic to the guest-worker program. Given his acute consciousness of the imperial history of border development, Paredes was wary of the contractual terms imposed on braceros.

The Shadow conforms to Paredes's inclination toward the long, historical view of border conditions, as seen elsewhere in his studies of the corrido and folklore. Paredes's novel clearly seeks to address the formation
of the migrant, transnational stream at its inception—in the campesinos'
incomplete transition from revolutionary to national subjects. Cuitla's concerns for the fate of the ejido date to his experience as a day laborer in the
cotton fields of Texas:

> It was in Texas he first heard men talk of revolution, men of his own
> sort, talk about striking off their chains, and of the imprisonment of
> starvation. Yes, he had got most of his education in Texas. In the cotton
> fields and the coal mines. (62)

Cuitla's work history reveals the commerce between the Texas fields and
the ejido economy, commerce not only in labor and goods but in revolutionary ideology. His political vision originates in his own exploitation
in the racial economies of Texas agriculture. But the fragility of that vision means that his men are destined to become braceros, their national
identity compromised by the explicitly racialized sale of their labor for the
rescue of a weak and dependent state.

Thus, Paredes's novel of the Revolution is not simply a Mexican American contribution to the modernist literature of postrevolutionary Mexico. It is an incisive interrogation of the processes of state formation and
modernization at the moment of transition from revolutionary reform to
nation-building. This moment was critical to the emergence of a modern,
bordered subject, neither Mexican nor "American." The creation of this
class of transnational, racialized migrants, defined by their itinerant labor
as failed national subjects, transformed the meanings of Mexican identity
in the United States, especially for the descendants of those disposed of
land and nationhood during the U.S.-Mexican wars of 1836 and 1848. Paredes's critique of the "institutionalized" revolutionary order granted him a
new point of departure for questioning the racial boundaries on citizenship that governed Mexican American identity and culture at the Mexico-
U.S. border.

The publication of *The Shadow* in 1998 reveals how Paredes's own thinking about border society changed during his lifetime. His more famous
masterwork, *With His Pistol in His Hand,* published in 1958, delineated a

form of border conflict that required a single male protagonist, whose defense of cultural rights entailed righteous action and vengeance. José Limón has argued that this earlier representation of South Texas is infused with a modernist "tragic sentiment" at the loss of a "heroic" age of border conflict and opposition to Anglo hegemony. Limón contends, "It is a tragic sentiment that eventually leads us to detect a tragic flaw in this work."[60] For Renato Rosaldo, as for Limón, Paredes's evocation of the masculinist poetics in the "Ballad of Gregorio Cortéz" founders in its failure to address the internal lines of political dissent and class antagonism that fragment Mexican border communities, by offering what he terms a "pastoral" vision of cultural unity and idealized patriarchal power.[61] With *The Shadow,* Paredes returns to, and significantly revises, his construction of masculine authority in its relationship to the social transformation of border society. In this text, the process of revolutionary transition engenders crisis not only for the formation of the national subject but also for the "pastoral" patriarchal order. It is much clearer in this novel than in Paredes's earlier work how ranching, so central to the tejano world he defends in *With His Pistol in His Hand,* relied on racial, class, and gender hierarchies and rationalized violence no less than the Anglo society that vanquished it.

In the novel, conflicts of race and class disrupt any notion of a univocal or "primordial" border community. *The Shadow* depicts the social fractures that the hacienda society engendered. Antonio Cuitla feels himself torn between old loyalties to Del Toro and his desire for acceptance within the governing class. Cuitla's association with the hacendado Don José María Jiménez allows Paredes to play out the contradictions between Mexican cultural nationalism, which valorized mestizaje and revolutionary militancy, and the lingering power of the oligarchic class. Cuitla, unlike Gregorio Cortez, is ultimately passive in the defense of his class. Jiménez offers a parodic inversion of the corrido hero of *With His Pistol in His Hand*: he voices his predilection for "the glories that were lost, the grandeur that was slipping away" from the descendants of Asturian hacendados, and his claim to the land is "sanctified with the fragrance of past generations" rather than his labor (23–24).

With his signature irony, Paredes dramatizes how the bourgeois classes managed to seize hold of the revolutionary state, schooling its emergent administrative leadership in the ways of paternalistic authority. Cuitla's sense of self is wholly dependent on this vertical arrangement of power and on his ability to distinguish himself as a "man of reason" from the campesinos to whom he refers derogatorily as "barefoot Indians" (7). Paredes captures the plasticity of racial discourse, the ways in which the prejudices of the colonial order reassert themselves in the processes of capitalist modernization and state-formation. Cuitla must disavow any identification with the indigenous culture of his men, even at the cost of his own sanity and his capacity to act.

Ultimately, Cuitla is undone by his own susceptibility to the mystifying discourse of development, and its segregation of the modern and the traditional, white and indigenous, scientific judgment and subjective experience. Fearing the actions of Del Toro, he sets out to shoot his rival, unaware that Jiménez has already hired a stranger to kill him. En route to Del Toro, Cuitla glimpses a strange, shadowy form in the underbrush of the chaparral but is unable to explain the presence of the "dense, shapeless mass of black rising out of the middle of the road, where no shadow should be" (10). The encounter divides him against himself by unsettling his faith in the rational and making him fear the ghost of the man whom he was about to betray. He falls ill with susto, which develops into consumption. He neither finds relief in medicines for the chill nor allows his faith in "progress" to be compromised by accepting the ritual cleansing offered by the local curandera [healer].

In refusing the old woman's cure, Cuitla brings on his own demise, unable to reconcile his scientific principles with his inner dread of the folk traditions that formed him:

> Everything would be all right then. The healing woman would come, and he would sleep afterwards without nightmares or fever, without the bottle of mescal. But then it would all be true. He could no longer speak against it, could never deny it. No. He would never sink that low. Sitting around the fire, telling silly stories. Passing on to the others the same fear and ignorance. (80–81)

Cuitla's death reveals the hollowness of his authority and becomes an allegory for the weakness of the new state. Cuitla's faith in modernity demands that he reject the feminizing ministrations of folk medicine. Through this conflict, Paredes points to the ways in which masculine authority defines itself against the feminine, which stands in for all that resists incorporation

into the progressive order of the new state. The more Cuitla resists his desire for the ritual healing, the more he lashes out with violence against his
wife. The women who inhabit the margins of *The Shadow* speak as figures
of contradiction in the masculine social order: the blind curandera loudly
contests Cuitla's attempt to retain control of the community after Del
Toro's death; meanwhile, it falls to Cuitla's wife to reconcile Cuitla's failures
with the demands of maintaining the household.

In the final scenes of Cuitla's feverish death, the dying commander
hears the familiar refrains of the corrido of "El Hijo Desobediente" being
sung around the campfire outside. The ballad tells the story of the prodi-
gal son of a rancher who violates his father's orders by fighting another
vaquero. When the disobedient son threatens his father with violence, his
father responds with a fatal curse, and the young man dies outside the
protected circle of his authority. Cuitla interprets the men's performance
of the ballad as a sign that they are already beyond the reach of his authority, "that to them he was already dead" (100). He views his own demise as
the passing of any possibility for the effective transition from the old regime to the modern social order. The men's song warns of the interrupted
transference of patriarchal authority from one generation to another, as
the heir dies disinherited by a traditional power too rigid to accommodate
his rebellion.

As the men's commander dies, Paredes depicts their singing as an urgent response to a situation of extreme social uncertainty:

> They were seated in a half-circle about the fire, their faces transformed,
> their mouths half open, their eyes shining in the light. Before them the
> singers sang, with their eyes shut and their heads thrown back, with an
> intense application to their task, as though they sang not from enjoy-
> ment, but from a compelling need. (100)

Paredes leaves the "compelling need" undefined, giving us only the texture
of the performance, the plaintive call of the guitar speaking "its invitation
to the voices" and their replies (100). Paredes describes a desire for narrative that reflects an anxious need to reestablish communal bonds sun-
dered by class and generational conflicts. Paredes underlines the tension
between the narrative certainty of the son's punishment in the ballad (and
thus the restoration of social order in the song) and the insurrectional

energies unleashed in this particular performance. What accounts for the urgency of the men's singing? In the men's repetition of the corrido we find a deep engagement with cultural memories "brought up north from the hot lands where they had been born" (99).

Herein lies the particular significance of vernacular performance for Paredes: its evocation of deep racial memory can become a material force for change. As it creates a contingent consensus of what was past, the vernacular performance is a collective retrieval of lived experience. Paradoxically, as the men's recitation of the past calls forth a new agency in the present, it will eventually undo their unity—by transforming the repressive social conditions that give them a sense of common destiny. By its contingent nature, identity formation is a process of differentiation in relation to the vanishing horizon of the past. "The simplest forms of verbal folk expression," Paredes tells us, "are names. . . . when we name things, we give them a life of their own; we isolate them from the rest of our experience."[62] In Paredes's ethnographic vision, the vernacular performance is a means to reckon with the immediate, subjective experience of loss and displacement accompanying the historical transformation of the border. "The appearance of an awakening sense of identity," Paredes cautions, "was coupled with a challenge to that same identity."[63] By taking the song into the body, and letting it emerge through their own voices, the men around the campfire experience that cultural sense of awakening and challenge.

In *The Shadow*, the men sing precisely at the moment when their commander's modernizing vision fails him, and when their revolutionary and productive labors are being coopted to serve the failing national project. As the song itself narrates the fated punishment of the son, the men's performance acknowledges too the changing context in which they sing. The song reawakens the indigenous resistance that still troubles the "progressive" state. The men's dramatic gesture of singing with their heads thrown back reclaims the racialized, laboring body from the experience of the commodification of their labor and the evacuation of their citizenship from the national body. As they enact the agency denied them as workers or citizens, the men's performance describes an insurgent possibility contained in the force of their vocalization.

The parable of dissent and retribution gives way to a more unsettling story of an interrupted succession of power. The father's own mortality is realized in the death of his disobedient son. If the father speaks as the paternal voice of the state, then his inability to discipline the son—who stands in for the revolutionary subject—except by killing him signifies the state's similar capacity for violence. For Paredes, the postrevolutionary government failed to compel the loyalty of its new citizens precisely because it could not integrate them into its vision for Mexican modernity. The song performance is thus a portent of the inevitability of the men's emigration.

Cuitla dies in his final effort to silence his men, just as automobiles —stock emblems of modernity's arrival—appear carrying state functionaries to disperse the crowd. In stark contrast to the narrative coherence of the corrido form, *The Shadow* breaks off at the scene of Cuitla's death. The novel suspends narrative closure by leaving the transition in community leadership incomplete. So, too, does the novel end without the final refrains of the men's song.

The Bracero Vernacular

Paredes understood that the vernacular is an inherently unstable construction, one that always surpasses authorial intention. The process of translation from the oral to the literary is one in which the vernacular signifies difference in excess. The written text acts as a cultural referent for an oral narrative; it comes freighted with the cumulative meanings invested in its ritualized transference from performance to performance and from speaker to speaker. The vernacular thus provides a form for mediating the problem of language for the unlettered, or for voicing what was once unutterable. For this reason, the vernacular form has so often erupted in association with emancipatory projects for social change.

Braceros brought a vibrant vernacular tradition into the fields, where it took root within the expanding discourse of communitarian struggle and civil rights. María Herrera-Sobek cautions against an "elitelore" that treats the bracero experience as unmitigated humiliation and that misses how, "in the lore of the bracero, the experience is a challenge and adventure . . . harsh but funny."[64] Making room for that complexity is critical to any consideration of the labor circuit and of the subjectivity of migrants within it. Migrant songs formed an alternate pedagogy to that of state and capitalist discourse. Ernesto Galarza recounted hearing this music throughout his travels to labor camps in the 1940s and 1950s. One bracero ballad from the 1940s, "La restrinción del azúcar" [The Sugar Ration], appropriated the discourse of binational friendship from the wartime contracts only to displace its framework of national service. In its place, the singer offers a frank celebration of proletarian desire, represented in the commodity of sugar:

Yo, como buen mexicano,	[Like the good Mexican I am,
vengo a traer la alegría	I come to bring joy
y a que más de algún	and so that more than one or two of
paisano	my countrymen
de mis tonteras se ría	can laugh at my inanities
Soy de la farsa el payaso,	I am the clown of the comedy,
soy clown de la palmomilla	I am the clown of the gang
de lo que hablen no hago caso,	what they might say I don't care,
ganando algo de pastilla.	as long as I earn a cent.
No se me agota el aliento	I'm never out of breath
para decir la verdad,	so as to tell the truth,
y si en lo que digo miento	and if I should say untruths
el público juzgará	the public can be the judge.
Hoy les hablo de bonanza	Today I talk about bonanza
y mañana de la crisis,	tomorrow about the crisis,
y siempre con la esperanza	and always with the hope
de que un día sean más felices.	that you'll be happier someday.][65]

The song eclipses the wartime emergency with a picaresque story of adventure, relaying the bracero's relationship to sugar in a meandering narrative that implies his imperviousness to the controlling design of the contract. The singer substitutes his capacity for play for his mere labor function: "I come to bring joy."

As a binational clown, the bracero knows that to speak of bonanzas or crisis is ultimately a passing matter for the laboring classes; the singer is concerned less with ideological truths than with the performative possibilities of his speech. In the arduous production of the sugar beet—described as "¡hijo de la remolacha!" [Son of a beet] (a swipe at Japanese Emperor

Hirohito)—his labor has social value because it makes life sweet during the rigors of the war. That quality of sweetness overtakes the commodity function of the crop and its place in the wartime economy. It encodes a desire unmet in the contract system and celebrates a human agency unquantifiable in company ledgers and development projects—the will to happiness. The humble refrain "que un dia sean más felices" [that you'll be happier someday] returns the abstract labor relation to the most basic expression of what Marx called "species being." It overcomes, if only momentarily, the estrangement of the bracero condition.[66]

With this expression of hope, the singer reclaims his labor from the contract system that made wealth for others but imposed privation on the emigrant class. The sweetness of sugar evokes, as an object of longing, a different value for his labor, that of productive activity in the service of real human need—what Marx termed "life-engendering life." For the bracero, interpellated into the transborder economy as the "production man" of agribusiness, indulgence of the appetite for sugar was a return to enjoyment of his body, outside the strictures that the labor relation imposed.

With the termination of the wartime contract in 1947, the contract system changed considerably. After a series of short-term extensions, the two governments formalized the labor loan in August 1951. Under Public Law 78, the U.S. government brought the Mexican National Program under the oversight of the Department of Labor. This measure intended to cover labor shortages during the U.S. involvement in the Korean War. In this new phase of the Bracero Program, labor protections were practically inoperative, and abuses were rampant in all aspects of the contract system. Workers no longer received the funds to return home and simply resettled in the border cities, where they could cross as day laborers into the United States. By the 1950s hundreds of thousands of unauthorized migrants labored alongside the legally contracted braceros; many of them were former braceros who had found it expedient to "jump" their contracts and sell their labor in the marketplace.

Mexican and U.S. officials were ill prepared to address the unauthorized migrations that the Bracero Program had stimulated. The rates of Mexican emigration skyrocketed during the 1950s, as "free-contracting" outpaced the legal extensions of the labor loans. The mass exodus of skilled and unskilled laborers proved debilitating to the Mexican economy, leading the Alemán administration to file formal complaints against the loss of nationals to unregulated contracting. Mexican officials sought to assert state interests by protesting illegal recruitment practices and contract violations endemic to the Bracero Program. But in practice, the Mexican ban on Texan contracts, and the implementation of new security measures along the border, proved largely ineffectual. Although the Mexican economy depended on migrant remittances, the actual Bracero Program gave the Mexican government few controls on emigrants' movements. Nor did Mexican officials have much leverage to mitigate abuses in the contract system, or in U.S. immigration law enforcement, when its trade partner revived the aggressive use of deportations to control Mexican immigration.

General Joseph Swing, who became INS commissioner in 1954, established a new campaign of immigration policing as a guarantee that the postwar Bracero Program would continue to fuel national development without permitting Mexicans to obtain permanent foothold in the domestic labor market beyond degraded stoop labor. Operation Wetback deployed the INS to inspect and police workplaces and undocumented settlements as a means to placate concerns about the Mexican threat to U.S. workers and the national standard of living. One State Department official stated that the INS would cut the number of Mexican visas, to make a clear distinction: "braceros would not be regarded as prospective immigrants."[67] This sentiment reflected the continuation of earlier policies that used immigration regulation to control the labor supply. The fact that Commissioner Swing was himself a participant in General Pershing's Punitive Expedition suggests continuity between U.S. military practice and its treatment of Mexican nationals in its domestic policies, even those recruited as "guest" laborers.

The binational trade in Mexican workers proved costly for both governments by the onset of the Cold War. In the early 1960s, U.S. unions and civil-rights leaders militated against the erosion of wages and labor conditions caused by the presence of temporary workers. Anticommunist sentiment revived anxieties about border security and the foreign presence within U.S. borders, leading anti-immigration groups and labor advocates alike to question the dangers of recruiting alien groups to work alongside U.S. workers. By this time, the mechanization of U.S. agriculture meant that fewer agricultural workers were needed in the labor-intensive work of cotton and food harvesting. The supposed excess of agricultural workers was not the only factor in turning the tide against the labor loan, however. No less a figure than Lee G. Williams, the Department of Labor official in charge of the Bracero Program, had declared that the labor loan supported a system of "legalized slavery."[68] Given the prevalent climate of opposition, the U.S. Congress made no move to renew the binational labor loan. The Bracero Program terminated on August 31, 1964. Despite its design as a temporary labor loan, the program left an indelible imprint on relations between the United States and Mexico, just as it transformed the Mexican presence in the United States.

However much power the contract-labor system gave to employers and the state officials who brokered the labor loan, the ideal of the temporary worker remained a phantasmatic projection of capitalist and state desire. The mass undocumented movement that accompanied the bracero period revealed the limits to state regulation and the will of migrants to evade the strictures of the contract. As studies by María Herrera-Sobek and others have shown, braceros passively accepted neither their designation as temporary workers nor their status as captive labor. They continually sought forms of collective bargaining, even at the most primitive level of work stoppages or complaints to consular officials, they skipped contracts, and they militated for lost wages and benefits. As "mojados" ["wetbacks"] they also formed families, brought co-nationals across the border, and established significant linkages between their places of residence and places of origin. Braceros did not go quietly into the recruitment centers or into the fields. They sought to craft the sale of their labor by using the medical exam, the tests, and the transport as occasions for improving their situation or taking possession, even symbolically, of their labor power. In this way, braceros participated in their interpellation as a mobile labor force, and the modes of their subjection—or of their refusals of subjection—have had a lasting impact on the migrants that came after and also on the communities that sent them out or received them as sojourners.

From the geographic and social distance of the labor camps, braceros created new markets for Mexican and Mexican American popular culture and for an industry of services catering to the mobile labor force, and that culture and industry remain entrenched in both national economies. Braceros left a complex record of their aspirations in song, chronicles, and poems; their mobility reshaped discourses of nation, community, and modernity in both Mexico and Mexican American barrios. At the start of the twenty-first century, the movement of former braceros to obtain reparations for lost Social Security payments constitutes one of the largest labor movements in the hemisphere, numbering in the millions of adherents.[69]

CHAPTER 3

No Constitution for Us

Class Racism and Cold War Unionism

> It is often forgotten to what extent women were the first labor-force of factory-based, industrial capitalism.... The maintenance of male prerogative, in the face of threats from women's employment, was conscious and was organized.
>
> —Doreen Massey, *Space, Place, and Gender* (1994)[1]

> No Constitution for us, who are neither citizens nor persons, but a freakish creation called "aliens."
>
> —Louisa Moreno (1950)[2]

The image of Luisa Moreno, the Guatemalan-born labor organizer and founder of El Congreso de Pueblos que Hablan Español [Congress of Spanish-Speaking People], author of "Caravans of Sorrow" (discussed in chapter 1), stands watch over the migrant City of Angels. Her portrait graces the world's largest mural, *The Great Wall of Los Angeles*, a massive cover for a flood-control channel in the San Fernando Valley.[3] The visual narrative of the mural chronicles the long sweep of California history, from the first emergence of animal life out of the sea in prehistoric times to the multiethnic spectacle of the 1984 Olympics. Artist Judith Baca placed Moreno between the picture of police brutality in the Zoot Suit Riots of 1942 and the arrival of Jewish refugees from Europe; she thus embodies wartime aspirations for an alternate racial and class order amid the abundance of the southwestern economy. For Baca, the migrant imaginary of the 1940s took female form in the life of Moreno, who countered anti-immigrant policies and class racism as a community organizer for CIO unions in Southern California.

Moreno's appearance in the mural precedes segments devoted to the "Forebears of Civil Rights," reminding viewers of the broader span of struggle that defined contestations over race, rights, and territory in the region. Rather than provide an evolutionary narrative of this history, the mural highlights the conflicting migrations and encounters of the many peoples who built California. In its production—which involved some four hundred youths from Los Angeles barrios, between 1976 and 1983—the mural project promoted cooperation and community formation. The history it tells is another matter. "Our people are the internal exiles," Baca wrote of the work. She then explained how her artistic vision transformed displacement into an aesthetic where "change, both social and personal, is not only possible—it has to happen."[4]

Luisa Moreno is an apt figure for such loss and transformation. She abandoned a girlhood of privilege in Guatemala to become an outspoken labor- and civil-rights activist in the United States, leaving behind her identity as Blanca Rosa Rodríguez López and the bourgeois constructs of feminine virtue and racial purity that her given name signified. Historian Vicki Ruiz interprets the political significance of Luisa Moreno's choice of the surname "Moreno" [brown-skinned] over her given name "Blanca" [white female], marking the young organizer's identification with the Latina/o laborers with whom she worked.[5] Moreno's reinvention of herself in transit to the United States embodies the migrant imaginary of her generation. Baca's depiction of Moreno contrasts the sharp angles of her face with the waving banners of marchers behind, offering an image of female militancy long absent from accounts of Latina activism and, in particular, of Latina politics in the pre-civil-rights period. Ruiz describes Moreno as "una mujer sin fronteras" [a woman without borders], "the only transcontinental Latina union organizer," whose activism took her to New York City garment shops, cigar factories in Tampa, pecan-shelling plants in San Antonio, and the canneries of Southern California.[6] Itinerancy was a tough trajectory for the single mother, one that included the task of finding care for her daughter, Mytyl, while she devoted herself to the CIO. Then and since, there have been few precedents for such commitment to the collective will of migrants, workers, and poor women of color.

That Judith Baca granted Luis Moreno a privileged place in her monumental narrative indicates both the centrality of Latina migrants to the formation of California and their vulnerability to erasure. Within the mural, Moreno figures a feminized migrant imaginary all but absent from official history and collective memory. In 1950, ten years after her "Caravans of Sorrow" speech, Moreno was forcibly repatriated to her native Guatemala. She was one of many Latina/o activists expelled from labor- and civil-rights campaigns during the Cold War. Moreno had long rejected the tenets of U.S. exceptionalism and liberal nationalism, having worked to expose racial discrimination and labor exploitation in the United States. But her removal also altered the terrain of oppositional politics and the pursuit of Latina/o civil rights.

This chapter is an examination of the combustible forces within the gender and ethnic politics that preceded El Movimiento Chicano, the civil-rights movement of the late 1960s. The fragmentation and dispersal of the radical left by government and anticommunist forces during the 1950s both incited new forms of ethnic militancy in the coming decades and foreclosed on transnational projects of class and ethnic solidarity. At the center of these conflicts were Latina activists who transgressed the restrictive gender norms of the post–World War II period. As the United States and Mexico alike hardened their national boundaries in the name of security, the "alien" emerged once again as a figure of provocation and subversion. Migrant women, whether waging class or gender rebellion, sought to expand the terrain of leftist struggle and met with state repression and male hostilities.

My account of Cold War iterations of civil rights thus begins with the scene of deportation, when the INS denied Luisa Moreno a place in the political mobilizations that were to transform the social landscape in which she had labored and struggled. Despite the new claims to ethnic solidarity that took shape in the postwar years, the emergent discourse of rights defined race and class as the public domain of politics but continued to subordinate gender to an apolitical, private realm of female service and endurance. The political autonomy and mobility of women emerged once more as a site of cultural conflict and political repression within both the movement for Latina/o civil rights and the nation as a whole.

Just as Moreno and other lesser-known Latina activists were embattled in the defense of their communities, so too were a group of women in Grant County, New Mexico. Between 1950 and 1952 the Mine-Mill Union struck against Empire Zinc, a bold expression of class struggle made all the more remarkable because the strike was carried by the wives, sisters, and daughters of the male miners. The strike against Empire Zinc provides a paradigmatic example of the domestication of Chicana militancy in the labor struggle and in its memory. In 1954, a filmic portrait of the strike, *Salt of the Earth*, was released and immediately censored for its portrayal of Mexican American women as labor militants during the height of Cold War red-baiting. A decade later, during the Chicano Movement, the film mobilized audiences to feminist, union, and antiracist causes through the figure of Esperanza, its Mexican American protagonist. And yet the film's very narrative of female empowerment eclipses a more complicated account of Mexican American women in the strike. This chapter reads the film as an expression of gender conflict over female autonomy within Chicana/o social movements of the 1950s and 1960s. The film's gestures of incorporation of women into the domain of class and ethnic politics anticipated the gender codes of ethnic self-determination operative in the ethnic nationalist discourse that gave form to El Movimiento Chicano.

Cold War Exile

Throughout her career, Luisa Moreno articulated a concept of rights that contested the importance of national sovereignty over the mobility of laborers and migrants. Through her work for the Congreso in the lead-up to World War II, Moreno articulated the decade's most radical position on migration, labor, and collective action. She rejected the discourse of scarcity and competition that blinded labor leaders to the needs of Mexican workers, while also indicting the dominant ideologies of "Americanization" that divided Mexican Americans from Latina/o migrants in the pursuit of civil rights. Her 1940 address, "Non-citizen Americans in the South West," as we have seen in chapter 1, marked a comprehensive assault on the limits of liberalism in the United States. It exposed the mass repatriations of Mexicans and Mexican Americans as a symptom of a broader crisis of freedom within racialized capitalism and the war against fascism.[7] Moreno's demand for the recognition of migrant rights went unfulfilled while the United States and Mexico colluded in the Bracero Program and used deportation as a mechanism of labor control and of political repression.

Soon after the war ended, Moreno herself became the target of INS persecution, when the Joint Fact-Finding Committee of the California Legislature on Un-American Activities designated her a "dangerous alien."[8] Moreno's activism had drawn the attention of the FBI since the 1930s, because her labor organizing linked her to known communist and Latin American radical groups. At her first hearing before Senator Jack Tenney and the Fact-Finding Committee, on September 10, 1940, she forced a confrontation with state authorities over her political allegiances to communists in the labor movement. When Moreno invoked her First Amendment rights, the committee deemed her a hostile witness, and Tenney warned he would send a report of the proceedings to the INS.[9] Moreno had recently filed an application for citizenship, following her marriage to the San Diego labor leader Gray Bemis, a U.S. national. She refused to be intimidated.

On September 30, 1948, the U.S. Department of Justice issued a warrant for Moreno's arrest, citing her political affiliation with organizations committed to the violent overthrow of the U.S. government. In early 1949, the INS began deportation proceedings against her. The FBI made her one final offer of protection: she could obtain citizenship by testifying against Harry Bridges, an Australian-born leader in the International Longshoremen's and Warehousemen's Union (ILWU). Moreno denied the request, refusing "to be a free woman with a mortgaged soul."[10] Moreno reported receiving violent threats against her safety while she pursued her appeal to the INS. Soon after, she was arrested and placed in detention at the Terminal Island Federal Prison of Los Angeles, where she was held for several days. Upon her release, she gave up her appeal. Rather than remain and be forced to incriminate friends and colleagues, Moreno chose voluntary departure over certain removal. She and her husband returned to her native Guatemala in November 1950 under warrant of deportation, on the charge that she had been a member of the Communist Party.[11] They soon immersed themselves in the progressive politics of Jacobo Arbenz, the leftist Guatemalan leader, but had to flee for Mexico City in 1954, following the CIA-sponsored coup that toppled the government. Moreno lived in Cuba and Mexico before finally returning to Guatemala, where she died in 1992.

Luisa Moreno understood her status in exile as a dimension of the fundamental condition of rightlessness that confronted racialized migrants and U.S. nationals alike: "We are right back in the pages of that revealing book on the 'Asiatic and the Alien,'" she wrote shortly before her departure from the United States. "No Constitution for us, who are neither citizens nor persons, but a freakish creation called 'aliens.'"[12] Her deportation was punishment for defying the imperatives of nationalization, a challenge that proved decisive in the Cold War. Many prominent Latina/o labor leaders and civil-rights activists lacked full naturalization, which left them vulnerable to deportation in the 1950s. The rise of anticommunist hysteria led to the expulsions or exile of the Latina/o architects of the Popular Front. The CIO and immigrant-rights organizer Bert Corona argued that the purges of the U.S. labor movement left Latina/o organizers particularly vulnerable and isolated; deportation proceedings and intimidation led to the departures of "Josefina Fierro, Refugio Martínez, Humberto Silex, Armando Dávila, Frank Martínez, Tony Salgado, and Fred Chávez to name a few."[13] The U.S. left and union leadership privileged the cases of indicted Euroamerican leaders, Corona recalled, over the defense of Latina/o activists. Although several prominent lawyers, writers, and labor activists, notably Carey McWilliams, had formed the Provisional Committee for Luisa Moreno Bemis, the taint of communism was enough to seal her fate, and she joined the number of Latina/o militants forced into hiding, prison, or exile.

It is worth considering what the anticommunist crusade cost Mexican American social movements in the decade preceding the full flower of the civil-rights movement. The forcible removal of migrant militants from the national scene—and, especially, from the leadership of community organizations and labor unions—had particular implications for Latina/o activism in the United States. The anticommunist repression of the 1950s did no less than remake the terrain of labor- and civil-rights struggle. State repression restricted the possible forms of dissent, restricting the possibilities for oppositional politics, as evidenced in the Taft-Hartley Act of 1947, which curtailed the authority and activities of unions in the name of national security and state interests. Just as antiunion legislation remade the relationship between the state and organized labor, Cold War policies also infringed on the internationalist vision that supported the most expansive claims to rights for Mexicans and Mexican Americans within the United States.

Even as the United States continued the legal importation of Mexicans and Caribbean nationals for farm labor, new immigration legislation cemented the use of naturalization to reinforce political boundaries within the nation. The McCarran Act or Internal Security Act of 1950 required all communist organizations to register with the federal government and established the Subversive Activities Control Board for domestic surveillance of persons deemed a potential security threat. This board was able to deny the members of these groups the rights of citizenship. The INS also gained new powers to reverse the naturalization of those deemed enemies of the state. The McCarran Act was a cornerstone of alien exclusion and deportation laws during the Cold War, allowing the state to curtail protected rights in times of war or cases of "internal security emergency."

Throughout the 1950s, U.S. immigration policy continued to treat "aliens" as the greatest threat to domestic security. The McCarran-Walter Act of 1952—which allowed the government to expel suspected subversives from the country and deny entry to those suspected of subversive intent—responded to the fear that migrants were carriers of communist ideology.[14] With the end of the wartime economic expansion, Mexican Americans became targets of renewed hostilities and suspicion. One group, the American Committee for the Protection of the Foreign Born (ACPFB) was especially important in the defense of Mexican migrants' rights.[15] Its Los Angeles chapter, in operation between 1950 and 1954, brought together Jewish and Latina/o radicals who shared a pluralist vision for the incorporation of migrants into U.S. society. Rose Chernin, an émigré from Czarist Russia, chaired the Los Angeles Committee and oversaw legal defense, public education, and political organizing despite her known ties to the Communist Party. In order to counter the separations of families and the removals of long-term residents in the United States, the ACPFB organized petition drives and legal proceedings that drew attention to the plight of citizen-children caught up in the deportation campaigns. The ACPFB estimated that as many as twenty-five to one hundred Mexican children, many of them U.S. citizens, were deported to Mexico daily from the Los Angeles

County area. These children were the unanticipated casualties of INS policies to repatriate undocumented Mexicans under Operation Wetback. In
the years between 1947 and 1954, David G. Gutiérrez writes, INS agents
apprehended an average of five hundred thousand unauthorized migrants
each year.[16] In this climate, the use of deportation as a threat to collective
action proved debilitating to the precarious transborder solidarity that had
guided Latina/o organizers during the 1930s.

Engendering Exile

A close colleague of Luisa Moreno during the 1930s and 1940s, Bert Corona
remembered her as "that rare human being for whom the human household is her family."[17] For Corona, not only did Moreno's loyalties transgress
the borders of the nation-state; they also transgressed the dominant vision
of female service to family and community, since Moreno chose political
solidarity over the primary bonds of kinship and ethnicity. Not only did
Moreno abandon the confines of her Guatemalan family for the migratory circuit; she also divorced an abusive husband and led a public life that
could not conform to period expectations of motherhood. In his remem-
brance, Corona reconciled Moreno's militancy to cultural ideals of female
virtue, but his very mention of the feminized domains of "household" and
"family" also exposed how the mobility of the woman activist—her *self-
imposed* exile from the domestic sphere—remained a source of anxiety for
even her close colleagues. The expulsion of Moreno from the United States
exacted a double punishment for her "subversive" politics: it suppressed
not only her internationalist vision of antiracist class struggle but also her
challenge to male prerogative in the political sphere.

The 1950s removals prevented migrant activists from bringing their
vision to the campaigns for social justice in the 1960s. One case among
many is that of Josefina Fierro, who settled in Guaymas in the 1950s, leaving behind a remarkable career of activism in the Hollywood left and El
Congreso. Fierro had played a decisive role in ending the Zoot Suit Riots
of 1942, when she enlisted the support of State Department officials for
the Los Angeles campaign against police brutality and racial terror. Not
only did deportation curtail the expression of transborder solidarity and

migrant militancy; it also represented an evacuation of communal and national memory. The expulsions of activists were an object lesson on the primacy of state sovereignty over their exercise of civil liberties, and despite militant resistance to INS activity, Latina/o social movements gave far less prominence to the migrant imaginary in the following decade. But the suppression of Popular Front militants had another, less visible consequence. The repression that forced Emma Tenayuca into hiding in the 1940s and that led Luisa Moreno and Josefina Fierro to leave the United States in the 1950s had a disproportionate effect on women of color in the labor and socialist left. With the removal of these women from the spheres of collective action, migrant organizing lost the most visible figures of Latina militancy. This loss effectively made the resurgence of feminist activism during the 1960s appear new and unprecedented to Mexican American and migrant social movements; it also marked the erasure of a distinctly feminized migrant imaginary, in which the gendered framework of labor and community organizing was far less restrictive than collective memory may suggest.

The absence of figures like Moreno, Fierro, and Tenayuca contributed to the gender conflicts that arose within Mexican American social movements in the late 1960s, when the imperatives of ethnic self-determination forced the subordination of women's autonomy to the communitarian ideal of *race as family*. If, as feminist historians have shown, the 1950s remasculinized politics and made female domesticity a matter of national security, Cold War ideological shifts also threatened working-class women of color who had never inhabited that idealized feminine realm.[18] The constructs of family and female domesticity held particular significance for migrant women and Chicanas, linked to the approximation of bourgeois citizenship but also to the private realm, which functioned as a front of struggle against class racism and state repression.[19] Male dominance within El Movimiento Chicano (1966–1974) is well established within feminist scholarship and revisionist histories of the period. But what deserves greater notice is that the reemergence of patriarchal constructs of family and ethnic community within the movement coincided with U.S. legal restrictions on the movement's migrant members. Women's political autonomy *and* transnational solidarity came under threat in the Cold War when nationalist ideologies reconfigured the very scope of rights and liberation in El Movimiento.

As Chicana/o historians have shown, women were active participants throughout the civil-rights movement; nonetheless, accounts of gender conflict over women's politics and feminism remain within the controlling frame of a gendered ideology of separate spheres, public and private, that can participate in the erasure of a more complex gender and class history, with its transnational dimensions. In its common usage, domesticity signifies a gendered division of space and labor, where women are responsible for the family and the home. It can also delineate a territorial boundary between the interior space occupied by citizens and the exterior domain of the foreign. Cold War nationalism mobilized powerful ideologies of domesticity in both its senses, both to forestall gender conflict and to bring citizens into the task of nation-building and self-defense. The connection between domesticity and nationalism was no less pervasive within the rhetoric of the Chicana/o Movement and no less coercive with respect to gender.

The Mine-Mill Union strike in Grant County, New Mexico, provides a case study of how the domestication of Latina activism within the labor left was also simultaneously a domestication of the transnational class struggle. Like the women of Doreen Massey's study of Irish cotton industries, working-class Mexican and Mexican American women met with aggressive opposition to their autonomy and mobility in the postwar years, as labor- and civil-rights leaders sought to maintain male primacy in political organizing. The suppression of migrant and Mexican American women's labor power and political militancy was conscious and it was organized.

Cold War Unionism and Mexican Self-Defense

Following a recession year for the metals industry in 1949, the price of zinc rose precipitously with the onset of the Korean War in June 1950. The wartime market put the New Jersey Zinc company at a decided advantage. With demand for domestic zinc only getting higher, the company's subsidiary Empire Zinc, of Grant County, New Mexico, stalled negotiations with representatives of Local 890 of the International Union of Mine, Mill, and Smelter Workers (Mine-Mill). Empire Zinc charged that the union representatives brought unreasonable demands to the bargaining table in order to provoke a strike.[20] From mid-July forward, accusations of communist infiltration and manipulation dogged the union effort at the bargaining table. In a September 30 proposal, Empire employees offered their final list of demands: "collar to collar" pay (meaning wages for each hour spent underground), the resolution of grievances on company time and pay, a raise of five cents per hour, an end to speedups, and six paid holidays a year.[21] The company flatly refused, and negotiations stalled.

At the core of the wage conflict were pay differentials between white and Mexican American miners. Mexicans constituted roughly 95 percent of the Empire workforce and were concentrated in the dangerous and arduous underground jobs. The lower "Mexican wage" also extended to separate and inferior housing, washing, and leisure facilities and to payroll lines.[22] Mexican Americans lacked indoor plumbing in their company housing, an issue that Empire Zinc refused to negotiate through the union. In his discussion of discriminatory practices in the southwestern mining industry, historian Zaragoza Vargas notes that although Fair Employment Practices Committee (FEPC) investigators had called for public hearings on the mistreatment of Mexican American workers in mining and metal industries in 1942, federal authorities had refused. The government feared that airing charges of racism would threaten U.S. relations in Latin America and, in particular, the ongoing negotiations of the Bracero Program.[23]

When Local 890 entered into contract negotiations in June 1950, its parent union was in a precarious position within the larger labor movement. In February of that year, the CIO had dissolved its association with the Mine-Mill for its association with the U.S. Communist Party. Mine-Mill had initially refused the Taft-Hartley requirement that all unions file noncommunist affidavits for their members; in the process, Mine-Mill lost its certification with the National Labor Relations Board. Although a later change in leadership led to a policy of compliance and gained the union its recertification, the Mine-Mill remained isolated and thwarted in its relations with employers, federal authorities, and organized labor alike. This gave New Jersey Zinc the upper hand as it approached the bargaining table. According to Local 890 lead organizer Clinton Jencks, Empire officials planned to starve out the weakened union in the hope of increasing the bargaining power of mining companies across the Southwest.[24] Jencks was certain that Empire's position reflected a clandestine accord among southwestern companies to destroy the leftist union.

Despite the clear antagonism of both government authorities and the local community toward the strike effort, Bayard miners voted for a walkout in October 1950. But, as Jack Cargill writes, the dual wage structure carried over to the labor action, as "only twelve of the ninety-two unionists who struck Empire were Anglos."[25] These ethnic divisions came to the surface throughout Grant County, as hostilities increased between Mexican American supporters and local whites who opposed the strike. The strike continued for fifteen months and brought only modest gains for workers, but it became one of the most dramatic labor conflicts in the southwestern border region's history.

As Chicana/o historians have noted, the Mine-Mill Union earned the steadfast loyalty of its Mexican American adherents, despite its communist reputation. Although many of the miners of Bayard County were from longstanding Hispano families, native to New Mexico, their labor struggle encompassed a transborder vision of class solidarity with Mexican workers and migrants.[26] During the 1930s and '40s, Mine-Mill had represented the vanguard in antiracist unionism, leading the CIO in contesting the dual wage system and job discrimination across the Southwest. The Mine-Mill newspaper, the *Union*, promoted the desegregation of the labor force by giving space to Mexican American unionists to speak for themselves. In 1951, writing under the banner headline "Es el tiempo para destruit [*sic*] la barrera" [It is time to break down the barrier], El Paso member José Fuentes invoked his wartime service as a rationale for ending the Mexican wage and racial divisions in the workforce: "Como va a ser posible que unos seres racionales, unos seres humanos, jovenes veteranos de la guerra estén contentos en ese ambiente?" [How will it be possible for rational beings, human beings, young veterans of the war, to be content in that environment?].[27]

Mine-Mill leadership cast the union's commitment to Mexican American civil rights within a transnational framework of antiracist, anti-imperial labor activism. Mexican American unionists, both rank-and-file members and lead organizers, were the pivotal force in this effort. At the time of the Bayard strike, Mine-Mill unionists in Texas were engaged in cross-border organizing with the Confederación de Trabajadores Mexicanos (CTM), in El Paso, while the national leadership pursued a North American accord among workers in the Canadian, Mexican, and U.S. metals industries. This internationalist strategy clashed with the official politics of the Good Neighbor era and went against the grain of the nationalism of most U.S. unions. When Mine-Mill signed "a pact of friendship and mutual assistance" with the Mexican Miners Union in Mexico City, on May 18, 1950, it was Cipriano Montoya of Bayard Local 890 who presented a copper plaque pledging solidarity among the unions. "We move toward coordinated action of all metal miners of the Americas," declared the U.S. delegates on behalf of Mine-Mill, "the dream of the hemisphere-wide labor solidarity."[28] Although the Canadian and U.S. delegation did not formally endorse all of the Mexican union's provisions for achieving this hemispheric unity, the delegate reporting from the conference, Morris Wright, articulated his union's position on the particular relationship of Mexican nationals to U.S. companies: "To the Mexican worker international solidarity means . . . something more. It means a step toward liberating his country from the semi-colonial status into which it has been pushed by the American owners of Mexican industry." Wright compensated for the paternalism of his remarks with a gesture of masculine friendship: "It is good to clasp hands with workers from across the border—men who stand in the same relationship to the bosses as he does."[29] His homosocial expression of shared interests and common character glossed over the more difficult question of the very different relationship of Mexican and U.S. workers to their corporate bosses.

During the trinational labor conference, Mine-Mill vice president Orville Larson used the forum to attack the U.S. Good Neighbor Policy in Latin America: "The growing cooperation between our unions . . . is of historic importance. It will lead to a new stage in the bargaining relations between our unions and the giant mining corporations that spread their grasping hands over all of North America."[30] The statement was a deliberate provocation of the capitalist interests that directed U.S. foreign policy in Latin America and that during the 1950s used U.S. diplomatic and military force to control labor in Bolivia, Chile, Guatemala, and elsewhere. The Mine-Mill conference coincided with debates over the renewal of the Bracero Program: in 1951 the U.S. Congress extended the labor loan under Public Law 78.

Although most of the rank and file of miners in New Mexico were not themselves migrants, they were well aware of the migrant chain that connected the two countries. Latina/o unionists associated with Mine-Mill organized across the border in order to unify the transborder labor market, but also in the service of anti-imperialism and labor insurrection. Their efforts drew INS harassment along with government surveillance. Federal authorities viewed the Mine-Mill-CTM alliance in the Southwest as evidence of a conspiracy to draw the CIO into an international communist plot. In his fascinating account of Mine-Mill organizing in El Paso, Zaragoza Vargas links the government's anticommunist campaign against the union to the coordinated INS suppression of binational labor solidarities and Mexican opposition to racial discrimination in the United States.[31] During the "little Red Scare" of 1939–41, cross-border labor activism led to conflicts among U.S. diplomatic officials, police, and Mexican consuls, when the local sheriff, Fox, arrested six organizers and brought the Un-American Activities Committee to investigate the alleged subversive presence in the border city. In an episode that anticipated the McCarthy hearings, Texas congressman Martin Dies brought investigative hearings against the Nicaraguan-born organizer Humberto Silex and the tejano Juan Peña in a show of force aimed at the laboring Latina/o class.[32] That the incarcerated labor unionists reported having experienced physical mistreatment and civil-rights violations while in the sheriff's custody was of no account to the anticommunist crusade. While Fox triumphantly declared his victory over communist plans to have "Mexican aliens inject their form of government into this country," the episode demonstrated the conflict between two contending projects for hemispheric unity: the pro-business Good Neighbor Policy and the CTM-CIO aspirations for classless unity among Mexican and Latin American peoples across the Mexico-U.S. border.[33]

Although such incidents of red-baiting cost the Mine-Mill opportunities for expanding membership and gaining exclusive union contracts, its Latina/o leaders developed successful organizing tactics that promoted ethnic ties and cultural preservation. At the onset of the Cold War, Mine-Mill unionists joined other CIO militants to form the Asociación Nacional México-Americana (ANMA), an organization dedicated to the concerns of Mexican Americans as a discriminated minority in the United States. The first ANMA conference took place in Phoenix in February 1949, and delegates went on to form chapters across the border states and as far north as Chicago. ANMA continued the work El Congreso had undertaken in the 1930s, adopting a platform for promoting civil rights in the areas of housing, education, employment, voting, women's status, and immigration;

ANMA's founders hoped their work would draw documented and undocumented migrants and Mexican Americans alike into a single movement. Historian Mario García describes ANMA as "a national organization for ethnic self-defense," which derived its praxis from the radical tradition of transborder Mexican activism.[34]

The Latina/o left encompassed migrant and U.S.-born workers in its sweeping claims for a new order of civil and human rights in the borderlands. Like the American Committee for the Protection of the Foreign Born, ANMA invoked the Treaty of Guadalupe Hidalgo (the agreement signed by both governments at the end of the U.S.-Mexican War in 1848) to make the case for redress of Mexican poverty and marginalization in the United States. The two organizations collaborated in combating deportations of Latina/o migrants and sought the repeal of the McCarran and McCarran-Warren acts. In 1959, the ACPFB produced the pamphlet *Our Badge of Infamy: A Petition to the United Nations on the Treatment of Mexican Immigrants*, which looked beyond the domestic government to the United Nations for solutions to the discrimination and injustices that Mexicans suffered north of the border.[35]

Mine-Mill organizers dominated ANMA's founding board, creating its platform for national civil-rights work on behalf of Mexican Americans, because, in their view, unionism was insufficient to the task of protecting the Mexican population in the United States.[36] ANMA adopted an ideology of defense and reform based in part on the tenets of cultural nationalism, stressing ethnic and cultural ties to Mexico and promoting a discourse of kinship and common experience as a basis for national unity. The Mine-Mill Union reported with approval the prominence given to cultural education at the first national conference in Los Angeles. Noting that "significantly, the culture panel's report excited the most interest," the author opined, "Here were representatives of a people whose ancestors were physically conquered, but whose culture lived through the years, despite all the attempts to degrade, abuse, scorn, dilute, and distort it."[37]

Mine-Mill members at the conference included several women staff members and organizers, including Aurora Casillas of Miami, Arizona, and Florence LaMarr and Bebé Grijalva, secretaries of Local 700 in Los Angeles.[38] ANMA president Alfredo Montoya was the son of a Mexican worker at the Kennecott smelter in Hurley, New Mexico, the scene of major organizing efforts. Addressing the chilling effects of anticommunist policies at the forty-sixth Mine-Mill convention, Montoya defended the special relationship between Mexican Americans and the union: "Mexican-American people are not going to be deterred in our struggle for human dignity and the rights to which we are entitled. We will take an active part in saving unions like Mine-Mill from being destroyed." Montoya noted that the convention marked the "first time an International union has given recognition to the Mexican-American people as a whole."[39] Both Mine-Mill and ANMA remained on the fringe of progressive organizations and unions, because their radicalism raised the threat of government retaliation. Nonetheless, both entities remained steadfast in their transnational labor activism and antiracist organizing.

ANMA's publications, *El Progreso* and *La Voz*, combined ethnic discourse with internationalist perspectives on labor rights and U.S. militarism. ANMA opposed Operation Wetback policies and militated against police brutality in the barrios. At a moment when more mainstream Mexican American organizations like the G.I. Forum viewed military service as a vehicle for overcoming second-class citizenship, ANMA declared its opposition to the Korean War and protested the disproportionate number of Latino casualties in the overseas conflict. ANMA countered the logic of Cold War militarism by naming war as a danger to development rather than adopting the prevailing view that U.S. aggression would bring global security and prosperity. Recognizing the centrality of the mining and metals industries to the war effort, ANMA supported the Bayard strike of 1950–52 and called for the end of hostilities in Korea.[40]

Government repression ultimately led to the demise of both Mine-Mill radicalism and the Mexican American civil-rights organization, which dissolved its national federation in 1954, following the costly legal defense of ANMA members called before the House Un-American Activities Committee in the early 1950s.

Female Militancy and the Empire Zinc Strike

People used to come and ask, "Who told you you could walk right there?" And we used to say, "We want to." And they'd ask, "Who is your leader?" "Jane Doe." "What is your name?" "Jane Doe." Even the little girls

came with their mothers to the picket line, every time someone asked,
"What's your name?"—"Jane Doe." . . . We are all leaders.
        —Mariana Rodríguez, captain of the Bayard picket line (1975)[41]

On October 17, 1950, Mine-Mill unionists set up two picket lines at entrances to the Empire Zinc plant in Bayard, New Mexico. Their contract
had expired on September 30, with little promise of improved negotiations
over wages, paid vacations, or housing conditions. Mine-Mill leaders anticipated a long strike and directed Local 890 to establish support committees to distribute benefits and weekly food rations to workers.[42] For
several months, the pickets continued uninterrupted as neither the company nor the union made a move to the bargaining table. Then, beginning
in early 1951, company officials began a concerted campaign to break the
strike, and they wrote workers urging them to circulate a "right to work"
petition. That June, with a reported twenty-eight petitioners requesting to
return to their jobs, Empire officials announced that the company would
reopen the mine.

    The union had blockaded the primary access road, and picketers con-
trolled traffic to and from the mine. Arguing that the highway was public,
Empire management asked district attorney Thomas Foy to declare the
mine-road picket illegal; Foy assented and ordered the highway cleared.
But as the mine moved to open on June 11, the picket line grew. Picketers
clashed with the police deputies, and a number of women were arrested
along with other protesters. In retaliation, the company obtained a strike
injunction from the New Mexico Sixth District Court, directing Mine-Mill
Local 890 to terminate all pickets against Empire Zinc or face legal sanctions. Strike organizers called an immediate meeting, and on June 11, strikers and their family members assembled en masse in the union hall. After
eight months on the line, most of the miners were unwilling to concede
their defeat. To continue the pickets against the court order, however,
would have incurred financial and legal liabilities that would have imperiled both the workers and their union. As deliberations went into the
night, three community members came forward with a proposal to save
the strike and still obey the injunction: the women of Bayard would hold
the line.[43]

    According to historian Ellen Baker, the proposal that Bayard women
should take over the miner's picket originated with Aurora Chávez, Virginia

Chacón, and Virginia Jencks. They had come to the meeting prepared with a plan for maintaining the strike action without violating the terms of the court order.[44] The three women were married to active organizers for Local 890: Augustín Chávez, Juan Chacón, and lead union organizer Clinton Jencks. In 1948, wives and other family members had formed the ladies auxiliary for Local 890 and earned certification as Auxiliary 209 in May 1949. Women had been visible participants in union activities throughout the local's history; their charter dictated that members "enlist the aid of all miners' families to further the principles of trade unionism, because they have a special interest in safety, health, compensation, political action, housing, education, and child welfare."[45] By the time of the injunction, women were members of strike committees, assisting with publicity and solidarity activities on behalf of the local. From the 1940s onward, these women had been active community organizers in Grant County; as Baker asserts, they were hardly new to political struggle.[46]

But because women were not actual members of the union, it was legal for them to conduct the pickets. Despite women's record of participation in the local, though, the proposal met with considerable objections from the male members; they questioned the women's capacity to withstand the dangers of the labor action and expressed concerns about how women would meet their childcare obligations while conducting the picket. Accounts of the meeting concur that the discussion broke down along gender lines. Only the paid Mine-Mill staff supported the women's initiative.[47] Nevertheless, because the international union permitted women to vote on the proposal, Local 890 endorsed the women's strike action.[48]

The miners' recalcitrance toward the women's picket likely stemmed from the stark gender relations of production in the mining economy of Grant County. The social relations of southwestern mining rested on a strict segregation of gender roles, both in waged labor and unwaged domestic tasks. Empire Zinc employed few women and certainly none in mining occupations in 1950. Although wartime labor shortages had led women into Grant County mines, companies maintained strict segregation of the workforce and expelled the women at the war's end.[49] Management and unions both classed women as unskilled workers and as supplementary wage-earners to men. Mining has most often been a particularly masculine trade: tradition in many mining communities around the world forbids women to work underground. Mining superstition holds that a female presence will cause cave-ins and disasters.[50] Bayard miners accepted the women's picket as an emergency measure, ceding women political ground with little recognition of their independent stake in the strike's success.

The auxiliary immediately elected strike captains and coordinated shifts for the pickets. On the following morning, June 12, hundreds of women and children from across Grant County set up a barrier against the replacement workers who intended to reopen the mine. The pickets became scenes of frequent violence, as police deputies sought to break through the women's barricade and to reopen the mine road to company traffic. Within a few days, local officials brought arrest warrants against several women picketers, charging them with assault and battery as they held off scabs. Then on June 15, 1951, the situation escalated: county officers lobbed tear-gas grenades at the women and children on the highway picket. In the skirmish that followed, the police arrested fifty-three women and locked them up with their young children in the Grant County Jail.[51] The group refused the sheriff's offer to release them on the condition that they return home and stay away from the pickets. Their disorderly conduct drew national press to the strike and later provided the most memorable scene of women's resistance in the 1954 film *Salt of the Earth*.

Strike coverage in the Mine-Mill newspaper, the *Union*, reflected the miners' ambivalent attitudes toward the women's takeover of the picket lines. Reportage alternated between celebrations of female heroism on the line and assertions of patriarchal authority over the new picketers. Two months into the women's action, for example, the *Union* trumpeted female militancy, with news that three of the women picket leaders had been jailed for their defense of the strike: "There's no question that the women of Bayard, Silver City, and other towns hereabouts have 'won their spurs' as far as Mine-Mill Local 890 is concerned." In the same article, Cipriano Montoya, president of Local 890, applauded the nomination of three women—Elvira Molano, Catalina Barrelas, and Carmen Rivera—to the official bargaining committee for the Empire Zinc workers, stating that the women "have earned the right by two months of around-the-clock picketing at Empire Zinc; by standing up to arrests, jailings, gunmen, blackjacks, and tear gas."[52]

The spectacle of jailed women and children reinforced the novelty of this picket line. Empire Zinc used the scene as proof of the communist manipulations of the local workforce, which officials claimed had led the desperate workers to abandon all decorum in the strike; and the union depicted these clashes as evidence of soulless corporate warfare against the workers' families. When fourteen-year-old Rachel Juárez, the niece of a striking miner, was struck by a company-paid deputy's car and dragged several hundred feet, the *Union* depicted her heroism as an act of filial duty, expressing both indignation at the routine assaults on women and children and applauding their stoicism before physical intimidation and injury.[53] Juárez's attacker defended his actions, stating that the girl had deliberately thrown herself onto the car and cursed him—a claim that would not excuse his actions but, if true, might account for why the young girl had sustained various serious injuries and been jailed twice in just two months.[54]

The *Union* accounts consistently omitted any mention of the women's own militant aggression, which would have made the spectacle far less appealing to a broader audience. The violence with which picketers fought the scabs, jumped on their cars, and pelted the company officials with chile peppers remained entirely absent from the stories of Bayard's "heroic women." Sympathy for the women was crucial to the union cause; Democratic senator James Murray of Montana, then a member of the Senate Committee on Labor and Public Welfare, wrote in protest to Mine-Mill president John Clark, "I have been greatly shocked by newspaper accounts of the jailing of pickets, including women and children."[55] Such concern rested on the notion that women and children were not themselves protagonists of the labor conflict but, rather, were the dependents of the absent male workers. But the same *Union* article that cited Murray's paternal concern also quoted a defiant picketer saying, "The only way the company could get us off this line would be to drop an atom bomb." These women clearly had no trouble speaking for themselves, so in the coverage of the strike, they had to be *made* the proper object of paternal sympathy, lest such expressions of boldness also lead to female insubordination in the union.

In fact, the *Union* also neglected to mention the women's prior history of labor activism. Articles listed picketers by their married names and affiliation to striking husbands or fathers and only very rarely quoted women directly. The July 16, 1951, issue, for example, placed the headline "Heroic Bayard Women Hold the Line" under an image of company-paid deputies tangling with picketers. Although Ramona Nañez appears to be wrestling

Bayard District-Wide Mine-Mill Union Strike [n.d.]. Photograph taken by Clinton Jencks. Jencks identified picketer Mary Pérez's attacker as Deputy Sheriff Louis Rhea, "former Co. gunman now stationed at Hanover." (Courtesy Los Mineros Photograph Collection, Chicana/o Research Collection, Arizona State University Libraries)

with the deputy Porter, the caption states that her attacker "threw [her] to the ground a moment after this picture was snapped."[56] That description suggests that the editors were as concerned to downplay Nañez's fighting posture as to denounce company tactics of intimidation. Although the article invoked the "brave women" in its opening sentence, it subordinated them to its story of the principal confrontation between male protagonists: "Every conceivable legal and extra-legal weapon was being used by the company and its stooges in local government in futile attempts to destroy the workers' morale and force them back to work."[57]

Within this account, the assaults on women constituted an injury to the male workers: the women functioned less as autonomous actors in the labor conflict than as proxies for the banned strikers:

But the story of the Empire strike is the story of courage and the determination of working men and their families not to let a greedy corporation force down their already inadequate living standards. This strike is a
fight for bread and butter. It is also in the best tradition of Mine-Mill.[58]

Such a model of familial struggle domesticated women's activism by cir-
cumscribing it within the sanctioned domain of domestic duty and female
service. Below the *Union* headline, the women disappeared, as their omission reinstated the prevailing division of labor and leadership within the
union movement. Most important in the context of the Korean War, the
article dignifies the women's participation by making their struggle a matter of "bread and butter" and not of ideology.

As the strike wore on, Cold War interdictions against radical unionism
made the Mine-Mill Union far more vulnerable than Empire Zinc to public
sanction. As Jack Cargill notes, the strikers' sole strategy was to outlast the
company in the labor standoff, while also working to prevent state officials from intervening against the workers' blockade. Public sympathy was
critical to this effort.[59] By promoting the labor action as an act of familial
solidarity against corporate greed, the union hoped to create allegiances
between the largely ethnic Mexican miners and the broader population
of Grant County. The racial division of the workforce made the task difficult, especially because the negative financial impact of the strike followed
on the recession year of 1949, which had hurt the mining-dependent local economy. Maintaining an image of female propriety and the normative
gender division of labor within the community became a paramount concern to Mine-Mill publicity. The spectacle of women outside the home was
enough to incite anxiety about sexual transgression—miners had objected
to the women's picket on the grounds that their wives might fraternize
too closely with other men. When the *Union* reported that the Silver City
courts planned to prosecute Virginia Jencks for "touching David Gray"—
the man who had beaten her and her daughter Linda on the picket line
—the paper took pains to contest any suggestion of female deviance, by
describing her as "the *attractive* Mrs. Jencks."[60]

For Mexican women, who were the majority of picketers, however,
the codes governing female conduct took a different form. *Union* reports
tended to depict women of color in terms that banished their sexuality
altogether. José Fuentes, writing for the *Union* about Mexican women's

activism, first had to establish the legitimacy of women's entrance into the public sphere: "They knew that the responsibility rested on them,—the responsibility that, because of technical questions of law, had been lifted from the shoulders of their husbands."[61] Fuentes made the women's activism a matter of legal contingency and, therefore, of a *temporary* reversal of gender roles. By depicting the women's motivation as one of maternal concern, Fuentes reinscribed their actions within the domestic front of ethnic struggle: "When they saw that the future of their homes hung in the balance, thinking only of the welfare of their children, nothing else mattered to them."[62] And, although his article celebrated the Mexican women's fighting spirit, it effectively denied them an autonomous stake in the union conflict by making their expressions of political will a matter of devotion to family. Though the strike marked a serious challenge to the ethnic division of labor, it did not intend to threaten the gender roles of production and reproduction. The strike's discourse of ethnic solidarity among Mexicans circumscribed female mobility by placing it under patriarchal surveillance:

> Among these women, there isn't a single sad face. Nor is there a single face that shows lack of confidence in victory. Among them we saw no signs of fatigue. Nor is there any hypocrisy. The only thing that is seen there is fraternity, cooperation, and the open comradeship that characterizes us Mexicans.[63]

At first glance, the passage appears to celebrate the female valor with equanimity and solidarity, but its insistent repetition of the verb "to see" hints at a watchful gaze that polices the women's actions on the line. Fuentes asserts that the women were fully competent in the struggle, but his depiction evacuates women's agency by denying them the expression of any independent feeling (sadness, doubt, fatigue) that might threaten the "fraternity, cooperation, and open comradeship" of ethnic kinship.

Mine-Mill unionists struck an uneasy balance between promoting women's labor activism and containing their problematic militancy to the domestic front of struggle. At the onset of the Empire Zinc strike, the *Union* published a single-image comic strip depicting a miner's wife discussing the labor conflict over the phone: the woman says, "She was telling me that my husband should leave Mine-Mill and go into steel, but she suddenly got a headache and went home."[64] The woman, dressed fashionably in a dress and pumps, stands chatting easily with a friend on the phone while clutching a broken vase in her hand. The joke is, of course, that the woman has just clubbed her impertinent visitor, but all the while she keeps up bourgeois appearances by gossiping about the harm that she has just inflicted as if it were a common feminine malady. The simple humor of the drawing captures the constraints on women's expression during the Cold War, when the feminized home became in the popular imagination not only a space of refuge from politics but also another site of struggle. The comic assents to the fact that women did engage in the fights typically reserved for men, but it insists on the absurd notion that they did so only in the veiled conventions of bourgeois domesticity. The artist's depiction of the Mine-Mill wife as a white woman in a middle-class home, enjoying the rituals of female gossip and visits (and the luxury of a phone!), when most of its members in Grant County lived in company-owned, substandard housing that often lacked indoor plumbing, suggests the power of bourgeois ideology even in the imaginary of the radical left. But the cartoon also conveys an awareness of female rage that could erupt from the boundaries of the domestic sphere. In its humor, the comic considered how to make that rage useful to the labor movement without disturbing male prerogative.

In the end, the women's picket lasted over seven months, but legal wrangling in the courts eventually sapped the energies and resources of the union. Negotiations stalled through the spring of 1951 as the district judge and justice of the peace consistently sided with Empire management in their rulings on the strike. Officials of the international union and Local 890 served jail sentences and paid steep fines, while numerous mediation efforts failed. Then, on August 23, hostile strikebreakers attempted a sudden end to the strike by driving their cars though the Empire picket lines.[65] This violence brought the strike national press coverage, as the union called for an industry-wide walkout in support of Local 890. Despite their antagonism to Mine-Mill, even the AFL and CIO locals respected the walkout in Grant County, which lasted two weeks.

As President Truman interceded, using provisions of the Taft-Hartley Act to set an emergency injunction against the miners' strike, Grant

County became convulsed with waves of anticommunism, including vigilante organizing and business-sponsored petitions for martial law. In December, police moved to reopen the mining road and took charge of the pickets, forcing Local 890 to obey the injunction to clear the highway to mining traffic. When management and union representatives finally reached a contract settlement a month later, both sides made concessions in the labor agreement. Workers gained increases in hourly wages, a pension plan, and new programs for illness and accident insurance. The company remained intransigent on the question of collar-to-collar pay and the demand for indoor plumbing in Mexican American housing. The company ultimately emerged victorious as it added a stronger no-strike clause in the new contract and then continued its lawsuit against the union for damages incurred during the plant shutdown. But given the weakness of the labor position in negotiations, Local 890 accepted the contract as a union success. According to Jack Cargill, Clinton Jencks reckoned that the results were not a workers' victory "on paper" but that "the recognition won by the women and the emergence of new leaders" could count as a triumph for the union.[66]

The strike took on new meaning in memory. In retrospect, the women's picket offered a powerful example of female empowerment and ethnic unity. The storied reversal of gender roles—women holding off scabs and men washing clothes—became a vehicle for drawing feminist concerns into the domain of labor- and civil-rights struggles. Spectators saw ordinary women mobilize to bring their interests over housing, plumbing, and health to the fore as legitimate labor concerns in the class conflict. But despite this recognition, the prevailing narrative of the strike still managed to set clear limits on women's autonomy in the movement. As Cargill demonstrates, women's actual roles in the negotiating committees were quite limited, and they had no say in the final union settlement with the company.

Mine-Mill's annual convention following the strike yielded a resolution on women's organizing that denied the auxiliary any role beyond service to an essentially male union: "Men cannot be wholehearted union members without the cooperation of their womenfolk. . . . our union needs their understanding, sympathy, and support."[67] By contrast, nearly a decade and a half earlier, El Congreso had issued a far more expansive statement on working women during its second convention in December 1939:

Whereas: The Mexican woman, who for centuries had suffered oppression, has the responsibility for raising her children and for caring for the home, and even that of earning a livelihood of herself and her family, and since in this country, she suffers a double discrimination as a woman and as a Mexican.

Be it Resolved: That the Congress carry out a program of . . . education of the Mexican woman, concerning home problems, . . . that it support and work for women's equality so that she may receive equal wages, enjoy the same rights as men in social, economic, and civil liberties, and use her vote for the defense of the Mexican and Spanish American people, and of American democracy.[68]

Rather than present domestic duties as natural extensions of Mexican women's gender identity, the 1939 resolution (whose authors included Josefina Fierro and Luisa Moreno) portrayed them as a burden and indicted the discriminated status of women within the Mexican community as well as without. Its authors demanded the full recognition of women's equality, independent of their relationship to men. Whereas the Mine-Mill statement used marriage as a figure for ethnic and working-class unity, El Congreso exposed the gendered division of labor as another front of struggle.

"A Crime to Fit the Punishment": Making *Salt of the Earth*

The determination of the Mine-Mill women, both in the face of the prevailing gender norms and the threat of violence, attracted considerable attention in progressive circles. Their story drew the attention of three Hollywood filmmakers, Paul Jarrico, Michael Wilson and Herbert Biberman, who were already embattled in their own struggle against anticommunist repression. The three associates of the Hollywood Ten chose to retell the story of the Empire Zinc strike "as a crime to fit the punishment" that the anticommunist proceedings had inflicted on their careers.[69] Film director Herbert Biberman had served six months in a federal prison for his refusal to testify before the House Committee on Un-American Activities (HUAC).

Jarrico and Wilson had also defied hearings. In 1951, Jarrico and Biberman had joined with other banned artists to establish the Independent Productions Corporation (IPC), a film company devoted to the aesthetics of socialist realism and stories of popular struggle.

Later that year, Paul Jarrico vacationed at a ranch near Taos, New Mexico, where he and his wife, Sylvia, met Clinton and Virginia Jencks, who were organizing for Local 890. Clinton Jencks seized the opportunity to invite the Jarricos to Bayard to assess the potential of the Mine-Mill cause for a film. Once Sylvia Jarrico marched in the ongoing picket, the two became convinced of the dramatic values of the miners' struggle. Paul Jarrico saw an analogy between his own conflicts in Hollywood and the Mine-Mill's expulsion from the CIO for its tolerance of communist membership. He promised the Jenckses that the IPC would return to make a film in a historic collaboration with the mining community; it would be, in his words, an account of "the dignity of women, labor, and a racial minority" struggling for economic justice and democratic rights.[70]

Back in Los Angeles, Jarrico persuaded Biberman of the value of the project. The two enlisted Michael Wilson, the author of the screenplay for *A Place in the Sun*, to write for the film. The filmmakers wanted the film to spark a revival of progressive filmmaking, one engaged with social justice in opposition to Cold War policies.

Filming began in January 1953, in a production process that involved the depicted community at a level unprecedented for a Hollywood film. The artists asked the townspeople to play themselves in the film, both out of a sense of reciprocity with their subjects and because of budget shortfalls for the production. Professional actors were hesitant about working with blacklisted filmmakers, and Hollywood unions withheld production crews from the film because of its political status. The improvised crew became the most integrated major film set of its time, employing African American and Latino tradesmen who ordinarily suffered a blacklist of another sort. The production process became a social movement in itself, breaking racial codes entrenched in mainstream cinema. Bayard residents pushed Jarrico and Biberman to cast a striker in the central role of the film. Ramón Quintero, the male lead, was modeled directly on the Mine-Mill organizer Juan Chacón, who was given the chance to play himself. The directors did not choose a local woman for the leading female role, however. Instead, they brought in Rosaura Revueltas, a noted Mexican actress who spoke fluent English, to play the part of Ramón's wife, Esperanza.

Throughout the production, community members educated the filmmakers in the realities of Mexican American life in the segregated county and exerted considerable pressure to obtain the filmic representation they desired. Wilson spent a month in Bayard, conducting interviews and gathering material for the script. He conceived of structuring the narrative around a Mexican American miner and his wife, whose marital relationship would reflect the social transformations unleashed in the strike. Wilson vetted the script among some four hundred members of the mining community, who rejected various elements of the plot as inauthentic or demeaning to them as Mexican Americans. Although they accepted the central marriage plot, community members rejected scenes of the husband's infidelity or drunkenness, arguing that such stereotypical images would detract from the dignity of their struggle. Members of Local 890 also rejected an initial plot that would have given the white union organizer Clinton Jencks primacy in the organizing effort and insisted that the grassroots leadership receive equal time onscreen.[71]

Well before the film's completion, *Salt of the Earth* attracted national attention for its defiance of the Hollywood censors. These "Reds in the Desert" sparked media attacks, with syndicated labor columnist Victor Reisel sounding the alarm, "not too far from the Los Alamos proving ground . . . [w]here you try to hide secret weapons . . . you find concentrations of Communists."[72] Entertainment-industry unions and studio executives closed ranks against the film—canceling insurance policies for the production crew, refusing contracts for processing or projecting the film, and mobilizing government officials against the filmmakers. On February 25, 1953, midway through filming, the Immigration and Naturalization Service seized Revueltas's passport. Claiming to find fault with the seals on her documents, agents drove the actress to El Paso, where they questioned her under armed guard. Revueltas returned to Mexico City under order of "voluntary" departure in circumstances similar to Luisa Moreno's deportation just three years earlier. The filmmakers resorted to creative editing as they continued production without her. Back in Grant County, on March 3, vigilantes fired on Jencks's car and led a mob onto the set, where they fought crew members and damaged camera equipment. The *El Paso*

Herald-Post praised the attackers "in their determination to clear away the pink overcast from their beautiful country."[73]

Despite the setbacks, *Salt of the Earth* finally opened on March 9, 1954, at private movie houses in New York and Los Angeles. The filmmakers had edited the footage in a secret cutting room and booked screenings without support from major motion-picture distributors. At its premiere, projectionists refused to run the film because of pressure from their union. As a result, the film enjoyed a run that proved all too brief. The drive-in theater near Silver City sold out for three weeks after the film's release, as the mining communities came out to see themselves onscreen. In Mexico City, *La Sal de la Tierra* earned laurels for Revueltas and incited popular sympathies for the unionists and the blacklisted artists. But the film did not survive the assault from the conservative film industry. Ultimately a coalition of Hollywood moguls, projectionist unions, and conservative organizations like the American Legionnaires succeeded in banning the further distribution of the film. In September, the film had one last theatrical booking in Menlo Park, California; screenings had been limited to one theater in Los Angeles, seven in Northern California, two in New York, one in Silver City, and two others in the Southwest.

Despite the long years of censorship that followed, *Salt of the Earth* re-emerged following the civil-rights movements of the late 1960s. In 1975, Sonja Dahl Biberman, who had been an associate producer on the film, obtained a special screening at an international women's cinema festival.[74] *Salt of the Earth* toured internationally in film festivals, union halls, and college campuses. Activists hailed the film as a resonant account of popular opposition to corporate greed and a moving depiction of women's collective action. That Esperanza, the film's central protagonist, was a poor, Mexican American woman made the film all the more significant as a chronicle of the culture of resistance that opposed the Cold War consensus. Audiences appreciated that the story the filmmakers and their interlocutors in Bayard chose to tell offered a vital prehistory of the social movements of the 1960s and '70s. The character of Esperanza embodied all the contradictions confronting Mexican Americans, especially women, as they struggled toward the national mobilization against racial segregation that became the civil-rights movement. In its story of a marriage and a strike, the film plotted the linked spheres of Mexican American women's struggles for full rights and political autonomy.

The Marriage Plot

> *Esperanza's voice*: We did not know what we had won in the strike. But
> our hearts were full. And when Ramón said . . .
> *Ramón (simply)*: Thanks . . . sisters . . . and brothers.
> —Michael Wilson, "*Salt of the Earth*: Screenplay"[75]

From the beginning, then, the film announces Esperanza's importance: she
is the symbolic device that supports the didactic function of the strike narrative, elevating the local story to political allegory. The multiracial, working-class women's mobilization commemorated in *Salt of the Earth* is an
example of what critic Jean Franco has termed "the tradition of women's
movements in Latin America," in which feminist concerns find expression
in relation to "other social and political issues." For these movements, she
writes, women's activism "is not only a question of individual liberation
but of social justice and democratization."[76] Esperanza fights for a voice in
the strike only to speak for the concerns of the collective, not for herself.

Salt of the Earth frames the women's takeover of the Empire Zinc picket
line through the story of marital discord between the timid Esperanza and
her overbearing husband, Ramón Quintero. As the miners organize the
strike effort, their wives gather to dispute the omission of their concerns
about sanitation conditions and plumbing from the men's list of demands
on the company. When Esperanza acknowledges that Ramón has dropped
their interests from the issues slated for arbitration, her companions suggest that the wives picket the negotiations, so "both sides will see we mean
business":

> *Teresa*: Come on Esperanza—how about it? We got to.
> *Esperanza*: No. No. I can't. If Ramón ever found me on a picket line . . .
> *Consuelo*: He'd what? Beat you?
> *Esperanza*: No. No. (17)

Esperanza's subjection to spousal control dramatizes debates over the
"woman question"—the relation of gender subordination to the capitalist
division of labor, which continued to vex union movements and communists during the 1950s. That the film frames Esperanza's story in relation to
the threat of retaliatory violence from her husband means that even as she

enacts her gender rebellion, her activism remains circumscribed as service to the broader familia, the ethnic community.

Esperanza's evolution as an independent actor dramatizes how women forced unions to expand the sphere of class conflict. In *Salt of the Earth*, the strike moves from a conventional labor dispute to a communal effort at checking corporate dominance and the racial and gender divisions that limit working-class unity. The film recounts the women's entry into the strike as an awakening of women's political potential, as they bring their anarchic energies to the men's labor conflict. Rather than making the *discovery* of women's agency, however, the film enacts the *containment* of women's power to the domestic sphere, even as it celebrates the women's new recognition as a political force. That is, the focus of the film's plot—marriage—forces a premature resolution of gender conflict by insisting on the complementary partnership between male and female spheres in the communal struggle. The marriage of Ramón and Esperanza naturalizes a gendered division of labor into distinct, cooperative fronts of collective unity against capitalist domination and racial subordination.

By omitting the longer history of Mexican women's militancy in favor of a developmental narrative of Esperanza's coming to consciousness, the film suppresses the living conflict over gender and labor roles. Instead, the film offers a more colorful, folkloric drama of Mexican American machismo. Although the story highlights women's efforts to prove themselves as militants, it continually subsumes those efforts within their status as wives. After the women lobby for their inclusion in the strike, the following scene narrates the men's negative reactions by cutting from one couple to another, in four vignettes in which each husband chides his wife for her initiative:

Sal: Why didn't you check with me? It's embarrassing!
Charley: But Teresa, you can't push things too fast. (26)

Only the Anglo organizer Frank Barnes gets an angry response from his wife. The three Mexican women say nothing. Thus, even as the film demonstrates the contradiction between the union demands and the women's disenfranchisement, it asserts the primacy of the marriage contract as the racialized domain of female struggle. In order to achieve a voice in public, the women must remake their men in private.

The film's depiction of "Mrs. Salazar" provides another lens on how gender ideologies figured in the construction of women's political agency. In her narration of the early days of the strike, Esperanza notes the "unwritten rule" forbidding the women from joining the picket line. Only one woman breaks ranks, bringing her knitting to the scene of the men's protest:

> *Esperanza's voice*: But then one morning Mrs. Salazar went to the picket line. Her husband had been killed in a strike many years before . . . and she wanted to be there. Nobody remembers just how it happened, but one day Mrs. Salazar started marching with them . . . and she kept marching with them. After a while some of the women began to bring coffee to their husbands . . . and maybe a couple of tacos—because a man gets tired and hungry on picket duty. . . . It was about that time the union decided maybe they'd better set up a Ladies Auxiliary after all. (28–29)

Mrs. Salazar can transgress the gender codes because as a widow, she is outside the surveillance or protection of a male partner. She takes the place of her absent husband beside the other men. Her presence on the line allows the other women to follow, although their actions are limited to supporting their husbands. Local 890 finally accepts the women into the union by forming the Ladies Auxiliary Committee, which commutes the women's bid for a participatory role in the decision-making process to one of serving the miners' material needs.

Decisions about casting for the film suggest another dimension to the gender frame delimiting the women's story. The filmmakers modeled the character of the widow on the activism of Elvira Molano, a leader in the women's committee and a strike negotiator, who had been married to an Empire Zinc miner. Molano served as the co-chair of the union negotiating committee, a fact that drops out entirely from the film's narrative of women's empowerment. All told, three of the five representatives to the negotiating team were women from the picket line. Molano was even named "the most arrested woman" during the Empire Zinc strike.[77] But these were not the stories that *Salt of the Earth* told. To play the widow Salazar, Molano appears onscreen dressed as an older woman, cloaking her gender rebellion in a long coat and headscarf. With these choices, the film unconsciously adopted the U.S. government's attitude toward the women picketers: their takeover of the strike was only possible because the U.S. law was unable to conceive of Mexican American women as political subjects. It is only because the court injunction did not address them that they were able to assume responsibility for the strike. This element of surprise at women's collective power also pervades the film and serves as a device for reducing the threat of female militancy onscreen.

The film portrays the Bayard women as newcomers to the union movement—theirs is a spontaneous show of resistance, rather than a product of the calculated, experienced planning that drew women like Elvira Molano, Henrietta Williams, Angela Sánchez, and Clorinda Alderette into the strike well before they reprised their historic roles in the film. Feliciana Montoya, for example, had been active in Communist Party circles during World War II and continued her political work after the Empire strike, until her murder in 1961. Mariana Ramírez, captain of the women's picket line, had extensive personal experience with the humiliations of the "Mexican wage":

> I was working with an Anglo lady. . . . we were doing the same thing. She was an Anglo, and she was getting fourteen dollars a week and I was getting seven. Sometimes we would work until nine o'clock, and the manager used to go out and get some sandwiches for the secretary, who was an Anglo, and the others, who were Anglos, and not a thing for me. When I got home I was hungry but I didn't feel like eating. Not because I was tired, but because I was hurt, from the very bottom of my heart I was hurt.[78]

But the hungers that women brought to the picket line—as wage earners, as leftist adherents, as discriminated citizens—disappear within the film's conventions of female domesticity. *Salt of the Earth* repeats the Mine-Mill rhetoric of feminine devotion to family to explain the women's participation in the labor conflict. As if to reinforce this image, the sisters of Local 890 discarded the modern clothes they wore on the picket in favor of more chaste dresses and shawls for the film. Numerous snapshots taken on the women's picket line center on the figure of a young woman dressed in a man's work shirt, denim pants, and boots, adopting a posture of defiance before the camera.[79] Her challenge to gender norms could not find

accommodation within the marriage plot structuring the film, not only because of its connotation of sexual difference but also because it disrupted
the public/private split that identified women's political interests with the
domestic sphere.

If the youthful defiance recorded in picket photographs hints at the
gender rebellion that animated the strike, then the somber figure of Esperanza functions as their resolution in the film. She is less the "composite" of
the women of Grant County than the archetype of feminine self-sacrifice,
an abstraction from the politically engaged miners' wives who helped negotiate the strike settlement. As Esperanza begins to exert greater autonomy from Ramón, the film invests her newfound independence with the
transcendent authority of the maternal. When Esperanza finally comes to
the picket line with the other women, she is in the advanced stages of her
pregnancy. Ramón, the picket captain, stands on the lookout for nonunion
workers breaking through the line. Discovering that one strikebreaker is
his old acquaintance, Sebastián Prieto, Ramón berates him for his betrayal, unaware that in his rage he has fallen into a trap set for him by the
company bosses. As the sheriff and his deputies handcuff him and lead
him away to a car for questioning, Esperanza suddenly feels the first pangs
of labor pains. The film then cuts between scenes of Esperanza calling for
assistance and Ramón's exchange with the deputies as he realizes their
intentions. The intercutting of the two scenes becomes more rapid, as
Ramón yells in pain from the deputies' blows and as Esperanza cries from
the contractions. The camera zooms into extreme closeups of Ramón's and
Esperanza's faces, as the two call out to each other:

Ramón: Oh, my God . . . Esperanza . . . Esperanza . . .
Esperanza: Ramón . . .
*Close up: Ramón. Now the two images merge, and undulate, and blur, as
with receding consciousness. And then darkness on the screen. We hear the
feeble wail of a newborn infant.* (40)

The purpose of the scene is to suture the two fronts of struggle, public and
private, through the bonds of marriage. Esperanza's wail merges these discordant figures.

As gender violence threatens the struggle, the film secures women's alliance to the cause by depicting Ramón's and Esperanza's suffering as equivalent, and thus complementary. They are both punished by the company for the strike: Ramón is beaten by the local corrupted police, and Esperanza undergoes childbirth without the attentions of the company doctor. Esperanza begs forgiveness for wishing that the child would never be born, in effect denying that her gender subordination would render her experience incommensurate with Ramón's. The newborn represents the productive union of male and female partners against domination, a union that is achieved by sublimating their conflict. The marriage plot sustains itself through rigid adherence to an ideology of separate spheres, just as its gender logic is inscribed in Ramón's and Esperanza's distinct forms of bodily suffering. In the subsequent baptism scene, the baby stands in for the broader ethnic collectivity, as the desired object of the marriage plot. The two are reconciled in their hopes for their son:

Ramón: A fighter, huh?
Esperanza: He was born fighting. And born hungry.
Ramón: Drink up Juanito, you'll never have it so good.
Esperanza: He'll have it good. Some day. (44)

Esperanza voices her emerging political militancy in the language of motherhood, but their jokes nevertheless demonstrate the couple's different conceptions of the maternal.

The mood of the film changes when the police jail the protesters, only to determine that it is impossible to treat the women like their male counterparts. The women sing, chant, and yell in jubilant opposition to the police, appealing for food and formula for Esperanza's baby:

Women: Queremos comida . . .
    Queremos camas . . .
    Queremos baños . . .
    Queremos comida . . .

    [We want food . . .
    We want beds . . .
    We want bathrooms . . .
    We want food. . . .] (70)

The women's demands prove too much for the sheriff to control. The anarchic energies unleashed in their protest demonstrate how women may deploy gender difference with strategic effects in the masculine public sphere. But it is a ploy that will only work once. The jail scene is based on the actual mass incarceration of women picketers in June 1951, which momentarily galvanized public sentiment in support of the strike. This episode provides the comedic element in the film that counterbalances the melodrama of the familial conflict. But it also glosses over the more threatening reality of the women's aggression on the line, as when women clashed with strikebreakers earlier that day. Mariana Ramírez recalled using the instruments of women's domesticity to far more menacing effect than the film scene suggests: "Everybody had guns except us. We had knitting needles. We had safety pins. We had straight pins. We had chili peppers. And we had rotten eggs."[80] Bayard women, children in tow, jumped the police cars, yelling, "¡No los dejen pasar! ¡No pasarán!" [Don't let them through! They will not get through!].[81] The film does not depict this scene at all.

The film does suggest, however, that the domestic sphere should function as a vital front of struggle. The climactic scene of the film comes when Esperanza confronts Ramón to demand his respect for her place in the struggle:

> *Esperanza*: Whose neck shall I stand on, to make me feel superior? And what will I get out of it? I don't want anything lower than I am. I'm low enough already. I want to rise. And push everything up with me as I go. (82)

Her speech reveals how the ideology of separate spheres suppresses women's insurgency—Esperanza voices her yearning not to rise up for herself but to "push up" those around her as she goes. When Ramón retaliates by threatening to strike her, however, Esperanza replies with dignity, "That would be the old way. Never try it on me again" (82). Her response is a moment of reckoning between them, one that announces the emergence of new sexual agency for Mexican American women and that suggests a "new way" of governing the conjugal partnership. In the final resolution to the film, the strike concludes with the fulfillment of the marriage plot, as the community comes together to resist the eviction of the Quinteros from company housing. The final confrontation with the company occurs not at the mine or on the picket line but in the workers' homes, where the gender divide dissolves into collective unity. Ramón echoes Esperanza's desire to "push everything up with us as we go," embracing her before the cheering crowd. The film ends by redirecting male violence toward its proper object, the corporation and the police.

Salt of the Earth concludes with a scene of ethnic resistance that resonated deeply with its Chicana/o audiences during El Movimiento, when urban redevelopment and police brutality were chief concerns for barrio activists. Through Experanza, the strike narrative thus anticipates another major shift in the politics of working-class Mexican Americans from its labor-unionist base of the 1930s and '40s to a communal, ethnic platform for civil rights. Mexican American movements could only achieve this change by incorporating Mexican American women. As Esperanza says to Ramón, "You can't win *anything* without me" (82). Paradoxically, the gender inclusiveness of the film narrative simultaneously expands the field of collective action *and* erases women's labor and political histories. The plot of Esperanza's personal empowerment eclipses the more interesting histories of Bayard women, of people like Virginia Chacón, Catalina Barrelas, Carmen Rivera, and Elvira Molano, whom she is meant to represent.

Memory and Forgetting

Why is it that the film, which purports to narrate the strike from the women's perspective, actually omits the greater part of women's activism within the struggle? Although the strikers had a major role in shaping the film narrative, it is nevertheless clear that the Bayard community shared no consensus about how the events had unfolded or about their lasting significance. As the strike passed into memory, Bayard women met with the retrenchment of male authority in their lives. Their militancy had posed a particularly potent threat to male primacy in Grant County society. If their struggle mounted an effective assault on racial divisions in the mining workforce, women remained at the periphery of the community's leadership. Even the locals involved in *Salt of the Earth* felt ambivalent about its story of female heroism. Although the film ultimately shaped public memories of the strike, Bayard women found that its script did not transfer easily into daily life. Virginia Chacón, whose husband portrayed the male lead in *Salt of the Earth*, recalled with some bitterness,

> The movie didn't make any difference. A lot of the women are still very much oppressed by the men. There's no difference in the home, I'm sorry to say. It didn't change my life. You can't teach an old dog new tricks.[82]

In fact, as various oral histories of the strike have demonstrated, the women who were married to the principal organizers, Virginia Jencks, Virginia Chacón, and Feliciana Montoya, were ultimately the most dissatisfied with its outcomes for women.[83] Jencks complained, "Is it enough for a union where the women saved a strike for seven months?"[84] For these women, the film was a source of ambivalence, as its story of female heroism impinged on their own, more complex set of memories. During an interview with Deborah Silverman Rosenfelt about the strike, Virginia Chacón interrupted to challenge Juan Chacón about his claims for women's equality: "Look at your own home. What about me?"[85]

Indeed, the story of female "rescue" threatened to eclipse the complex history of women's protracted struggle for autonomy and full equality within union and civil-rights movements. Ellen Baker documents the cases of gender violence within the striking community, citing Mine-Mill organizers' testimony that they often overlooked cases of domestic abuse within the local.[86] Virginia Chacón recounted that the women whom she organized through home visits often expressed a reluctance to join the auxiliary out of fear of their husbands.[87] Although Cipriano Montoya, president of Local 890, publicly asserted that women had gained a place on the union bargaining committee by their own merits, he expressed discomfort with his wife's militancy. Despite his assertions of respect for women's organizing, Montoya later recanted, stating that the directive had come directly from the Communist Party and that he had never thought women belonged on the picket line. Montoya made these statements after his arrest for the shooting of his estranged wife, Feliciana Montoya, in July 1961.[88] He explained to police that he killed her because of her CPUSA membership, which he believed made her a danger to the couple's children. This episode of gender violence entwines patriarchal rage with Cold War anticommunism to reveal how the domestication of women was an artifact of much broader political processes than a matter of persistent male dominance in private life. The domestic sphere was neither autonomous from wage-earning and political spheres nor a refuge from relations of social repression.

When viewed against the broader landscape of contemporary Mexican American women's roles in the Mine-Mill Union, the ANMA, and the United Cannery, Agricultural, Packing, and Allied Workers of America (UCAPAWA), it seems clear that the film enacts the reentrenchment of gender ideologies restricting women's political activity to the domestic sphere. Perhaps the women's takeover of the strike in effect heralded the crisis of the masculine subject as the central protagonist of class struggle. The reassertion of female domesticity at the film's end signaled the reconsolidation of male authority just at the moment of emergency.

Through the iconic image of Esperanza, the film constructs a social-realist aesthetic in which idealized womanhood and ethnic color converge to depict Grant County as isolated and traditional Hispana/o country. Herbert Biberman wrote that the Bayard community "was such a beautiful group of people . . . that well photographed they will just knock people out of their seats with their strong and clean and incredibly attractive character."[89] For the filmmaker, their aesthetic value derived from their geographic and social isolation, far removed from the cosmopolitan urbanity of Hollywood. However powerful, the figure of Esperanza contrasts sharply with the worldly militancy of the actual Bayard women. These women brought the local struggle national and international attention, in defiance of the cultural logic that made their militancy unimaginable and surprising to the company, the union, and government officials alike. *Salt of the Earth* also makes no mention of the Korean War, which gave the labor conflict its impetus.[90] Nor does it acknowledge the involvement of Local 890 in transnational organizing. Instead, the story that the filmmakers told is decidedly local, grounded by the racial and gender frames that converge in the figure of Esperanza.

But the film is not merely the product of Biberman, Jarrico, and Wilson's imagination; it is also the creation of the strike participants themselves. The story was local in part because of the miners' own perspectives. Although they understood that their labor struggle was bound up in international matters of state and corporate expansion, they also viewed themselves as humble people caught up in larger forces of conflict.[91] The New Mexican community was not immune to the pressures of Cold War nationalism. In telling their story, Bayard residents accepted the frame imposed by the Hollywood filmmakers. But through the film, their struggle acquired significance beyond the limited gains of the strike and became a testament to Mexican American desires for full civil rights in the United States. The strikers passed on a narrative of collective action that endured and inspired the generation that followed them.

As they forged a new grammar of communal struggle in the shadow of the Cold War, Mexican American unionists gave renewed force to an ideology of race as family and of heterosexual marriage as the ideal unit for ethnic self-defense. This discourse laid the groundwork for the ethnic nationalism that shaped El Movimiento in the late 1960s; in the process, it also foreclosed on the more radical possibilities of the migrant and female imaginaries that fell outside the nationalist frame. The deportation of Luisa Moreno in 1950 deprived the coming movement of its most ardent advocate for migrant, working-class, and racialized women. Her memory was entirely absent during the Chicana/o Movement. In her place stood the more ambiguous figure of Esperanza, a character so abstracted from the actual women who saved the Bayard strike as to be unrecognizable. She represented a far more restrictive view of Mexican American women's political work. The deportation of Rosaura Revueltas in 1953 indicates just how dangerous the character of Esperanza was to the U.S. government as a figure of opposition to Cold War cultural politics. But in retrospect, Revueltas's failure to complete the part could also signify just how difficult it was for the outspoken Mexican actress to embody the role. Just as the filmmakers had to complete their script with a double, no single Mexican woman could live up to Esperanza's ideal in the struggles ahead.

Bordered Civil Rights

Migrants, Feminism, and
the Radical Imagination in
El Movimiento Chicano

> ... These are warriors
>
> distancing themselves from history.
> They find peace
> in the way they contain the wind
> and are gone.
>
> —Lorna Dee Cervantes,
> *Emplumada* (1981)[1]

"At some point the people themselves must define their reality," wrote Elizabeth Martínez in a letter to the *New York Review of Books* dated February 12, 1970. Martínez, then editor of *El Grito del Norte*, a prominent newspaper of the Chicana/o civil-rights movement, had dispatched an exasperated corrective to a review article devoted to books about Mexican Americans and the land-rights movement in New Mexico. In 1967, members of the Alianza Federal de Mercedes, led by Reies López Tijerina, had raided the Rio Arriba County Courthouse of Tierra Amarilla to demand the restitution of historical land grants to the descendants of Spanish and Mexican settlers in the region. They staked their claim to property and other rights promised in the Treaty of Guadalupe Hidalgo, signed at the end of the U.S.-Mexican War in 1848. Writing from northern New Mexico, Martínez expressed concern that Anglo-Americans were unprepared to address the longstanding grievances of

"La Raza" [the Race], given their relative ignorance of Mexican realities in the United States. "If white America feels it has just passed through a ten-year trauma . . . of learning about black consciousness and the meaning of the black experience," she warned, "it is going to find itself up against something even more elusive as it tries to dig the Chicano movement."[2] Martínez had joined the Alianza Federal de Mercedes in 1968, leaving a leadership position at the New York office of the Student Nonviolent Co-ordinating Committee, one of the principal organizations behind the African American movement for civil rights. As a former editor for Simon and Schuster and a frequent contributor to the *Nation*, Martínez was well connected to the cosmopolitan society of New York publishing. Her letter faulted the *New York Review of Books* for allowing its "urban middle-class white liberal" optic to define the struggles of her people. Already a seasoned activist and researcher of liberation movements, Martínez was acutely conscious that Mexicans were largely invisible to the larger U.S. society, but also that their political demands fell outside the existing frameworks for civil-rights reform.

For Martínez, the aspirations of La Raza belonged to "another country":

> Starting with a language difference and moving on to cultural values of all types, La Raza is even less "American" than black people in the United States. . . . The weight and the intricacy of family and other social relationships, with roots that are centuries old, create a Raza society in which layer after layer of truth can be peeled away—still leaving an outside observer with the feeling that the fundamental has yet to be grasped. Even in urban Raza areas, which seem more familiar to the non-Raza perception, there are human forces at work that will not be understood by comparison to either white or black life.[3]

The Chicana activist echoed the pervasive complaint of the civil-rights era, that leading intellectuals often ignored or misrepresented the racial disparities and cultural differences that set communities in struggle apart. Martínez made the issue of representation—of controlling perception—a central point of contention in the larger conflict over minority rights in the United States. As Chicana/o militants sought redress for decades of discrimination, adopting many of the claims made by African Americans and Native peoples before them, they insisted on the singularity of their community and their fight.

Adjudicating the demands of Mexican Americans for full rights as U.S. citizens required a new definition of the ethnic community, Martínez argued, one that conformed to the liberal framework of civil-rights reforms. But this was no simple task. Just as "the fundamental" difference of Mexican American communities had "yet to be grasped" by the larger U.S. society in 1970, it remained no less elusive for Mexican migrants and Mexican Americans. Throughout her career, Martínez encountered opposition from within the Chicana/o left for her expansive definition of Mexican American peoplehood, her defense of migrants, and her trenchant feminism.

This chapter examines the Chicana/o civil-rights movement within the context of unresolved conflicts over the migrant presence in Mexican American communities. I begin this inquiry with Elizabeth (Betita) Martínez because her long career describes a singular commitment to the global dimensions of Mexican and Mexican American struggles for land, political rights, and cultural autonomy. The issue of immigration and immigrant rights divided the leadership of El Movimiento, the political struggle that emerged from 1965 to 1975, just as it had split unions and earlier civil-rights campaigns. Although U.S.-born Mexican Americans constituted the majority within the ethnic Mexican communities in the United States, the foreign born formed a significant portion of the overall population. "This demographic reality," argues David G. Gutiérrez, "continued to exert a powerful influence on both ethnic politics and attitudes about immigration and ethnicity among Mexican Americans during this volatile period of American history."[4] No single view of immigration or ethnicity unified the various fronts of the movement. The demand for an inclusive framework of redress to class and racial discrimination would necessarily reveal the limits of liberal reforms, and the capacity of the nation-state to act as the guarantor of civil rights for the transborder community. In the wake of 1965 legislation that ended much legal segregation in the United States, the more localized mobilizations of Mexican American communities across the southwestern United States gave rise to cohesive demands by Mexican Americans for full citizenship.

As a writer and photojournalist, Betita Martínez lent an eloquent voice to La Causa [the Cause]. Born in 1925, she grew up in Washington, DC, where her Oaxacan father worked as a secretary to the Mexican Embassy.[5] As a young child Martínez experienced first-hand the Jim Crow practices that supported white supremacy in the southern United States when she and her father were forced to ride at the back of a public bus. Educated at Swarthmore College, Martínez obtained a degree in history and literature. From 1948 until 1963, she worked at the United Nations in New York researching decolonization movements for the secretariat until her supervisor and other colleagues were fired for allegedly "having past or present connections with Communism."[6] Martínez traveled to Cuba in 1959 shortly after the success of the revolution, beginning decades of travel to scenes of popular struggle in the socialist republics of the Soviet Union, Poland, Hungary, China, and Vietnam. Martínez and María Varela were the sole Chicanas to occupy positions of leadership in the Student Nonviolent Coordinating Committee. As a photographer, fundraiser, and organizer, Martínez made scenes of the antiracist struggle visible across the country, particularly during her participation in the Mississippi Summer Project (Freedom Summer) of 1964.

When Martínez moved to New Mexico in support of the land-grant movement in 1968, she began a sustained engagement with a social movement unlike any other of the Chicano Movement. In Tierra Amarilla, the Alianza Federal de Mercedes had waged a militant conflict with the state over communal properties held by Hispanas/os over generations. For Martínez, the demand for land surpassed the bounds of the civil-rights conflict: "The movimiento in Nuevo Mexico," she wrote, "evolved within the framework of a long, popular struggle against U.S. colonization and for land—that is to say, nothing less than the means of production."[7] This struggle unfolded far differently from the Bayard strike of the early 1950s, located hundreds of miles to the south; the reach of the historical grievances in Tierra Amarilla dated back to the colonial decimation of indigenous nations and predated either Mexican or U.S. national claims to the territory. "The roots" of the movement, Martínez explained, "include social relations, economic traditions, political forms, artistic expression, and language—everything that defines peoplehood." But the author made a clear distinction between *people* and *nation*: "It was not primarily cultural, not exclusionary of other peoples, not 'Mi raza primero' (my people first)."[8] Because she often departed from the nationalism that came to dominate the movement, Martínez was sometimes subject to censure from other Chicana/o militants during the 1970s. Still, her long historical view eventually ensured the enduring relevance of her documentary and activist projects.

Perhaps El Movimiento's greatest challenge to liberal racism in all its gender and class dimensions came from Martínez's print journalism during the war in Vietnam. Together with movement lawyer Betty Axelrod, Martínez founded *El Grito del Norte*, an independent newspaper that linked the local struggle to Chicana/o mobilizations in other parts of the United States, as well as to indigenous rights, black liberation, labor campaigns, and prisoner-rights movements. Using the theme of land struggle, *El Grito* forged alliances with revolutionary movements across the Third World, sending reporters to Vietnam, Cuba, and China. Its staff of Chicana journalists, which included Enriqueta Vásquez, set a feminist agenda for the paper, publishing articles such as "New Life for La Chicana," alongside "We Are Not Alone: A Survey of Movements around the World" and "Vietnam, Vietnam." The October 1969 issue featured the young author Valentina Valdés in the first of several articles devoted to Vietnamese society. Valdés opened her essay with a direct appeal to Chicano soldiers: "Why are you going to fight this war?"[9] A year later, *El Grito* featured a report on Martínez's trip to the scene of conflict that drew analogies between the plight of Vietnamese peasants and poor Mexicans: "La historia de la Guerra en Vietnam empezó por la tierra" [The history of the war in Vietnam began over land].[10] *El Grito* stood out among war reportage because its articles explored the war beyond the question of Chicanos in combat.[11] Martínez drew her readers into the broader historical conflicts in Southeast Asia and promoted alliances between antiwar activists and their counterparts in Vietnam.

Betita Martínez clashed more than once with Chicano nationalists over her internationalist vision. In an essay about her experiences in New Mexico, Martínez recalled controversy over the graphic history she compiled in 1976 for the Chicano Communications Center (CCC) in Albuquerque, *450 Years of Chicano History in Pictures*.[12] The book won wide recognition as the first bilingual volume devoted to photographs of Mexican life in the United States. The community around the CCC, however, split over the book's representation of Mexican Americans as a people. The August

Twenty-Ninth Movement (ATM), a Marxist-Leninist group that in Los Angeles commemorated the Chicano Moratorium against the war, took issue
with the editors, because "the book did not declare Chicanos to be a nation; the CCC people were not yet convinced of it."[13] The ATM had taken
a Stalinist position and determined that Chicanas/os were not a racialized
minority but a distinct nation; in retaliation against the CCC, the group
ordered the second printing of the book destroyed. The episode illustrates
how nationalists could draw on the militaristic postures of official, Cold
War Americanism to defend their position in La Causa; all too often, they
made their targets other left organizers and, in particular, the Chicanas.
Martínez's refusal of the nationalist position links her to the historical position of radical feminism within Mexican American social movements: like
Tenayuca or Moreno before her, she was willing to imagine that Chicana/o
liberation would take another form.[14]

Many competing discourses of rights, freedom, and collective action gave
rise to the various fronts of El Movimiento Chicano. Still, Chicana/o nationalism has come to define our current historical and cultural understandings of the civil-rights struggle. The following pages examine the ascendancy of identity-based politics over other forms of antiracist struggle
to argue for a more expansive, and less cohesive, narrative of Chicana/o
militancy. In challenging the primacy of ethnic nationalism—its imagined
racial unity—I argue that migrants remained a structuring absence in its
discourse. The arduous conflicts over feminism that dogged the movement
were another kind of boundary discourse. Even as they named Chicanas
their political partners in struggle, ethnic nationalists sought to control
their insubordinate will. Interestingly enough, Chicana feminists provided
the most trenchant assault on racial and class inequality, because they insisted on moving sex and gender out of the private realm. They also held
a longer historical memory, one that predated 1848 and the nation form.
As such, many were more attentive to the migrant presence. "More than
anyone else," wrote Evangelina Márquez and Margarita Ramírez in 1977,
"women cherish revolution and socialism."[15] Three decades later, I cannot
make this claim for women alone. But in my story of civil rights, Chicana
feminists are the least satisfied with the world they were given.

Cold War Nationalism and Chicana/o Militancy

The Chicana/o civil-rights movement is most commonly described as the singular political awakening of Mexican American people to their collective power in the United States.[16] For one scholar, the period from 1965 to 1975 witnessed "una militancia sin precedente" [an unprecedented militancy] on the part of Mexican Americans, who pressed local and national authorities for social justice in schools and universities, prisons, and farm-labor camps.[17] The new tide of labor and community organizing among Mexican Americans corresponded to national conflicts over racial and class disparities; it also reflected worldwide mobilizations in opposition to Cold War militarism, sexual repression, and colonialism. When, on September 16, 1965—Mexican Independence Day—the United Farm Workers Union launched a strike against grape growers in rural California, Mexican American politics entered a new and in some ways more militant phase. During Easter week of the following year, strikers and supporters staged the Peregrinación [Pilgrimage], a 340-mile march from Delano to the state capitol in Sacramento, declaring their intent to redeem the humiliation of the thousands of Mexicans consigned to stoop labor: "They have imposed hunger on us. Now we hunger for justice."[18] El Plan de Delano, a manifesto drafted for the march, invoked a long history of racial wounds, combining rites of penitence with Mexican revolutionary discourse: "We are suffering. We are not afraid to suffer in order to win our cause. ¡VIVA LA CAUSA¡ [Long live the cause]."[19] The statement resonated with meaning for the emergent leadership of what became El Movimiento Chicano, as participants in the national civil-rights and antiwar movements began to articulate their own demands for first-class citizenship. The fledgling mobilization surpassed the bounds of a labor dispute and sparked wider revolt within Mexican American communities.

El Movimiento soon recast longstanding opposition to labor abuses, segregation, and police brutality, in terms that privileged the tenets of ethnic nationalism. Adherents called for various fronts of resistance to unite in the pursuit of self-determination for la raza. Militants also announced their rejection of the more "reformist" Mexican American politics of the 1940s and 1950s in favor of revolutionary action. But as we have seen, the post–World War II decades were hardly periods of political quietism for Mexicans and Mexican Americans in the United States. As Chicanas/os forged a new language of communal destiny in the wake of the grape strike, they also drew selectively from older traditions of struggle. The most significant campaigns of the 1960s built on earlier civil-rights projects, like the Community Service Organization (CSO) of California, which had given organizers like César Chávez and Dolores Huerta their start in the early 1950s. Binational organizing by leftist unions, including the Mine-Mill and the Asociación Nacional México-Americana (ANMA), helped set the radical agenda of the later movement. These organizations had been as attuned to the imperialism guiding U.S. military interests in Asia during the Korean War as Chicana/o nationalists were in the Vietnam era. Historian Ernesto Chávez argues that ANMA influenced the conduct of Chicana/o militants in Los Angeles, particularly those linked to the Centro de Acción Autonoma (CASA), whose leaders—including Bert Corona—distanced themselves from Movement nationalists and continued the work of organizing immigrant workers.[20] The postwar activism of figures like ANMA president Alfredo Montoya, labor organizer Ernesto Galarza, and migrant activist Luisa Moreno both enabled and remained critically removed from the nationalism of 1960s mobilizations. The rallying call "¡Mi Raza primero!" [My people first] invoked the historical unity of Mexicans against discrimination but gave primacy to racial solidarity as a vehicle for its expression.

The discourse of ethnic nationalism during the 1960s overtook the memory of other political traditions, represented in Emma Tenayuca's Workers' Alliance, Luisa Moreno's Congreso de Pueblos de Habla Española, and Bert Corona's CASA. This proved a matter not only of forgetting but also of closing off other imaginaries of peoplehood, of rights, of collective destiny. Chicanas/os presented their grievances as an oppressed racial minority, a development that was tactically important, since it allowed them to petition the federal government for relief as a discriminated group. Movement demands led to radical confrontations with the state over the Vietnam War, agribusiness, and cultural theft. But as these conflicts developed, Chicana/o activists set a political agenda that most often left the concerns of migrants behind. Even as El Movimiento opened new claims to group rights and political autonomy for the ethnic community, these claims were largely bounded by the limits of liberal nationalism. The historical challenges that Mexicans had posed to the transnational reach of racialized capitalism—which had been the basis for transborder labor and community solidarity from the 1920s onward—were more muted in the Vietnam War era. The ascendancy of probusiness unionism, and the repression of the radical left, had undercut the older political base out of which the Chicana/o Movement arose. As a result, the migrant imaginary found only limited expression in the insurgent challenge to liberal racism in the United States.

Even nationalist manifestos that opposed "capricious frontiers on the bronze continent" downplayed the migrant presence and narrated ethnic history in terms that overlooked the diverse histories that had drawn Mexicans across the Mexico-U.S. border.[21] Throughout the 1960s, Chicana/o leaders who invoked the territorial losses of 1848, citing violated treaty rights as the origin of racial discrimination, provided a narrative that did not extend easily to the situation of migrants who had entered the United States by routes other than that of forcible annexation. As a result, the political life of the civil-rights movement diverged sharply from that of the migrant-led labor campaigns of prior decades. Reies López Tijerina may have mobilized Hispanas/os in defense of land titles under the revolutionary slogan of Emiliano Zapata—"Tierra o Muerte" [land or death]—but his vision of community was one of generations of settlement, not of migration and itinerant labor, despite the fact that Tijerina himself had harvested beets as a migrant farmworker during his childhood. The United Farm Workers Union (UFW) was even less accommodating of migrants. Having fought the Bracero Program in defense of Mexican American labor rights, César Chávez and union supporters regularly rooted out recently arrived migrants whom they saw as scab workers. In 1969, the union marched through the Imperial and Coachella valleys to protest growers' use of undocumented laborers; then, in 1974, the UFW set up the infamous "wet line" along the Arizona-Mexico border to prevent migrants from crossing for work as strikebreakers. Still, as migration from Latin America continued unabated after 1965, Chicana/o bids for full U.S. citizenship were made more complicated by the undocumented presence. Chicanas/os were racialized by their association with unauthorized migrants, and immigration agents regularly failed to distinguish among legal residents, citizens, and undocumented Mexicans when making arrests. Debates about immigration divided civil-rights leaders. Radical labor organizers countered the more centrist United Farm Workers Union with strategies for cross-border mobilizations of both migrants and citizens alike. But such efforts were difficult to sustain in a political climate dominated by the liberal national-ism of the U.S. and Mexican governments.

As Cold War militarism shaped both national and international politics during the postwar period, the United States and its Latin American al-lies—including the ruling party in Mexico—pursued a belligerent policy of anticommunism and counterinsurgency across the hemisphere. In the view of U.S. policymakers, the political geography of the Cold War made the U.S.-Mexico border an absolute divide: to the north was U.S. prosperity and democracy, and to the south, the turmoil of the "developing" world. Chicanas/os were expected to achieve civil rights within the territorial and political boundaries that the state set on U.S. citizenship. The delib-erate suppression of transborder movements by U.S. and Mexican agents also had an impact on civil-rights strategies. Surveillance and intimida-tion by FBI agents at times quelled leftist dissent, threatened solidarity among ethnic militants, and contained radical visions for transforming the nation-state. In 1968, FBI agents helped Los Angeles police arrest thirteen Mexican American activists linked to mass strikes of high-school students in East Los Angeles. The charges of conspiracy against these college stu-dents, Brown Berets, and community organizers were overturned in 1970, but the message remained clear: the U.S. government would not hesitate to use tactics of intimidation against its own citizens, just as U.S. allies in Latin America were jailing and torturing dissident students. That summer, the Mexican military repressed student dissent in a campaign that culmi-nated in the Tlatelolco massacre of October 3, 1968.[22]

In 2006, the release of new documentary evidence revealed the extent of the U.S. government's knowledge about the Mexican government's "dirty war" against suspected subversives during the late 1960s and 1970s; the U.S. State Department offered tacit approval of the repression, in part to keep social unrest from spilling over the Mexican border.[23] President Luis Eche-verría Álvarez had ordered the student killings in 1968, in his capacity as Secretary of Government for the administration of President Gustavo Díaz Ordaz. Echeverría became a close associate of President Richard Nixon af-ter assuming the executive office in 1970. During a state visit to Washing-ton on June 15, 1971, Echeverría used the threat of Chicana/o militancy to press Nixon for the financial resources he needed to promote economic growth and halt the spread of communism in his home country. Echeve-rría complained of rising discontent among Latin Americans:

these events that take place in Latin America—when solutions are not found—are reflected within American society itself in Mexican-Americans and Puerto Ricans and other minority groups, such as other racial minority groups, and therefore we either find the balanced economic solution to the problems of our neighbors to the south or there will be events in these countries that will have repercussions within your own borders here.[24]

Echeverría did not specify the relationship between the problems in the South and racial minorities in the United States—he did not have to. Like other Mexican presidents before him, he used the proximity of Mexico to the United States for political leverage with his powerful neighbor. U.S. enmity toward Cuba and the Soviets meant that the two executives shared a vital interest in monitoring their common border. Nixon understood perfectly and thanked Echeverría for his vision of hemispheric unity: "Because Mexico . . . provides not only the U.S. border with Mexico but the U.S. border with all of Latin America." For the two presidents, the boundary was alternately a strategic barrier and a source of connection: "Mexico also . . . is the bridge," Nixon continued, "the bridge between the United States and the rest of Latin America."[25] By extension, Mexican migrants and Mexican Americans were seen as either the sanctioned agents of the border-bridge or threats to the border-barricade.

The exchange suggests something more, that at this critical moment, the two governments colluded in dividing ethnic Mexicans in the United States from Mexican society. The discussion differentiated Mexican Americans from migrants as distinct problems for the two governments; migrants remained outside the domain of political rights, while Mexican Americans were made into "a racial minority group" belonging only to the United States. Echeverría made clear that although his government would take responsibility for Mexican migrants, Mexican Americans were solely the concern of U.S. leaders. This binational understanding set a clear political boundary between the concerns of migrants and those of Mexican Americans—this despite the fact that large segments of the ethnic Mexican population in the United States comprised both groups. It assured that Mexicans in the United States could only appeal to the U.S. government for relief from racial discrimination and labor abuses.

The two statesmen did not consider addressing Mexican-origin residents of the United States as parts of a single transnational population composed of both Mexican and U.S. citizens. But President Echeverría was not done with the issue of Mexican Americans. He cautioned Nixon against allowing civil-rights activists to become involved in Latin American affairs. In advance of his trip to Washington, the Mexican president had been warned about the activities of "so-called 'Chicano' groups in the United States" who had joined forces with Angela Davis and the Black Panther Party to press for the release of political prisoners in Mexico.[26] Echeverría admonished the U.S. president to prevent the cross-border alliances of ethnic minorities in the United States to radical elements in Latin America: "if time goes on and solutions are not found, communism will [be sold] as a possible alternative. And that will be reflected in the United States, too." Pressing for a new binational agreement on "the problem of the wetbacks," Echeverría once again admonished Nixon not to allow civil-rights activists to set the agenda for dealing with migrant workers: "The attitude of the radical Chicano groups in California and Texas has been changing as far as these illegal immigrants are concerned. They're starting to help them now."[27]

Echeverría's callous attitude toward the Mexican American civil-rights movement showed a complete disavowal of the ethnic unity claimed by Chicana/o nationalists with Mexico. Echeverría pressed further: "So you have your problem of a minority that is growing in the United States."[28]

When Nixon deferred comment on Echeverría's demand for an agreement on migration, he was nonetheless conscious of the need to turn Chicanas/os away from their international commitments—in Asia as in Latin America. Nixon was fully aware of the "problem" that Chicana/o radicalism posed for his administration. The war in Vietnam had become a referendum on Chicana/o civil rights in the United States. By the time of the Tet Offensive in January 1968, Chicanos had suffered a disproportionate number of casualties on the frontlines of combat. The war became a focal point for demands for full citizenship, as Chicanas/os refuted the legitimacy of the overseas conflict by pointing to grave inequalities in the United States.[29] So, too, did the imperial dimensions of the war mobilize Chicana/o solidarity with the Vietnamese—Chicanas/os began to describe themselves as "an internal colony" of the United States. From November

1969 to August 1971, the National Chicano Moratorium Committee staged mass protests against the war. At the height of the Chicano Moratorium, on August 29, 1970, a crowd of thirty thousand convened in East Los Angeles, where police provoked violent clashes with demonstrators and used tear gas and batons to subdue the protest. Three people were killed, among them the beloved journalist Rubén Salazar. The events galvanized the wider Chicano movement, but they also incited intimidation and surveillance from the highest levels of government. Of critical concern for the Nixon administration was the possibility that black and Latina/o militants would forge effective ties to international movements that ran counter to U.S. policy interests. Nixon made a highly visible show of appointing Mexican Americans to positions in government, in an appeal to moderate elements of the rights movement. Throughout the period, government officials combined counterinsurgency tactics with efforts at appeasement, in order to bring civil-rights leadership in line with state-led reforms of racial inequality.

Although political repression narrowed the allowable forms of dissent, Mexican Americans nonetheless used the framework of liberal reforms to obtain new forms of political redress for wrongful discrimination. Chicana/o militancy found its most emphatic expression precisely as Mexican Americans made legal advances toward equal citizenship in the late 1960s. With landmark decisions that overturned legal segregation in U.S. public schools—*Mendez v. Westminster* in 1947 and *Brown v. Board of Education* in 1954—citizens of Mexican descent acquired new instruments for countering legal and extralegal barriers to their social mobility. As soldiers returned from wars in Europe and Asia, the first generation of students educated on the G.I. Bill earned university degrees. These soldiers were among the most visible advocates of Chicana/o civil rights. In 1960, the G.I. Forum and others promoted Mexican American voting through the Viva Kennedy! campaign. The Civil Rights Act of 1964 and the Voting Rights Act of 1965 gave Mexican Americans new access to the electoral process; Chicanas/os exercised their political influence in both the Democratic Party and the independent Raza Unida Party of southern Texas. Taken as a whole, the demise of legal segregation gave Mexican Americans new cause to invest in their citizenship and focus on the formal political sphere of the nation. Liberal reforms had a paradoxical effect in the domain of immigration law: although the Immigration and National Services

Act (Hart-Cellar) of 1965 removed racial and national quotas in favor of numerical limits, it placed such a low cap on the number of Mexican migrants who could enter the United States legally that it guaranteed the continued growth of undocumented migration in the wake of its passage. The law did offer Mexicans in the United States incentives to naturalize and become citizens, however, offering new provisions for family reunification that would also promote Mexican American citizenship.

In short, the contradictory processes of social and political reform in the 1960s both created and delimited cultural pluralism in the United States. The federal government promoted the formal equality of Mexican Americans and simultaneously reracialized them through other discourses of deviancy, poverty, ignorance, and need—terms that masked persistent liberal racism in the U.S. polity. At the height of the Cold War, as the United States promoted its interests across the Americas, Chicana/o activists found new bases for collective action, but also repression, as they sought to protect the integrity of transborder communities. This contradiction cost El Movimiento its coherence as a radical challenge to the global logic of racial capitalism. As the movement adopted a liberal framework for attaining civil rights, it also faltered with respect to two vital elements: its connection to the migrant imaginary and its investment in Mexican women's militancy.

On the Borders of Aztlán

The Mexico-U.S. border remained a structuring presence for all fronts of the Chicana/o Movement, with the most radical and utopian projects calling for the eventual dissolution of the geopolitical marker separating Mexican Americans from the larger territory of Mexico. Recognizing that their political marginalization originated not only with the seizure of Mexican lands in 1848 but also with U.S. political hegemony throughout the Americas, Mexican American activists and intellectuals had to contend with the disciplinary apparatus of the political border while simultaneously disavowing its interpellative power. This precarious operation led ethnic nationalists to construct their own oppositional narratives of peoplehood as a means to contest the state's monopoly on producing political subjects.

The desire to efface, at least in symbolic terms, the boundary between Mexico and the United States arose alongside a new discourse of nationalism anchored firmly within the boundaries of U.S. citizenship. At the height of the Vietnam War, Chicana/o militants contested the prevailing discourse of militarized national power through works of imaginative geography. The two signature manifestos of the student movement, *El Plan de Santa Barbara* and *El Plan Espiritual de Aztlán*, drafted at youth conferences in 1969, subverted the Mexico-U.S. border in declarations of pan-American racial unity against second-class citizenship and police repression. Notwithstanding their ardent expressions of affinity with Mexican *cultural* life, however, student militants gave Mexican *politics* little attention in the struggle. Their refusal of "assimilation" was more a rejection of white primacy than a defense of the sovereignty of transborder communities. As ethnic nationalists imagined establishing a new Chicana/o homeland out of the territories ceded in the U.S.-Mexican War, their vision made little mention of migrants, or the problems of U.S. immigration policy. Their Aztlán was a decidedly *national*—not transnational—figure of ethnic community; its borders fit comfortably within the boundaries of the U.S. Southwest and left the modern Mexican nation-state aside.

The ascendancy of ethnic nationalism over other ideologies of communal self-defense did not only displace the migrant imaginary within the struggle for civil rights, however. It also signaled a marked remasculinization of the liberation struggle. The historical dispossession of Mexicans from their lands gave rise to expressions of ethnic unity that, in the words of Cynthia Enloe, "typically sprung from masculinized memory, masculinized humiliation, and masculinized hope" for restitution.[30] The national expression of "the people," argues critic Anne McClintock, "aligns itself inevitably with the notion of a 'race' structured around the transmission of male power and property."[31] Nationalist claims during the 1960s and '70s were based on a vision of Chicanas/os as a distinct race; these claims derived in large part from the writings of José Vasconcelos, whose 1925 publication *La raza cósmica* had helped define the cultural politics of the postrevolutionary order in Mexico. The writers of *El Plan Espiritual de Aztlán* used his concept of mestizaje [racial hybridity] to declare their insurgency as "a bronze people with a bronze culture." Ethnic nationalism in its purest form denied the legitimacy of Chicana militancy beyond a limited sphere of female service and domesticity. Although Chicana activists resisted such a limited construct of female value, it has remained the controlling thread of memory and historical narrative, even under critique.[32]

The Chicana/o student movement crystallized in 1968 amid confrontations with state institutions over everything from prisoners' rights, police abuses, and education to welfare rights and residential segregation. The new student movement crafted its discourse in the form of manifestoes, which outlined an emerging cultural politics and mandated ambitious, nationalist projects of racial uplift. In April 1969, one hundred students convened in Southern California to draft "A Chicano Plan for Higher Education," which set the foundations for the new discipline of Chicano Studies. The proposal, known as *El Plan de Santa Barbara*, sought to democratize public universities through joint initiatives for the recruitment of Chicana/o students, the formation of community centers, and the establishment of new Chicana/o-centered curricula. Its authors outlined a visionary proposition for educating communities with limited claim on institutions of higher learning. The declarative statements of the manifesto placed academic programs at the service of an identity-based mandate for self-determination:

> Culturally, the term Chicano, in the past a pejorative and class-bound adjective, has now become the root idea of a new cultural identity for our people. It also reveals a growing solidarity and the development of a common social praxis. The widespread use of the term Chicano today signals a rebirth of pride and confidence. Chicanismo simply embodies an ancient truth: that man is never closer to his true self as when he is close to his community.[33]

El Plan announced the unification of the disparate Mexican American communities, divided by class and region, into a single, national entity.

The authors of *El Plan de Santa Barbara* articulated their identity project through the spatial imaginary of the nation, as the manifesto located its "rebirth" in the reformation of "our people and our community, el barrio and la colonia." Chicanismo described a politics of affect, a racial brotherhood that superseded any other political affiliations or loyalties. The barrio became the anchor for ethnic unity; its boundaries marked the protective space of home, rather than of racial and class confinement. Furthermore, the performative praxis of chicanismo specified a *male* interlocutor, so that the totality spoke its will in the singular voice of the race man—who, in turn, achieved full selfhood in the community. The metonymic substitution of "barrio" for "people" territorialized the community and made it a bounded nation, as opposed to the more fluid concepts of diaspora, ethnic collectivity, or class. In 1939, Emma Tenayuca had taken pains to reject the designation of nation; in 1969, Chicano students viewed nationhood, however metaphorical, as the best horizon for their political aspirations. The document invested this idealized ethnic domain with gendered meanings, by promoting the barrio as a site of cultural regeneration. Their vision of carnalismo [racial brotherhood] required the idealized notion of a sheltered domestic sphere of social reproduction and maternal care.

The cultural geography of ethnic nationalism achieved its fullest expression in *El Plan Espiritual de Aztlán*, the manifesto of the First Annual Chicano Youth Liberation Conference, convened in Denver by Rodolfo (Corky) Gonzáles in March 1969. The meeting grew out of Gonzáles's tireless organizing for the Crusade for Justice, a community advocacy program he had founded in 1966 to address the needs of Chicanas/os in the Denver area. The Crusade for Justice devoted much of its resources to youth services, administered through the Tlatelolco School, which offered students instruction in Chicana/o history and socialism and preparation for college. After leading a procession in the Poor Peoples March on Washington, D.C., with Tijerina in 1968, Gonzáles sought a national Chicana/o political platform that would unite the various factions of the movement. *El Plan Espiritual de Aztlán*, ratified at the conference, articulated a national program for self-determination—but it was the document's preamble, written by San Diego poet Alurista, that had the most enduring impact on the movement.

El Plan Espiritual de Aztlán announced that the imagined community of the nation had already arrived:

> In the spirit of a new people that is conscious not only of its historical heritage but also of the brutal "gringo" invasion of our territories, *we*, the Chicano inhabitants and civilizers of the northern land of Aztlán from whence came our forefathers, reclaiming the land of their birth and consecrating the determination of our people of the sun, *declare* that the call of our blood is our power, our responsibility, and our inevitable destiny.

The manifesto represented the ultimate use of the performative: the language creates the very action it describes. The declaration obliterates time, collapsing precolonial, colonial, and postcolonial history into one another, to construct a single, univocal "we" that stands against time to claim its "inevitable destiny." The text thus enacts the rebirth of the "mestizo nation" as a *male* genesis. *El Plan Espiritual de Aztlán* subsumes all difference —of time, space, or gender—as it "commits all levels of Chicano society . . . to La Causa." Just as the authors of the manifesto refused to recognize "capricious frontiers on the bronze continent," they also denied gender or class conflict within the imagined community. *El Plan* allocated freedom and sovereignty to the privileged masculine subject of the struggle for self-determination: "Brotherhood unites us, and love for our brothers makes us a people whose time has come . . . with our heart in our hands and our hands in the soil, we declare the independence of our mestizo nation."

The anxious reiteration of "brotherhood" reflects the authors' preoccupation with gender conflicts erupting within the national project. Throughout the 1960s and '70s, nationalists promoted a heterosexual model of race as family, suppressing sexual difference in favor of an ideology of separate, complementary fronts of masculine and feminine social action. The discourse of El Movimiento hailed women as the symbolic mothers of citizens and bearers of culture. Through their domestic labors, women would defend and redeem la raza. The coercive force of the nationalist trope of *race as family* did not exclude women from political activity but, rather, delimited their participation so as to foreclose the capacity of Chicanas to voice their interests with any autonomy. When the new generation of activists remembered Luisa Moreno, Josefina Fierro, and Emma Tenayuca at all, it remembered them as exceptional figures and largely overlooked their trenchant critiques of gender inequality.

During his political appearances, Gonzáles repeatedly issued numerous warnings against Chicana feminism, arguing that women of la raza would find their sole fulfillment in service to the national project. Accordingly, the political resolutions adopted at the 1969 conference placed the feminized domestic sphere, and with it women's political agency, in the service of its imagined, horizontal brotherhood. Even the session devoted to "The Woman of La Raza" ended in the active suppression of concerns for gender equity, when the workshop elicited the statement that "the Chicana woman does not want to be liberated."[34] The redundant articulation of the generic "Chicana woman" doubly fixed Mexican American women's agency: they were identified first as racialized subjects, whose gender interests were supplemental to their primary status as Chicanas.

Chicanas did not simply accept their gender subordination to La Causa, at the Denver conference or elsewhere. Chicana activists contested the male-centered logic of ethnic nationalism and its rigid segregation of gendered spheres of political action. Female activists reminded their compatriots of the longer history of Mexican and Mexican American women's militancy and brought gender concerns to bear on the movement's struggles over labor, immigration, and civil rights. But the force of male reaction often succeeded in subordinating feminist energies to a masculinist program of community self-defense. Enriqueta Longeaux y Vásquez's response to the Youth Liberation Conference, entitled "The Woman of La Raza" demonstrates the contradictory loyalties Chicanas felt in their embrace of its influential platform.[35] Published in the foundational *Sisterhood Is Powerful* (1970), her essay is a cautionary statement to the Women's Movement, as she argues against a simplistic framework for "liberating" women of color.[36] Recounting her participation in the Denver meetings, Longeaux y Vásquez admitted her distress at the gathering consensus that Chicanas had no interest in liberation:

> As a woman who has been faced with living as a member of the Mexican American minority group, as a breadwinner and a mother raising children, living in housing projects, and having much concern for other humans plus much community involvement, I felt this as quite a blow. I could have cried. Surely we could at least have come up with something to add to that statement. I sat back and thought, Why? Why? Then I understood why the statement had been made and realized going along with the feelings of the men at the convention was perhaps the best thing to do at the time.[37]

The grammar of Longeaux y Vásquez's expression of her identity conveyed the depth of the split in her racial and gender identity: she called herself a woman *living as* a Mexican American. Not only did she find it impossible to articulate woman and Mexican American together, but her own political engagement as a wage-earner, single parent, and community activist defied the construction of the Chicana as a *passive object* of the feminist project—"the Chicana woman [who] does not want to be liberated." Certainly, she asserted, the desires of Chicanas for liberation would find expression in some other form than feminist struggle. Longeaux y Vásquez made her peace with the conference by determining the strategic value of accommodation to the men, once again separating gender interests from those of the ethnic collective.

Even as she described the "double oppression" of Mexican American women, Longeaux y Vásquez fell captive to the masculine grammar of ethnic nationalism. She responded to the conference statement on the role of Chicanas with a gesture of self-censorship: "I could have cried." She proceeded to consider the material concerns of gender in terms that consigned Chicanas to a realm of utter dependency on men:

> How the Chicana woman reacts depends totally on how the *macho* Chicano is treated when he goes out into the "mainstream of society." If the husband is so-called successful, the woman seems to become very domineering and demands more and more in material goods. I ask myself at times, Why are the women so demanding? Can they not see what they make their men do? But then I realize: this is the price of owning a slave.[38]

Her statement adopted the spatial imaginary of ethnic nationalism, setting the feminized domestic sphere apart from the "mainstream of society." But Longeaux y Vásquez's portrait contradicted entirely her earlier self-description: as a breadwinner and activist, she was an active participant in the public realm in her own right. (Nor would a resident of public housing be likely to view home as the nationalists did, as the inviolate space of ethnic renewal.) More puzzling still, she denigrated women's political expression as mere complaint. The dependent Chicana of her essay espouses only self-interested material desire. The author's iteration of Chicana servitude equates freedom with manhood and Chicana agency with the entrapment of the male partner, the legitimate protagonist of the struggle. As in *Salt of the Earth*, her vision of Chicana liberation rested on "what they make of their men."

The self-censorship of the essay makes sense if we understand its reliance on the doctrines of El Movimiento. Longeaux y Vásquez delivered a strategic performance of female abnegation in order to make Chicana concerns legible within the limited script of ethnonationalism. She followed her withering critique of women with an incisive platform for addressing the pressing costs of meeting the material demands of social reproduction: food, clothing, housing, employment, childcare, and social companionship. Her conclusion sought to explain how these demands pertained to the liberation struggle:

> The Mexican-American movement is not just that of adults fighting the social system, but it is a total commitment of a family unit living what it believes to be a better way of life in demanding social change for the benefit of humankind. When a family is involved in a human rights movement, as is the Mexican-American family, there is little room for a woman's liberation movement alone. There is little room for having a definition of women's roles as such. Roles are for actors and the business at hand requires people living the example of social change.[39]

Longeaux y Vásquez resolved the gender conflict by commuting the categories of ethnic and gender particularity to the universal terrain of human rights, arguing the principal value of fighting for "the benefit of humankind." (She did not write *man*kind.) Her argument thus contained a muted critique of how the "woman question" relegated Chicanas to a supplementary part in El Movimiento. Her ultimate articulation of race as family can be seen as a bid for Chicana power that would dissolve gender difference altogether.

But the ideology of separate spheres underlying her construction of race as family could not permit this dissolution. Her essay ends this way:

> The Mexican-American movement demands are such that, with the liberation of La Raza, we must have a total liberation. The woman must help liberate the man and the man must look upon this liberation with the woman at his side, not behind him, following, but alongside of him, leading. The family must come up together. . . . When a man can look upon a woman as a human, then and only then, can he feel the true meaning of liberation and equality.[40]

Once again, the marriage plot placed Chicana liberation in the service of the totality, as the essay equates women's fulfillment with assistance to their male partners. Longeaux y Vásquez repeated almost to the word Esperanza's desire in *Salt of the Earth* "to rise and push everything up as I go," so that the family would "come up together." The logic of complementary spheres of male and female political action displaced yet again the problem of gender and sexual inequalities. Longeaux y Vásquez's final objective is less the emancipation of Chicanas in struggle than the reiteration of their dependence on men. The essay ends painfully with Chicanas awaiting the recognition of their human status. Here it is exclusively the masculine subject who will ultimately enjoy the "true meaning of liberation and equality." The tortured grammar of her elocutions conveys the strong suggestion of male coercion behind the author's accommodation to male primacy in El Movimiento.

Chicanas did find other ways to modify nationalism's essentially masculine script, however. Throughout the mass mobilizations of El Movimiento, Chicanas took vocal positions to secure their public presence in political confrontations. Chicanas found themselves forced to conduct their activism in deference to the presumed primacy of male leadership, at cost of expulsion from organizations or more severe retribution. Chicana newsletters from the movement proffered familiar assurances—from "the importance of family unit" to "the strength of men and women working together" —terms that feminist historian Vicki Ruiz aptly describes as a "mantra of justification and affirmation" of patriarchal norms.[41]

Relegated to the domestic sphere of the nationalist imaginary, Chicanas contested the sexual objectification of their political role in the movement. In February 1970, women in the East Los Angeles chapter of the Brown Berets formally dissolved their relationship to the community self-defense organization, citing their expulsion from its leadership.[42] In her cogent analysis of the episode, historian Dionne Espinoza makes the case for a structural approach to gender inequality in the nationalist phase of the movement: "What is needed . . . is not an examination only of attitudes and behaviors or of cultural nationalism as an oppressive ideology for women, but also how gender inequality was *institutionalized*."[43] Chicano militants had made the sexual contract a central feature of the Brown Berets, staging "weddings" to define women's roles in the organization. The Chicana Brown Berets not only opposed the sexism of male militants but also fought for control of movement resources. Gloria Arellanes and her colleagues fought to bring the Beret-operated Free Clinic under autonomous female leadership and to provide reproductive services and counseling for Chicanas. The clinics became a critical domain of women's organizing, fostering what Espinoza terms "collective identification," outside their male-defined roles in the movement.[44]

These struggles were repeated in different forms across the spectrum of Movement campaigns. But the conflicts over sex and gender roles were not only due to male dominance. The prevailing prohibition of sexual difference and feminist identification generated profound divisions among women in struggles for civil rights, as lesbian and socialist feminists staked out positions on women's rights that defied the heterosexist and patriarchal structure of La Causa. In 1971, approximately six hundred women gathered in Houston for the First National Chicana Conference. Their intent was to address the specific concerns of Chicanas within the larger liberation struggles against race and class oppression. But the delegates split over resolutions calling for reproductive freedoms and egalitarian marriage, because some participants maintained that feminist demands would weaken the primary bid for ethnic unity. The conference ultimately endorsed the symbolic platform of the ethnonationalist project, *El Plan Espiritual de Aztlán*, which had become the defining framework for the ethnic nationalist project. As a result, the women delegates displaced the question of gender conflicts within the nationalist agenda altogether. The conflict reflects the ways that ethnic nationalists dictated the erasure of Chicanas' labor history and made female-headed households invisible to their political projects. The sometimes painful debates over the status of Chicana feminism within the civil-rights project bears out Paul Gilroy's suggestion that "gender is the modality in which race is lived."[45]

Despite accommodating the primacy of the nationalist program, the Chicana delegates did issue radical propositions for addressing the gender and racial subordination of Chicanas. One participant, Mirta Vidal, opposed Longeaux y Vásquez's rejection of feminism, arguing that women's liberation would expand, rather than divide, El Movimiento:

> The appeal for "unity" based on the continued submission of women is a false one. While it is true that the unity of La Raza is the basic foundation of the Chicano movement, when Chicano men talk about maintaining La Familia and the "cultural heritage" of La Raza, they are in fact talking about maintaining the age-old concept of keeping the woman

barefoot, pregnant, and in the kitchen. On the basis of the subordination of women there can be no real unity.[46]

Vidal, the national director of Latina/o projects for the Young Socialist Alliance, which retained the international vision of the prewar left, issued a trenchant assault on the equation of race with family. In her view, ideologies of domesticity were simply instruments of patriarchal control over women's labor and political will. Even as women delegates endorsed *El Plan Espiritual de Aztlán,* they added a supplementary resolution on "Sex and the Chicana" that challenged the ideology of female domesticity. Their resolution called for immediate access to "full legal abortions and birth control."[47] The authors insisted that access to reproductive rights and companionate marriage were the only means to achieve full equality for women.

Writing in the aftermath of these debates, the sociologist Betty García-Bahne drew on Marxist theory to dismiss nationalist claims for family unity: "The form of the contemporary family, like other institutions . . . has been influenced by and reinforced to correspond to the capitalist mode of production."[48] As a social scientist, García-Bahne understood the connection between the home and work to be one of gender repression: "This combination of contingencies impact the woman in such a way as to facilitate her exploitation within the family and in the marketplace."[49] For socialist feminists, sexuality linked women's service to the family and their service to capitalism. García-Bahne concluded, "The family legitimizes sexuality for women and channels men's sexual expression, thus playing a necessary role in the sexual repression required by capitalism. . . . The family and marriage get viewed as the only vehicles by which a woman can validly find expression of her values regarding her sexuality, thus binding her to childbearing and maintenance of family cohesiveness."[50] In the 1970s, sexuality emerged as the terrain on which activists could draft a new movement script, one in which Chicanas could exert collective power by exposing the intersections of racial, gender, sexual, and class subordination.

The Houston Conference resolutions reflected the urgency that many Chicanas felt in bringing issues of sexuality to the Movement agenda. After their efforts to raise issues of reproductive rights, welfare, and families at various Chicana/o Movement conferences were frustrated, another group

of Chicana activists founded the Comisión Femenil Mexicana Nacional
[National Mexican Commission on Women] in October 1970. In 1973, eight
hundred members of the Comisión gathered to set an ambitious agenda
for "organizing women to assume leadership positions within the Chicano
movement and in community life."[51] If they did not protect their autonomy, Comisión leaders argued, Chicanas would lose ground on the many
urgent concerns they faced as women of color. They were acutely aware of
the sexual dimensions of racial repression in the United States. During the
civil-rights period, racialized women were the frequent targets of state designs on their bodies. Chief among their demands was an end to coercive
sterilization practices by health-care agencies.

Liberal racism in the 1960s gave rise to a new discourse of social pathology that fueled programs for regulating the fertility of poor women of
color. During the Johnson administration's War on Poverty, Senator Daniel
Patrick Moynihan had issued his 1965 study "The Negro Family in America:
The Case for National Action," which argued for aggressive federal intervention to offset what he described as the "total breakdown" of black urban communities. The incendiary report, which decried the "disorganized
and matrifocal" structure of "the Negro family," led to policies that targeted
female-headed households among Latinas/os as well as among African
Americans. New welfare policies were perhaps the less punitive aspect of
a larger project to control racial minorities and the urban poor. Amid a revival of eugenics approaches to public health, U.S. medical centers across
the country subjected Latinas to nonconsensual sterilizations.

The Comisión made no distinction between migrants and citizens in
their campaign to obtain full reproductive choice for Mexican women
in the United States. Chicana activists were conscious that inherent cultural bias made public health services an instrument of anti-immigrant
policies, particularly in the realm of population control. In 1974, Dr. H.
Curtis Wood Jr., a medical consultant and former head of the Association
for Voluntary Sterilization, made the case for curtailing poor women's
fertility:

> People pollute, and too many people crowded too close together cause
> many of our social and economic problems. These in turn are aggra-
> vated by involuntary and irresponsible parenthood. As physicians, we
> have obligations to the society of which we are a part. The welfare

mess, as it has been called, cries out for solutions, one of which is fertility control.[52]

Wood's justification of sterilization epitomized the liberal racism of public institutions. As a stand-in for the paternal authority of the state, the doctor could claim to be working for the women's own best interests. Metaphors of pollution were common justifications for restricting welfare benefits to poor migrant women.

In 1975, members of the Comisión organized protests against sterilization abuses, and they joined in a class-action lawsuit against involuntary sterilizations of Mexican and Mexican American women in Los Angeles. Their lawsuit led to public hearings on incidents of abuse dating from 1971 to 1974 at the USC Medical Center. On May 31, 1978, Antonia Hernández and other Chicana/o civil-rights lawyers working with the Comisión brought a civil suit for damages against the Los Angeles Medical Center's Department of Obstetrics and Gynecology. The plaintiffs in *Dolores Madrigal et al. vs. Dr. E. J. Quilligan, et al.,* alleged that eleven doctors at the Medical Center had performed surgical sterilizations on ten Mexican women between 1971 and 1974 without obtaining their consent or educating them about the procedure.[53] Nine of the ten women named in the suit were poor migrants from rural Mexico who presented their testimony in Spanish at the trial, a process that underlined their status as "alien citizens" within the legal system.[54] Before handing down his opinion in favor of the doctors, Judge Jesse W. Curtis told the court, "We all know that Mexicans love their families."[55] In his ruling, Curtis emphasized that doctors' failure was one of misunderstanding, rather than of institutional negligence. The judge went on to express his sympathy toward the plaintiffs, whose social status, he argued, derived from their capacity to produce children: "If for some reason she cannot, she is considered an incomplete woman and is apt to suffer a disruption of her relationship with her family and husband."[56] In other words, the court determined that the injury to the women lay in the loss of childbearing capacity, rather than in the doctors' violation of women's control over their bodies. The exercise of racial and patriarchal dominance by doctors went unchallenged in the final ruling. The judge's admission of cultural difference into the proceedings did not, in the end, dislodge the institutional power of liberal racism, but, rather, it sanitized its image.

As the Chicana/o Movement entered its later years, other narratives of family emerged to contest the prescriptive rhetoric of ethnic nationalism. In the realm of expressive culture, Chicana authors found new forms for imagining community and narrating the struggle. For Lorna Dee Cervantes, poetry provided a form of cognitive mapping of the barrio—in the sense that Fredric Jameson gives to the imaginative process by which the individual subject situates him- or herself within "that vaster and properly unrepresentable totality which is the ensemble of society's structures as a whole."[57] In Cervantes's signature collection, *Emplumada*, the physical layout of her barrio becomes both a measure of her confinement and the key for a larger, elusive map of the world.[58]

Emplumada

> We were a woman family:
> Grandma, our innocent Queen;
> Mama, the Swift Knight, Fearless Warrior . . .
> Myself: I could never decide . . .
> I became Scribe: Translator of Foreign Mail
> —Lorna Dee Cervantes, "Beneath the Shadow of the Freeway"[59]

In a 1985 interview, Lorna Dee Cervantes located the inspiration for her most celebrated poem, "Beneath the Shadow of the Freeway," in the debates over gender roles that took place in San José State's first Chicano Studies courses during the early 1970s:

> The poem . . . was written specifically to address the whole notion of *machismo*. I started the poem when I was very young, I was 17. . . . But the whole reason why I wanted to write that poem [was] that at that time I was taking a lot of Chicano culture and sociology courses, and the whole notion of the family of the patriarch . . . I could not buy at all. It was not the situation of a lot of my friends I was growing up with.[60]

Cervantes's poetry of place refuses the idealization of race-as-family as the central trope for ethnic collectivity. In its stead, she offers the "woman family": three generations of Chicanas coping with the economic and racial marginality that has excluded the poor Mexican American community of San José from the benefits of urban progress, symbolized throughout the poem by the long shadow that the Freeway 280 casts over the barrio. In his inspired study of the effects of urban renewal on Mexican communities, Raúl Homero Villa illustrates how the freeway served Cervantes as an icon of "the historical violations (and the violations of history) done to the greater Californio population through intercultural conquest and the violations done specifically to Chicanas through intracultural gender conflict."[61] *Emplumada* moves seamlessly between these two subjects: poems about the historical dispossession of Californias/os [nineteenth-century Mexican Californians] and their Chicana/o descendants, and poems that offer searing depictions of family discord. Far from representing a space of cultural renewal, the feminized domestic sphere exists under the constant threat of gender violence that divides the women against one another. Her grandmother derives her authority in sharp contrast with traditional iconography of the maternal: "She built her house / cocky, disheveled carpentry, / after living twenty-five years / with a man who tried to kill her."[62]

Growing up in San José, California, Lorna Dee Cervantes started as a self-taught poet in the theatrical arts of El Movimiento. In 1974, she launched the small literary journal *Mango*, while working for the Centro Cultural de la Gente in San José. That same year she traveled to Mexico City for the International Chicano-Latino Theater Festival, where she gave the first performance of her poems. In 1981, she published her first book, *Emplumada*, to critical acclaim, receiving the 1982 Before Columbus Foundation prize for her poetic exploration of the cultural geography of the San José barrio Sal Si Puedes [Get Out If You Can]. That neighborhood had also been the place where César Chávez began his organizing career in the early 1950s, and it had been home to the many migrants since the 1920s whose presence helped define Cervantes's perception of Mexico and of California's history.

Throughout *Emplumada*, the freeway cuts through this Mexican American community, becoming a metaphor for the gender conflicts that make the Chicana/o idealization of familia impossible for the poet. By drawing attention to relations of dominance within the domestic realm, Cervantes destroys the gender binary promoted by ethnic nationalism and, along with it, the notion that men and women inhabit complementary spheres.

In doing so, she depicts San José as urban space broken by deindustrialization and urban renewal as well as by migration and displacement. For Cervantes, the barrio is in no way a homeland or a separate, inviolate territory. Thus, her representation of space contradicts the fundamental tenets
of the nationalist manifestoes.

Though separated from the youthful writings of Américo Paredes by
time, space, and gender, the poems of *Emplumada* share many of Paredes's concerns as they explore culture as an arena of social conflict. Cervantes stages several border crossings in the collection, to inquire what
it is that makes her Mexican. In "Barco de refugiados/Refugee Ship," the
poet depicts the granddaughter of a Mexican immigrant as "a captive /
aboard a refugee ship."[63] Like Paredes, she represents Mexico and the
United States as two distinct ontological worlds, with herself positioned
as a migrant continually subject to displacement: "The ship that will never
dock / *El barco que nunca atraca*."[64] The repetition of the metaphor in
both languages conveys the unrelenting nature of her punishment: to be
Mexican American is to be permanently deprived of home and citizenship.
The poem invokes a child's sense of alienation, "orphaned from my Spanish name," but embeds her family story of broken kinship ("Mama raised
me without language") within a political narrative of statelessness.[65] The
poem fuses the subjectivity of the migrant with that of the discriminated
racial minority. As in the case of the "Mexico-Texan," hers is a citizenship
that cannot be embodied.

For the displaced subject of "Refugee Ship," writing becomes an ambivalent search for refuge. But writing also stages an encounter with loss,
the loss of a native language. The speaker of the poem "Visions of Mexico
While Writing at a Symposium in Port Townsend, Washington" confesses,
"I don't want to pretend I know more / and can speak all the names. I
can't."[66] She is equally at the mercy of English in the United States: "I need
words / simple black nymphs between white sheets of paper . . . words I
steal."[67] The images conjure a fugitive relationship to language—she perceives the power of words by their absence. For the subject of the poem,
the border marks an absolute divide between Spanish and English and, by
extension, between Mexican and U.S. nationalities. Positioned between the
two, and belonging to neither, she occupies a position anterior to language.
The sense of dispossession recalls the loss that defined border identity for
Paredes in the 1930s. Although *Emplumada* maintains a strict segregation

between Spanish and English, the poet depicts writing as a form of border crossing. Hers is a creative destruction: "as pain sends seabirds south from the cold / I come north / to gather my feathers / for quills."[68] This complex chain of images depicts writing as simultaneously an act of survival and of self-inflicted wounding—elsewhere, the poet describes herself as the plumed bird (Emplumada), whose plumage is both armor and writing instrument. The quills she takes from her body could serve as pens or arrows, since the poem commands language as a weapon of self-defense. The poem reverses the route of birds' migration south for refuge, as the speaker returns to the inhospitable climate of the north, where she recovers language. But her return is an ambiguous achievement. In order to obtain her livelihood, the writer is forced to move, and violate her better instinct, since, she admits, "I don't belong this far north."[69] Cervantes implies that Mexican migration is itself an equally unnatural process of displacement. But the poem is also an implicit homage to the capacity for self-invention that belongs to migrants alone.

Through its stories of displacement and interrupted kinship, *Emplumada* develops an imaginary entirely distinct from that of the nationalist project, in order to make visible the complex social agency of Chicana subjects. Her poem "Meeting Mescalito at Oak Hill Cemetery" embeds the emergence of a girl's poetic consciousness within a narrative of domestic abuse, linking her entrance into language to threats against her sexuality.

> Sixteen years old and crooked
> with drug, time warped blissfully
> as I sat alone on Oak Hill
>
> The cemetery stones were neither erect
> nor stonelike, but looked soft and harmless;
> thousands of them rippling the meadows
> like overgrown daisies.[70]

The girl experiences the awakening of consciousness only through the evacuation of her body, and its material context. The drug transforms the nihilism of the cemetery landscape as the tombstones become a flowering meadow.

In ways that challenge the tenets of cultural nationalism, Cervantes upends the indigenismo of the Chicana/o Movement—its reliance on static Aztec cultural iconography—to fashion a more personal recovery of ancestral Mexican landscapes:

> I picked apricots from the trees below
> where the great peacocks roosted and nagged
> loose the feathers from their tails.
> I knelt to a lizard with my hands
> on the earth, lifted him and held him
> in my palm—Mescalito
> was a true god.[71]

The poet's vision of the poem remains decidedly nonnational. The girl's drug-induced fantasy nourishes an imaginary impoverished by familial disorder. In the poem Cervantes delivers the story of the girl's entrapment in the domestic sphere with condensed violence:

> Coming home that evening
> nothing had changed. I covered Mama on the sofa
>
> with a quilt I sewed myself, locked my bedroom
> door against my stepfather, and gathered
> the feathers I'd found that morning, each
> green eye in a heaven of blue, a fistful
> of understanding;
>
> and late that night I tasted
> the last of the sweet fruit, sucked the rich pit
> and thought nothing of death.[72]

The girl's pursuit of liberatory knowledge and the signs of her emergent artistry are indivisible from the sexual danger present in her home. Here Cervantes underlines the latent threat of gender violence that was entirely absent from celebratory accounts of Chicana domesticity. The girl who thinks "nothing of death" tastes her freedom in the solitude of a room locked against her family; it is a solitude wholly incommensurate with the communal imperatives of ethnic nationalism.

Cervantes links Chicana confrontations with gender violence within the home to their encounters with other threats to bodily integrity and spirit. Her portrait of the barrio insists on viewing the full gender dimensions of the proletarianization of Mexican female labor in the postwar decades, an issue missed by most Marxist critiques of labor during that period. The poem "Cannery Town in August" invokes the silencing effect of gender domination on the Chicana industrial workforce:

All night it humps the air.
Speechless, the steam rises
from the cannery columns. I hear
the night bird rave about work
or lunch, or sing the swing shift
home. I listen, while bodyless
uniforms and spinach speckled shoes
drift in monochromatic down the dark
moon-possessed streets. Women
who smell of whiskey and tomatoes,
peach fuzz reddening their lips and eyes—
I imagine them not speaking, dumbed
by the can's clamor and drop to the trucks
that wait, grunting in their headlights below.
They spotlight those who walk
like a dream, with no one
waiting in the shadows
to palm them back to living.[73]

Cervantes renders the factory as a masculine apparatus that robs women of their bodily agency, as the constant rhythm of production in the peak season mirrors sexual penetration. In marked contrast to the aesthetic of socialist realism, which dignified the industrial labor force during the 1930s, here only the "night bird" sings to the labor process. The women do not even achieve speech through the poet's intervention but are rendered silent by the mechanical discipline of the factory. Their bodies bear the imprint of their exploitation; their smell of "whiskey and tomatoes" suggests their own self-censorship for economic survival. The cannery women lack access to the outside agency that would restore their will, to "palm them back into the living."

The silence inscribed in Cervantes's poem recalls the violent suppression of Chicanas' labor insurgency in the cannery strikes of the 1930s, and in particular, the workers organized by Luisa Moreno.[74] Cervantes was one of the very few young artists who attended to the long tradition of women's employment and labor organizing in the barrios. But the silence also suggests the loss of a grammar for encoding that insurgent will in language, since the poet only *imagines* that the women are not speaking. Chicanas in fact remained ardent in their campaigns against abuses in both the food-processing companies and labor unions during the crises of deindustrialization in Northern California. Cervantes sets the stage for the cannery women's rebellion, but the silence of her poem also anticipates the weakness of the nationalist framework governing union and civil-rights activism in confronting the changing industrial economy of the 1970s and '80s. The poem marks a moment of transition, when the international dimensions of the labor market began to move Chicanas and Mexican migrants into a new domain of conflict.

Cervantes's final offering, "Emplumada," completes the poetic cycle with an allusive contemplation of aesthetics and sex. The poem comments on the creative powers of each by observing a pair of hummingbirds hovering over a flower garden. Its opening line signals the presence of death amid the scene of abundant fertility: "When summer ended /the leaves of snapdragons withered."[75] Cervantes then introduces the protagonist of the poem, the gardener, who must contend with her own thwarted desire: "She hated / and she hated to see them go."[76] The decline of the flowers threatens the gardener's own creative powers with dissolution, until she catches sight of an alternate source of inspiration:

> two hummingbirds, hovering, stuck to each other
> arcing their bodies in grim determination
> to find what is good, what is
> given them to find.[77]

The hummingbirds offer a light counterpoint to the oppressive pairings of men and women contained in the earlier poems. Cervantes approves of their instinct for pleasure, their modest desire for "what is given them to find."

Since the title of the poem references the identity that Cervantes has constructed for herself as plumed bird and scribe, the hummingbirds represent an alternate mode of creative existence. Cervantes closes with a comment on her own restless enterprise:

. . . These are warriors

distancing themselves from history.
They find peace
in the way they contain the wind
and are gone.[78]

The birds evoke the Aztec god Huitzilopochtli, "the hummingbird of the south." This god of war was both a herald of death and a guide for journeys. As "warriors," the birds grant the poet a new relationship of autonomy from the past. Theirs is a freedom acquired in flight, in migration without settlement. The fleeting arrival of the hummingbirds contrasts with the rootedness of the flowers, now in decline. The birds' constant motion inverts the sense of confinement that Cervantes conveyed in "Refugee Ship," by making a virtue of mobility and remove from history. Through the hummingbirds, the poet recovers an aesthetic of migration for Chicana/o literature. It is no less an answer to the losses that shaped her community in the course of El Movimiento: "They find peace / in the way they contain the wind / and are gone."

As she narrated the transformation of the San José barrio by urban development, Cervantes could not have anticipated the changes yet to come, when mass migrations from Mexico and Central America would remake her native city during the 1980s and '90s. But even as she began her writing career in the 1970s, Chicana labor struggles throughout the southwestern United States already showed the portents of the profound dislocations in the politics of gender, work, and citizenship yet to come.

Holding the Line at the Mexico-U.S. Border:
The Farah Strike

> They put me on two machines. You set up one machine, to sew, and
> then when you start to sew you turn and set up the second one but you
> always have to keep an eye on both of them to make sure that they are
> doing right. Then they tried to make me run three machines but that
> was too much.   —Estela Gómez[79]

In May 1972 Chicanas set another picket line against class racism in the
southwestern United States. Far from Cervantes's San José, garment workers struck against the Farah Manufacturing Company of Texas, and in the
process, they combined labor demands for collective-bargaining rights
with a volatile alchemy of ethnic solidarity, women's organizing, and border
conflict.[80] Although unions had largely ignored Mexican women—especially at the border, where immigration status complicated the organizing
effort—many of these workers brought the political traditions of Mexican
and Chicana/o social movements to the struggle. Chicanas protested with
signs bearing the slogans "Viva La Unión, Viva La Causa, Viva La Raza"
[Long Live the Union, the Cause, the People]. For most of the women who
struck, their income was either the single source for their families or was
vital to the survival of their households.[81]

Farah was then the second largest employer in El Paso, with a primarily female and ethnic Mexican workforce. The company enjoyed a high
profile in the industry, supplying cambray shirts and denim pants to national stores like J.C. Penney, Sears, and Montgomery Ward. Its owner,
Willie Farah, was the son of a Lebanese immigrant who had begun the
business with a small shop in the city's South Side during the Great Depression. During the 1960s, Farah opened new factories in San Antonio,
Victoria, and Las Cruces, with nearly ten thousand employees by the time
of the strike. Company officers represented the business as a united family, cloaking their management practices in a paternalist authority. But in
fact, Farah hired Anglo men to supervise the Mexican and Chicana workforce; women reported a pervasive pattern of sexual harassment and intimidation on the shop floor. For many women, the price of promotion
was accepting the unwanted sexual attentions of their bosses. The abundance of low-wage workers in the twin cities and the Texas "right to work"

law permitted the company to sustain a high turnover in employees. The company thereby evaded the responsibility of paying pensions to senior workers and could eliminate insubordinate workers with impunity. Farah proudly asserted that he employed only legal residents and U.S. citizens, but the labor force included undocumented women as well. During the strike, the company used Mexican workers to break the union effort.

Willie Farah was notorious for his opposition to unionization. When San Antonio workers staged a walkout in March 1972, the company began a long and repressive campaign against the strike. Four thousand garment workers walked out; 85 percent of them were women, and most were residents of El Segundo Barrio, one of the poorest communities in the United States. Many workers also crossed the border bridge for work from the colonias of Ciudad Juárez. These women had few economic or political protections to fall back on during the strike beyond their social networks of mutual assistance. After years of frustrated organizing efforts at Farah, the Amalgamated Clothing Workers of America (ACWU) coordinated a national campaign in support of the workers, calling it an unfair-labor-practice strike. Picketers complained of low wages, frequent speedups in production, poor safety and health conditions, and pervasive labor abuses. Workers suffered bladder and kidney infections from sitting long shifts without bathroom breaks, bronchitis from the lack of ventilation, and injuries to their fingers and eyes from the sewing machines.

The ensuing conflict tested women's resolve to claim new rights in the racially segregated and patriarchal border city. The walkout lasted two long years. Farah hired private guards to patrol the factory entrances with dogs and interfered with the protests by invoking an 1880 ordinance that made picketers stand fifty feet apart from one another. Police arrested nearly one thousand strikers, most of them women, and set bail at punitively high levels. The workers' primary source of leverage came from the union boycott of Farah pants that gave their struggle visibility at the national level. AFL-CIO members organized pickets against Farah products at department stores, raised relief funds for the strikers, and held massive rallies across the country for "Don't Buy Farah Day" on December 11, 1971. César Chávez addressed the picket lines on behalf of the UFW, drawing close connections between Mexican American agricultural workers and the Chicana garment workers. Farah workers and their supporters formed the independent caucus Unidad Para Siempre [Unity Forever], hoping to make labor representatives responsive to local concerns and to build grassroots leadership within the union.

Finally, with company profits falling precipitously, the National Labor Relations Board tipped the conflict in favor of the workers, issuing a decision against Farah for "flouting the [NLRB] Act and trampling on the rights of its employees."[82] Willie Farah conceded and recognized the ACWU as the bargaining agent for company employees. Workers found that they obtained small gains as a result of the two-year walkout, when ACWU and company management reached a rapid agreement on the new contract without offering workers much time for deliberation. The new terms raised wages, established a company medical-insurance plan, improved job security and seniority provisions, and set up a grievance procedure. Despite workers' hopes for consolidating their hard-won labor power, Farah soon initiated mass layoffs, dismissing five thousand of his nine thousand employees. The most militant strikers were the first to lose their positions during the plant closings.

Farah employees were soon hurt by rapid changes in the garment industry and in the structure of border manufacturing. In 1965, Mexico had inaugurated the Border Industrialization Program (BIP), establishing a factory system based in Ciudad Juárez and other Mexican border cities that created export-processing zones in partnership with U.S. corporations. BIP attracted foreign investment to the Mexican north to create jobs and capitalize on Mexico's proximity to the United States. El Paso companies like Farah exploited the new economic integration, drawing immigrant workers or subcontracting production to the Mexican side of the border.

The Chicanas who built communal ties on the picket line challenged elite economic interests during the initial phases of border industrialization. But the labor conflict exposed divisions in the transborder working class, as Farah employees had to confront the arrival of company scabs, who were nearly all more recent migrants from Mexico. The strikers were more often than not migrants or daughters of migrants, with close kinship and cultural ties to Chihuahuan communities. But as the economic depression of 1973 hit the border, these bonds proved fragile before the demands of protecting their meager hold in the industrial workforce. U.S. unions were ill prepared to meet the challenge that transnational capitalism posed to labor organizing. Farah workers signed a contract with

ACWU, only to see their union weakened by the southern shift of industrial capital in the 1970s.

The gains and losses of the Farah strike encapsulated the migrant Mexican women's labor activism that fell outside El Movimiento's campaigns for ethnic self-determination and racial brotherhood. Garment workers at the Farah plant were subject to Taft-Hartley restrictions on strikes. Had the ACWU bolstered the independent organizing efforts of the Farah women in Unidad Para Siempre, perhaps the union would have been able to sponsor more effective, transnational opposition to exploitative conditions in the border factories. Their militancy represented an assault on Cold War business unionism, as it divided obreras [female workers] from male workers, and white and Latina/o communities. The Farah women, and the Mexican women whom the company brought in as scabs, were the very image of the "Non-citizen Americans" whom Luisa Moreno had dignified in her campaign against the repatriations of the 1930s. With the recession that followed the Farah strike, however, it was not the obreras themselves who were sent out of the country; it was their jobs. The emergence of new transnational divisions of labor assured that civil-rights organizations and organized labor would be hard-pressed to recover the migrant imaginary that Moreno and her colleagues in El Congreso had once brought to U.S. labor- and civil-rights activism. The transnational ties that animated the Popular Front were sorely absent precisely at a moment when the mobility of transnational capital seemed beyond restraint.

Sin Fronteras

Recently the labor struggles of women at Farah Pants, a garment factory in El Paso, Texas, and the women from Tolteca Foods, a tortilla factory in Richmond, California, have shown the determination, militancy, and consistency of the Mexican woman worker. The women at Farah maintained the strike for one and a half years, while the Tolteca workers completely shut down the plant. In both places over 90 percent of the labor force were Mexican women fighting for the right to unionize in Texas and at Tolteca fighting for the expulsion of an unrepresentative union. In both strikes undocumented and documented workers stood side by side in solidarity and mutual protection.

—Evangelina Márquez and Margarita Ramírez,
"Women's Task Is to Gain Liberation" (1977, 191)

Although the Farah strike proved transformative in the lives of the Chicana participants, it produced few lasting structural changes for Mexican women in the border labor force. In the aftermath of the Farah campaign, Chicana unionists did stake out new terrain for El Movimiento by articulating women's labor concerns from a perspective that favored internationalism, rather than nationalism. Their mobilizations took place at the tail end of the Chicana/o civil-rights movement, and they anticipated the harsh reactions against the reforms of the 1960s that emerged in the Reagan years. Their internationalism reflected an assessment that civil-rights legislation had been an insufficient challenge to liberal racism. Rejecting ethnic nationalism as insufficiently attuned to the primacy of capitalist domination in the lives of Mexicans in the United States, members of the Centro de Acción Social Autonoma-Hermandad General de Trabajadores [Center for Autonomous Social Action—General Brotherhood of Workers, CASA-HGT] drafted a platform for class struggle centered on the plight of Chicana workers. Precisely because the nationalists blurred the definition of national and transnational solidarities, Chicana/o socialists sought to distance themselves from the identity-based projects of the student mobilizations.

Rather than view Mexican Americans as an internal colony within the United States, the radical left of the Chicana/o labor movement saw the border as a false divide splitting the integral unity of Mexican revolutionary struggles. CASA-HGT organizers adapted Third World socialist revolutionary principles to the contingencies of labor organizing at the Mexico-U.S. border: "NO BORDER STOPS WORKERS' STRUGGLES," read the banner of their newspaper, *Sin Fronteras*, in 1977.[83] The organization viewed the U.S. government as an imperial instrument of capitalist interests, which oppressed Mexicans both as a nation *and* as a class; Mexicans would achieve liberation by recognizing that "we are the largest Spanish-speaking population in the World."[84] Writing in the same issue, Evangelina Márquez and Margarita Ramírez issued the unapologetic demand "Women's Task Is to Gain Liberation," pointing to the high levels of Mexican women's integration into the U.S. workforce. Opposing movement discourse on gender roles, they wrote, "One out of every three Mexican workers in the U.S. is a woman. . . . This is a critical point because contrary to the myth of women not having to work, one out of every seven women is a sole provider for her family, since 14 percent of Mexican women are heads of households."[85]

Citing the North Vietnamese revolutionary leader Ho Chi Minh, Márquez and Ramírez argued for increasing women's activism in the public sphere:

> Despite the incorrect conceptions and manifestations of women as inferior, despite the predefined expectations of a "woman's role," resistance, consciousness and concrete actions themselves take place during the process of social production. It is here we see the link and essence of women's oppression, how women's role is defined by her relation to the means of social production in society, not in her relations to men at home. This is why the demand for the right to work is a revolutionary demand which must be fought for if women are to actively build their movement for liberation within the ranks of their fellow workers fighting the class struggle. . . . Our interest is for our class and for our nationality. We seek equality to learn, to educate, to organize, to fight and to build a better society with the real equality of the whole working class.[86]

Rather than reconcile women's leadership through a revalorization of women's domestic roles, as other Chicana organizers had done, here the CASA-HGT organizers insisted that the full span of women's labor, in waged and unwaged work, formed part of the "liberation of the working class and the struggle against national oppression." The article reviewed the history of Mexican women's labor in the United States, linking women's exploitation to the use of immigrants as a temporary workforce: "Like immigrant workers, women are seen as a potential labor force to be mobilized into production when necessary."[87] The authors reminded readers that Mexican women were also laid off and deported from agricultural and assembly work. For the organizers at CASA-HGT, women's incorporation into waged labor during World War II was critical to the revival of progressive social movements: "These few years in the workforce for women, however, were extremely important for they produced new progressive attitudes related to the collectivity of society's production."[88] But the essay also warned of the vulnerability of Mexican women to forced sterilizations, sexual violence, and immigration abuses.

Looking ahead to the near future in which "Mexicans will outnumber the black population in the country," the authors imagined the conditions for new collective power as a Latina/o majority: "We are young, we are increasing, and we are organizing."[89] Theirs was, by the late 1970s, a rare, uncompromising voice for an expansive vision of struggle. Their work connected with the vision of Moreno and others and stood in contrast to the writings of authors such as Richard Rodriguez, who soon became the most celebrated interpreter of Mexican immigration in the United States. It is significant that the fullest articulation of feminist thought within El Movimiento took on transnational form, reviving the migrant imaginary within its vision of liberatory struggle. If the Farah strike demonstrated that the border could in fact *stop* workers' struggles, the new migrations of the coming decade showed that migrants could also *transform* the "capricious frontiers" of transnational capitalism.

CHAPTER 5

Tracking the New Migrants

Richard Rodriguez and Liberal Retrenchment

The real task, even for those of us
who as diasporics think of seceding,
is to contemplate that difficulty.
Of how in our minds we allow
ourselves to believe that it was ever
possible to find a place of withdrawal.
It is also, inevitably, a problem of
collectivity, far beyond individual
issues or nations.

—Amitava Kumar,
Passport Photos (2000)[1]

I am on my knees, my mouth over
the mouth of the toilet, waiting to
heave. It comes up with a bark.
All the badly pronounced Spanish
words I have forced myself to sound
during the day, bits and pieces of
Mexico spew from my mouth, warm,
half-understood, nostalgic reds and
greens dangle from long strands of
saliva. I am crying from my mouth in
Mexico City.

—Richard Rodriguez,
Days of Obligation (1992)[2]

With this grotesque gesture, the Chicano essayist Richard Rodriguez revisits Octavio Paz's *Labyrinth of Solitude* (1961) in a collection of autobiographical essays that explore the cultural and political distance inscribed in the Mexico-U.S. border.[3] Published a decade after his 1982 memoir *Hunger of Memory* and Lorna Dee Cervantes's *Emplumada* (1981), Rodriguez's *Days of Obligation: An Argument with My Mexican Father* (1992) inaugurates a new self, the atravesado—a border crosser—not undocumented or of the Chicana/o underclass but a middle-class, disaffected intellectual.[4] Rodriguez commemorated the quincentennial of Columbus's arrival on American shores with a personal memoir of the European conquest. His writings mark a radical departure from the migrant imaginary that enlivened the works of his predecessors, Luisa Moreno, Américo Paredes, and Emma Tenayuca. Like other Chicana/o writers formed during the civil-rights movement, Rodriguez's essays examine the predicament of the mestizo in the United States; his writing addresses the cultural confusion that Paz expounded in his meditation on Mexican national character. For Rodriguez, however, collective identity as Mexicans in the United States offers no shelter from the wounds of racism.

In his second memoir, Rodriguez offers himself up as a translator of tragic Mexico to an English-speaking media hungry for images of cultural authenticity. But Rodriguez is far more interesting for his refusal of ethnic affiliation, his renunciation of what Latina/o anthropologists have termed "cultural citizenship."[5] Like the diasporic subject of Amitava Kumar's *Passport Photos*, Rodriguez "dreams of seceding" from the racialized bonds of the ethnic collective. However, as Kumar writes, his fantasy is a problem not only of his own imagining but of racial formation and nationalism in the post-civil-rights, postcolonial era.[6]

Like the poet Lorna Dee Cervantes, Richard Rodriguez came to maturity during the civil-rights movement of the 1960s. But his formation as a public intellectual diverged sharply from Cervantes's participation in community-based cultural organizations for popular theater and small literary presses. Born in 1944 to working-class Mexican parents, Rodriguez grew up in Sacramento and attended Irish Catholic schools. He continued his education at Stanford and Columbia universities and won a Fulbright to study in London, where he began to elaborate the arguments on immigration, schooling, and language that formed the basis of his 1982 memoir, *Hunger of Memory: The Education of Richard Rodriguez*. In 1975, he was completing a doctoral program in Renaissance literature just as higher education was being transformed by demands for increased representation of people of color in school admissions, faculty hires, and administration. In response to the radically altered relations of race and class in the U.S. academy, Rodriguez withdrew his candidacy for hire in English departments. Choosing "Romantic exile" in protest of affirmative action, Rodriguez turned down teaching positions he felt were offered him solely for his "Hispanic" surname, over and above his individual talents and qualifications.[7] The career that followed has included the patronage of conservative institutions interested in opposing bilingual education, multiculturalism, and affirmative-action policies won during this period. "This was my coming of age," Rodriguez confessed in the oblique phrases that pervade *Hunger of Memory*. "I became a man by becoming a public man."[8]

With the publication of his first memoir, *Hunger of Memory: The Education of Richard Rodriguez*, in 1982, the young author gained a level of renown then unknown for a Latina/o writer in the United States. The book earned such prestigious awards as the Christopher Prize for Autobiography, the Gold Metal for Non-Fiction from the Commonwealth Club of California, and the Anisfeld-Wolf Prize for Civil Rights. *Hunger of Memory* went almost immediately into serial printings as a mass-market paperback, and it has been reissued in numerous editions for use in schools, libraries, and book clubs. In the years following its publication, Rodriguez received the Frankel Medal from the National Endowment for the Humanities, the International Journalism Award from the World Affairs Council of California, and television journalism's highest prize, the George Foster Peabody Award, given to him in 1997 for his cultural-essay segments on the *MacNeil/Lehrer NewsHour* of the Public Broadcasting Service network. Rodriguez earned these laurels for his incisive power of observation and his disarmingly frank, confessional prose. The Chicana/o Movement had embedded Latinas/os more fully in U.S. national culture, so that Rodriguez was well positioned to receive broad acclaim for his literary achievements. But as Ronald Reagan's presidency entered its second year, Rodriguez was equally visible because of his dissent from key platforms for Latina/o civil rights. However subtle the author's criticisms of bilingual education and minority set-aside programs, Rodriguez's public persona helped authorize the politics of resentment that undercut the legitimacy of racial-reform projects that derived from the Civil Rights Acts of 1964 and 1965.

Richard Rodriguez's evolution as a public intellectual occurred during the important shifts in U.S. social policy and race relations that came to define the Reagan years. In his writings following *Hunger of Memory,* he maneuvered through various identities—Hispanic, mestizo, Indio—in order to consolidate his position as a commentator on Latina/o immigration and Mexican American society. As a journalist, Rodriguez became an influential observer of the cultural politics of the post-civil-rights-movement era. By presenting himself as the son of Mexican immigrants, Rodriguez staked out a central position in coming debates over border security and the growing Latina/o influence in U.S. culture and society.

Although Latina/o scholars have considered him a reactionary figure for his attacks on minority claims to rights, I consider his liberalism less an aberration from U.S. minority discourse than an embodiment of what Norma Alarcón has termed the "constitutive contradictions" of ethnic inscription in the post-civil-rights era.[9] Precisely because his career unfolded during the conservative turn in leftist politics of the post-Vietnam era, Rodriguez's visibility signaled the narrowing promise of oppositional politics during the 1980s. That is, his critique of minority politics pointed to the contraction of the "meaning of freedom within liberalism's already narrow account."[10] Rodriguez's views on immigration, education, and affirmative action were significant not only because of their implications for Chicana/o cultural politics. They also unmasked new constructions of race that emerged within the international division of labor during this period, as the governments of Mexico and the United States pursued free-market reforms. Rodriguez's increased visibility in popular media derived in part from his willful denial of his membership to a Chicana/o collectivity, but his reportage also revealed the limits of civil-rights reforms within the strictures of liberalism and racial capitalism. His attention to the differences between migrants and U.S. citizens of Latina/o descent were often meant as an assault on identity-based claims to group rights; still, the author also gave U.S. audiences an uncomfortable reminder of the national desire for the racialized migrant, both as a pliable source of labor and as a cultural resource in the economy of consumption.

During the 1980s, many critics reviled Richard Rodriguez for repudiating civil-rights efforts for social reform. Rodriguez embraced the fiction of "unmarked" citizenship, in willful denial of the ways that the state's ideal of assimilation produced racial, gender, and sexual difference in order to maintain class hierarchies. In 1982, his critique of affirmative action and bilingual education set him apart from his cohort of Chicana/o intellectuals; but by the start of twenty-first century, legal challenges had radically curtailed these programs, and the resurgence of cultural conservatism moved the author well into the mainstream of Latina/o cultural politics. Rather than a subjection of his writings yet again to a discussion of "assimilation" and cultural particularity, what is more interesting are the ways that Rodriguez contended with liberal racism during the Reagan and then the Bush era of neoliberal reform and conservative retrenchment.

But Richard Rodriguez did not only position himself in the public eye as a critic of ethnic identity claims. By the time he published his second memoir in 1992, the growing public resentment toward undocumented people offered him a different role. In *Days of Obligation*, Rodriguez remade himself as the interlocutor for the new migrants; their presence, he believed, would remake the nation and expose the insufficiency of the category of "the minority." "Every day and every night," he wrote, "poor people trample the legal fiction that America controls its own destiny."[11]

This chapter examines the implications of profound political and cultural transformations of the post-civil-rights era for Mexican and Mexican American communities in the United States. I address these changes through the writings and public declarations of arguably the most prominent Latina/o author of the period. But Rodriguez did not confront the challenges of this period in isolation. His adopted city of San Francisco was home to a vibrant Latina/o community that responded to the combined challenges of the conservative backlash, the AIDS epidemic, and the Central American wars, with unparalleled creativity in the arts and in political mobilizations.[12] My discussion accordingly references other artists and writers whose works shaped the context in which Rodriguez wrote, and whose efforts signal other possible answers to the dilemmas of the period.

If Rodriguez's insistent assertion that "there is no such thing as a Hispanic" fails to deflect racism, as I argue, it nonetheless points to the insufficient relief that identity politics provides to racialized groups. Indeed, the author's career as a public intellectual has exposed the failures of liberalism to deliver on its promises of equality amid the global restructuring of racialized classes in the past quarter century. Despite Rodriguez's long flirtation with the neoconservative demand for a "color-blind" society, his reflections on the migrant presence undo his personal accommodations to the liberal ideal. Rodriguez's aspirations to full, unmarked citizenship notwithstanding, his interest in the undocumented reveals the continued salience of Latina/o critiques of liberalism, when delivered from another quarter, from within the migrant imaginary.

Neoliberal Entrenchment

The political philosophy known as neoliberalism took hold after the oil crisis and recession of 1973.[13] Its principal tenet is that economic growth, sustained through a free-market system freed from government intervention, is the best platform for democratic reform and social justice. In neoliberalism's strictest application, its policies dictate privatization and the removal of state controls on economic investment and production.[14] U.S. foreign policy during the 1980s and 1990s followed suit and promoted the opening of foreign markets through a combination of political and economic pressure and incentives.[15]

In Latin America, such incentives for economic liberalism included the leveraging of foreign loans in exchange for the removal of protective barriers to trade. But the United States also used military force to achieve its economic and political ends, as the Reagan and Bush administrations provided millions of dollars in aid to military juntas and dictatorships in Central and South America.[16] The brutal civil wars of the 1980s forestalled popular challenges to oligarchic and corporate class power in El Salvador, Guatemala, and Honduras. The U.S.-sponsored Contra war in Nicaragua helped depose the revolutionary Sandinista government that had come to power in 1979.[17] In Chile and Argentina, authoritarian regimes pursued rapid economic restructuring in a period of brutal repression, waging protracted "dirty wars" against their own civilian populations.[18]

The transition to democracy in Argentina in 1983 and in Chile in 1990 occurred in a climate of political uncertainty and financial crisis, as poverty rates rose precipitously in the final years of both dictatorships. By the conclusion of the Contra war in 1990, the signing of the Salvadoran Peace Accord of 1992, and the end of the thirty-six-year civil war in Guatemala, the Soviet Union had collapsed, and socialism no longer held its political purchase as a viable alternative to globalized capitalism.[19] But the economic and social disparities that fueled the armed conflicts have remained largely intact, and Central American states still comprise some of the poorest countries in the region.

As the U.S. government pursued its political and economic objectives under the "Reagan Doctrine"—not only in Latin America but also in Afghanistan, Cambodia, Angola, and Mozambique—neoliberal reforms also altered the domestic economy and political landscape of the United States. Although its proponents portrayed neoliberalism as a practical philosophy that could transcend ideology, its application worked to concentrate class and political power in the hands of economic elites. The Reagan and Bush presidencies pushed the U.S. government toward "laissez-faire" practices— namely, the deregulation of markets and industry—and began the systematic dismantling of the welfare state.[20] Conservative appointments to the Supreme Court and the National Labor Relations Board supported a frontal assault on collective-bargaining rights and the power of trade unions, while the government legislated profound tax cuts, all in keeping with a philosophy that would transfer the responsibility for social investment and public welfare out of the state and into the private sector.

The economic shocks were immediate: income inequality reached new levels in the country in the 1990s, while economic growth and corporate profits peaked. As President William Clinton fought for the North American Free Trade Agreement of 1994 and the welfare-reform bill of 1996, he touted the burgeoning stock market as a leading indicator of national economic health. The official title of the legislation that severely curtailed welfare programs, the Personal Responsibility and Work Opportunity Reconciliation Act, epitomizes neoliberal social principles, by transferring the burdens of poverty away from the state and onto the individual.

The 1990s saw the ascendancy of what Amartya Sen termed development *as* freedom.[21] Traditional liberalism, from the Enlightenment onward, has located rights in individual persons; its adherents imagine that since individuals defend their self-interests, their actions would naturally function as the guarantee of democratic, participatory governance. Neoliberal reforms extended this logic to its limit and put the very *substance* of civil rights into crisis, by transferring responsibility for social welfare from the government to the private sector.

During the 1980s, civil-rights advocates in the United States found themselves forced to defend the welfare state against federal cutbacks. Ceding the critique of the state in order to defend the recognition of minority protections or entitlements, these organizations were largely unable to address the persistent class and racial inequalities that U.S. nationalism and free-market capitalism continued to produce. In this way, leftists were often forced to abandon the urgent concern of how the state, even in its decentralized and apparently shrinking form, administered the crises of contemporary capitalism through yet another racializing practice of social control and domination.

Neoliberal restructuring of the state and its controls on the free market left Mexican Americans vulnerable to further social exclusion and economic exploitation. While residents of Mexican origin had the highest rates of labor-force participation among workers in the United States, they also experienced the greatest degree of economic stagnation and occupational segregation.[22] Their lack of social mobility even in the wake of civil-rights victories, exposed the limits of civil-rights legislative reforms that did not provide structural changes in the system of racial capitalism. Income polarization reached unparalleled levels in both the United States and Latin America during the 1980s, creating forms of social inequality that paralleled the effects of legal racism before 1965.[23]

For Latinas/os, this conservative turn had devastating effects. The immigration reforms in 1986 and 1996 once again racialized migrants as a threat to national security and economic health.[24] Massive immigration from across Latin America and Asia made the question of "Americanization" and citizenship far more complex than it had been at any previous moment. Political transformations throughout the hemisphere facilitated the mobility of transnational capital on a scale that radically altered the nature of government and the institution of citizenship. The accelerated pace of neoliberal reforms meant that those displaced from agricultural and industrial occupations could find little relief from their governments. As a result, unprecedented numbers of migrants entered the United States as a population precluded from both naturalization and full political rights.

In 1980, fourteen million Latinas/os resided in the United States; within two decades that number had risen to an estimated thirty-five million, with most of this growth owing to new immigration from Mexico, Central and South America, and the Caribbean.[25] Of the more than seven million people of Mexican origin counted in the 2000 census, over half were foreign-born.[26] The 2000 census estimated the foreign-born population of Central Americans in the United States at over two million, and by 2004, the American Community Survey placed the number at 2,836,362.[27] The census did not count the unauthorized population, which the Pew Hispanic Center numbered at 1.3 million in their survey of March 2005.[28] New immigrants transformed older Latino barrios.[29] Refugees from the wars in Central America brought with them a clear understanding that nation-states were capable of deliberately suspending civil rights in their bids for capital investment and development. These migrations diversified the U.S. Latina/o population and simultaneously reconfigured the politics of latinidad.

During this period of rapid population growth, the Latina/o left split on the question of migrant rights. Latinas/os took leading roles in demanding amnesty for Central American refugees and undocumented migrants, but leading civil-rights organizations and unions also saw migrants as a major threat to the primacy of U.S. workers in a job market already weakened by deindustrialization.[30] The amnesty provisions of the 1986 Immigration Reform and Control Act (IRCA) drew broad support from Latina/o civil-rights organizations and labor unions. Following its passage, Mexicans naturalized and registered as voters at record levels. But the legislation also codified security provisions and penalties that ultimately corroded the capacity of new migrants and Latina/o citizens to secure full civil rights.[31] Amid the uncertainties provoked by changes to the U.S. labor economy and immigration policy, Latina/o migrants took the lead in revitalizing U.S. unions, particularly in the service sector. The Justice for Janitors movement of the Service Employees International Union (SEIU) took off in 1990 after police assaulted immigrant workers on strike against a multinational janitorial-services company in Century City, Los Angeles. Their movement pointed to the possibilities for expanding the rights of U.S. workers by placing immigrants and service employees in the lead of justice campaigns.

However vital their role in the service economy, the new migrants encountered the virulent revival of a racial discourse that constructed Latina/o migrants, economic or otherwise, as aliens ineligible for naturalization. Growing intolerance toward migrants fleeing the Latin American debt crisis and the Central American wars led Congress to introduce various legislative measures to curtail illegal immigration. In September

Protest at Mexico-U.S. border wall in Nogales, Mexico. Punitive anti-immigrant measures introduced in 1996 met with opposition on both sides of the boundary. Photograph by Pablo San Juan, taken in August 1996. (Corbis)

1996, President Clinton signed into law various immigration reforms that further limited the capacity of undocumented migrants to improve their political status in the United States.[32] The Welfare Reform Act denied both illegal and legal immigrants access to various forms of federal assistance, including many types of Social Security benefits. The Illegal Immigration Reform and Immigrant Responsibility Act (IIRIRA) imposed severe criminal penalties on unauthorized migrants, while also limiting opportunities for political asylum and other forms of legal relief. New detention and deportation policies, including those contained in the Anti-Terrorism and Effective Death Penalty Act of 1996, gave license to punitive regulation and enforcement, so that the rates of incarceration and removal of migrants rose precipitously.[33]

Within this climate of economic and political insecurity, Latina/o communities were ill prepared to confront the changes that new immigrants were bringing to the barrios. But immigration alone could not account for the persistent poverty and low levels of educational attainment that persisted for Mexicans: sociologist Susan González-Baker noted that second-generation migrants tended to fare better than the first generation, but third-generation Mexican Americans fared worse.[34] Nor did limited English account for these problems, since those populations showing high rates of language retention, like Cubans, showed higher levels of economic and educational advancement. Although proponents of tighter immigration controls charged Mexican migrants with resisting naturalization, studies of migrant communities suggest that, in fact, Mexicans tended to meet the state's criteria for successful acculturation: they learned English, participated in public institutions, and paid taxes. Immigrant workers revived the flagging labor movement in California and beyond, shifting the center of labor militancy toward service industries, in which migrants made up the majority of the rank and file. Migrants' disfranchised status contrasted sharply with their ardent efforts to incorporate themselves into the societies where they settled. But, as Luisa Moreno noted in 1940, legal barriers on naturalization have far-reaching, negative consequences for citizen and noncitizen Latinas/os alike.

Not only did the forms and meanings of mexicanidad change dramatically with these new immigrations, but alterations in the welfare state left civil- and migrant-rights mandates unfunded and out of pace with the emergent economic and political order. As we shall see, new migrants brought with them their own, particular accounts of their racial insertion into the U.S. labor market and national polity, accounts that diverged from the identity narratives of the heirs to the ethnic nationalism of the Chicana/o Movement.[35] But as criminalized nonnationals, migrants could not defend their rights in the courts or official spheres of citizenship; their mass presence as "illegal" subjects tested the limits of the civil-rights framework of antiracist struggle.

The mass migrations also produced new forms of cultural expression. Beginning in the 1980s and into the 1990s, the Central American refugee crisis captured the imagination of Chicana/o artists and writers. New works by visual artists, playwrights, and novelists drew analogies between racial repression in the United States and the U.S. sponsorship of the brutal counterinsurgencies in El Salvador and Guatemala. The San Francisco muralist Juana Alicia, for example, created her 1983 tribute *Las Lechugeras* [The Women Lettuce Workers] on the corner of York and Twenty-Fourth

streets, the heart of the Latina/o Mission District. The massive painting features a crop-dusting plane showering toxins over the Chicana/o
field workers in an explicit reference to the aerial bombardments of the
scorched-earth campaigns in Guatemala. Her inclusion of an unborn fetus
within the fertile body of a lechugera links the farmworker struggle to the
campaign against the Mayan genocide.[36] Alicia's portraits of the women
emphasize their indigenous features, just as her vibrant color palette links
Mexican and Mayan aesthetics. The image suggests a shared plight for
both campesino populations, made the victims of U.S. agribusiness and
its political allies. Alicia later completed a mural in Managua, Nicaragua,
continuing her work in solidarity with popular struggles in the region. In
the 1992 play *Heroes and Saints*, Cherríe Moraga narrated the United Farm
Worker campaigns of 1988 in MacLaughlin, California, by similarly using
the image of the Guatemalan killing fields to depict the devastating effects
of pesticide poisonings on migrant workers.

In 1993, the Chicana artist Ester Hernández rendered the ikat weave
of the feminine rebozo [shawl] in a print that commemorated the missing victims of the Central American wars. Her *Tejido de los desaparecidos*
[Weaving of the Disappeared] integrates the skeletal remains of the disappeared into the warp and weft of the fabric, so that the cloth becomes sat-
urated with their memory. The alternating bars of helicopters and skele-
tons use the repetitive nature of decorative patterning to reveal how death
is naturalized in war. Vivid red bloodstains interrupt the pattern, disrupt-
ing the process of aestheticizing violence. The rebozo both displays the
virtuosity of indigenous textiles in Mexico and Central America and serves
as a humble female garment. As a symbol, then, the *Tejido* constructs a
shared feminine imaginary of political struggle and solidarity across the
hemisphere. Hernández, the daughter of Mexican migrant farm laborers,
is best known for her 1982 painting *Sun Mad*, which also indicts the use of
pesticides in California agribusiness.

For Hernández, as for Alicia and Moraga, the Central American crisis revitalized an artistic commitment to the unfinished projects of the
Chicana/o Movement. The movement to halt U.S. support for repression
in Central America revived a sense of the transnational field of struggle,
expanding the campaign for racial justice beyond the nation-state. In an
installation devoted to the victims of pesticide poisoning, Hernández drew
attention to the particular place of the Mixteca/o population in the diverse

arena of Latino cultural politics. Describing her use of photography to document farmworker life, Hernández invested her mestizo subjects with the vitality of the migrant imaginary:

> I'm going out for the next few weekends to do photography. In particular, I'll be looking for the Mixteco Indians. One of the things I'm interested in is how when people immigrate or travel, they carry something with them that tells them who they are. It could be a medalla or a picture of children. It keeps our spirit going.[37]

In keeping with the communal aesthetics of the farm-labor movement, Hernández crafted her ethical vision from the vernacular culture that sustains migrant people. Her movement between the "they," the Mixtecas/os, and the "we" of "our spirit" permits the new migrants to retain their cultural particularity while also admitting them into the ethnic collectivity of shared class struggle. Her art allows her subjects to reveal what they wish of themselves; she is neither their interlocutor nor their judge. Her migrant aesthetic refutes the notion that mobility and resettlement mean the loss of meaningful connections to origins, or the rupture of memory. Migrants are carriers of cultural value, she argues, making visible the migrants' assertion of presence that "keeps our spirit going." Hernández's homage to farmworkers also alluded to the death of César Chávez on April 23, 1993. For her, as for the many Mexican Americans who mourned his passing, the new migrants would carry forward the dignity of field work that the UFW struggle had defended.

These works demonstrate the active labors of many Chicana/o artists to expand their repertoire of advocacy and dissent in relation to the new migrant presence. In contrast to this revival of the migrant imaginary by Chicana artists, Richard Rodriguez constructed his relationship to the new migrants in opposition to the discourse of collective solidarity. For him the border crossing entailed remaking the self; the migrant in his accounts is a shadow figure for his own self-fashioning. In the spheres of official culture, the political and economic transformations of the 1980s and 1990s necessitated a sanctioned interpreter in the news media and in the classroom: Rodriguez has been that voice—on television, in magazines, and as the author of the exemplary "Hispanic" autobiography. His narrative of tragic acculturation accompanied a photographic spread on gang warfare in

Harper's magazine in 1990; Insight Media marketed his video *Victim of Two Cultures* in its catalog for "Diversity Studies," making him the representative "Hispanic" subject that his memoir famously refused to perform.[38] Rodriguez shared with so-called multiculturalists (whom he repudiated), but also with Chicana artists and writers, a vision of hybridity and cultural impurity as the defining future of national life: its recognition, he writes, marked "the last Discovery of America."[39]

El Atravesado

In *Days of Obligation*, Rodriguez staged a series of border crossings not in the interest of recovering the Mexico lost to him in his parents' migration but, rather, to banish it to the distant past. Rodriguez exploited the disappointments of racial politics in the post-Movimiento period via the reassertion of a rigid separation of the public and private spheres—this was the signature gesture of his virulent opposition to multiculturalism. His first memoir, *Hunger of Memory*, signaled his refusal to claim membership to a larger Chicana/o collectivity, when Rodriguez absented himself from struggles for civil rights and affirmative action by publicly disavowing his own ethnicity; a decade later, *Days of Obligation* turned on the unshakable belief that conquest and immigration inevitably result in the severing of meaningful ties with Mexico for "Mexico's children." But just as *Hunger of Memory* hinted at family secrets that troubled his insistence on separate spheres for citizenship and cultural affinity, his second book dodged the problematic forms of racial inscription that made Mexicans a temporary workforce ineligible for naturalization. The fragmentary essays on migration, Catholicism, San Francisco's Castro district, conquest, and memory that make up *Days of Obligation* are seasoned with pieces of a cynical exchange with "Mother" Mexico:

> I lower my eyes. I say to Mexico, I say . . .
> I cannot understand you.
> Do not pretend to understand me. I am just a figure of speech to you—a
> Mexican American.[40]

Although Rodriguez's journalism positioned him as a champion of im-migrants, his essays also strategically deployed his refusal of ethnicity, as he anxiously asserted his U.S. citizenship and his status as "an American writer."[41]

Nor did Rodriguez offer any articulation of a Mexican American iden-tity apart from its fragile construction as a "figure of speech." The open-ing paragraphs of *Days of Obligation* destroy the conventional story of the return to roots, as he denounces the desire of Chicana/o nationalists to recover their lost homeland.[42] Rodriguez is on his knees, vomiting up his guts in the colors of the Mexican flag. This scene frames the author's anxi-eties about identity, citizenship, and authenticity, and about his status as the "voice of 'Hispanic America.'"[43] The author suffers the attack of nausea while on a trip through Michoacán with a BBC television crew filming a documentary on the United States and Mexico. Acting as "presenter and translator," Rodriguez guides the crew through his parents' home state in search of his family's origins in a "village [he] has never seen."[44] The irony is not lost on the writer whose fame was built on the disavowal of his eth-nicity: "A man who spent so many years with his back turned to Mexico," he demurs, "Now I am to introduce Mexico to a European audience."[45] In vomiting the colors of his parents' flag, Rodriguez literally voids his body of his Mexicanness, ridding himself of the "nostalgic reds and greens" of his cultural inheritance. The vomit can also be read as failed speech, a vulgar metaphor for his inability to speak for Mexico—as Rodriguez is haunted by his "badly-pronounced Spanish" and the "half-understood" words that surround him.[46]

Rodriguez's failure to locate the "village of childhood imaginings" could be interpreted as a cogent critique of Chicana/o nationalists who sought to dispel anxieties about the present by invoking a heroic, mythical past. His refusal to claim Mexico challenges standard sociological assumptions of ethnicity as stable and unitary, a naturalized category in social-scientific preoccupations with "group solidarity, traditional values, family mobility, political mobilization" and language.[47] Read this way, the episode might reveal how ethnic identification is overdetermined; Rodriguez's inability to identify as Mexican could signal his unwillingness to perform the role of "native informant" for the BBC.[48] Rodriguez's work tantalizes readers because it hints at a variety of evocative interpretations. But the author ultimately undoes these possibilities. He is only interested in recording his experience in his parents' country as an episode in his own production of himself as a deterritorialized subject.

> The village was constructed around a central square. Passage toward the center was narrow; just room enough for a van filled with our television equipment to pass. Most of the doors of the village were open. We saw a few people about; those few more curious than friendly, more Indian than mestizo.[49]

This parodic inversion of the pilgrimage home reinstates the authority of the imperial gaze, as Rodriguez indulges the BBC's request for images of a premodern, remote Mexico: "This is perfect I kept saying from the back-seat, perfect."[50]

As translator, Rodriguez acts as the agent of what anthropologist Renato Rosaldo has termed "imperialist nostalgia," a yearning in which "people mourn the passing of what they themselves have transformed."[51] The travelers marvel at the picturesque quality of the figures in black standing in front of a crumbling church, until their loud music disturbs what is revealed to be a funeral procession and they are asked to leave. Rodriguez's exaggerated attention to the contrasts between the Bobby Brown song playing in the van and the aged plaza bell tolling for the funeral mask the actual economic inequalities that underwrite his tour. Thus, even as Rodriguez delights in the absurd juxtaposition of the van wheeling down the cobbled roads of the nameless village, he becomes complicit in a long line of colonial narratives that relegate Mexico to a place without history.

"Mexico was memory," he (the son of immigrants) writes, "not mine." The country of his parents exists only as past. In this small scene, the conquest of Mexico is called up and reenacted, the first of the book's multiple repetitions and deformations of the imperialist plot of modernity meeting premodernity in the peripheral village. The episode in Michoacán concludes as Rodriguez's renounces any interpretation that he might offer as a "native" observer. Rather than establish communication with the townspeople, he ignores the distance between the metropolis and the village (and his own distance from his "roots"):

My vision of the Mexican village—yellow doors, wet gutters, children with preternaturally large eyes—floated backward. The crowd of mourners in the village square became smaller and smaller and smaller.[52]

Narrating the events in Michoacán through this hallucinatory language, his own desire converges with that of the television audience, until he becomes the instrument that satisfies their voyeurism. Despite the distance that he constructs between himself and the "native" Mexicans he encounters, however, Rodriguez's account is authenticated by "experience," as his cannibals—the villagers—act as the mirror of the Other in himself, his Caliban. "Mexico," Rodriguez repeats, "is memory," and it ceases to exist for him once he turns his gaze.

As in *Hunger of Memory*, Rodriguez assumes that the simple gesture of refusal—in this case, the refusal to satisfy the imagined audience's appetite for a performance of ethnic authenticity—subverts the liberal apparatus that regulates the production of ethnic identity. Nevertheless, this position of refusal does not hold, nor can it insulate him from the neocolonial chains of signification circulating in the encounter. The artifice he ascribes to memory does not absolve him of any responsibility to history, as he might wish; rather, it produces contradictions he seeks to resolve by retreating into narcissistic reflection. For Rodriguez, difference is only permissible in the fictive, enclosed realm of the personal.

The opening scene of vomiting up his parents' flag is emblematic of the ways *Days of Obligation* repeatedly brings the terms of racial, sexual, and national identity to crisis, only to reinscribe the normative boundaries of public and private that police the expression of difference. This narrative strategy of repression tests the political limits of postmodern border theories from the 1980s that represented migrants as oppositional subjects. Border theories seized the figure of the border crosser as the prototype of a radical subjectivity for the migrant's ability to negotiate the space where two competing cultural systems meet.[53] The particular conditions that allowed Rodriguez to perform this identity, however, suggest that his "biculturalism" was itself accommodated within, or in fact constructed by, the nation-state in the conservative retrenchment following the civil-rights movement. Not only did the category of "the minority" function as a site of opposition to social norms and state power; it also functioned to incorporate and reconstitute marginal subjects within the liberal nation-state. During the 1980s, the U.S. media aided in racializing Mexicans as illegal subjects—images abounded in television and news stories of parasitic undocumented immigrants and irredeemable gang members.[54] Rodriguez became the sanctioned Mexican American interpreter for narrating the apparent clash of Mexican and U.S. cultures at the Mexico-U.S. border.

Rodriguez's exemplary use of the "American" autobiographical genre allowed him to fulfill this role of translator to perfection. *Days of Obligation* confidently addressed "'We' Americans," by condensing five centuries of cultural rivalries in a form self-consciously modeled on the ironies of Montaigne's *Essays*. Both memoirs encode Rodriguez's singularity with their strangely idiosyncratic systems of references and the display of intellectual mastery. Nevertheless, his faith in what critic Rob Wilson termed the "regenerative plot of self-invention" means that his work enacts the very Americanization that the author attributes to immigrant communities.[55] Thus, Rodriguez's narrative strategies of defamiliarization, parody, and irony consolidate national ideals of citizenship, while also undermining the idea of identity as a coherent, stable entity.

Against what he terms the confines of "minority culture," Rodriguez argues for a more privatized, individual experience of ethnic affiliation:

> Ethnicity is for me something much more private, [having] in some sense, a theological dimension. I don't think of it as tacos and serapes and weekend trips to a Mexican resort town. I think of it as having to do with my very soul, and the nature of my relationship to my god.[56]

In transposing the process of subjection from the state to his god, Rodriguez denies that ethnicity is used by the state to maintain social hierarchies. His position relies on an absolute distinction between public and private spheres. All articulations of ethnicity are confined to the private spaces, to "personal" life; in contrast, subjects enter the arenas of commerce and politics as free, political actors, unmarked by race or class distinctions. For Rodriguez, proponents of minority rights disrupted the boundaries between private and public, in his view the very condition of freedom and social mobility. Private language and cultural celebration of origins could not share space with the blank slate of the public self. For this reason, Rodriguez opposed bilingual education because it consisted of "using family language in the classroom."[57] Rodriguez willingly admitted the severity of this position, which made citizenship a matter of cutting cultural and linguistic ties to the "private" sphere of familial origins.[58] His argument against bilingual education was not about learning in and of itself but about schooling as a necessary site for interpellating national subjects. Rodriguez's assertion was a developmentalist one, meaning that he understood nationalization to mean cultural deracination (at least in public) for those racialized migrants deemed "failed subjects" for their class and ethnic difference from the liberal ideal of citizenship.

Liberal Retrenchment

In 1992, the United States celebrated the quincentennial of Europe's arrival in the Western Hemisphere with a marked upsurge of anti-immigrant and nativist sentiment. As Rodriguez penned *Days of Obligation*, the new migrations in the wake of Mexico's worsening economic crisis mobilized U.S. fears of a full-scale border invasion. The rapid emergence of Latinas/os as the largest ethnic minority in the new century—and in California, the threat that Mexicans would *overtake* the majority white population—provoked a crisis of national proportions.

In 1994, California governor Pete Wilson won reelection on the strength of his promises to bolster law enforcement, both through anticrime policies targeting low-income, racialized communities (the so-called inner cities) and demands for tighter border security. His notorious advertising campaign, which featured video of undocumented migrants leaping into freeway traffic, mobilized his supporters for the state election. That year, 59 percent of California voters approved Proposition 187, a sweeping "Save Our State" ballot initiative that denied unauthorized immigrants access to social services, health care, and public education. The measure required all law-enforcement agents to report immigration violations, in effect making police officers into an arm of the Immigration and Naturalization Service. It restricted all public benefits of welfare, health services, and education (save the emergency medical care required under federal law) to those who could prove their legal status. In an important manifestation of tensions among ethnic groups, a significant portion of minority voters—including Latinas/os and naturalized immigrants—voted for its passage.

Save Our State entered the ballot as "the first giant stride in ultimately ending the ILLEGAL ALIEN INVASION."[59] Supporters hoped that the measure would set an agenda for broader reforms at the federal level. Against Proposition 187, a diverse grassroots campaign did mount considerable opposition to the law, but its work proved inadequate against the bleak politics of fear and nativism that gripped the state. A California judge issued an immediate restraining order on the legislation, pending challenges to its legality. Final relief from the measure came from the Ninth Circuit of the U.S. District Court of Appeals, when Judge Mariana Pfaelzer overturned the measure in 1998. Newly elected governor Gray Davis then reached an agreement with legislators not to appeal the decision further. Although Proposition 187 never went into effect, the measure achieved its major objective by sending a clear message of intolerance toward the growing Latina/o majority in the state.

The anti-immigrant assault was a strategic bid for conservative power in California and in the larger nation, which aimed to exclude the noncitizen population and isolate the Latina/o citizenry. The defeat of progressive organizing in the 1994 campaign marked the escalation of social conservatism, as Republican leadership capitalized on popular resentment toward the perceived gains of racial minorities from civil-rights legislation. The bid to seize control of the border corresponded not only to new anti-immigrant aggression but also to conservatives' defense of a particular brand of white, Christian, and monocultural nationalism against the challenge of cultural pluralism. During the Reagan era, immigration reforms militarized the border to an unprecedented degree, to a higher level than any other international border between states not at war. This coincided with debates in Congress over a constitutional amendment to make English the official language of the United States.[60] Although the 1981 English Language Amendment never came to a vote in the national legislature, twenty-three states have since enacted statutes and constitutional amendments that make English the sole language of government. At the local level, cities and counties have also pursued English-only laws. In 1995, the U.S. English movement, chaired by Mauro E. Mujica, lobbied state by state for English-only laws and for passage of HR 123, a bill that would declare

English the official government language, require all governmental business to be conducted in English, and end federal funding for bilingual education.

A common rationale for these discriminatory laws is, ironically, that English is "the language of equal opportunity": these measures thus appropriate the discourse of civil rights in order to impose a single trajectory of Americanization on the diverse, non-English-speaking polities of migrants and ethnic minorities.[61] The sponsors of some of these bills claimed to be defending immigrant rights in the United States, while actually working to ban non-English speakers from the U.S. polity. The bills would severely restrict immigrants' access to the primary institutions of citizenship and social mobility. Under these provisions, voting materials, court services, public education, and welfare benefits could no longer be translated to other languages. That Richard Rodriguez, the son of immigrants, who had begun his schooling in Sacramento with fifty words of English, could end his education as a Fulbright scholar in the British Library meant he embodied the notion that new citizens were best formed in cultural isolation.

English-only measures had their liberal proponents as well, who argued for the necessity of forcing immigrants to adopt the official culture of the United States as a means to defeat ethnic divisions and bring language minorities out of the shadows of their cultural enclaves. Such measures followed the logic common from the 1880s into the 1930s, of prohibiting the use of native language in Indian schools; here, federal authorities held out the promise of citizenship at the cost of severing students' familial and cultural ties. In 1995, a routine child-custody case in Amarillo, Texas, revived the logic of "kill the Indian to save the child" when Judge Samuel C. Kiser issued an order to deny Martha Laureano parental rights following her divorce. The state district court judge reprimanded Laureano for speaking Spanish to her five-year-old daughter, which he equated with neglect, or worse:

> If she starts first grade with the other children and cannot even speak the language that the teachers and the other children speak and she's a full-blooded American citizen, you're abusing that child and you're relegating her to the position of housemaid.[62]

In issuing his order, the judge infringed on clear constitutional protections of free speech, and yet his position rested on a belief that the daughter's civil rights could not find full expression in any other language than English. His denial of Laureano's parental rights stemmed from a conception of a single public sphere of citizenship located in the English-only school; rather than make it the obligation of state institutions and civil society to accommodate the child, Kiser set the full responsibility on the immigrant mother. In severing the mother's claim to her daughter, the court asserted the primacy of state interests (a sovereignty defined by English usage) over the familial rights of the immigrant and her child. His logic was built on a caste system that appeared fixed and immutable: to speak Spanish is to be a housemaid.

As it happened, not even the state could uphold its own language mandate. In his final admonition to Laureano, Judge Kiser stated, "Now get this straight, you start speaking English to this child because *if she don't do good in school*, then I can remove her because it's not in her best interest to be ignorant. The child will only hear English."[63] Although the judge apologized for his grammatical slippage and his slight against domestic workers, he never repudiated his order. One could argue that Texas is the state with the longest history of educating Spanish-speaking children, but it has done so in a school system whose implicit intent has been the maintenance of the racial division of labor. Texas public schools remained in violation of desegregation orders well into the 1990s, under legal challenge from the Mexican American Legal Defense Fund (MALDEF) and other civil-rights advocates.[64]

Proposition 187 and the English-only measures were just two instances of post-civil-rights projects of racial governance in the late twentieth century. During the 1980s, the incarceration rates of black and Latina/o populations rose precipitously with the "War on Drugs" as a renewed discourse of social pathology also disfranchised poor communities of color. The triumph of liberalism over the more radical challenges of the civil-rights movement now permitted neoconservatives to cast the instruments of social reconstruction—affirmative action, antipoverty programs, and school desegregation—as, at best, unnecessary interference by the state or, at their worst, deterrents to *true* antiracism. The 1978 Supreme Court decision in the *Bakke* case held that the University of California could not apply "fixed racial quotas" in order to pursue affirmative action in accordance with the 1964 Civil Rights Act. Opponents to minority set-aside programs and affirmative action used the demand for a "color-blind" society to undo the project of state-mandated desegregation. The turn toward privatization that drove the neoliberal phase of U.S. economic development is thus also a politics of reaction against civil-rights gains, against minority directives to use public resources to ameliorate racial and class inequalities.

As a journalist and contributing editor at *Harper's* magazine, Rodriguez opposed the legislative initiatives that would have curtailed the civil rights of immigrants, sexual and racial minorities, and prisoners, as he wrote essays that indicted the political right in California for its efforts at social engineering. Rodriguez could not sanction legislation that would have excluded migrants from the possibility of national belonging. Proposition 187 not only identified Latinas/os and immigrants as threats to the integrity of the state, but in doing so, the initiative would have coopted public institutions of education, culture, health care, and the law from their function to incorporate new national subjects. But because of his investment in unmarked citizenship, Rodriguez fell short in his critique of the conservative assault on Latina/o civil rights.

The dismantling of bilingual curriculums in the public schools did not facilitate Latina/o integration into the public sphere of citizenship as Rodriguez would have it; it was far more a tactic to differentiate the population by race and immigration status as a means to reproduce class divisions of wage work, reproductive labor, and commerce. By identifying English as the official language of citizenship, the state foreclosed on the recognition of *multiple* public spheres of social interaction, spheres maintained by immigrant and racial communities at the margins of the formal market and political arenas. As we will see, these *counterpublics*—by which I mean alternate subnational or transnational spheres of communication and politics—had long been critical to the sustenance of migrant communities within the racialized apparatus of the nation-state.

In what follows, I examine the strategies of self-fashioning at work in *Days of Obligation* in order to disentangle how the public/private binary structured the author's articulation of citizenship, racialized desire, and the role of cultural translator.

Mexico's Children

Throughout the 1990s, Rodriguez commanded a leading position in public discussions of the rising presence of Latinas/os in the United States. From his vantage point as a renowned author, he looked back on the trajectory of Latina/o activism, only to pronounce that there was no possibility for collective action under the sign "Chicano." His critiques of the civil-rights project hit home precisely at the moment of crisis for civil rights; but rather than draw on the more radical democratic traditions of the migrant imaginary, Rodriguez's writings refused to engage the problems of racial governance. The author claimed, instead, to voice his assault on identity politics from a position outside ideology, as "the comic victim of two cultures."[65]

Rodriguez saw claims to collective unity as inevitably separatist and limiting because they threatened to foreclose the exercise of membership to the broader ("unmarked") public. His articulation "We Americans" wrested the nation from its identification with normative whiteness by remaking it in the image of Asian and Latin American immigrants; however, his reductive distinction between public and private reduces mestizaje to yet another racializing vehicle for assimilation. *Days of Obligation* presented mestizaje in its postmodern guise of market-driven relations of consumption: eating tacos and donning serapes. Even as Rodriguez rejects the name Chicano, however, his own writing serves as the representative voice of Hispanic life in U.S. schoolrooms and college seminars.

In 1982, Rodriguez phrased his criticisms of ethnic politics in *Hunger of Memory* with trepidation and ambivalence. A decade later, these restraints gave way to a triumphant repudiation of all forms of collective Chicana/o struggle. He systematically reduced the diverse community mobilizations of the 1960s and '70s to a middle-class, adolescent crisis of identity:

> Mexican Americans of the sixties had no myth of themselves as Americans. So that when Mexican Americans won national notoriety, we could only refer the public gaze to the past. We are people of the land, we told ourselves. Middle-class college students took to wearing farmer-in-the-dell overalls and they took, as well, a rural slang to name themselves: Chicanos.[66]

This acid depiction of the utopian energies of the civil-rights movement turns on Rodriguez's use of his education to abandon his own working-class roots. Here he derides college-educated students for their participation in labor politics, speaking of their identification with farmworkers as inauthentic. The "we" of his statement authorizes him to reduce all Chicana/o claims to collective unity to a simple yearning for the past, ignoring the history of Mexican American social activism that produced the demand for Chicana/o civil rights, as well as the movements in which the connection to land was much more a stake in class struggle than it was a symptom of nostalgia. In effect, his dismissal of social movements makes electoral politics the sole venue for political development, once more reinscribing the nation-state as the singular engine of modernization.

For Rodriguez, any expression of ethnic solidarity with the legacies of 1848 is automatically rendered inauthentic, because Chicana/o nationalists "used the language of colonial Spain to declare to America that they would never give up their culture. And they said, in Spanish, that Spaniards had been oppressors of their people."[67] Here Rodriguez addresses the indigenismo of Chicana/o power, its identification with heroic native resistance to colonial domination. Rather than make the thorny issue of language indicative of the inherent contradictions of a legacy of multiple conquests, Rodriguez uses it to cancel the possibility of claiming Chicana/o identity altogether. Rodriguez's own account of "the Indian" derives from the same colonial narrative that fueled Chicana/o nationalism; here he is less a critic of indigenismo than of its anticolonial posturing.

Rodriguez faults Chicana/o nationalists for their clownish appropriations of Mexican nationalism, but he himself claims to be "Indian" in his own strategic performances. This claim is a function of his antinationalist agenda, staged precisely to evade the problem of his hyphenated Mexican American identity and the taint of ethnic nationalism. Following the publication of *Days of Obligation*, Rodriguez positioned himself as an advocate of immigrants, identifying himself with new populations arriving from Asia and Latin America: "Today, Los Angeles is the largest Indian city in the United States. . . . On any day along Sunset Boulevard you can see Toltecs and Aztecs and Mayans."[68] A significant segment of the mass migrations of the 1990s were indigenous peoples from Mexico's interior. Rodriguez extends the category "Indian" to include all new immigrants, in order to mark their difference from the "settled" populations of Chicanas/os whom he so distrusts. Still, he calls them by the same pre-Columbian names invoked by the ethnic nationalists, rather than naming their distinct political affiliations as Mixtecas/os, Zapotecas/os, Chinantecas/os, or Purépechas.

Rodriguez deploys a racializing discourse even as he parodies it in Latino struggles for self-definition:

> Puerto Ricans, Mexicans—we are the earliest Latin American immigrants to the United States. We have turned into fools. We argue among ourselves, criticize one another for becoming too much the gringo or maybe not gringo enough. We criticize each other for speaking too much Spanish, or not enough Spanish. We demand that politicians provide us with bilingual voting ballots, but then we do not vote.[69]

While the descendants of "immigrants" debate the trivial, the new immigrants, fresh from the homeland, become the bearers of authenticity. The author fails to account for the imperial history that has made culture a site of social conflict. Rodriguez calls his migrants peasants, once again calling up the tropes of the clash between the primitive and the modern, masking migrants' recruitment for labor in the industrialized fields and factories of the United States. Rodriguez's argument turns on his facetious assault on the Latina/o counterpublic, the bilingual sphere in which the ballot box is only one among many sites for claiming expansive democratic rights.

Responding to Chicana/o activists' claims to the status of a discriminated minority, Rodriguez has argued that their insistence on "separatism" is in fact the greatest indicator of their assimilation. This kind of reversal is typical of his rhetoric, which may contain a kernel of truth but evades entirely the terms of that "assimilation" and the historical relations of power shaping Chicanas/os' economic and political marginality. Rodriguez provides an important corrective to Chicana/o nationalist discourse by acknowledging the diversity of Latina/o life in the United States, but he has marshaled that insight in the service of his narrative of Americanization. He may oppose the criminalization of undocumented migrants, but his own narrative reinscribes a boundary on national community, by differentiating between proper immigrants (entrepreneurial migrants) and failed national subjects (Chicanas/os). Immigrants, valued for their traditional work ethic and stubborn self-interest, function as the prototypes of his own rejection of origins:

> The notion of "legal immigrant" allows us to forget that all immigrants are outlaws. Immigrants violate custom; they assault convention. To be an immigrant is to turn your back on your father and your village. You break your mother's heart. The immigrant is as much a scandal to his ancient mountain village as to suburban Los Angeles.[70]

The trip north as depicted here repeats the family drama that structures Rodriguez's flight from home in *Hunger of Memory*. Rodriguez transposes immigrants' outsider status before the law onto the social realm to describe a position of agency defined by individual self-interest. This slippage allows him to represent the "Indio" immigrants (of the "ancient mountain villages") as uninterested in the past, so long as it is a past defined by static tradition and bonds of affect. In fact, fully half the newer migrant population was female, a trend Rodriguez elides by conflating immigration with masculine rebellion. Similarly, the family he describes differs vastly from the transnational communities of migrants that sustained complex social and economic networks across borders, networks intimately linked to shifts in labor and political economies.

The signifier "Indio" therefore functions both as a rejection of Chicana/o identity and as the key to Rodriguez's interest in the aesthetics of colonial conquest, which serve as a veil for contemporary articulations of race and nation:

> I think it may be too early to tell what the story of Columbus means. The latest chapter of the Columbus saga may be taking place right now, as Latin American teenagers with Indian faces violate the U.S. border. The Mexican kids standing on the line tonight between Tijuana and San Diego—if you ask them why they are coming to the United States of America, they will not say anything about Thomas Jefferson or *The Federalist Papers*. They have only heard that there is a job at a Glendale dry cleaners, or that some farmer is hiring near Fresno.[71]

With his enigmatic style, Rodriguez describes the division of labor that spills over the Mexico-U.S. border in terms of the colonial encounter. He intends to deflate nativist projections of "brown hordes" which would undermine the exceptional democracy of the United States; he also permits new immigrants to define U.S. nationhood in terms that depart from the monolithic myth of Anglo origins. But in doing so, Rodriguez depicts the undocumented as unthreatening youth, disinterested in politics. This denies them their militancy as laborers, obscuring too the political interests that make the policing of immigration a matter of policing class and race relations as well. (The undocumented may well construe democracy in terms that ask how it is that dry cleaners, agriculturalists, building contractors and restaurants show such a predilection for Mexican workers). This episode demonstrates the author's new role of interlocutor for the undocumented, who he constructs as outside the public sphere, transient and voiceless with respect to their rights as laborers. They are most appealing to him as agents of aesthetic, not social change: their "Indian faces" are turning California brown.

By contrast, Chicanas/os are simply failed national subjects, by virtue of their perceived lack of productivity: "California does not have an immigrant problem. California has a native-born problem. I worry more about the third-generation Mexican in Boyle Heights than about the newly arrived Mexican immigrant."[72] Rodriguez's dismissal of the Chicana/o Movement reinscribes a vision of the Chicana/o community as a "univocal, unthinking mass" (and dangerous) and erases the long history of Mexican American politics in which the articulation of hyphenated, transnational community has expanded or subverted the monocultural, unitary structure of U.S. citizenship.[73] His logic presumes that no real thinking takes place within the close-knit bonds of family and culture. Whereas Chicana feminists used their critiques of nationalism to reconfigure the repressive boundaries of family and ethnic community, Rodriguez leaves no alternative but intellectual remove from the collective.

In the 1980s, critics dispensed with the fiction of the unitary subject, as postcolonial and feminist scholarship converged with poststructural theory to produce a new paradigm for examining the conflictual ways that race, gender, sexuality, and class operate in relation to one another to form the subject. Gloria Anzaldúa's *Borderlands/La frontera: The New Mestiza*, published in 1987, became the paradigmatic account of the nonunitary subject of consciousness; her theory located a radically decentered agency in the figure of the queer woman of color.[74] By contrast, the fixity of the public/

private split in Rodriguez's thought accommodated the author's project within the neoconservative assault on civil-rights reforms, suturing the gap between his gay, Chicano self and that ideal construct of "unmarked" citizenship. Nowhere is the instability of that self-construction more evident than in Rodriguez's narrative of his travels in Tijuana, where the author struggled to contain the dissolution of himself as citizen-subject amid the various and contradictory signifiers given to his brown body.

Close Encounters at the Mexico-U.S. Border

There is a turnstile.
Through which American tourists enter Mexico as at a state fair . . .
I pass through the turnstile.
Already the sun feels older . . . Hands and voices, beseeching eyes and rattling cups gather to surround me as I tread the gauntlet of pathetic enterprise . . . In Tijuana as in Bombay.
The point of the United States is distinguishing yourself from the crowd. The point of Mexico is the crowd. Whatever happens in Tijuana, I tell myself, do not imagine you have been singled out. You have entered into the million.
—Richard Rodriguez, "In Athens Once," *Days of Obligation* (1992, 80)

In *Days of Obligation*, Rodriguez depicts the border crossing in reverse; his passage through the turnstile threatens with dissolution the individuality that he prizes so highly. His chapter on Tijuana represents the border as the site of indeterminacy (is it Mexico or India?). His series of anecdotes recalls colonial narratives with their trope of cannibalism, as Rodriguez imagines being swallowed up by the brown hordes. In the United States, Rodriguez's brown face stands out as a sign of his individuality; in Tijuana, its exoticism fades into the "million." The tale of Rodriguez's crossing relays the constant friction between two ontological worlds north and south of the turnstile. In his effort to preserve the integrity of the individualism that he purchases as a citizen of the First World, Rodriguez puts the Mexican under erasure, reducing it to the mute, anonymous other. Throughout the chapter, Rodriguez deploys a postmodernist aesthetic that foregrounds the artifice inherent in representation, in order to disarm the reader but also to preserve his own innocence as he turns away from the gross inequities that confront him as he moves through the border space.

And yet the repressed returns with monstrous allure in the "unclean enchantments, whirling platters of melon and pineapple, translucent candies, brilliant syrups, charcoaled meats, black and red . . . all tempting, all inedible" of the open air mercados.[75] At a café with a hostess from the Comité de Turismo, Rodriguez almost relents from his abstinence. His kind companion offers him a drink.

> No I say . . . But suddenly I fear giving offense. I notice apothecary jars
> full of improbably colored juices, the colors of calcified paint.
> Maybe some jugo, please.
> Offense to whom? That I fear drinking Mexico?[76]

The signifiers for "Mexico" travel from the mute landscape to his polite hostess to the strange drink, taking on allusions to a predatory feminine sexuality embodied in the female representative of "Mother" Mexico as the situation turns sinister.

> Ah.
> We are all very pleased. It's a lovely day. I put the glass to my lips.
> But I do not drink.[77]

Rodriguez inverts the trope of cannibalism as he fears the effects of drinking or eating anything Mexican. He refuses to taste in order to preserve inviolate the boundaries of his identity as U.S. citizen from the country that threatens to corrupt his individuality.

Rodriguez's trip to the border takes place during the Catholic Holy Week, and his account exploits its ritualized language of sacrifice, pilgrimage, and sacrament to gloss the violence of the scene. Appropriately enough, it is Good Friday when Rodriguez joins a press tour of the U.S.-Mexico border, organized by the border patrolmen themselves. Seduced by the scene unfolding before him, he alternates between reports of migrants waiting for night to cross and local reenactments of the Crucifixion in Tijuana's hills:

> We come upon a posse of border patrolmen preparing to ride through the canyon on horseback. I get out of the truck; ask questions; pet the horses in the dark—prickly, moist, moving in my hand. An officer we meet obliges me with his night-vision telescope, from which I am encouraged to take a sample of the night. He calls me sir. He invites me so close to his chin, I smell his cologne as I peer through the scope. It as though I am being romanced at a cowboy cotillion.[78]

The undocumented recede silently into the dark, natural features of the landscape against which Rodriguez stages his initiation into the eroticized workings of state power. Night duty at the border becomes a Western romance as the cowboys make their roundup of border crossers. The author takes interest in the undocumented for what they reveal about the border guard, whose racialized, masculine authority fascinates him. (He does not comment on the Chicana/o agents who make up a sizeable percentage of the Border Patrol.) The routine arrests provide an erotic script for this theater of social dominance.[79] Calling the immigration agents "cowboys," Rodriguez calls up the history of border lynchings by Anglo "posses" only to displace the hint of violence onto the terrain of sexual fantasy. Rodriguez is all too aware of his own transgressive desire. His accommodation to the coercive apparatus underwriting his own U.S. citizenship requires his disavowal of the migrants' presence; but it is the vulnerability of these same migrants that props up the masculine power that so attracts him.

Observing the arrests of the undocumented, Rodriguez enjoys a border spectacle in which the evening roundup facilitates the erotic exchange between himself and the guards:

> You can take your pictures, the patrolman says.
> I stare at the faces. They stare at mine. To them I am not bearing witness; I am part of the process of being arrested. I hold up my camera; their eyes swallow the flash—a long tunnel, leading back.[80]

Even as Rodriguez subverts the documentary pretensions of journalistic narrative, he remains silent about the use of force that the nightly roundup truly represents. As a voyeur, Rodriguez imagines that he plays no role in what he observes, but for those arrested, he is indistinguishable from the migra. His inability to bear witness repeats his strategy of evacuating writing of its political service to others. Again and again, Rodriguez denies the dialogic dimension of his writing: "As a journalist I am allowed to come close. I can even ask questions," he writes; only "there are no questions."[81] Rodriguez's refusal signals the role that the undocumented play in his memoirs: they are merely the conduits for his performance as interpreter, a performance for a national arena that excludes migrants from speaking for themselves. The scene functions as a display of his narrative mastery; he alternately seduces and is seduced by the white border guards in an erotic exchange relayed through the undifferentiated brown bodies.

Here, the undocumented remain silent actors in Rodriguez's individual drama of self-discovery. Rodriguez cloaks his silence in the apparent isolation that he inhabits as an intellectual, but his reticence marks the place where the construction of the authorial persona stands in for his formation as a gay Chicano of the educated class. The incident recalls an episode in *Hunger of Memory* in which a summer construction job working alongside Mexican laborers reawakens sexual desires inhibited by his isolation at Stanford University, an institution of white, upper-class privilege. Rodriguez describes how his boss exploits the Mexicans, only to conclude that, by virtue of his own citizenship and education, he would never be one of them. Most important for him, his distance from their life as "los pobres" [the poor] makes him a man: no longer afraid that his education would make him effeminate, he marvels at "the pleasing sensations of [his] maleness."[82] Even as he acknowledges that his muscular body is now indistinguishable from the working-class masculinity to which he aspired, he notes that his summer adventure could not undo his difference from them. His class privilege transforms the significance of his brown body into a symbol of cosmopolitan leisure and upward mobility. The spectacle of the working men grants him access to his own masculinity. This masculinity is defined by the racial economy that valorizes the normative whiteness of the "unmarked" public sphere and confines the racialized migrant laborers to the subaltern counterpublic.

Just as the undocumented in *Days of Obligation* serve as a conduit to Rodriguez's sexual identity, they also serve as a measure of his distance as an intellectual from the ethnic squalor of the Tijuana streets. Rodriguez's insistent descriptions of the credit cards he carries, the cab rides he takes, and his pleasure in "the complaisancies of the Inter-Continental Hotel" serve not so much to make explicit his privilege as a cosmopolitan subject but to render transparent his choice of isolation and social disengagement. "The theme of city life is the theme of difference," Rodriguez writes, but for him, as for the liberal nation-state, the discourse of difference and cultural pluralism masks structures of dominance.[83]

During the 1980s, liberal discourses of multiculturalism and diversity constructed difference as a resource to be enjoyed in the logic of consumer society; for Rodriguez, recognizing "race" does nothing to disturb the unitary structure of U.S. nationality. In the words of Renato Rosaldo, for Rodriguez, "one achieves full citizenship in the nation-state by becoming a blank slate."[84] The logic of consumption does not do away with racialism but remakes it as an eroticized token of exchange. Rodriguez can only tolerate his racial subjection, figured here as his brown face, if it makes him unique, exotic. Rodriguez's refusal to act as a witness, then, is the price of his removal. Here, his privilege masquerades as what critic Eve K. Sedgwick calls "originary, passive innocence."[85] He retreats to the refuge of the cosmopolitan hotel away from the anonymity of Mexico's streets: "Because Mexico is brown and I am brown, I fear being lost in Mexico."[86]

Liberal Mestizaje

> Representation is possible only because enunciation is always produced within codes that have a history, a position within the discursive formations of a particular space and time. The language of binary oppositions and substitutions will no longer suffice.
>
> —Stuart Hall, "New Ethnicities" (1988)[87]

Even as Rodriguez has contested the primacy of whiteness in U.S. national culture, his celebration of the "browning of America" falters on the material logic of liberal racism. Because Rodriguez embraces the ideal of unitary citizenship, his discourse of mestizaje is at best muted in its attack on "the American paint box": "The price of entering America is an acid bath, a bleaching bath—a transfiguration—that burns away memory. I mean the freedom to become; I mean the freedom to imagine oneself free."[88] This enigmatic passage is typical of the author's oracular prose: does he mean to indict the national equation of whiteness with freedom or is he writing to instruct Latina/o immigrants on house rules? His use of color to denaturalize fixed racial polarities signals his utopian intent—"the deliverance of the United States of America from race."[89] Rodriguez commutes skin color, shifting it from what historian George Fredrickson terms "the practices, institutions and structures that a sense of deep difference justifies or validates" in support of "*a racial order*, a permanent group hierarchy," to an erotic resource.[90] In his 2002 volume *Brown: The Last Discovery of America*, Rodriguez encapsulates his vision of the proverbial melting pot:

> When I began this book, I knew some readers would take "race" for a tragic noun, a synonym for conflict and isolation. Race is not such a terrible word for me. Maybe because I am skeptical by nature. Maybe because my nature is already mixed. The word race encourages me to remember the influence of eroticism on history. For that is what race memorializes. Within any discussion of race, there lurks the possibility of romance.[91]

As a voice for mestizaje in the new millennium, Rodriguez remakes the black-white binary of U.S. racial discourse; he marshals the new immigration from Asia and Latin America to undo national myths of ethnic separateness, racial purity, and Anglo-Saxon origins: "The future is brown, is my thesis; is as brown as the tarnished past."[92] But this romance has often stumbled on the terrain of history: in Chicana/o discourse, as in Mexican nationalism, the term "brown" revives, rather than undoes, racial thinking. It makes the indigenous subject an object of fantasy, rather than an equal in political struggle. If, as Rafael Pérez-Torres writes, "within Chicano critical discourse, the mestizo body serves as a locus of identity whose refashioning foregrounds the political and relational valences of race," it is all too often a body abstracted from history. In Rodriguez's formulation, brown is timeless, both past and future.[93]

The mass migrations from Mexico that followed the country's sustained economic crises during the 1980s and '90s forced Chicanas/os to take a new look at Mexico and revise the tenets of ethnic nationalism. Mexico was not the ancestral past but an uncomfortable and diverse present. New Mexican arrivals reshaped the cultural landscape of Latino barrios and raised fears of competition in the low-wage workforce. During the years when Rodriguez sought to revise Chicana/o indigenismo, the Mixteca/o population of southwestern Mexico surpassed the Navajo (Dineh) to become the largest indigenous language group within the United States. "Brown" is hardly a liberatory term for this largely undocumented group; for indigenous populations, sovereignty is often a weightier term for identity than color. In her essay "Who's the Indian in Aztlán?" María Josefina Saldaña-Portillo aligns Chicana/o discourse with Mexican indigenismo: "in our Chicano reappropriation of the biologized terms of mestizaje and indigenismo, we are also always recuperating the Indian as an ancestral past rather than recognizing contemporary coinhabitants not only of this continent but of the neighborhoods and streets of hundreds of U.S. cities and towns."[94] Precisely because neither immigration officials nor immigrant advocates have ever differentiated among Mexican migrants, Mixtecas/os —and other indigenous groups—have remained largely invisible within the transnational circuit. Although mestizaje signifies differently within the racial codes of the United States than in Mexico, it has most often been expressed as an accommodation to the demand of liberal pluralism, by fixing group identification and making difference intelligible to the state.

As Mixtecas/os helped establish new migrant outposts in the southern and northeastern United States, they confronted a double prohibition of their cultural and language differences—both as migrants and as indigenous people. In 2005, the Juvenile Court of Wilson County, Tennessee, awarded temporary custody of an eleven-year-old girl to a foster family who had petitioned to adopt her. Her mother, Felipa Berrera was a Mixtecan migrant from the state of Guerrero, now residing in Lebanon, Tennessee. She had been charged with neglect of her parental obligations. During the legal proceedings, Berrera had difficulty communicating with the court because she had been assigned a Spanish translator, although her sole language was Mixteco. When she requested that the court arrange family counseling for her, the presiding judge, Barry Tatum, ordered that she learn English at a fourth-grade level within six months or lose her parental rights permanently. As in the 1995 custody case in Texas, the court reserved the right to classify the use of a maternal language other than English as child abuse. The order read,

> The court specially informs the mother that if she does not make the
> effort to learn English, she is running the risk of losing any connection

legally, morally, and physically, with her daughter forever. If the mother is able to learn English, she will be able to speak to her daughter for the first time *in a substantive manner* and will show her that she loves her and is willing to do anything necessary to connect with her.[95]

The court made more of her lack of English than of the original charge of neglect. In a subsequent hearing, Berrera made her plea to the court through a Mixtecan translator: "I don't hit my daughter, I love her." But for the court, the expression of maternal feeling in any language other than English would forfeit its moral status as "love."

The court order inverted familial roles by casting the mother in a submissive role to the child; as a U.S. citizen, the girl was treated as her mother's superior. According to the Southern Poverty Law Center (SPLC), a civil-rights agency engaged in the case, the fact that Berrera spoke only Mixteco meant that the court denied her the chance to speak on her own behalf: "The fact that it was hard to speak to her meant that they didn't," reported the SPLC attorney, Mary Bauer. "None of this would have happened if she had not been a poor immigrant and spoke English. They never spoke to her."[96] But in fact, her identity was *precisely* Tatum's justification for his ruling: in his court, the non-English speaker was a person without status, whose rights could be abridged in order for the state to meet its obligations to U.S. citizens.

Judge Tatum reportedly issued orders mandating English training in at least four other custody cases during his first term on the bench. His decisions tended toward coercive social intervention: in one incident, Tatum not only instructed an eighteen-year-old mother to learn English but also suggested that she use birth control. The woman was a recent migrant from Oaxaca, Mexico, who had been reported to the Department of Children's Services for missing pediatric appointments and failing to keep up with scheduled immunizations for her U.S.-born toddler. This was enough to warrant the charge of neglect. "A parent has the right to raise a child the way they [sic] see fit, but government gets involved at some point," Tatum told the *Tennessean*. "I'm concerned about the civil rights of the child and what will happen to her."[97]

The judge's rulings reflected the consensus of the Wilson County community toward the new immigrants. Lebanon, a small town on the outskirts of Nashville, Tennessee, has a population of twenty thousand; the arrival of some twelve hundred migrants for jobs in agriculture and manufacturing since the 1990s has provoked intense conflict over language use and local identity. Despite charges from civil-rights organizations like the American Civil Liberties Union that such rulings were unconstitutional, Tatum received considerable support from local residents who perceived his opinions as a defense of their group identity as Americans: "The general sentiment is, if people are going to be in this country, we all have a moral obligation to speak the language," stated Bob Bright, a Lebanon insurance agent. Bright's syntax was confused perhaps because he did not want to appear prejudiced, but in asserting the primacy of English as an objective fact, the speaker conflated language with race: "I know if I was in Mexico, I would make an effort to learn Hispanic [sic]."[98] The demand for English thus functions as a racializing project in a region that scholars have termed "the new South."[99]

The small minority population of Mixtecan speakers is particularly vulnerable to exclusion, even by other migrants. Mixtecans' local advocate, the Latino minister for Lebanon's First Baptist Church, Alexis Andino, told the *Los Angeles Times*, "They don't know how to do basic things. They're way behind."[100] Such a position inverts the codes of Chicana/o indigenismo; but in either case, Latina/o cultural discourse has often cast the indigenous subject out of the present into the past, constructing the Indian as a belated arrival to modernity, or as the *anti*modern. That Latinas/os commonly adopt the coercive fiction of "Americanization" in their confrontations with the newer Latin American immigrants suggests that their own precarious citizenship is predicated on their disavowal of the stigmatized "illegal alien." When the unauthorized migrant is a member of the family, as in the custody cases, the exclusionary structures of citizenship can threaten to rupture the apparently indestructible bonds of family and ethnic community.

Rodriguez's career as the "voice of 'Hispanic' America" cannot be understood apart from the contestations over identity, autonomy, and rights during the last decades of the twentieth century. His border crossings exploit gaps in both liberatory articulations of resistance and nativist imaginings of white primacy. Because his postmodernist critique of origins appears to work against the essentialism of the state's racial discourse, it is tempting to identify with his efforts to position himself outside the liberal apparatus that produces and regulates ethnicity. However, his critique of Chicana/o politics is only concerned with revealing the contradictions that arise from the paradox of racial formation within the liberal state. Never admitting that he also benefits from, and is subject to, the same processes of racial subjection, he adopts a posture of exceptionalism. His disavowal is fascinating because it occurs just as contemporary identity politics has come up against the limits of liberal individualism and reached an impasse.

Scholars ascribe this impasse to the increasingly corporatist politics of feminist, gay, lesbian, and ethnic movements during the 1980s and 1990s under the Reagan and Bush presidencies. In *States of Injury*, the political theorist Wendy Brown suggests that these movements' appeals for special rights have tended to increase their dependency on state power.[101] Precisely at this juncture, the political left surrendered its critique of the state as a site of domination and repression. As a result, Latina/o civil-rights organizations were unable to mount an effective challenge to the racializing processes that followed from neoliberal restructuring of politics and the economy.

Identity-based claims to rights have faltered, Brown argues, on their claim to oppositional ground, their "promise to address a social injury or marking that is itself constitutive of identity."[102] Identity-based movements are ambivalent about their relations to the state; they argue that differences are a result of conditions of domination, but they simultaneously deploy difference as a source of agency born out of their particular experience of oppression. For these movements to be effective, they must transform the social relations of domination that generate subjects constituted in difference at the risk of losing their particularity. If identity-based movements expand the political arena by introducing new actors, they may also reify difference in ways that mask its relation to a particular regime of power. In calling for special protections, they risk extending the legitimacy of the regime by empowering the state to act on their behalf. In so doing, they deflect awareness of how difference (as marginality and inequality) may be produced within and for the state. Corporatist politics thus mask the state's complicity with social violence toward the alien and the queer, in the sense that the call for state sanctions against discrimination comes belatedly to the issue of redress. That is, it does not effectively counter the violating force of subjection itself.

Rodriguez's persistent faith in privacy ultimately renders him passive before the forms of subjection that deny particular subjects the rights of liberal citizenship. If "the right to privacy" enshrines the liberal ideal of personhood and freedom, its very construction remains incommensurate with the forms of racial and sexual subjection that have targeted racialized migrants and sexual minorities in the post-civil-rights period. In "Beyond the Privacy Principle," legal scholar Kendall Thomas rereads *Bowers v. Hardwick*, the notorious Supreme Court case of 1986 that denied consensual gay sex the protection of the doctrine of constitutional privacy.[103] I reference Thomas's discussion here to suggest how a liberal defense of minority rights, as it appeals for state protection, may in fact legitimize a system of formal and informal sanctions that curtail the civil rights of certain groups. Thomas narrates the history of harassment and police terror leading up to Michael Hardwick's arrest in his bedroom for violating Georgia antisodomy statutes in order to argue against the "language and logic of sexual privacy" that dominated discussions of the case.[104] The arresting officer, Torick, systematically pursued Hardwick for weeks prior to his arrest; as a result, Thomas concludes, the separation of Hardwick's private sexual activity from his public sexual identity cannot hold as a defense of his constitutional rights. Hardwick was vulnerable before the law, Thomas argues, precisely because his homosexual identity made him susceptible to both sanctioned police surveillance and prosecution, and because of the "lawless and random aggression" of the beatings before his arrest.[105]

The criminalization of sexual difference, Thomas writes, is thus a matter of a complex "constellation of prohibitive practices" that interdicts identity with behavior, so that "the regnant emphasis on abstract, private personhood can never provide more than a partial account of the actual individual against whom . . . [various, constellated mechanisms of social control] operate."[106] Since the law permits, or actively provokes, violent recriminations against queer subjects, Thomas writes, "we must, in short, force privacy to go public."[107] Queer social movements have echoed this injunction by finding innovative ways to make the "private" domain of family relations, sex, and desire matters of public discourse.

The price of Rodriguez's admission into the "unmarked" public, then, is his passivity before the spectacle of state-sanctioned repression against immigrants, the urban underclass, and queer people. Both immigration status and sexual difference make subjects vulnerable to vigilante violence, as anti-immigrant and homophobic assaults have sought to maintain the subordinate status of these communities, in ways that confirm state interdictions against their membership to the protected sphere of citizenship. By consigning ethnicity and sexuality to the private sphere, Rodriguez became complicit with a regime of power that Thomas argues "enlists the unauthorized, unofficial disciplinary power of private actors and the authorized, official police power of state institutions" to curtail the exercise of full civil rights.[108] In maintaining the fiction of the private, Rodriguez places the political under erasure. In every case, his gestures of refusal position him less as the interlocutor for an expanded U.S. national culture than as the voice of conformity to the state, a public figure who embodies a sanctioned expression of minority subjectivity. Nancy Fraser reminds us that the public sphere of the liberal nation-state requires the pretense that interlocutors bracket "inequalities of status, set aside differences . . . and speak to one another 'as if' they were social and economic equals."[109] Rodriguez's retreat to individualism ultimately proves unsustainable. The "English-only" vision of national culture that he advocates would deprive migrant subjects of a vital resource for exercising rights beyond the boundaries of liberal citizenship.

But the systematic exclusion of difference from the national public sphere is not, and cannot be, absolute. Ethnic, sexual, or class difference is threatening to liberalism precisely because it *does* inhabit the public sphere, and it is dangerous not because it divides social space but because difference multiplies public space into *publics*. The migrant, the queer, and the urban poor traffic the gaps between the official and the indeterminate, remapping social space. Theirs is a politics not reducible to the silent privacy of Rodriguez's narration. They are not spoken for.

Nomadic Counterpublics

In closing, I turn to the poetry of Francisco X. Alarcón as a case for nomadic counterpublics—for locating political and cultural agency beyond the sanctioned boundaries of liberal nationalism. Like Richard Rodriguez, Alarcón is a writer possessed of a tremendous command of language, a gay resident of San Francisco, and the son of Mexican immigrants. But Alarcón demonstrates another mode of response to the experience that Rodriguez has marshaled to legitimate his strategy of representation. Alarcón's poetry is spare and measured, but finds lyricism in the shifting vocality of bilingualism:

soy	I am
un nómada	a nomad
en un país	in a country
de sedentarios	of settlers[110]

Alarcón writes of a life conditioned by difference, lived in the space of contradiction:

un nopal	a cactus
que florece	that flowers
en donde	where one
no se puede	can't
ni se debe	and shouldn't
florecer	flourish[111]

His strategy of self-inscription resists naming in favor of metaphors that rework and surpass oppositions. Always, he locates the "nomadism" of his "naturaleza criminal" within the social imperatives that define his separateness from the "unmarked" status of "los sedentarios" [the settled, sedentary ones]:

soy	I am
una herida	history's
todavía viva	fresh and
de la historia	living wound
mi crimen	my crime
ha sido ser	has been being
lo que he sido	what I've been
toda mi vida	all my life[112]

The "crime" (for Rodriguez as for Alarcón) is to be both a Latino immigrant and gay. Alarcón's nomadism captures his positioning both within and outside formations of family and nation. Alarcón's is a subjectivity that inhabits the wounding force of subjection but finds beauty there, in the flower of the nopal blooming amid the spines of cactus in dry earth.

Alarcón's aesthetic privileges the rearticulation of the terms of subjection through the reinscription of social space. Noncitizens may be barred from the official political sphere; they nonetheless create spaces of action throughout the migratory circuit.

Written from the Mission District of San Francisco, Alarcón's "Gramática/Grammar" codifies the law governing the Latina/o barrio as a nomadic counterpublic, peopled by migrants:

en mi mundo	in my world
hay poco lugar	there's little room
para adjetivos	for adjectives[113]

His is a grammar of immediacy, governed by necessity. The landscape is rendered in scenes of "beef stew / cooked daily / on stoves" and "clothes . . . / dried from windows," the domestic arts of transforming scarcity into plenty.[114] The poem enacts a project without completion, for

| en las calles queda | so much remains |
| tanto por nombrar | to name on the streets |

en mi mundo	in my world
todos los nombres	all names
se vuelven verbos	become verbs[115]

All names become verbs as the law of identity is subverted by the grammar of contingency. The condition of violation becomes the very possibility of movement and change, of vibrant conjugations in other publics:

y todos los verbos	and all the verbs
· se conjugan igual	conjugate the same
que el verbo "vida"	as the verb "life"[116]

PART II

Border
Crossings

Frontiers of New
Social Conflict

X-ray of truck entering United States with smuggled migrants. Photograph taken
June 20, 2000. (Sygma/Corbis)

CHAPTER 6

Narrative Acts

Fronteriza Stories of
Labor and Subjectivity

My name is María Guadalupe Torres Martínez.
I am from the city of Matamoros, Mexico, which
is on the border between Mexico and the United
States. . . . I started working in the maquiladora
twenty-eight years ago. I came from the town
of San Luis Potosí, which is in the interior of
Mexico. My mother came from the country and
I have always been a country woman at heart.
However, we had to leave San Luis Potosí to earn
a living—my mother was a widow and there was
no decent paying work for us where we lived. My
mother wanted us to go north toward the Mexican border because she wanted us to cross into
the United States to look for work there. In the
United States, we worked as domestic employees
in wealthy homes, but I never liked it. When we
found out the first maquiladora factories were
arriving in the border city of Matamoros, I said
to my mother, "Let's return to Mexico!" I thought
that since they were American factories, they
would pay well, and that the work would be
cleaner. I thought I was going to like it.
—María Guadalupe Torres Martínez (1995)[1]

María Guadalupe Torres Martínez nar-
rated her life of labor for the 1995 Global Tribunal on Accountability for

Women's Human Rights, in Huariou, China. She represented the global industrial workforce that had radically altered the social worlds of Asian, Latin American, and African women over the course of three decades. Torres's testimony on behalf of the Comité Fronterizo de Obreras [Border Committee of Women Workers] contributed to the United Nations–sponsored global campaign to expand human-rights protections for women and counter sexual and labor exploitation, human trafficking, and gender violence worldwide. The tribunal formed part of the United Nations Fourth World Conference on Women in Beijing, in which 189 governments, and over five thousand members of nongovernmental organizations set demands for fulfilling the promises of legal, economic, and cultural improvements in the status of women that were established at prior world conferences.

Torres opened her testimony on the labor struggles of Mexican women with an account of her insertion into the industrial labor force. Various narratives of gender intersected within Torres's biography: those of economic displacement, migration, urbanization, and the feminization of the border working class. But this obrera [female worker] did not merely describe the influence of these broader forces on an individual life; her testimony engaged in a struggle over their meaning and consequences far beyond the scope of her personal story. Her narrative exposed those human elements of desire, pain, and resiliency that resisted Torres's subjection by factory discipline. In her narrative, Torres's laboring body became the site from which she contested corporate and national ideologies of development and refuted the gendered and racialized structures of class domination at the Mexico-U.S. border.

A native of the rural altiplano of San Luis Potosí, María Guadalupe Torres's life history encompasses transformations in the Mexico-U.S. border region after 1965, when rapid industrialization drew mass migrations to northern Mexican cities for work in maquiladoras, or assembly plants.[2] Like many fronterizas [border women], her work experience included emigration for domestic work in the United States and a more permanent settlement in the border city. Her mother's widowhood initiated a trajectory of loss that ruptured the family's rural connections, altering her primary sense of self. If Torres had "always been a country woman at heart," the meanings of both gender and home were irrevocably changed in her journey north.

Torres's life story did not conform to the "regulative psychobiography" that industrialization imposes on women and migrants: for Torres, factory wages and the relative autonomy they bring did not mean progress over the life she left in her hometown.[3] Torres presented her work history in terms of her expectations of each situation and their eventual disappointment: she loved the countryside but found no viable employment; she rejected being a domestic employee in the United States; the maquiladoras were not the clean factories she had imagined. Her modest statement of what she expected to "like" in each job veils the profound dislocation and difficult adjustment, as each job entailed changes in residence, income, and political status. Torres hints at humiliations she chooses not to relate —the harassment and exploitation common to migrant women's labor experience. Her departure from "wealthy homes" implies her assertion of labor power within a limited framework of choice.

Torres's move into the maquiladoras remakes her subjectivity, however, as she is exposed to chemical and safety hazards in a factory operated by Kermet de México. The plant radically alters her sense of bodily integrity:

> I began work in a maquiladora factory called Kermet—a capacitor factory which was a subsidiary of Union Carbide. I remained at Kermet for eighteen years. I worked in many areas of the factory, but most of the time I was preparing epoxy, which is a kind of adhesive. Other workers didn't call me by my name, Lupita Torres, they called me Lupita Epoxy. Conditions in the maquiladora factory were primitive. We never had enough material to meet the production quotas. We had to invent ways of meeting them. For example, there were only 10 molds to make 3,000 pieces a day we were required to make, so we took the pieces out of the molds before they were cured. We burnt our hands every day —just to meet the production rate. Once in a while the ovens would overheat and explode, and everyone would run out of the factory in a panic.[4]

Torres becomes "Lupita Epoxy," a name that conveys the gothic humor of workers confronting the toxic conditions of the plants. The name Lupita Epoxy calls to mind an ultramodern superheroine, one whose special skill is wholly identified with the labor process. Like the superheroines of fiction, however, she finds that her powers bind her irrevocably to the demands

placed on her. They erase her given name; her private self as Lupita Torres becomes a constitutive absence. Her renaming relates the simultaneous transformation of her body as the toxins enter her bloodstream. The
chemicals that saturate her body mimic the process by which her work
consumes her identity. In contrast to the ultramodern image of the new
technology she produces, Torres finds the factory conditions primitive and
deficient. Obreras like Torres may deploy their inventive skill to meet production quotas at physical cost to themselves and to the ecology of the
border. Because they must get paid, they sometimes have to violate their
most basic interests. Economic need functions as a mechanism of corporate control and exploitation. In the maquiladoras, obreras contend with
labor conditions designed to make them feel like the consumer goods they
produce: expendable objects to be used up to the point of extinction. Torres relates the splitting of her consciousness from her body: "we burnt our
hands everyday," she says, describing conditions in which the obrera's body
and conscious will turn against each other.

The explosions in the ovens at Kermet, a subsidiary of Union Carbide,
conjure the chemical explosions and mass deaths that occurred in 1984 at
the Union Carbide plant in Bhopal, India. In the course of three days, leaks
at this pesticide factory killed 8,000 people and injured 120,000 others,
becoming emblematic of what Samir Amin termed "maldevelopment."[5]
In 1996, the International Medical Commission on Bhopal found that "as
many as 50,000 survivors may still be suffering from partial or total disabil-
ity as a consequence of the Bhopal disaster."[6] The industrial devastation of
Bhopal and the unregulated contamination of both workers' bodies and
the border landscape of Matamoros are inextricably linked; the mobility of
capital allows companies to recover far more quickly than the communities that house their operations. This regime of accumulation uses time
and space to differentiate the capitalist class from the laboring class—the
company enjoys a mobility and flexibility of time-keeping utterly different
from the tenure of a Mexican woman in the factory.[7] The obrera may mark
time by how long her body can endure the routine and may measure space
by the confinement of the industrial plant. This divergence in the qualita-
tive experience of time and space reflects how the postmodern phase of
global capitalism is not so much a rupture from the modern world order
but a reinauguration of its imperial design. The scene in Matamoros repeats, at a lesser scale, the horrors of Bhopal:

No one had ever told us that the liquids were dangerous—to this day the warning labels are always in English. Workers in the maquiladoras don't have time to go to school to learn other languages. In my workers' group I could see how my fellow workers hoped to put an end to poor working conditions by organizing. We took the warning label off one of the chemical barrels at Kermet and sent it to a church worker in New York. She explained to us that we were washing components with methylene chloride, a substance which causes miscarriages, cancer, and extreme skin irritation. I spent eighteen years washing components in methyl chloride, dipping my hands in it without gloves or any kind of protection. Finally I understood that the same substance that had been stripping the oils from the metal components had also been stripping my skin.[8]

For Torres, la toma de conciencia [coming to consciousness] is also the moment of reckoning with the loss of bodily integrity. Her growing awareness of class domination enacts a symbolic reentry into the body, as in their testimonies obreras set limits on corporate capital's access to their bodies.

In countering their construction as the "nimble fingers" and "fragmented bodies" of global assembly, obreras engage the rationality of development at the bodily site of its claim to their labor power and corporal agency. This chapter explores the uncertain terrain where obreras' stories of subjectivity contended with the regulatory force of the labor market and political economy during the 1980s, a period—as we have seen in the previous chapter—when neoliberal restructuring made the Mexico-U.S. border a highly contested site of class struggle for both countries. The border industries were a central, but mostly occluded, force in the politics of immigration and civil rights that Richard Rodriguez sought to capture in his writings. The highly profitable production system accelerated the social and economic transformations of U.S. labor markets and also linked the vastly disparate terrain of U.S. cities and border towns in a chain of production and consumption of far-reaching consequence for both countries. As I will show in these two final chapters, the border cities were a crucial locus of human transit within the migratory circuit, and developments at the border had a profound impact on the political life of both countries from the 1990s onward.

I begin this chapter by discussing the competing discourses that constructed Mexican women as the new class subject of the global assembly line: the "Third World woman," also known as the "global woman." I read the testimonials of obreras in relation to very different narratives—of development and capitalist expansion—that subjected migrants and border residents to the economic imperatives of free-market capitalism. Financial agreements that established free trade and economic integration in the region also stimulated labor migrations to and across the northern border. The North American Free Trade Agreement (NAFTA) of 1994 remade Mexican national space as maquilatitlán, a platform for cheap, feminized labor. In this era, migrant earnings became an ever-greater resource for the Mexican economy. The development of the maquiladora system and the concurrent feminization of the industrial and service labor force in the transborder region reconfigured the aims of Chicana feminism in the 1980s. That decade witnessed a renaissance in creative and critical writings by feminist women of color; these authors explored the subjective worlds of Third World women.

The chapter concludes with two narratives from the 1990s, by the Los Angeles poet Marisela Norte and the Chihuahuan author Rosario Sanmiguel, each of whom intervened—from alternate sides of the border—in cultural contests over the laboring bodies of fronterizas. Obrera testimonials and women's literature reveal a distinct female imaginary operating in the border space, one that moves with ambivalence and caution through competing claims of family, class, and nation in the transnational arena. Women and children are increasingly protagonists of the border crossing, rather than simply dependents left behind by male breadwinners. Their accounts reveal how social relations structuring kinship and community are not simply reconstructed over transnational space but often fail to provide sufficient refuge from the perils of the cross-border passage.

The Reorganization of Global Capitalism and the New Class Subject, 1973–1989

The world economic recession of 1973 spurred the dramatic reorganization of late-twentieth-century capitalism. The result, in David Harvey's words, was a shift toward a "new regime of accumulation, coupled with a quite different system of political and social regulation."[9] Industrialists sought to overcome the inefficiencies of Fordist systems of production by restructuring the labor process and dispersing manufacturing sites to industrializing nations that volunteered a ready supply of inexpensive workers.[10] The move toward what Harvey terms "flexible accumulation" was not based on the abandonment of assembly-line mass production but, rather, on its reorganization across geographical space.[11] These new factories, located on the periphery of the world's advanced capitalist consumer societies, may have taken advantage of technological innovations, satellite communications, new financial services, and emerging consumer markets, but they also exerted longstanding forms of labor control over a vastly dispersed population of workers. As the labor historian Jefferson Cowie demonstrated in his study of electronic giant RCA, the migration of capital within and across national boundaries was part of a "continuous struggle to maintain the social conditions deemed necessary for profitability," which permitted companies to transfer their adjustment costs to working-class communities.[12] Capital mobility during the 1970s and 1980s remade the international division of labor, when outsourcing and so-called offshore manufacturing allowed companies to pursue a tightening profit margin by demanding new concessions from workers. Companies managed volatile markets by coordinating highly differentiated modes of production and segmented labor markets across a wider geographical terrain, forcing workers to adapt to new levels of job competition, a degradation of skilled labor, and the erosion of union power.

The resurgence of multinational capital during this period necessitated the recruitment and consolidation of a new global workforce; in the electronics and textile industries, this population tended to be young, immigrant, and female.[13] Sweatshops in the "global cities" of Los Angeles, Miami, and New York employed Filipina, Chinese, Korean, and Vietnamese women alongside Latina workers from the Caribbean, Central America, and Mexico.[14] Many more thousands of workers migrated from small towns and rural zones to urban factories within the Caribbean, the Philippines, and Mexico; these migrations, as Saskia Sassen and others have shown, revealed that the vast mobility of labor corresponded to the movements of capital.[15] Although women of color were not new to the industrial workforce, women from Africa, Asia, and Latin America played a highly visible part in the reformation of industrial production worldwide.[16]

The capitalist fantasy of a pliable global workforce necessitated the invention and recruitment of the new class subject, the "Third World/global woman."[17] This category, located between tradition and modernity, gained significance both as a figure of acquiescence and contestation in the interwoven systems of representation and systems of production that devised the new international division of labor. The capitalist discourse of *flexibility* that financiers used (to describe corporate design and the new systems of accumulation) found its echo in political rhetoric about the emerging power of women in the "developing world."[18] Transformations in countries with high indexes of poverty and weak economies brought the agency of poor women—as breadwinners, as nurturers, and as producers of social change—into relief precisely at a moment of impasse in standard economic models for growth and development. Policymakers associated women's multiple responsibilities for familial welfare and economic survival with particularly female virtues of creativity, resourcefulness, and pragmatism.

But this construction of global, racialized womanhood had an even broader purchase in the terrains of culture and global civil society. Investment in export-processing zones occurred precisely as the United Nations launched its Decade for Women (1976–1985) with an international mandate for "integrating women into development."[19] Feminist critiques of traditional economics, most notably Ester Boserup's *Women's Role in Economic Development*, as well as those raised by international feminist movements, focused new attention on women's productive and reproductive labors.[20] Feminists countered the patriarchal structure of economic models by arguing that women's subordinate economic status and political marginality was not a function of inherent cultural or gender traits but a function of patriarchal oppression and male bias in political and economic structures.[21]

Still, as many critics of development noted, feminists concerned about the status of Third World women were often insufficiently critical of developmentalist rationality itself. Arturo Escobar has argued that "development" constitutes "the historically produced discourse" that emerged in the post–World War II era "as an extremely efficient apparatus for producing knowledge about, and the exercise of power over, . . . subject peoples."[22] If we take Escobar's definition, then the incorporation of women into the framework of development merely extended the legitimacy of development through the uncertainties of the capitalist crisis of the 1970s. Development agencies and international financial institutions set their sights on poor racialized women as a new category of need, as clients for development. This opened new avenues for cultural and economic intervention in dependent states. In an effort to strengthen women's economic agency, development projects designated domestic and informal economic spheres as sites of investment. These programs often met vital practical aims and challenged the primacy of male wage-earning power in development models. Still, their aggregate effect was to forestall more radical assaults on economic inequality, as development bureaucracy (what James Ferguson termed the "anti-politics machine") produced a homogenized subject, the "Third World woman" as its client.[23]

The pervasive representation of women of color as the "cultural and composite Other of western modernity" all too often displaced class and anti-imperial critiques of women of color's particular relationship to processes of global economic restructuring.[24] A news article from the UN conference in Beijing, entitled "The Second Sex in the Third World," demonstrated how the turn toward "small production units" of women and peasants in development programs during the 1980s exemplified this revival of colonial rationality, a rationality that fixed racialized women within a particularly rigid account of female agency. Responding to controversies among conference participants, journalist Barbara Crossette reported,

> While women in the rich nations bicker over history, women in the poor ones fight for goats and tools. . . . In the last few years a bold new idea has caught on—that women are the key to development. . . . Poor women turn out to be surprisingly good investments everywhere.[25]

Even as Crossette wrote with intended irony about the splintering of female solidarity at the Beijing conference, her depiction cast the gendered struggles of poor women within a limited frame of development, separating economic need ("goats and tools") from ideology ("history"). As an isolated category of social agent, "poor women" simultaneously expands the possibility of development by integrating new actors into its field of operations and serves as development's limit, a reminder of all that stands outside its influence. The development imperative remains unexamined in Crossette's account; the pragmatism of solving immediate hungers with "good investments" displaces the more fundamental question of how inequality continues to be produced and managed in a global economic field.

Multinational operations followed the same developmentalist rationales in their recruitment of poor, racialized women into the industrial workforce: these women, contractors also argued, were good investments. Garment and electronics assembly followed a longstanding industrial trend of feminizing those labors that mimicked domestic tasks, as companies sought to exploit the greatest advantage in labor control by recruiting workers with a subordinate status in the labor market.[26] But the location of these factories mattered as well: managers could exploit the economic needs that made women available to work at home, to do "piecework," and informal services that extended beyond the space of the factory and increased the flexibility of production. At the onset of the new export-processing system in the mid-1960s, the economic linkages between multinational corporations and factories in industrializing countries followed established patterns of colonial extraction: companies employed poor workers for labor-intensive operations, manufacturing commodities on the other side of the border for consumption by advanced capitalist countries. Rather than mechanize assembly, corporations increased their profits by obtaining labor at lowest cost, with minimal investment.[27]

The contract between host nations and foreign investors relied on a shared conception of who the ideal worker was for the rigors of the assembly line. In the new factories, the labor process was fragmented into a series of minute, timed, and repetitive tasks; the gendered and racialized labor market required the simultaneous fragmentation of the laboring body into "nimble fingers" and "watchful eyes."[28] In Mexico, contractors recruited "jóvenes, bonitas, y baratas" [young, pretty, and cheap women] on the assumption not only that young women were less likely to join unions or demand a family wage but that they were conditioned by nature and society to perform labor requiring dexterity and care.[29] A factory supervisor in Ciudad Juárez articulated the managerial discourse of "nimble fingers" typical to this period of export processing:

These women have natural qualities that make them ideal for these types of jobs; their delicate hands allow them greater precision in carrying out the minute procedures. . . . Furthermore, women are more psychologically suited for repetitive tedious tasks.[30]

Such claims legitimated the exploitative design of the labor process. Even more damaging, they also undercut women's labor power by transferring restrictive patriarchal ideologies onto the scene of production. The sexism that devalued the unpaid domestic work of women was built into the construction of the factory line. The managerial discourse of "nimble fingers" represented Third World women's high levels of productivity as an effect of innate racial and gender traits; managers defined these qualities not as skills but as the inevitable social conditioning that happened to be ideal for factory work. Managers cast themselves in a tutelary role with their female employees, claiming that they were improving women's status by giving them skills and training along with decent wages.[31] Such a posture masked the deliberate recomposition of race and gender difference *within* the labor process and the organizational structure of the corporation. The forms of capitalist discipline that required workers to endure monotony and repetition in the fragmented productive process relied on a neocolonial configuration of capital in relation to Third World women's bodies.

Viewed together, it becomes clear how the rationale of both development and industrial discourses redefined and reinforced the perceived racial and gender difference of Third World women, in order to harness it as an economic resource during the capitalist restructuring of the 1970s. The metaphors of freedom used by development agencies and corporations alike—in which they depicted market-led modernization as a key to educational advancement and material gain—masked a more archaic system of labor extraction tied to the appropriation of poor women's bodies. In this process, the nation-state played a critical role in the procurement and regulation of the ideal labor force. At the Mexico-U.S. border, the relative proximity of the "Third World" to the consumer market and investor companies intensified the neocolonial relationship between the development scheme and the exploitation of women's labor power. Spectacular levels of productivity in the plants became legendary: "With Mexican girls," a plant manager reported to the scholar Devon Peña, "I can double or triple production every six or eight weeks."[32]

Maquilatitlán

The Mexican government established the Border Industrialization Program in 1965 to provide employment for returning male emigrants at the end of the Bracero Program. Despite this design, the maquiladoras employed a predominantly female workforce through the 1970s and into the mid-1980s. Mexican officials promoted Mexican obreras in terms that tied female productivity to modernization and growth. In 1982, when Mexico's political economy virtually collapsed, the state used the obreras' cheap labor as a lure to attract much-needed foreign investment. By the late 1980s, the expansion of the maquiladora sector brought greater parity in the numbers of men and women employed in the factories; nevertheless, the factories were strictly segregated by gender, continuing the feminization of various manufacturing sectors. Not only did the export-processing zones transform the Mexican economy; they also became essential to the reorganization of the gendered division of labor in the region. Women's industrial work made them the vulnerable, and mostly invisible, partners in the volatile processes of economic and political integration that linked the maquiladoras with multinational investors, Mexican industrialists, and two national governments.

An advertisement from a handbook for maquiladora investors, from the mid-1980s, clearly exploits the uncertainties of economic restructuring for the debt-ridden nation. The corporation, Grupo Frisa, promotes its excellence as a "constructora de ciudades" [builder of cities], a function that aligns its services to investor firms with the task of social engineering. "Spatial products," writes Keller Easterling, "are imbued with myths, desires, and symbolic capital. . . . their recipes for organization are also recipes for political constitution, and the disposition of that organization embodies a capacity for collusion, persuasion, and aggression."[33] Frisa manages the desires of a market system for limitless production, in which untrammeled growth is an end in itself, a goal symbolically aligned with progress, order, and innovation; its spatial plans impose a grid of legibility and control over the disordered landscape of Tijuana, where the industrial parks sit like islands amid the sprawl of shantytowns, open waste sites, and the contaminated Río Bravo. The unruly bodies of migrants and poor women enter the plants and are reconfigured as productive beings.[34]

In the advertisement, Frisa industrial parks appear as the central architecture of a new, progressive Mexico, but ultimately, national imperatives recede before the demands of capital, as the ad proclaims, "Sus parques industriales cumplen con las más altas expectativas que requiere el mercado" [Our industrial parks meet the highest expectations that the market requires]. The advertisement exploits the new program for national development, reflecting how the liberalization of the Mexican economy following the debt crisis of 1982 oriented the nation-state and private entrepreneurs alike to the vicissitudes of the international market. Just as Frisa offers an array of secondary services to industrialists in East Asia, Europe, and the United States—by arranging for financing, property insurance, and building permits—its marketing mimics government efforts to promote Mexico as a viable site for foreign investment.

In fact, Frisa marketing is itself a form of diplomacy: the advertisement mutes a description of the company itself in favor of an argument for locating industrial operations in Mexico. The corporate logo appears at the bottom of the page, with only the briefest suggestion of what Frisa actually sells: "Industrial Parks, Facilities, Construction, Consulting." As the operators of one of the largest industrial centers in Tijuana, Baja California, the company appears far more concerned with the image of Mexico than its own competitive status in the building industry. The image stages a confrontation between two moments of national transition—using the terms "Mexico Then" and "Mexico Now"—and their distinct ideologies of modernization. Political observers depicted the neoliberal programs of the 1980s as "Mexico's second revolution" not so much for their promise of social advancement but for their stark contrast to the revolution of 1910.[35] Whereas the nation-building reforms of the Mexican Revolution promoted economic restructuring in the name of redistributive reforms, the austerity programs of the 1980s subordinated social reform to economic growth. The advertisement thus aligns the interests of foreign investors (North American, European, Japanese, and Korean) with the antistatist tenets of economic liberalization, contrasting them with the economic nationalism of the postrevolutionary period. "Mexico Then" depicts a dirty, disorderly work scene with machinery suggestive of the contested petroleum enterprises nationalized by Cardenas in the 1930s. As the male workers gaze confrontationally at the camera, their somber faces threaten an unruly, unproductive workforce, the products of a degenerate Mexico. The anti-imperialist, anticapitalist threat captured by the photograph is the masculine image of Mexican nationalism and trade unionism.

Half a century later, "Mexico Now" illustrates a new vision of a cooperative partnership between domestic and foreign capital. Men no longer occupy the center of the frame, having been replaced by women as the primary workers in export processing. (Men are only present at the margins of the image, as the technicians of the new industrial plants.) The women stand in a straight row in white lab coats, their heads bent before the advanced technologies of the new factory system. They are the vision of an efficient and submissive workforce, the embodiment of productivity. The image promises that modernization will arrive with a harmonious relationship between the state, the productive obreras, and multinational investors. Even the light emanating from the clean workroom suggests progress. "Times have changed south of the U.S. border," the ad states (interestingly erasing Mexican national space), signaling that, under the hegemony of neoliberal reform, Mexican industry is once more a safe investment. Most important, the feminization of the workforce signals the feminized posture of the nation toward foreign trade partners as Mexico transitions to an open economy.

This advertisement reveals the gendered implications of state development for women's political identities as citizens and as workers. Development strategies are themselves an ideological projection, as we have seen, of a particular distribution of wealth and route toward capital accumulation. That is, they articulate class interests through the arrangement of productive and reproductive processes within a seemingly "neutral" regulatory framework.

Even as neoliberal policies dictated the transfer of state enterprise to private control, the liberal version of capitalist growth has not meant the shrinking of state authoritarianism. It has meant quite the opposite, as President Miguel de la Madrid made clear in a 1983 address before the Mexican congress. Discussing the themes of women and development, de la Madrid ignored the actual participation of women and their class interests:

I would not wish to omit to mention in a direct manner the essential topic of [the Mexican] woman . . . to underline the centrality of her role

in society, its transcendental importance as well as its insufficient protection at a practical level. [Her] role is decisive in the maintenance
and strengthening of our principles, values, and familiar and social
structures. Responsible for the sustenance and preservation of our traditions, [the Mexican] woman cannot continue to be the object of our
prejudices.[36]

Though already in the second decade of maquiladora production, the voice
of the state refuses to modify the essentially masculinist formula of development. De la Madrid depicts the Mexican woman solely in terms of her
service to others, just as state discourses often negate women's political
interests even as they avow the centrality of women to the preservation
of the nation-state. The phrase "her *transcendental* importance" denies
women a *corporal* presence as national subjects; the deliberate erasure of
women from the public sphere is a function of their coercion within it. Developmentalism, which insists that the capitalist wage system will usher
women into productive citizenship, legitimated the state's wholesale transfer of the burdens of economic restructuring to poor women. In the 1980s,
the worsening debt crisis in Mexico forced women and adolescent girls
to assume primary responsibilities both as wage earners and as provid-
ers of the unwaged domestic labors that would ensure their households'
survival.[37]

During the 1990s, the maquiladoras continued to expand, leading independent unionists in Mexico to question the commitment of the Mexican
government to state-led development. Neoliberal policies, argued critics,
journalists, and satirists alike, had converted the Mexican homeland into
Maquilatitlán [Maquilaland]—a platform for cheap labor.[38] In the early
2000s, the newspaper *La Jornada* published its indictments of the maquiladora system online in its edition *La Jornada Sin Fronteras* (this edition features news geared to issues of emigration, social conflict, and international solidarity). For the writers of *Jornada Sin Fronteras*, emigrants
constitute el otro México [the other Mexico], co-nationals who inhabit
the boundaryless terrain of the global market. In articles such as "Los
derechos del que migra y el derecho de no migrar" [The Rights of the Migrant and the Right Not to Migrate], journalists and unionists stage a contest over the absent body of labor—both those who experience the erosion of their labor power in the border factories and those who depart the

Still image from the 2006 documentary film *Maquilapolis* (City of Factories). Carmen Durán and other factory workers display the products they
assemble. Photo by David Maung. (Courtesty of filmmakers Vicky Funari
and Sergio de la Torre)

nation-space altogether.[39] At the heart of their concern are the "hijas de
Maquilatitlán" [daughters of Maquilaland]: girls recruited into the global
assembly in direct violation of their rights as Mexican citizens. "Acá su-
frimos bien harto" [Here we suffer hard], comments Teresa, a fourteen-
year-old garment worker at a costume factory in Tepeji del Río, Hidalgo,
telling her interviewer, "Todavía tengo sueños de niña" [I still have a girl's
dreams].[40] However paternalistic the journalist's posture toward the young
obreras, Teresa's response resonates beyond the limited frame of the article. Her account relates a precocious awareness of the subjective split that
her labor imposes: she is both obrera *and* child. Her membership to one
category, the working class, annihilates the other, that of childhood. Sewing Halloween costumes for export in an unregulated maquiladora both
threatens her adolescent laboring body and enacts the symbolic destruction of her "sueños de niña." Like Lupita Epoxy, Teresa experiences factory discipline as a threat to her integral self, as the abstract labor relation
both materially and symbolically impinge on the autonomy of her body.
Teresa's struggle to retain her girlhood—even in fantasy—punctures the

capitalist fantasy that constructs her as a body available for appropriation, mere "nimble fingers" detached from consciousness.

Testimonials of the Laboring Body

Discourses about the "Third World woman" during the United Nations Decade for Women were not a one-way conversation, however. Throughout the 1980s, working-class and poor women from across Latin America demanded the democratization of their societies in a variety of social movements linked to urban conflicts, housing, ecology, labor, and citizenship. The Mexican maquiladoras also produced a subaltern discourse, contesting the state's corporate authority. Telling their stories through union-organizing drives, human-rights forums, the media, and ethnographic studies, obreras anchored their labor politics in the laboring body. The forms of embodied consciousness that obreras articulated in their accounts of the labor process revealed how capitalist discipline relied on the very humanity of the workers that companies sought to control.

During the mid-1980s, the writer Sandra Arenal conducted interviews with garment and electronics workers of northern Mexico, which were published in 1986 in the volume *Sangre joven: Las maquiladoras por dentro* [Young Blood: Inside the Maquiladoras].[41] Born in Mexico City in 1936, in the 1960s Arenal moved to Monterrey, Nuevo León, where she wrote on behalf of labor causes, subaltern groups, and the rights of children. Arenal, who wrote in the tradition of the Mexican left (and was connected at one time to the Mexican Communist Party), adopted the form of the testimonio in her panoramic chronicles of popular struggle. *Sangre joven* indicted the maquiladoras for their systematic abuses of women's labor rights, in a project of direct advocacy for women normally absent from national politics. But Arenal's principal concern was to negate the notion that Mexican women were merely docile members of the new labor economy. In his preface, Fernando Carmona assured readers, "La mayoría de las 200 mil trabajadoras de esta reciente forma de explotación no volverán a ser nunca 'abnegadas' y 'sufridas' mujeres mexicanas" [The majority of the two hundred thousand workers in this recent form of exploitation will never revert to being "self-sacrificing" and "suffering" Mexican women].[42]

For Carmona, as for Arenal, women's exposure to wage discipline, however harsh, had made them unable to conform to patriarchal gender codes. In this belief, Arenal shared the Marxist faith that proletarianization could function as a developmental project; it initiated the concientización [coming to consciousness] of women otherwise invisible to the public realm of national life.

Arenal's text retains the oral character of the testimonial form and mutes her own authorship in favor of her subjects. The book consists of fifteen narratives, under headings excerpted directly from the interviews, such as "El trabajo en sí no es pesado" [The Work in Itself Is Not Burdensome] and "me gustaba mucho bailar" [I Used to Love Dancing]. Although Arenal provided little information about the text's production, she emphasized her interest in "creación colectiva" [collective creation], so that the orality of the text becomes a collaborative exposition of the labor struggle within the plants. As such, Arenal's narrative authority evaded entirely the prevailing national debate about the maquiladoras, which focused simply on whether they were good or bad for the Mexican economy, or for women. "Como no somos economistas ni estudiosas del tema," Arenal wrote, "no damos nuestra opinión al respecto" [Since we are neither economists nor students of the subject, we do not give our opinion on this issue].[43] Instead, her text proposes to use obreras' narratives to illustrate "el drama cotidiano" [the daily drama] of "el ejército de 200 mil personas" [the army of two hundred thousand people] as a means to insert obreras into national discussions of economic crisis and dependency on U.S. capital. Behind her apparent deferral to academic authority, Arenal staged a collective demand to shift the discourse on development. For the author and her collaborators, the purely economic questions mattered less than the social and political status of women within the national project underwriting the maquiladora system. As a gesture of political contestation, *Sangre joven* presented an alternate view of Mexico's political economy, theorized through the laboring bodies of the obreras. The testimonies made obreras visible not in aggregate as a factor of production but in the full plurality of their lived experiences.

The obreras' testimonials elaborate women's sense of displacement from their own laboring bodies; their bodies are not entirely their own but become the crossroads between productive and reproductive labors, formal and informal economies, private and public subjection to patriarchal authority.[44] Through their litanies of physical pain, obreras refuse the instrumental value assigned to their productive capacity. The testimonio converts the sometimes compliant body into a figure of defiance. Obreras narrate their coming to consciousness as political agents through a discourse of the body, opposing its material needs and hungers to the logic of capital accumulation and masculinist authority. The circulation of workers' discourses about their bodies contains a protracted negotiation with what Foucault named the "microphysics of power":[45]

> Tengo 22 años, llevo trabajando seis años en las maquilas, he durado más que otras—nos dice, al tiempo que nos muestra sus manos: dedos con deformaciones en los huesos y con un enorme callo que le va de la punta del dedo pulgar (de los dos) por el dorso, casí hasta la muñeca, de color amarilliento café (como si fueran capas superpuestas de piel, una encima de la otra). Ante nuestra expresión agrega: "Éste es el costo de trabajar ahí."

> ["I am twenty-two years old, and have been working in the maquila for six years. I've lasted longer than the others," she says, at the same time showing us her hands: fingers deformed in the bones, with enormous calluses stretching the length of both her forefingers to her wrists, a yellow-coffee color. (They look as if they were formed by layers of skin, one layer over another.) Responding to our expression, she adds, "This is the cost of working there."][46]

This exchange between Arenal and the obrera involves the reader in a scene of horrific revelation, as the young woman unmasks the violence of the factory. "I've lasted longer than others" and "This is the cost of working there" are neutral, self-effacing statements that become testaments of wounding when joined to her deformed hands. Her wounded body speaks where her speech withholds her story. Arenal's text records the relay of the message, from the young woman's body to the gaze of the interviewers and to the reader, forming a circuit of communication that is both within and outside language. As the obrera exposes her injury, she implicates her readers in the economy of bodies that sustains the market in consumer goods: she has paid her price for her job, but her readers must also pay theirs. In this sense, the production of the book is itself an act of contestation to the obreras' other productive labors. The book circulates as a commodity, but unlike most commodities, which lose value as they are used, this book accrues value through consumption. The symbolic function of the testimonio is to restore the obrera's body as a locus of value, a value not determined by her productive capacity but by her social relatedness. In compelling readers to react, the testimonio seeks to construct a prosthetic body, one that can stand in for the wounded body of the obrera.

Deploying a discourse of pain, obrera testimonials expose circuits of production and exchange that target the laboring body as a locus of value. But they also depict the women's protracted, bodily engagement with the external authorities that also have an effect on the assembly process: the corporate and police surveillance, border checkpoints, and immigration institutions that define obreras' residency in the border space. Whether or not the stories that women recount of cancers, physical impairment, and anxiety are statistically representative of actual factory conditions, their performance enacts a form of oppositional consciousness that opposes the materiality of the body, its debility, to the abstractions of economic rationality and scientific management. The circuits of rumor and suggestion about sudden deaths in the plants, about the toxicity of solvents, reveal how the labor process functions as a crucial site of conflict in the reproduction of social relations of dominance. The factory not only produces consumer goods; it also aims to produce proper subjects who will conform to social relations of consumption and exchange. The laboring body sets its own limits on this rhetoric of capitalist domination on the global assembly line—flexibility, mobility, and productivity without end:

> Yo soy de familia campesina, mi padre es jornalero . . . me vine a trabajar cuando me enteré que para hacerlo no exigían estudios sino solamente saber leer y escribir un poco y tener más de 16 años. Me presenté y me aceptaron.
>
> Cuando me presenté luego luego me sentaron a una máquina a coser y ya desde los quince días me exigían cuota, pero yo no podía por más que me apuraba, así que me sentía muy mal, me presionaban mucho. Me acuerdo mucho todo los días me exigían más y más y yo no podía darla.

Aquí ni siquiera la preparen a uno bien, la cambian de lugar sin más ni más, exigiendo que una sola aprenda, así que nos quedábamos, a veces, hasta las nueve o diez de la noche y no nos pagaban horas extras.

[I come from a rural family, my father is a dayworker. . . . I came to work [in the maquiladoras] when I found out that the factories did not require much education, that employees only need to know how to be able to read and write a little bit, and to be over sixteen years old. I applied and they accepted me. When I started, sooner or later they sat me down at a sewing machine and after fifteen days they expected me to meet the quota, but I couldn't do it, no matter how fast I worked, and so I felt really bad because they pressured me a lot. I remember that they demanded more and more from me every day and I couldn't give it to them. Here they don't even prepare you very well, and they move you around without notice, expecting you to learn by yourself, so sometimes we used to stay as late as nine or ten at night, and they wouldn't pay us overtime.][47]

The young seamstress refuses her subjection as mere nimble fingers. Her narrative of selfhood begins in negation: for the campesina, entry into the factory is a function of displacement, from the familiar landscape of interior Mexico and from the protection of her father's role as primary wage-earner. The repeated pressure from the managers to make the quota enacts a scene of failed interpellation: "I couldn't do it no matter how fast I worked." Despite the futility of their demand, the factory managers insist on the quota, converting the factory into a theater of social conflict waged over the women's bodies. The obrera comes to understand that she herself is under production, forced to internalize the profit imperative.

In the factory, market rationality dissolves as the discipline becomes useless suffering:

Al principio cuando entré y ahora lo vi con mi hermana cuando la traje, yo tuve muchos meses pesadillas. Como creía que sólo a mí me pasaba, me daba harta vergüenza y a nadie le contaba, y me aguantaba en las noches cuando soñaba que unas enormes tijeras se me venían encima y me perseguían, y yo veía sus picos que se me iban a clavar en el pecho y entonces gritaba y veía a mi compañera de al lado cosiendo, clavada

en su máquina y yo por más que le gritaba no lograba que volteara,
era horrible, porque se repetía muchas veces y por muchos meses tuve
esos sueños; incluso llegué a pensar que me estaba volviendo loca, así
que mejor me callaba, me daba vergüenza platicarlo, además ya no me
hubieran dejado venir, así que mejor me callaba . . . Ahora resulta que
todas creíamos que nos estábamos volviendo locas. ¡Qué barbaridad!
¿Verdad?

[At first when I started, and now I saw it in my sister when I brought
her, I had nightmares for many months. Because I thought that they
were only happening to me, I was very embarrassed and didn't tell anyone, and put up with them at night, when I would dream that some
gigantic scissors were coming at me, hunting me, and I could see that
their points were going to stab me in the chest, so I would cry out, and
I saw my co-worker sewing next to me, pinned to her machine, but no
matter how hard I yelled, she wouldn't turn around. It was horrible, because the dream was repeated many times and so for many months I
had those nightmares, I even began to think that I was going crazy, so
I kept my mouth shut, I was ashamed to speak of it, and anyway, they
wouldn't have allowed me to continue, so it was better that I keep quiet.
Now it turns out that all of us thought we were going crazy. How cruel!
Right?][48]

The nightmare image of the scissors makes literal the potential bodily
harm from the physical hazards of the repetitive motions of deskilled production. The obrera experiences the "terror of the machine" precisely as the
U.S. industrialists Frederick Taylor and Henry Ford imagined them.[49] Their
discourses of scientific management conceived of an ideal workforce for
whom "repetitive operations hold no terrors."[50] But in Ciudad Juárez, as in
Los Angeles, Fuzhou, or Manila, obreras understand the wage relationship
as one of sanctioned violence. The scissors, representing the technology
of garment cutting, doubles as the threat of both physical fragmentation
and psychic fracture, as the obrera comes to doubt her own sanity. But her
encounter with the sinister machinery of her exploitation is also the scene
of her repression: in the dream she cannot make her co-worker hear her,
and in her waking hours she remains silent about her night terrors lest she
lose her job. The testimonial narrative enacts a final cutting, as the speaker

separates herself from her prior self, the obrera whose silence permitted and extended the relations of power in the plant.

Obreras' testimonials narrate the slow disintegration of the body, the evacuation of its force, and the concurrent loss of identity and motive will. Writing about the mechanics of torture, Elaine Scarry tells us that extreme physical pain "destroys a person's self and world, a destruction experienced spatially as either the contraction of the universe down to the immediate vicinity of the body or as the body swelling to fill the entire universe." Bodily pain obliterates language along with the self, so that for Scarry, "that which would express and project the self is robbed of its source and subject."[51] As the testimonial narrates the monstrosity of a body violated by agents for which the worker has no names or proof, the experience becomes an allegory for the place of women in the neoliberal regime of development and capital accumulation. For the obrera, the terrors of the machine entail the theft of her capacity to command the self, her voice, and the meaning of her labors; and yet the testimonial can effect a kind of reversal. As the obrera uses her pain to indict the sped-up labor process, she articulates an alternate account of female value and integral personhood. As the impaired body begins to speak itself against appropriation, it becomes the source of a contestatory agency, however fragile, for establishing a new ecology in the border space.

Chicana Feminism in the Integrated Circuit

If, as Donna Haraway writes, "the machine is us, our processes, an aspect of our embodiment," then we must attend to the particular terms of that embodiment.[52] The publication in 1985 of "A Manifesto for Cyborgs," Haraway's treatise on gender, technology, and power, elaborated a new feminist imaginary for the regime of flexible accumulation, anchored in the figure of the cyborg. This cybernetic organism, a hybrid of body and machine recasts the "Third World/woman of color" of global assembly as the figure for a radical nonunitary agency: "'women of color,'" Haraway wrote, "might be understood as a cyborg identity, a potent subjectivity synthesized from fusions of outsider identities."[53] Within the cyborg "myth," the relative social marginality of women of color, and their difference from privileged categories of whiteness and maleness, offers the prototype of an oppositional agency. Haraway predicated her claims for the power of the cyborg on what Chela Sandoval termed "flexible identity."[54] Chicana feminist writings were central to Haraway's formulation of the woman of color as *outsider*.[55] But, we must ask, an outsider to whom? And from what places? The "integrated circuit" of Haraway's imagining dissolves into texts and surfaces in a mobile series of associations: "young Korean women in the sex industry and in electronics assembly," "U.S. black women," "home-workers," and even La Malinche. In offering this decontextualized array of references, Haraway mimics the processes of information retrieval and sig-nification that define "the informatics of domination," the tactics that she ascribes to global capitalism.[56]

"A Cyborg Manifesto" is a provocation to practice a new order of soli-darity appropriate to the technological age, what Donna Haraway use-fully termed "affinity politics." Her repudiation of identity politics opens a broader field of social action by recognizing the plural and contingent nature of subjectivity under late capitalism. In 1985, Haraway read the de-colonizing project of Chicana feminism as a model for the radical revision of the unitary subject of liberal humanism, a humanism complicit with capitalist, imperial, and patriarchal domination. Haraway reminded her readers of their complex interconnections in a global network of alliances —which she called "the integrated circuit" of global capitalism. These alli-ances have been produced not only by political and social relations of in-equality, but by the technological processes that remade the environment and the body, making them available to operations of power on an unprec-edented scale. The machine is us.[57]

And yet Haraway's vision fails to engage with the obreras' own pro-tracted struggle to enunciate their opposition to capitalist domination. The obreras seek their agency from another place in the integrated circuit: not the place of information retrieval or writing but the place where the motherboards and circuitry were made under harsh production quotas. The "Manifesto" figured the political energies of women of color by re-course to language that mimics precisely those functions of assembly and disassembly that obreras performed in global factories, so that the bound-ary between their own narrative of subjectivity and the capitalist fantasy disappeared. The obreras of Arenal's volume of interviews narrated the splitting of consciousness in ways that complicate the idealization of nonunitary subjectivity; at the very least, their performance marked a gap between the flexibility of subjectivity as it was lived in the maquiladora and as it was enunciated within the emancipatory projects of women-of-color feminists in the United States. For the seamstress who dreamt that her co-worker was absorbed into the sewing machine, the cyborg represents a capitalist nightmare that threatens her embodied self with annihilation: the common refrain in Arenal's volume is "we are not robots."

During the 1980s, Chicana feminists contended with the postmodern cultural turn with perhaps more trepidation than Haraway's "Manifesto" suggests. Following the civil-rights movement, Chicana scholars developed new critical perspectives on power and subjectivity. The decade marked a watershed in feminist and lesbian scholarship; the publication in 1987 of Gloria Anzaldúa's *Borderlands/La frontera* articulated a new discourse of border subjectivity linked to the "new mestiza."[58] Through the Third Woman Press, the preeminent Chicana scholar and editor Norma Alarcón published over thirty works by Latinas and other women of color, creating a new field of knowledge at the intersections of feminist and ethnic studies.[59] Drawing on the same migrant imaginary that had animated the efforts of Emma Tenayuca and Luisa Moreno before them, Chicana feminists reclaimed the liminal space of the borderlands as a site from which to intervene in nationalist and patriarchal discourses. Their theories contended with geopolitical boundary that defined them as misplaced subjects, caught between two, unequal nation-states. Just as pressingly, the border served as a metaphor for the conflicted site where race, gender, sexual, and class power materialized in relations of domination and exclusion. The critic Sonia Saldívar-Hull called for Chicana feminism to be a "bridge feminism," arguing that it could connect the First and Third Worlds through the figure of the migrant woman of color. Her work affirmed the stake of Mexican American women in a cultural politics "that deconstructs geopolitical boundaries," as it recognizes and protects the precarious agency of the migrants who traverse national borders.[60] For Norma Alarcón, a new emancipatory politics followed from Chicanas' distinct formation in the border space: Chicanas come to critical consciousness by acknowledging that they are both citizen *and* noncitizen, Mexican *and* non-Mexican, inhabitants of an in-between space that disrupts the boundaries of First and Third Worlds. For all these reasons, she argued, the very notion of political agency had to be revised to accommodate a historical consciousness forged in the "multiple migrations and displacements of women of 'Mexican' descent."[61] Saldívar-Hull's bridge feminism subverted the boundaries of citizenship that marginalized Mexican women and Chicanas alike as she charted the global terrain of solidarity, born out of a commitment to working through difference and to overturning the imagined homogeneity of the national community.

Rather than privilege the autonomous, self-constituted sovereign subject, Chicana feminism drew agency from the shifting lines of identities engendered and raced in "los intersticios" [the interstices]. Anzaldúa wrote,

> In the Borderlands
> you are the battleground
> where enemies are kin to each other;
> you are at home, a stranger,
> the border disputes have been settled
> the volley of shots have shattered the truce
> you are wounded, lost in action
> dead, fighting back.[62]

The long history of border conflict inscribed its violence directly on the body, a mestizaje born of contradiction and ambivalence. Gloria Anzaldúa described a condition of absolute negation, a subject "wounded, lost in action" as the source of a differential agency that was "dead, fighting back." In *Borderlands*, she used the figure of the wounded mestiza body to demonstrate sexuality's central role in the subordination of Chicanas, in relation both to state powers materialized in the border and to Chicanas' subjection to patriarchal institutions of family and community. Lesbian eroticism emerged in Anzaldúa's enunciation of mestiza agency as a discourse of opposition. In a luminous essay on Cherríe Moraga's *Loving in the War Years*, Yvonne Yarbro-Bejarano reminds us that racial and class hierarchies are "inflected by constructions of dominant and subordinate sexuality," so that "lesbian desire and the body themselves become the field of negotiation and (de)construction."[63] This construction of a borderless subjectivity anchored the articulating capacity of a coalitional, feminist practice in the body as site of racial and gendered wounding. The body, subjected to the fragmenting authority of the patriarchal state, could be recuperated as the "body-as-bridge," Anzaldúa's metaphor for a new racial and gender agency formed in the border space. The vision of the "crossroads" invested the marginalized mestiza with a plural agency: "To survive in the Border-lands / You must live sin fronteras / Be a crossroads."[64] Although Haraway also posited the "integrated circuit" as a crossroads, the site for an affinity politics, her conflation of multiple sites of gendered struggle diluted the particular realities of the U.S.-Mexican borderlands. Chicana claims to a distinctly bordered subjectivity derived from the specific site of the geopo-litical frontier and the embodied experience of displacements arising from the border's longer colonial formation.

Chicana feminists, in dialogue with other U.S. feminists of color, elabo-rated models of subjectivity that privileged the multiplicity and irreduc-ibility of racial, sexual, gender, and class identities. Chicana claims for the "Third World/woman of color" aimed to decenter Western epistemology and the privileged, sovereign subject of modern social theory.[65] Their work broke an impasse reached by identity politics by proposing that identity constituted a provisional claim to a social location formed as an effect of variously constellated discursive positions (namely class, race, gender, and sex), rather than being a stable, empirically verifiable object. Thus, Norma Alarcón situated the Chicana subject in "the locus of *la différend*, . . . the site of a conflict . . . opposed to anything that presupposes for its inter-pretation an inherent monological rationality."[66] Alarcón usefully located Chicana agency in a dialectic of identification and disidentification—in the necessity of occupying diverse subject positions and at the same time undermining their oppressive logic. In her foundational work on Chicana subjectivity, she contested the prevailing conception that social agency resided exclusively in the unitary, citizen-subject of modern social theory. But she did not dismiss the utility of identity, since the subject-in-process enunciates her opposition, however "provisionally," from this contingent social location. This location becomes the name by which the subject is called, and answers power. What separated Alarcón's subject-in-process from the subject of (essentialist) identity politics was her *tactical* con-sciousness, her capacity to "recognize . . . and exploit difference" by vir-tue of her "differential theorization" of the experience of racial and gender subjection, marginality, and exploitation.[67] The key to utilizing this appar-ent mobility of identification, however, is a particular social conditioning. The substance of that conditioning implicitly gave form to (and for identity politics *authorized*) the strategic enunciation of opposition. This process involved a particular movement from material location to subjective experience, to conscious resistance. The fragmenting effects of late capitalist culture, with its hyperdifferentiated forms of social stratification, were thus already familiar to Chicanas, who had experienced a longer trajectory of colonial displacements and loss.

Transformations in the borderlands since the 1980s have forced Chicana scholars to contend with the limits of tactical consciousness to create social agency. The militarization of the border region, coupled with the severe economic effects of neoliberal restructuring, placed ever-greater burdens on migrant women and Latinas in the border region in the final decades of the twentieth century.[68] Mass migrations to and across the border during the 1990s and early 2000s remade its social and political geography once again, bringing with them new global actors in the management of space and commerce in the region. Violence linked to human trafficking, and the trade in arms and drugs, alongside unprecedented levels of police surveillance, made the border crossing far more dangerous than it had ever been for migrants and fronterizas. Since the inception of Operation Gatekeeper in 1994 (which is discussed in the next chapter), thousands of migrants have died in the arduous crossing, at the hands of coyotes or from exposure to the extreme conditions of the Sonoran desert.[69]

But even more than border militarization, the feminicidio in Ciudad Juárez has irrevocably changed the discourse of agency attached to fronteriza subjects. The term "feminicidio" describes the systematic murder of girls and women because of their gender; it references a social context of extreme gender inequality and misogyny. Since 1993, an estimated four hundred women and girls have been killed in extreme acts of gender violence, and another thousand have disappeared.[70] The impunity with which these crimes have been perpetrated against poor girls, women, and migrants raises the specter of a new governmentality in the region, what scholars Rosa Linda Fregoso and Lisa Lowe each termed a *necropolitical* order.[71] As civil society has failed to halt the serial assaults on girls and women, the normal bonds that unify society in the promotion of life have been replaced by atomizing fear and asocial violence.

But even in the 1980s, obreras' testimonials demonstrated the limits of agency in the nonunitary subjectivity of racialized women. Obreras' stories of subjectivity, and their demands for bodily integrity, exposed the material violence that produced the category "Third World woman/woman of color" as a different order of subject. The values of "flexibility" and "mobility" that defined oppositional agency for Chicana feminists in the 1980s and 1990s are precisely the same values praised by factory owners and proponents of development. However different their inflection in Chicana feminist critique, for obreras, these were the alibis that sanctioned their exploitation and bodily theft. From the 1970s onward, it was these ideals that patriarchal culture, the neoliberal state, and multinational capitalism invoked as they sought to remove border women from the spheres of rights.

In 1987, Gloria Anzaldúa described the border as "*una herida abierta,* ... a vague and undetermined place created by the emotional residue of an unnatural boundary. It is in a constant state of transition."[72] At the opening of the twenty-first century, the borderlands witnessed another moment of profound indeterminacy in the social ecology of the Mexican frontier. Unspeakable forms of violence produced new narratives of subjectivity, declarations enunciated from a border space whose political reach far exceeded the binational institutions charged with its regulation. Anzaldúa's command to live sin fronteras located fronterizas at the center of a global traffic that threatened to overpower even her plural, expansive conception of difference in the border space.

New Narratives of Fronteriza Subjectivity

It was a Holiday Inn
downtown El Paso
where she crossed the line daily
paso por paso
mal paso que das
al cruzar la frontera

There was the work permit
sealed in plastic
like the smile
she flashed every morning
to the same uniformed eyes
                    —Marisela Norte, "Act of the Faithless" (1991)[73]

We have explored the various discourses of the 1980s that constructed
Mexican women as the new class subjects of global assembly, and we have
seen obrera and feminist struggles to interpret the extraordinary transformations in gender, labor, and social space that remade the border during
that period. Next, I want to consider alternate imaginaries of the border
space by examining literary productions by Mexican and Chicana authors
that contested the violent border crisis at century's end. Like the obrera
testimony in *Sangre joven*, these narratives depict female mobility in ways
that recognize the differential consciousness of fronteriza subjects and expose the debilitating limits that the geopolitical boundary sets on their social agency. As fiction, they surpass the confines of testimony, by opening
speculative realms that permit the authors to reimagine female subjectivity in the border space. For this I turn to texts by Marisela Norte and Rosario Sanmiguel, which narrate how the border crossing, and the change
in political status it implies, produces intimate fractures in the forms of
kinship, class, and ethnic solidarity among Mexican women and Chicanas.
Both authors inscribe fronteriza subjectivity in the political geography of
the Puente Libre [Bridge of the Americas] that joins Ciudad Juárez to El
Paso and yet divides these polities of Greater Mexico. In the 1991 spoken-
word composition "Act of the Faithless," Marisela Norte portrayed the relationship between a young Chicana girl and her uncle's girlfriend, a Ciudad
Juárez woman who crosses the border daily for work in a luxury hotel in El
Paso.[74] Rosario Sanmiguel depicted the emotional and physical estrangement between a Mexican domestic worker and her daughter in "Las hilanderas (The Spinners)," a story that appeared in her 1994 collection *Callejón
Sucre y otros relatos* [Sugar Alley and Other Stories].[75]

The critics María Soccoro Tabuenca Córdoba and Debra Castillo assert
that in postmodern border theories "cities like Tijuana and Juárez almost
too neatly conflate symbolic geographic and moral exclusions from the
healthy body of the state."[76] In contrast, Norte and Sanmiguel refute this
dematerialization of the actual crossing in their writings. Theirs is a border space defined less by *alterity* to the nation than by its coercive imbri-
cation within the nation's economic and social order. Both texts feature
working-class protagonists for whom the border crossing is a constant,
almost daily feature of life; its very repetition undoes the construction of
the border as a space of exception. For Norte and Sanmiguel, the infor-

mal service and leisure industries that employ Mexican women as maids are far more central to the official, national economies than the women's illegal status would suggest. Indeed, both tourism along the border and migrant remittances remain vital to Mexico's GDP and to the commerce of the southwestern United States.

The fronteriza characters of Norte's and Sanmiguel's stories confront the limits of their own bodily agency as they come up against the political and social strictures imposed by the geopolitical boundary; as adolescents, these young women develop a sense of self against the dominant construction of fronterizas as bodies available for appropriation. Both narratives depict the precarious passage from youth to womanhood as a movement wholly defined by the border crossing; for both protagonists, the transformation implies the attainment of new powers and the simultaneous threat of loss. Neither story fulfills the expectations attached to the generic migration plot: for the young protagonists, the movement north is merely one part of a longer itinerary of personal and familial displacement. Norte and Sanmiguel continually defer the moment of arrival, as Norte's young protagonist says, "I mean / I'm just passing through here."

A leading figure in spoken-word performance and Chicana/o literature, Marisela Norte is an "Eastside Girl," a voice for urban Los Angeles. Born in 1955 to Mexican parents who immigrated to Southern California in the 1930s and 1940s, Norte grew up in a community with strong kinship and cultural ties to Ciudad Juárez.[77] "Act of the Faithless" first appeared in recorded form in 1991, on the poet's compact-disc recording *Norte/Word*. Rather than publish her compositions in book form, Norte chose to circulate her performance texts in a format that would make them available to broader audiences and retain the texture of her voice. Norte's poem exploits shifts in narrative time and perspective in order to convey the multiplicity of female subjectivity in the border space. By appropriating a working-class, migrant vernacular, it delineates the complex alterations of female agency and perspective that occur in the border crossing. Because the poem stages the process by which a young Chicana comes to critical consciousness in the borderlands, it provides a different perspective on the fronteriza subject of Chicana feminism.

In Norte's narrative, the environs of Ciudad Juárez and El Paso appear as sites of economic and personal transactions that convert Mexican women into commodified beings. Norte's story of a young Chicana's relationship to her uncle's girlfriend embeds the relationship in a longer tale of family, danger, and desire at the Mexico-U.S. border:

> The story would have to begin with her.
> She worked as a maid
> in the El Paso Holiday Inn.
> El Paso
> Mal paso que das   [The bad step you take
> al cruzar la frontera   when you cross the border]
> I mean
> I'm just passing through here.

Norte tells us that if she were to tell her story straight, it would begin with the aunt cleaning rooms in the luxury hotel, "twenty stories high" above the squalor of the urban frontier. Their crossing into El Paso, told as a momentary departure from the confines of class, is described in the Spanish passages as a "bad step" or a "wrong move." For the protagonist, the border crossing acts as a change in cultural identity and a passage from girlhood to maturity. The girl's consciousness emerges as she reckons with her separation from the maternal figure of her aunt.

Norte recognized the border crossing as doubly hazardous, because mexicanas are pressed into the service of a foreign and punishing racial system in the United States but also, for the young narrator, because it signifies loss:

> El paso con la frontera   [The passage through the border
> Por vida   For life
> con safos   with safety[78]
> más vale   it's better]
> as it is written
> up and down that border
> that runs up and down our backs
> like a bad tattoo

The severing of national ties symbolized in the border forces us to understand Chicana/o identity as a violation, the "bad tattoo" that marks the difference of Mexican Americans. The racial inscription of the migrant's body is analogous to the division of social space by the national boundary. "Por vida / con safos," the tags of graffiti that adorn the border bridge, are ironic articulations of presence and ownership; they are written into the interstices of nation and property, formations that exclude migrant subjects.

"The acceptance of difference," for Norte as for Ramón Saldívar, "does not diminish the pain of separation that difference implies," a loss that resides at the heart of identity.[79] Norte's poem turns on jagged inflections of loss within the gestures of intimacy between family and workers. "She was an aunt / I would know too briefly," Norte warns us from the beginning. Norte's poem enacts the dialectic of identification and disidentification that Saldívar prescribes, as she continually delivers an affirmative statement, "she cleaned up / decorated their home," only to communicate more effectively its negation, "with objects of rejection."

As Norte's narrator visits the Holiday Inn with her aunt, her trip features an ascent "in the hotel elevator / from the basement / to the honeymoon suite," a crossing of class boundaries that far surpasses the physical distance of her journey from home. The young girl quickly perceives that this visit has significance beyond her entertainment, as her aunt shows her the workings of leisure and bourgeois values:

A slow curtain is pulled
by the delicate hand
holding the heavy gold cord.
Slowly and deliberately
she will expose,
letting out a little sigh.
She cannot believe it herself.
This is what it could all look like,
this view from twenty stories high.

Like a magician, the aunt ceremoniously presents her niece with a glimpse of a world of privilege wholly distinct from life as it is lived on the ground floor. The view signifies more than just the romantic disengagement from worldly cares promised by the tourist industry; here it is described in spatial terms as the industry's deliberate construction of an insular social landscape. As the "delicate hand" that services this fantasy, the maid experiences the crossing of class boundaries as a kind of cognitive dissonance —even as she reveals it to her niece, "she cannot believe it herself."

The view alternately figures a space of possibility beyond the social restrictions of the border and reinscribes the aunt and niece's outsider status within this cosmopolitan realm. The statement "this is what it could look like" reminds us that the landscape can only reflect the gazers' own social position. Looking out, the narrator situates herself in relation to the luxury that encloses her by reading the storefronts:

> There was a dance hall
> called El Peor es Nada,
> Better than Nothing,
> and then there was
> that narrow stretch of nothing,
> the remains of a dried out sewer.
> She told me it was El Río,   [She told me it was The River
> El Grande grande.   The grand Grande]
> Surely these were the things
> bad dreams were made of.

The place-names signify the absolute negation of the social mobility manifested in the gilded ornaments of the luxury suite. Even the river, made heroic in border legend, betrays its name by serving as the washed-out basin for pollution and waste generated by the tourist trade and the maquiladora industry. The repetition of "nothing" inscribes the landscape with a fatalism that diverges sharply from Chicana feminist constructions of the border as a crossroads.[80] This nothingness exerts a material force on its subjects—for the narrator, it is the substance of nightmares. Norte's border insistently spatializes the racial and gender formations that make up the neocolonial tourist economy.

The maid offers her niece the hotel stationery, a gesture that encapsulates the whole drama of the girl's formation as a writer. The girl's aspiration to authorship is figured as trespass and theft, as the aunt urges her niece to record her experiences on sheets of paper stamped with marks of privilege. The aunt insists,

> Look at the traffic.
> Look how tiny
> the cars look,
> and the people, too.
> Look!

Although the aunt symbolically grants her niece the means to write, she also urges the girl to note how her remove transforms the very process of seeing and recording the landscape below. The act of looking is not neutral but implies both a privilege and a burden.

The narrator's first instinct is to experience her ascent to the luxury suite as an escape, and to close her eyes:

> I only wanted to lay down
> and shut my eyes
> to the annoying Texas sun
> in the sky
> and make these feet
> leave the ground
> for one moment
> and imagine the afterlife,
> eternity at twenty stories high

Abandonment of her place under the "annoying Texas sun" connotes not only relief but a kind of death. The girl's fantasy—to abandon her class for the status of the tourist—is rendered as immobility and stasis, not mobility or freedom of choice. The girl's lesson continues in a trip to the rooftop swimming pool. "If there's no one up there," the maid tells her, "you can take your shoes off / and put your feet in the water." This episode speaks to the innumerable hidden acts by which migrant women contest the dehumanizing control of their labor. The act of putting her feet in the pool alleviates tiredness from long hours spent standing; it also transgresses the boundaries between the domestic worker and the customer. For the niece, getting her feet wet is an experience of what it means to be a tourist.

Their moment of transgression occasions a struggle between them over the meanings of the girl's transnational identity:

You are not from here,
nor are you from over there,
you understand m'hija?   [you understand, daughter?
¿Entiendes?   Understand?]

The aunt understands her niece's identity as a condition of homelessness, of estrangement from both Mexican and U.S. national unities. She ascribes a particular cognitive advantage to the girl's binational status, but also an utter lack of a coherent identity. The narrator counters with a recitation that, in the words of Emma Pérez, reclaims the border as the sitio y lengua (place and language) that both authorizes and gives form to her utterance.[81]

¿Los dos idiomas?   [Both languages?
Claro que sí.   Of course.
Que no soy de aquí   I'm not from here
Que no soy de allá   I'm not from there

But I can speak
the language, I insisted,
both of them.
¿Entiendes?   Understand?]

One important detail of this exchange is the way the aunt distinguishes between her own border identity and that of her niece. The niece belongs to both worlds on either side of the border; "she speaks both languages" and her aunt does not. The maid merely travels to render her services at the hotel. The whole of the girl's adventure in the pool foreshadows her future travels beyond the confines of her border existence. This transient destiny is shaded with both pleasure and danger: "mal paso que das / al cruzar la frontera," she warns; "I mean, I'm just passing through here."

The young girl expresses trepidation at her first incursion into the realms of privilege and mobility:

My feet in the water,
I still hadn't learned to swim
(too scared to take the plunge).
How good they felt up here

where they didn't belong
twenty stories high.

Norte's narrator takes pleasure in transgressing the boundaries of privilege. But as she imagines her immersion in the luxury pool, she is pulled back to the present by the sight of her aunt performing her duties as a maid, wiping down the patio furniture: "I watched her body move inside the uniform / . . . / the sound of her nylon stockings." Immediately she senses her separation from her aunt's status as a worker and wishes to repudiate her fantasy. Her aunt, observing the girl in her dark glasses, laughs at her pantomime of the role of U.S. tourist: "Ahora sí pareces turista americana" [Now you do look like an American tourist]. Her niece, threatened with the gulf of difference opening between them, hands the sunglasses back:

> She began to laugh, but I shook my head.
> I don't belong here and neither do you.
> I'm just passing through here, remember?
> I'm not from here and neither are you.

The niece recognizes that her play creates a separation between her aunt, who is a worker, and the mobility of her own identity. She refuses to identify as a tourist, seeking instead to make her aunt share in her own position of "passing through." But the aunt knows better. Contained in the maid's laughter is a prescient knowledge of the girl's future; as the older woman moves efficiently around the pool, she acknowledges her place in the border labor economy.

Rather than assume that kinship unites the girl and her aunt within a shared class position, Norte allows us to see precisely how the labor of the maid influences her niece's future as a writer. The poem contrasts the relative social mobility of the Chicana niece and the Mexican maid. In a moment of great poignancy, the aunt reveals how the lesson that she gives her niece plays a part in her own gendered class struggle:

> She gave me a pair of sunglasses
>   to wear
> "Toma, cuidate los ojos   [Here, take care of your eyes]
> take care of your eyes.
> There's so much you should see.

The sunglasses signify both the trappings of class privilege and a shield against the potential harm of exposure that the girl faces in her formation as a writer. The aunt prepares her niece to bear witness but, in a moment of great generosity, also to protect herself. As Michelle Habell-Pallán notes, the warning to protect her eyes holds a double-edged meaning: the niece's privileged sight creates possibilities of both reward and punishment.[82]

Norte separates the moment of seeing from the act of writing, so as to show precisely where the differential agency of the writer/critic differs from that of the migrant domestic worker. The writer, whose mobile identifications enable her to "pass through here," never elides the division of labor that makes race, gender, and class a matter of wounding, of captured labor. In the final scene of the poem, the narrator relates the conclusion to her poolside fantasy. As the maid pushes her cart toward the door back to the elevator, the voice of a U.S. tourist calls her back:

> Excuse me. Señorita, can you come here, por favor?
> . . . .
> He waves an empty glass at her.
> The wife looks up at him smiling
> The "He's all mine" smile.

The girl's critical consciousness is thus formed within an ongoing conflict over the terms of sale for mexicana labor. Opposed to the maid and her niece are a white tourist and his wife, who play out their heterosexual travel adventure against the backdrop of the luxury hotel. Norte dramatizes the maid's prescribed role within the tourists' honeymoon, just as she notes the importance of the honeymoon to the girl's emerging sense of her place within a racial economy that values mexicanas for their service:

> Señorita. The name stings like the sun.
> My aunt smiles at him
> and cusses him out real good
> in Spanish under her breath.

Norte concludes her narrative of authorial self-fashioning with the aunt, as the maid contends with her exploitation at the hands of the tourist. Language is simultaneously the source of violation and of subversive agency, both in this scene *and* in the very act of narrating the event as a poem.

For this reason, the poem lingers on this final image of the aunt and niece together, in which the aunt's gesture of defiance gives way to the girl's future vocation as a writer and performer.

> She puts the sunglasses on
> and leads me back to the elevator
> where I stand beside her
> leaving a trail of wet prints behind me.
> I hold her pretty hands.

The maid pointedly refuses to respond to the beckoning tourist, opting instead to put the sunglasses on. This simple gesture suggests that she too must protect her eyes; she too must struggle to bear witness. Her "pretty hands" figure a body not wholly claimed by the labor discipline; they also represent her protective presence in the life of the young girl. The trail of prints that the niece leaves behind hints at the writing still to come as they call to mind the graffiti left by border crossers at the international bridges.

This final scene reveals how the struggle over writing and interpretation shares space with the class struggle over labor power:

> I tug at her arm.
> I point at the man now silent.
> "There is too much to see," she said.
> "Too much to remember."

By leaving open the possibilities for seeing and narrating, Norte "problematizes women's discursive practices" in the border space: saying "there is too much to see / too much to remember."[83] The girl's formation as a fronteriza separates the cognitive agency of "knowing" and "seeing" from the security of kinship and rootedness. Adolescence here demands another boundary crossing, in the painful process of separation from the maternal figure of the aunt. The girl's "passing through" is a process of both personal transformation and leave-taking, dislocating her from the resourceful aunt whom she "would know all too briefly." For Norte, the border crossing entails loss, figured in the rupture of kinship, even as it allows the girl to assume a new status in the United States.

Rosario Sanmiguel was born in Benavides, in the northern state of Chihuahua, a town located at a short distance from the Texas-Chihuahua border.[84] Very nearly the same age as Marisela Norte, Sanmiguel's formation as a writer was also shaped by cultural shifts in the concerns and visibility of women authors in Mexico and the United States, and by the efforts of so-called minor literatures to shed their minority status in the literary market. As the preeminent female author in Chihuahua, Sanmiguel has contended with the exclusions of border culture from Mexican literary society. Sanmiguel rejects the costumbrismo of regional literatures in favor of a tactic that, as critic María Socorro Tabuenca Córdoba notes, "takes the border space as constructed by the metropolis in order to subvert it *from the borders.*"[85] Both Sanmiguel and Norte claim intimate connections to the urban landscapes of the border cities of Ciudad Juárez and El Paso, but they came to those places from different migrant trajectories—trajectories made different by their distinct nationalities.

The central protagonist of Sanmiguel's stories is the border city itself, which brings together many different subjects, all in transit: urban migrants, longtime border residents, and emigrants headed to the United States. Her city is both a terminus and a point of departure. Even though its social geography caters to impermanence, it also retains a large, resolutely immobile population of native Juarenses. The title story of her 1994 collection, "Callejón Sucre" [Sugar Alley], embodies this paradox: located in an alley that intersects with the central tourist drag, Avenida Juárez, the story depicts a distinct urban subculture that is neither fully embedded within the commercial and sexual trade of the city nor opposed to it. The bars, hotel rooms, and domestic interiors of Sanmiguel's narrative undo the categories of center and periphery by reflecting on the cultural and material sedimentations of urban life, the refuse that accumulates in places of transit. That is, her characters contend with those elements of social life that tend to be discarded or repudiated within the national imaginaries of Mexican and U.S. society; they occur at a distance, in spaces unseen from the maquiladoras or the river itself. But in Sanmiguel's narration, the border brothel loses its exoticism and becomes as ordinary as a railway depot. Her stories suggest that the home, the train station, and the brothel can equally stage scenes of estrangement, displacement, and excessive consumption. Ultimately, the isolation of the border space comes from the imposition of a social grid that deliberately renders border life unintelligible to the national imaginary.

By necessity, the fronteriza writer narrates the border crossing differently from the emigrant or the Mexican American. If the girl of Norte's poem achieves a new status in the border crossing, the protagonists of *Callejón Sucre* experience the liminality of the border space as a form of confinement. In Sanmiguel's narrative, the transgression of the political boundary is an endlessly repeating scene of subjection. Her protagonists pass over the bridge or through the river knowing that the migra [border patrol] lies in wait for them, but they also know that theirs is a journey with no clear starting point and no clear end. Their repeated ventures into transnational space, for wages or for family, do not conform to the idealized trajectory of the immigrant because the move never advances them beyond the interstitial location of the boundary.

"Las hilanderas" [The Spinners] portrays the migratory route from the Chihuahuan town of Malavid, through Ciudad Juárez, and into El Paso as one of stasis rather than transformation.[86] A girl, Fátima, crosses with her mother, Manuela, to work as a maid, only to find that her childhood home and the home of her employer are qualitatively the same—both are places of confinement and tedium. The story opens with the adolescent girl swatting away flies while waiting for the train at the depot in Malavid. The town, whose name references a "bad vine" but also a "bad life," represents a place in which time has lost its meaning; the grapevine that yields no fruit corresponds to the loss of the regenerative processes of the harvest cycle. (Sanmiguel's portrait echoes the stillness of Juan Rulfo's Comala or of Américo Paredes's ejido, Los Claveles, but invests the landscape with a distinctly feminized vision of stasis.) As Manuela sends Fátima to ask what has become of the train, the girl recognizes her surroundings as a geography that only becomes meaningful in its relationship to other destinations. For the two of them, life is elsewhere:

> Son las doce del día. Todos esperan. Unos la partida por el único camino que conduce a geografías diferentes; otros, la llegada de algún bulto o del periódico de la ciudad.

[It's twelve noon. Everyone waits. Some await their departure on the only route that leads to other geographies; others await the arrival of some package or newspaper from the city.][87]

The story opens in a third-person, omniscient narration, but with the arrival in El Paso, the narrative shifts to the voice of Fátima, who recollects that her first border crossing also marked the end of her childhood: "cuando los senos empezaban a definírseme bajo la blusa" [when breasts began to appear more defined beneath my blouse].[88] Even this passage lacks determinacy, as the girl remarks on the changes in her body as if from an impersonal distance, narrating the event in a voice devoid of affect. She claims no ownership of her emerging sexuality and barely perceives her change except in relation to her work status. Fátima's one hope is that the move will draw her closer to her mother, but that reconciliation never materializes. Manuela remains aloof, seemingly indifferent to the daughter who functions more as an apprentice in domestic work than as a relative.

The narrative suggests that the particular domestic arrangement attached to their labors in the house of the "gringa" [white American woman] is a further cause of the mother's estrangement. In order for Fátima to join her mother, Manuela must take on sewing in addition to cleaning to earn their keep. As Manuela marks time with her stitches, her daughter notices that her gaze always rests elsewhere, on a horizon that does not include her:

> Ella siguió habitando su mundo de voces. Hablaba para sí misma mientras yo crecía solitaria en aquellos corredores ajenos, entre los muebles que las dos bruñíamos a diario con aceites perfumados.

> [She continued to live in her world of voices. She talked to herself while I grew lonely in those strange corridors, among the furniture that we both polished daily with perfumed oils.][89]

In Norte's poem, the aunt uses her labors in the hotel to nurture the younger girl's growing sensibility of her place in the networks of kinship, labor, and ethnicity that define her gender in the border space. But even as

Fátima and Manuela are bound by shared work obligations, the monotony of their routines only separates the mother further from her daughter.

Fátima is only minimally aware of her mother's designs: "Mi madre era una hilandera que conducía la rueca de los días por un cauce inalterable" [My mother was a spinner who turned the spindle of our days along an inalterable course].[90] Sanmiguel's depiction of sewing departs entirely from the values that her contemporaries attached to the needle trades: "Las hilanderas" are not the militants of the Farah strike, defending their worth as skilled workers, nor do they resemble Yolanda López's portrait of her grandmother as the Virgen de Guadalupe seated at a sewing machine.[91] In Sanmiguel's narrative, sewing is an act devoid of creativity, because it occurs in the context of service to their employer's household. Manuela marks time with her stitches, time experienced as the evacuation of the self. For Fátima, Manuela controls the passage of time and the meaning of their labors; she has no idea why her mother has brought her to El Paso, where the passage of time only repeats her subjection to the routine of cleaning the enormous house. The tedium of cleaning obliterates time, impinging on the girl's growth as an adolescent. Precisely as Fátima realizes that her mature body now resembles that of her mother, she discovers Manuela's design, to leave her daughter behind with the gringa. Once again, the narration marks her condition as one of stasis: her passage to womanhood is not one of transformation but is merely the assumption of her mother's duties: "yo tomé su lugar en la casa" [I took her place in the house].[92] Fátima, in other words, becomes her mother, as the labor role of the Mexican maid effaces her own subjectivity.

Manuela's abandonment of her daughter signals a betrayal of filial obligation in the service to the domestic labor economy. The absent mother represents a nomadic subjectivity willing to trade kinship for survival. The story suggests a deformation of mothering by the transborder market in the bodies of Mexican girls and women. It also allegorizes the ways that the U.S. labor demand transfers the costs of social reproduction onto the Mexican working class; Manuela can leave her employer only by substituting her own daughter for her position in the household. The neoliberal regime permits the rupture of a social contract at its most intimate relation; Fátima refrains from condemning Manuela, perhaps because she now has to inhabit her position: "entonces era yo quien tejía el transcurso de las horas en las habitaciones de la casona" [Then I was the one who wove the passage of hours in the rooms of that house].[93]

Sanmiguel's story is a troubling one, since the metaphor of spinning suggests the women's own capacity for self-exploitation, for abnegated service to the consumer economy that the well-furnished house represents. Fátima settles into the routine: "Al paso del tiempo mi vida tomó el curso que correspondía a una sirvienta joven como yo" [As time passed my life followed the path that fit the situation of a young maid like myself].[94] Fátima experiences her life passively, describing the passage of time as a trajectory not of her own making. As she begins to find friends among other maids, her crossings to Ciudad Juárez in her leisure time inscribe a new urban landscape in her memory. She begins to feel more alive on Sundays in the streets of Juárez, where she can wander the city without a fixed destination and take pleasure in its entertainments. Almost immediately, a letter from her mother threatens her newly awakened self. Manuela writes to warn her daughter to stay in the home of her employer, saying that in Mexico, she has nothing. For Fátima, the message provokes a crisis of identity:

¿Y en El Paso? Me preguntaba yo, un pobre salario, un cuarto con baño y una television prestada. Nada era mío, nomas la zozobra de ser atrapada, en cualquier momento, por la migra.

[And in El Paso? I asked myself, a meager salary, a room with a bathroom and a borrowed television. Nothing was my own, only the fear of being caught at any moment by the border patrol.][95]

Fátima feels an overpowering sense of loss that ruptures the temporal unity of her routines. At the movies with her friends, she feels with sudden urgency the need to return home. The film's images of the ocean provoke a phenomenological reduction: "Sin poder evitarlo la imagen de mi madre me acompaño durante todo el tiempo que duró la proyección" [Without my being able to avoid it, the image of my mother accompanied me for the whole duration of the film].[96]

Fátima's crisis of identity resolves itself only through a regression to childhood, as she reverts to her status as the mere extension of her mother's being. The film provokes her desire for union with Manuela: the images of the sea invoke the neonatal stage of oceanic unity between mother and baby. As a newborn, the child knows no boundaries between its own existence and that of the mother. In psychoanalytic terms, this moment precedes the developmental phase that Jacques Lacan termed "the mirror stage," when the child becomes aware of its individuality apart from the mother. The baby's capacity to recognize its own reflection marks its recognition of a new bounded identity and entails the loss of the prior boundless self.[97] When the young women are detained by the border patrol on their return to El Paso, Fátima falls asleep in the fetal position in her cell, dreaming that she is floating in the ocean. Her dream state figures a form of death: "Trataba de nadar, pero me cansaba mucho" [I tried to swim but I got very tired].[98] In the morning, the other maids make their way back across the river, but Fátima refuses, detained by her reflection in the muddy water of the Río Bravo: "Al verlas reflejadas en el agua quieta yo también me vi, desde el primer día, cuando cruce de la mano de mi madre, hasta ese momento" [Seeing them reflected in the still water, I saw myself too, from the first day that I crossed holding my mother's hand, up until that moment].[99] Fátima stays behind, refusing to perform the crossing that will complete her separation from her mother and from her childhood. Sanmiguel marks the moment by shifting back to an omniscient narration, so that Fátima's voice disappears along with her emigrant self. The story ends with Fátima's return to Malavid only to find that her mother has died; the last lines hold the merest suggestion that here, too, Fátima will inhabit her mother's place, as she goes to sleep beside a man who sits napping at her mother's table. She stands at the brink of a sleep that is itself another crossing, into death.

These narratives, like the testimonials of obreras, depict the border traffic in Mexican women in terms that banish any fantasy of the border's dissolution or easy permeability. Through the protagonist's fond recollection of the aunt whom she has lost, Norte gives voice to the "longing for unity and cohesion" that critic Rolando Romero ascribes to Chicana/o narrative, even as her story belies any hope of an organic class or kinship unity among Mexicans, migrants, and Mexican Americans across the boundary.[100] For Sanmiguel the border is a fixed and dominating presence that impinges on the most intimate life of the border dwellers. In these and other writings, Norte and Sanmiguel detail the intimate and often conflicted relationships among women in the clandestine and authorized

labor economies, relationships complicated by the constant presence of
sexual danger, transgressive erotic relations, and personal violence that
accompany the transnational sale of women's labor.

The narrative agency of fronteriza subjects cannot be understood apart
from the material conditions of its own production, its place in a chain of
labors that are simultaneously performed and contested. Just as lived social relations necessarily exceed authors' capacities to relate them, narra-
tors inevitably remain fallible: "there is too much to see / too much to remember," Norte insists. But the narrative act engages language as another
terrain of struggle, so that an alternate knowledge of self and way of seeing
may emerge. The border in its extravagant dangers provides not only a site
of enunciation but also the form of the message.

CHAPTER 7

Migrant Melancholia

Emergent Narratives of the Border Crossing

> Today more than ever, as productive forces tend to be completely de-localized, completely universal, they produce not only commodities but also rich and powerful social relationships. These new productive forces have no place, however, because they occupy all places, and they produce and are exploited in this indefinite non-place. The universality of human creativity, the synthesis of freedom, desire, and living labor, is what takes place in the non-place of the postmodern relations of production.
>
> —Michael Hardt and Antonio Negri, *Empire* (2000)[1]

> Migrants would make wings if they had to.
>
> —Padre Ademar Barilli, director of Casa del Migrante, Tecún Umán, Guatemala (2006)[2]

On May 10, 1948, Concepción Zapata presented her retablo to the Santísima Virgen de San Juan de los Lagos

Retablo of Concepción Zapata, San Luis Potosí, May 10, 1948.
Reproduced from *Miracles on the Border: Retablos of Mexican Migrants to the United States* by Jorge Durand and Douglas S. Massey, © 1995 Arizona Board of Regents. Reprinted by generous permission of the University of Arizona Press and Jorge Durand)

as a testament to the saint's protection during her sojourn in the United States.[3] The retablo, or votive painting, is a popular form of devotion that renders compensation for the miraculous intercession of the patron saint. The paintings, rendered in oil paint on wood or tin, typically depict an individual reckoning with a personal ordeal. The votive practice records a private act of supplication and gives witness to the person's deliverance from illness or danger. For Mexican migrants, the retablo combines a holy image with a visual rendition of perils faced in the border crossing, forming a closed narrative of departure and return once the painting is deposited in its shrine. As the patroness of Los Altos de Jalisco, the highland region to the northeast of Guadalajara, La Virgen de San Juan de los Lagos has heard many stories of emigration and made many border crossings of her own.[4] Alongside accounts of averted deaths and wondrous cures, this guardian of migrants knows the particular gender terror of the passage northward.

In her account of divine protection, Concepción Zapata relates:

Dedico el presente RETABLO a la Sma. V. de San Juan de los Lagos por aberme salbado de un TEXANO que me llebara, me escodi [*sic*] debajo de un arbol con mi hermanito ala orilla de la carretera.

[I dedicate the present retablo to the Holiest Virgen of San Juan de los Lagos for having saved me from a Texan who tried to carry me off. I hid under a tree by the side of the road with my little brother.][5]

Unlike conventional votive paintings, this retablo depicts not the traumatic encounter itself but Concepción's act of devotion after the fact. The image places the kneeling figure of Concepción just beyond a drawn curtain, as if the viewer is looking in on a confessional. Staged this way, this public disclosure of the young woman's experience reinscribes the private, unspeakable nature of sexual aggression. The anonymous artist painted the nationality of the aggressor in capital letters, "TEXANO," as if to locate the threat of gender violence en el otro lado, on the other side. The story describes the peril of a young woman traveling alone, her younger brother too small to act as her guardian or chaperone. Concepción's narrative leaves open the question of what might have happened: she describes the male threat in the verb "llevar" [carry off] ("un TEXANO me llebara"), a taking that is both rape and capture. The verb shows how the sexual violation is discursively linked to disappearance, a taking from which there is no return. The story ascribes the agency behind the young woman's evasion of harm to the saint, rather than to her own resourcefulness. Concepción's escape under the tree anticipates the enclosure that awaits her upon her return home. The narrative figures the border as the open road, "la carretera," in opposition to the protective closeness of the interior space rendered in the painting.

In its reticence toward depicting Concepción as a fully autonomous agent in her border crossing, the retablo presciently anticipates current concerns about Mexican women's mobility through transnational space. Women's perceived sexual availability and vulnerability incite social anxieties about the nation's exposure at the northern frontier. As women's migration has increased since the 1980s, this anxiety has become all the more acute. The question of women's autonomy of movement takes on greater urgency at the international boundary, where disappearance can also be a matter of a change in political status altogether. The story of Concepción Zapata's miraculous deliverance speaks to us from midcentury San Luis Potosí as a testament to the ways sex has historically been constructed as a woman's price for a successful border crossing.[6]

Zapata traveled north to Texas at the height of the Bracero Program, a period of mass emigration, which as we have seen centered almost exclusively on men. During these years, women's mobility remained invisible in public discourse, rendering women migrants doubly undocumented. Some fifty years later, we should inquire into the strategies for rendering these journeys visible and intelligible: by what means may artists, political activists, and scholars elucidate the complex relationships linking women's bodies, processes of deterritorialization, and the fabric of transnational social bonds?

This final chapter examines the discourses that produce what I call *migrant melancholia*: an emergent mode of migrant subjectivity that contests the dehumanizing effects of the unauthorized border crossing. The mass exodus from Latin America in the new century produces new rites for mourning the necessity of emigration. Migrants do not only mourn the deaths of their conationals, or the violating injuries of theft, coerced labor, and sexual assault that can define the passage north; migrant melancholia also marks the loss of a social contract, the democratic ideal anchored in the Latin American nation-state.[7] Behind their willful journey away from the spaces of communal belonging and citizenship, the specter of state failure looms large.

As in every crisis, the migrant imaginary articulates what citizens and state actors have only begun to comprehend—that the ethical imperative of *survival* cannot conform to the geopolitical fiction of sovereign borders. Schemes for deterrence have consistently failed. Since 1986, when the United States implemented its first comprehensive program of amnesty, border militarization, and punitive immigration law, annual rates of unauthorized migration have continued their precipitous climb.[8] Desire and need lead migrants to find ways to circumvent the barriers on human mobility. The keeper of La Casa del Migrante in Tecún Umán, Guatemala, observes, "Migrants would make wings if they had to."[9]

Migrant determination has continuously remade the social ecology of the border. For Mexicans living a precarious permanence in the United

States, the border operates as a critical juncture for imagining community and exerting claims on either nation. In this context, the crossing *itself*—in its various legal, economic, cultural, and social aspects—shapes the political disposition of the larger transnational community of unauthorized migrants and noncitizens in the United States, and in their hometowns in Mexico. Here I refer not only to the political apparatus of the border, as it regulates the mobility of peoples or their access to rights and citizenship, but also to the broader binational space that contains the institutions devoted to national security, immigration, and trade at the boundary checkpoints. Not only is the transborder corridor the largest urbanized region in Mexico; it is one of the fastest growing sites of settlement in the hemisphere.[10] The complex communal ecologies of this space do not simply give the border an internal sense of distinction and shared identity; they also influence the form that broader transnational linkages and communities may take. Border cities also socialize migrants in their passage from citizenship to noncitizenship, authorized status to unauthorized status. As greater numbers of people find themselves stranded in the border space because of failed crossings or deportation, or the availability of jobs in service work and export manufacturing created by neoliberal development, the normative force of this movement to the transnational corridor increases.[11]

The first years of the twenty-first century marked the tenth anniversaries of Operation Gatekeeper and the North American Free Trade Agreement, as well as mass migration in the transborder region; we may ask what the government policies may signify for current understandings of migrant mobility and transnational community. The combined regime of heightened border surveillance and socioeconomic integration recast migrant subjectivity in a decidedly melancholic direction. This turn made the problem of how migration is to be narrated and understood a matter of urgent concern for contending with "the new era of Mexican migration to the United States."[12] Alongside established accounts of transnational labor and remittances, other narratives of loss and wounding have always coexisted in tension with the legitimating discourses of international cooperation, development, and economic opportunity that depict the sojourn in the United States as a matter of elective choice.[13] The narration of migrant sorrows constitutes a political act cast against the prerogatives of neoliberal development and the global division of labor—in particular, the erosion of substantive citizenship and communal belonging but also the resurgent forms of racial governance in both countries.[14]

Bounded Nations/Boundless Economies

With the launch of the North American Free Trade Agreement (NAFTA) in January 1994, the governments of Canada, the United States, and Mexico heralded the establishment of the world's largest "free trade area," a zone of investment and commerce that would facilitate both "the special bonds of friendship and cooperation among their nations" and "contribute to the harmonious development and expansion of world trade and provide a cat-alyst to broader international cooperation."[15] The multilateral agreement oversaw trade liberalization among the three countries, canceling tariffs and setting terms for the integration of North American commerce, indus-try, and agriculture. The text of the accord weds commerce to progress, enlightened governance, and international good will. As many observers have noted, the legislation made no provision for the movement of people within its pledge to "facilitate the cross-border movement of goods and services between the territories of the Parties."[16] Although the trade pact includes side agreements on environmental and labor cooperation, they were not designed to create uniform levels of labor and environmental protections among the three nations. Labor was not invisible to the nego-tiations over market integration; still, workers were not to enjoy the same freedom of mobility as the commodities that they helped produce.[17]

Although Mexican officials and financiers may argue that the first decade of NAFTA brought Mexico new foreign investment and jobs with the added dividend of the democratic transition from PRI dominance, the actual economic and political benefits accruing from neoliberal reforms have largely bypassed the poorer sectors of society. Even the expansion of the manufacturing sector and the growth of the maquiladoras in the wake of the trade agreement did not offset the displacement of workers in both agriculture and industry. Mexican agriculture proved unable to com-pete against the giant, well-subsidized agribusiness to the north. The rapid restructuring of Mexican agriculture has only exacerbated the historical process of out-migration from the countryside and small towns. The relative weakness of Mexican industries on the open market has likewise resulted in the emigration of the urban working class. As the promise of NAFTA went unfulfilled, the benefits of trade liberalization failed to curtail the rise in undocumented immigration, whose effects were already being felt in both countries.

In fact, by 1994, concerns about illegal immigration led the U.S. Immigration and Naturalization Service (INS) to install a new program of border law enforcement that effectively shut down traditional migrant routes through Southern California. On October 2, the INS blockade of the San Diego–Tijuana boundary shifted policing further toward an emphasis on militant deterrence, as opposed to the primary focus on capturing migrants already on U.S. soil. (This strategy is sometimes called by the somewhat revealing title of "territorial denial.")[18] If U.S. officials celebrated the new era of economic integration with gestures of friendship, their rhetoric on Operation Gatekeeper tended toward metaphors of war: migration constituted "invasion," and U.S. cities were "under siege."[19] This language was nothing new, since U.S. media, policymakers, and politicians alike have long resorted to attack imagery when depicting Mexican immigration.

Nevertheless, the new reach of U.S. law enforcement in the 1990s was unparalleled in the history of the frontier. In 1994, the sixty-six-mile stretch that made up the San Diego sector of the two-thousand-mile border accounted for more than 40 percent of the Border Patrol's annual apprehensions of unauthorized migrants.[20] Seeking to establish a more effective barricade at the Tijuana–San Diego juncture in order to shift migrant traffic eastward, the INS deployed its agents in a highly visible show of dominance at the crossing. Operation Gatekeeper then expanded to encompass the full boundary, concentrating enforcement at high-density crossing points like that of Ciudad Juárez–El Paso.

Increased rates of interdiction at the Mexico-U.S. border, along with unprecedented levels of undocumented migration from Mexico and farther south, added to the perils of the border crossing and settlement in the United States in the first decade of the twenty-first century.[21] Migrants confront the travails of the desert and anti-immigrant hostilities along the frontier as a passage through a space of death, or what Luis Alberto Urrea calls "the devil's highway."[22] After 1996, migrant fatalities rose 500 percent with the incremental growth of U.S. border policing and the expansion of

organized crime in the border region.[23] In the following decade, an estimated three thousand migrants died in attempts to enter the United
States through the far greater hazards of the Sonoran desert. According
to Roberto Martínez, a longtime human-rights advocate in San Diego (one
could say he is the conscience of the U.S. Border Patrol), an average of two
migrants die in transit every day.[24] Many more deaths go unreported and
undiscovered. The space of death is not confined to the border but incor-
porates the limited spheres of agency that are afforded undocumented
people in the United States. Mexican consuls have had to apportion ever-
greater percentages of their budgets to the forensic identification and repatriation of bodies, both of migrants who perished in transit and of those
who died in the United States; consuls have also faced increased demands
for assistance from families searching for missing relatives, now numbering in the thousands.[25]

The numbers of missing migrants reveal changes in migrant behavior
that correspond to the effects of border militarization. The intensification
of border surveillance radically shifted migrant movements and disrupted
the longstanding circular pattern of seasonal migration practiced by many
Mexicans.[26] The proximity of Mexico to the United States had traditionally allowed many migrants, particularly agricultural workers, to enter the
United States for work and then return home for months at a time. But
the new hazards of the border crossing created a far more permanent
presence of undocumented people in the United States.[27] Mexican border
states have also felt the impact of the blockade: deportees and aspiring
migrants tend to remain in the northern cities while they gather the necessary funds to pay coyotes for another attempt at the crossing.

Even so, Operation Gatekeeper failed to meet its own objectives. In 1996,
the Department of Justice's Office of the Inspector General (OIG) launched
an investigation into allegations that the Border Patrol had falsified data
on migrant apprehensions in order to convince the public of the program's
success. The charge came from Border Patrol agents themselves, who tes-
tified before the California Assembly about rampant fraud in the surveillance operations. Officials from the Border Patrol Council, the union representing the agents, described the initiative as an "operational failure."[28]
For agents, failure meant the rising numbers of unauthorized migrants
making a successful entry into the United States and their own increasing
exposure to assault by traffickers; for migrant communities, failure meant

an escalating death toll and a growing climate of racial hostility and intolerance in the United States.[29]

In his study of immigration policing in the 1990s, Joseph Nevins called Operation Gatekeeper "the pinnacle of a national strategy that has achieved historically unprecedented levels of enforcement along the Mexico-U.S. boundary," only to observe its apparently contradictory relationship to the political economy of free trade. "That such an effort is taking place at a time of also unprecedented levels of economic and demographic growth within the border region," he continued, "one marked by a rapidly intensifying transborder socioeconomic integration—a process that many assert is making international boundaries increasingly irrelevant—makes Gatekeeper seem all the more paradoxical."[30]

Paradoxical indeed—but perhaps only in the bifurcated rhetoric with which the U.S. government conducted diplomatic relations with its southern neighbor. As we have seen, the design of NAFTA repeats a longer historical pattern of transborder cooperation among Mexican and U.S. elites; the movement of capital and goods through the region has most often been tied to the fantasy of a regulated border. Both Mexican and U.S. architects of the Bracero Program fought for the means to delimit the mobility of workers through border checkpoints, to labor camps, and to and from job sites. The national boundary could hardly be *less* irrelevant in the age of free-market capitalism. However ineffective border policing appears as immigration *law enforcement*, official sanctions against unauthorized entry function effectively as instruments of *labor regulation*. The difficulty of the border crossing produces migrants less willing to risk deportation, just as the threat of return delimits their social integration and keeps their wages low.

Migrants understand U.S. immigration policy as a check on their labor power and their capacity to defend their rights as workers. The case of day laborers in the United States provides a vivid illustration of how the current regime of border governance serves as a form of labor discipline. Day laborers, a floating population of workers for hire on an informal basis, are a visible fixture of the transnational migrant circuit. Men and women seeking employment in private homes as domestic workers, gardeners, and handymen share street corners, parking lots, and hiring centers with skilled tradespeople awaiting hire by a contractor for jobs in construction or landscaping. Their wages and work conditions depend on what the market will bear, or on their own capacity to contest the racialized terms of the informal transaction. Latin American migrants continue to fill the fantasy of a pliable, disposable workforce: brown bodies available for appropriation.

In a groundbreaking study of the day-labor market, "On the Corner: Day Labor in the United States" (2006), researchers reported consistent patterns of labor exploitation that correspond to the vulnerable status of unauthorized migrants. The social marginality of this population, they argued, helped foster intolerable conditions of abuse in the expanding informal labor market:

> Our findings reveal that the day-labor market is rife with violations of workers' rights. Day laborers are regularly denied payment for their work; many are subjected to demonstrably hazardous job sites; and most endure insults and abuses by employers. The growth of day-labor hiring sites combined with rising levels of workers' rights violations is a national trend that warrants attention at all levels of government.[31]

According to the authors, a national survey of 2,660 day-laborers returned shocking statistics: in 2005 day laborers earned a median income of ten dollars per day but often earned much less due to the volatility of working conditions. Nearly one-half of the respondents reported experiencing the nonpayment of wages at least once during the two-month period preceding the survey. One in five laborers had been injured on the job, and of these, fewer than half received any medical attention. Forty-four percent had been refused breaks or food and water during their work time.[32]

Such working conditions raise ethical and legal concerns about the rights of over six million undocumented people working in the United States.[33] They point to the existence of a laboring caste of migrants whose exposure to severe violations threatens their capacity to act as free workers. The criminalization of the undocumented in U.S. immigration law has had the perverse effect of encouraging their employers to flout U.S. labor law without fear of reprisal. Employers who disregard the codes governing wages, and health and safety, do so knowing that undocumented workers are unlikely to risk exposure by reporting violations to the National Labor Relations Board. Moreover, beginning in the 1990s, the U.S. Supreme Court issued rulings on a number of cases that restricted noncitizens' access to various constitutional protections that would cover their rights to organize, resist arbitrary search and seizure, or seek legal redress for grievances.[34] In the 1990 case *United States v. Verdugo-Urquidez*, notes the legal scholar Michael Wishnie, the Court declared that "many noncitizens are excluded from the protections of the First Amendment" because they are not among "the people" for whom the Constitution was framed.[35]

The expulsion of the noncitizen from the national community follows from the competing demands of the free market and nativism in the United States. The "bounding of the United States" under the auspices of 1996 immigration reforms and Operation Gatekeeper installed a regime of immigration regulation that sought to protect a new rule of law, one that would attempt to satisfy demands for a guarded national community on the one hand (one insistently identified with white cultural primacy) and meet the consumer and capitalist demand for cheap labor on the other. This precarious balance was to be achieved through border regulation. This contradiction has led to an impasse between the boundary-less spheres of free trade and the bounded spheres of U.S. nationalism. Not only has this led immigration officials to infringe on the basic rights guaranteed to noncitizens under both U.S. and international law; it has also meant the distortion of civic life in places where large numbers of undocumented migrants work and reside without the rights and privileges enjoyed by the larger society. Migrants occupy the legal minefield between labor- and human-rights protections on the one hand and U.S. immigration policy on the other.

The conflict over undocumented migrants has also introduced new actors into the field of border policing. As longstanding patterns of border life reasserted themselves in opposition to Operation Gatekeeper, and as human need and practical realities outpaced the drive to close the border, southern Texas and Arizona emerged as the focal point for conflicts between armed ranchers and border crossers, provoking a spate of vigilante violence that has resulted in numerous migrant deaths and injuries. Both the paramilitary and migrant presence showed the final impossibility of imposing an absolute order on the diverse social and political geography of the border region. The Minutemen, the leading civilian patrol group to emerge from the Texas-Arizona ranch patrols, reveal the violence embedded in the concept and operation of the "rule of law" within a space of such radical dissymmetry in wealth and power.

By the banks of the Rio Grande in South Texas, in midsummer 1997, Dob Cunningham held an AR-15 semiautomatic weapon against the temple of a young Mexican man. The sixty-three-year-old rancher had seized the border crosser where the boundary of his pasture dissolved into shallow water and had ordered him to strip naked. Cunningham, who wore a combat jacket and military fatigues, then emptied his gun clip into the air above the brush where he imagined his captive's companions to be hiding. In Spanish he asked the youth if he wanted to live or die and then ordered him back across the muddy river. "I told him to tell his buddies they [were] lucky they weren't all killed," Cunningham informed a reporter for the *Houston Chronicle.* "I told him I was a Marine from Presidio. I told him President Clinton sent me down here to kill you guys." Cunningham went on to become an officer for the American Patrol, a citizens' action group conducting border vigilance.[36]

On May 13, 2000, Samuel Blackwood shot and killed Eusebio de Haro and wounded Javier Sánchez when the two migrants wandered onto his isolated property near Brackettville, Texas, some forty-five miles north of the Mexican border, and begged for water at the door of his house trailer. De Haro pleaded for assistance from his assailant. A woman came out of the house and suggested that he stick his finger in the bullet wound to stop the bleeding. She then watched as de Haro fell silent and died. In response to the initial charge of murder, Blackwood pleaded self-defense and was later indicted on the lesser charge of deadly conduct, despite the fact that de Haro was shot from behind. Blackwood was convicted of homicide by an Eagle Pass, Texas, court but was given a sentence of only 180 days, drawing an official complaint from the Mexican Ministry of Foreign Relations.[37] During these and numerous other incidents of vigilante action against migrants since 1994, landowners have claimed to be carrying out the work of citizenship, upholding the law and protecting property rights where the U.S. government has failed to do so.

Responses to the American Patrol and the Minuteman Project have tended to view their activity as a consequence of the contradictions of globalization, resulting from the inevitable tensions that private citizens experience as the United States seeks both to protect its borders and to pursue economic growth in the free market of labor and capital. But these explanations tend to obscure how the diverse and multilateral violence characteristic of border conflict has arisen both as an effect of state building (not simply as its failure or absence) and from racial limits on the institution of citizenship. Following official complaints from Mexican consuls in 2000, government officials warned the civilian patrols that they have no legal rights to enforce the laws of the United States and that further actions would invite prosecution. Nevertheless, the Border Patrol used the paramilitary "Vigilance Operation" as a justification for expanding the scope of its own operations, demanding new technologies, military and police cooperation, and significant increases in personnel. Following the attacks of September 11, 2001, the U.S. "war on terror" brought border policing under the newly formed Department of Homeland Security. The new security mandates have made antiterrorism a new discourse for the surveillance of migrants and management of the southern boundary.

By its very nature, vigilante violence erodes the boundary between state and citizen, collapsing the distance between abstracted citizenship and the individual citizen. Through the expanding "war on terrorism," the Bush administration officially sanctioned this process. The new definition of homeland security explicitly militarized the exercise of citizenship. Launching the U.S. offensive against Afghanistan on October 7, 2001, Bush addressed the U.S. public in language that enacted the state's interpellative function: "Every American is a soldier, and every citizen is in this fight." The Minuteman Project, which cites this address in their recruitment literature, clearly discerned that the "war without end" would authorize their paramilitary presence as a parallel engagement to the wars in Afghanistan and Iraq.[38] No less a figure than Oliver North received an endorsement from the Minuteman Project for calling the Mexican border "America's Back Door to Terror."[39]

The changed political climate brought the Minuteman Project new political legitimacy. In August 2005, two governors issued declarations of a state of emergency on the southern border. Having criticized the actions of the Minutemen, Governor Bill Richardson of New Mexico and Governor Janet Napolitano of Arizona reiterated the civilian patrols' claim that their southern counties were in a state of war.[40] Both officials cited undocumented migration as a drain on state resources and cited new levels of criminal activity in the border region linked to drug smuggling and human trafficking. Less than a year later, President George W. Bush stationed National Guard troops on the border and signed legislation authorizing

funds for a rapid increase in the number of Border Patrol agents.[41] The National Intelligence Reform Act, which Bush signed into law on December
17, 2005, was designed to add ten thousand new border agents over five
years, doubling the number of officers serving U.S. Customs and Border
Protection.[42]

Justification for the increase in border policing included the need to
quell the activities of vigilantes. But in fact, the augmented Border Patrol
simply reinstates the state monopoly on the sanctioned violence against
border crossers. The injuries inflicted by armed ranchers on migrant "trespassers" number far fewer than those suffered at the hands of Border Patrol
agents themselves. In 1993, Americas Watch reported a "protective climate
of impunity" in the Border Patrol, which had given license to the battery,
shootings, and sexual assault of migrants by the official border guard-
ians.[43] In its summary report, the human-rights agency noted the case of
Agent Michael Andrew Elmer. On June 12, 1992, when Elmer was on patrol
in Nogales, Arizona, he and fellow agents homed in on three men whom
they suspected of being lookouts for area drug traffickers. As the men fled,
Elmer fired on the suspects, hitting Darío Miranda Valenzuela twice in
the back. He then hid Miranda Valenzuela's body in a hollow tree trunk,
leaving him there to die. Elmer's conduct is no different from that of the
vigilantes; but unlike the ranchers, his law-enforcement badge protected
him from prosecution. Even though his trial uncovered prior incidents of
violent conduct on the job, Elmer was acquitted on grounds that he had
acted in self-defense. In contrast, the agent who reported the incident was
fired. Whereas migrants have had some success in countering the acts of
vigilantes, it is almost impossible for them to obtain redress for the abuses
of government agents.[44] The war on terror has only exacerbated concerns
about human-rights violations. In December 2006, when the Inspector
General for Homeland Security, Richard L. Skinner, made his semiannual
report to Congress, he produced an internal audit that showed a marked
increase in the arrests of department employees for crimes including murder, rape, and corruption.[45] Cases involving the Immigration and Customs
Enforcement (ICE) topped the list of severe crimes.

The vigilante demand to declare the Mexico-U.S. boundary a new front
in the war on terror brought the protocols of U.S. imperialism full circle after 2001. Projects for securing the border may have aligned "security" with
the contingencies of "the post-9/11 world," but the ideologies and practices

for national defense (such as preemptive war) were in part the products of the nation's historical interventions in Latin America. Historian Greg Grandin contends, "Latin America was where the United States learned how to be an exceptional empire, extraterritorial . . . without actual direct colonialism."[46] The militarization of the Mexican border occupies no less a part of that history; if we accept Grandin's assessment that U.S. foreign policy under the administration of George W. Bush constituted a "new imperialism," then the southern frontier was a vital staging ground for its discursive and material formation. In the drive for a regulated border, the U.S. government rehearsed the "promotion of free market capitalism [and] a sense that the United States has a special purpose in the world to advance democracy or freedom."[47] These policies authorized the exercise of violent domination of territory and subject populations.

The interdiction of hundreds of thousands of Central American migrants by U.S. immigration authorities from the 1990s onward constituted a continuation of a state of war that predated this boundless war on terror. The U.S.-Mexican border functions as a final crossing point for sojourns that begin much farther south, in Central and South American countries. As the U.S. government sought to bring its southern boundary under military control, it also promoted the militarization of Latin American borders. According to the National Institute of Migration (INM), the detentions of undocumented migrants within Mexico rose by 75 percent between 2002 and 2006, drawing international attention to the inhumane treatment of migrants within the country.[48] The dangerous crossing of the southern Mexican border is a violent rehearsal for the longer trek north for work in the United States or Canada. This exodus grew ever more critical as a strategy for income generation for the Southern Hemisphere: statistics from the Inter-American Development Bank calculate migrant remittances to Latin America and the Caribbean at $54 billion in 2005, a sum that exceeded the sum of all direct foreign investment and aid during the same year.[49] Padre Ademar Barilli, director of the Casa del Migrante, a house of refuge in Tecún Umán, Guatemala, reported in 2006 that the shelter received nearly sixteen thousand migrants over the course of twelve months, most of them from Central America.[50] Rising concerns over transnational gangs that link El Salvador, Guatemala, and Honduras with migrant settlements across the United States produced another discourse of criminality linked to unauthorized migration.

Since 1994, border law enforcement and migrant detention centers have imposed a singularly punitive framework for contending with the unauthorized movement of peoples. This new governmentality partnered sending nations in Central America, countries of transit like Mexico, and destination countries like the United States in a military response to the economic and social contradictions of unequal development in the hemisphere. States have colluded to construct the unauthorized migrant as a legitimate military target for violent interdiction, even as all parties recognized the centrality of the migratory labor circuit to the political economy of the region.

This situation has allowed new capitalist enterprises to move into the militarized zones of border traffic: mafias that trade in drugs, arms, and people in the service of a boundless consumer economy. Contracting with "coyotes" has become vital for migrants; criminal organizations are responsible for the heightened violence in the region, as the movement of people becomes more and more lucrative.[51] "These governments are enriching a network of human traffickers," argued the head of the Guatemalan bishops' migrant pastoral program, Padre Mauro Verzeletti, in 2006.[52] The new migratory circuit sustains a broad array of small-time smugglers and large-scale operatives. For the trafficker, as for the sending country and the U.S. labor contractor, neoliberal reforms and border militarization in the 1990s combined to assign a dollar value to the migrant body—converting persons into profitable objects of exchange.[53]

Migrant Melancholia

U.S. immigration policies and border policing have effectively canceled the option for circular migration, making Mexicans much more likely to pursue permanent settlement in the United States. The coercive aspect of these developments warrants further inquiry. In fact, studies show that most migrants do not wish to stay: "Left to their own devices, the vast majority would return to participate in Mexico's growth as an economy and a society."[54] The prevailing metric of immigration studies, centered as it is on the economic and social productivity of the migrant, cannot measure the melancholic aspect of the shift from circular migrations to a "national population of settled dependents scattered throughout the country."[55] A focus on the relative economic integration between migrants and sender communities, measured in remittances, may obscure the social upheaval and deformations of kinship that extended migrations impose on sender households.

In his 1917 essay "Mourning and Melancholia," Sigmund Freud addressed the ways individuals contend with the death or absence of a beloved person, object, or idea. He noted that distress leads the mourner to deny the loss but that the healthy person will eventually relinquish the attachment and recover a capacity for everyday life. The melancholic person, he argued, refuses to relinquish the lost object and cannot therefore overcome the psychic burden of loss.[56] For Freud, melancholia arises from a pathological or thwarted process of mourning, in which the absent object becomes constitutive of the melancholic self. Recent scholarship has applied Freudian models of mourning and melancholia to forms of subjection or abjection enacted in the political sphere.[57] The border crossing implies a psychic wounding for migrants and invests their nostalgic desires for return with political significance.

If current conditions make the option of circular migration unavailable to many migrants, then the notion of "home" may take on the qualities of the beloved object, whose loss threatens the integrity of the border crosser's personhood. In the same way, the migrant's departure may constitute a catastrophic separation for the sending family and community. In the 2001 documentary *Beyond the Border/Más Allá de la Frontera,* about a family in rural Michoacán that sent three sons to Kentucky for work, the mother of the young men describes a sense of desperation at her economic dependence on her children's remittances: "Yo sé que me va a ayudar, pero para mí cada partida es una muerte" [I know that it will help me, but for me every departure is a death].[58] Marcelo, the last son to leave, describes his trip to the United States through the Sonoran desert as an indelible trauma:

Yo no sabía si podía aguantar. Pasé tres días sin alimentos, tomando sólo traguitos de agua. El sol era tan caliente. Tenía tanta sed. Mi mamá estaba llorando. Eso me afectó mucho. Creo que me afectó psicológicamente.

[I was not sure if I would make it. I went three days without food, taking only small sips of water. The sun was so hot. I was so thirsty. My mother was crying. This affected me. I think it affected me psychologically.]

This exchange offers a rare pedagogy for U.S. viewers on migrant subjectivity. Marcelo's reflection on his border passage captures exactly the process of melancholic incorporation that Freud describes: as the son recalls the hardships of his desert passage, he makes no distinction between his mother's grieving and his own. Although his mother remained behind, the son narrates his experience as if his mother traveled alongside him in the desert—as a source not of comfort or protection but of the profound guilt and distress that Freud ascribed to the melancholic person.

By extension, we may consider how undocumented status itself might constitute a melancholic condition for migrants in the United States. In 2004, I participated in an effort to uncover a confidence scheme to defraud undocumented migrants of thousands of dollars through the sale of false papers. That summer, a friend of mine who migrated to New Haven, Connecticut, from Veracruz, Rita (a pseudonym), told me that a woman for whom she worked had offered to assist her in obtaining legal status for herself and for her family. Soon after, while cleaning the woman's home, Rita observed her employer operating a business in immigration documents out of her house. This woman, a Latina resident of Hamden, posed as a New York immigration official, offering to process paperwork "under the table" and expedite her clients' legalization process. Dozens of Latin American migrants came from New York, Connecticut, and New Jersey to pay fees of as much as twenty-five thousand dollars for the "green cards" that they thought would permit them to work legally, sponsor family members, and move freely between the United States and their home countries.[59]

Rita paid her employer approximately twenty-five hundred dollars to process paperwork for her husband, herself, and her four-year-old son, all of whom had entered the United States without authorization three years earlier. She grew alarmed when I communicated my doubts about the legitimacy of the woman's credentials and my concerns that Rita and her family could get in trouble because of the scam. At the time, Rita was a client of Junta for Progressive Action, an advocacy center that serves the primarily Latina/o neighborhood of Fair Haven. Having seen the number of people taken in by her employer's false promises, Rita made the courageous decision to report the criminal operation to local law enforcement. Junta's director, attorney Kica Matos, mediated between the migrants and the police to make sure that the police would not pursue the immigration cases of the people caught up in the fraud.

As I translated for the victims during their exchanges with Hamden police, I came to understand how easy it was for the imposter to persuade her clients that she could help them circumvent the most elaborate and impenetrable apparatus of U.S. law enforcement, that of immigration. The people from whom she stole were hardly naive—they had experienced theft at the hands of coyotes, employers, immigration lawyers, and other migrants—but they were unwilling to relinquish the fantasy of reunion with the lost objects that haunted their residence in the United States: family and citizenship. The perpetrator of the scam had intimate knowledge of their melancholic disposition as a Puerto Rican migrant herself, and she knew just how far it would lead her clients into her trap. Even after she was exposed, having abandoned her Hamden residence without delivering the papers, many of her clients remained unwilling to accept the reality of their situation. In January 2006, the alleged perpetrator of the crime, María Agosto, a fifty-five-year-old resident of New York, was arraigned on charges of first-degree larceny and criminal impersonation. Rita was the chief witness in the proceeding. Rita continued to confide to me after her testimony that she was certain that the police proceeding was a mistake and that perhaps the woman would return with her documents if she withheld her charges. "Cada noche sueño que estoy en la casa de mi mamá," she said. "Hasta puedo oler su perfume" [Every night, I dream that I am in my mother's house. I can even smell her perfume.].

Proponents of anti-immigration measures commonly represent the undocumented as people with no respect for the rule of law. This assumption reflects a total misunderstanding of what "law" means for the unauthorized migrant. One could say that the undocumented come from countries where bribes are routinely paid to expedite state services; however, this explanation is, in my opinion, an inadequate answer to the question of how so many migrants came to pay unimaginable sums for the dream of legalization. It is precisely because of their investment in legality, both in practical and moral terms, that the victims of the Hamden scam could invest so heavily in false papers. The migrants did not deliberately seek to circumvent state authority when they paid the imposter to act on their behalf; rather, they sought incorporation into the state through the only means available. Beyond their desire for the goods of citizenship, for freedom of movement and for better wages, working conditions, and health care, the migrants were easily deceived because of their profound desire to be recognized as legitimate subjects, to inhabit the status of citizen. Even in simple economic terms, the theft of migrant earnings represented an enormous crime: the price of twenty-five thousand dollars for false papers represents an inordinate number of labor hours for a network of migrants and relatives who joined together in the vain hope of bringing children north from Ecuador or Guatemala and making them into U.S. nationals.

The Hamden incident reminds us that it is easy to exploit migrant desire. For many migrants, the costs of entering into the United States for work preclude the seasonal visits to Mexico that might placate the sense of loss and isolation. In New Haven, far from the ethnic centers of the Southwest, nationality is easily reduced to a consular card and the vague promises of protection that it confers. For Mexicans here, U.S. citizenship or legal residence represents the single best option for securing a livelihood and retaining viable connections to family and hometown over time. And yet the vast majority of the undocumented are unlikely to obtain such a prize.

The material and psychic hungers that propel migrants to abandon the most basic elements of sociality—residence, kinship, language, culture, and landscape—in short, *home*, for wages exert a violence that immigration scholarship and state discourse have yet to fully address. The condition of being "undocumented" does not simply imply a lack of legal protection or status but rather entails the active conversion of the migrant into a distinct category of stateless personhood. This peculiar status emerges with the contradiction between market demands for mobile labor and consumable goods and the immobility of rights beyond the bounds of the nation-state. Mexican migrants, like other displaced peoples, continually invent forms of agency within that space of opposition. It is a melancholy task. Stories of border mortality and disappearance are a means to narrate the other kinds of death that Marcelo's mother describes, the leave-taking that extinguishes one form of connection to make way for another. In this ritual of departure, the family enacts, in intimate form, the migrant's detachment from the state, a severing of citizenship that is also a death, a death that produces.

Lost Citizens

In the days following the destruction of the World Trade Center, members of El Asociación Tepeyac de New York, an advocacy center for Latino immigrants, found themselves inundated with calls from households across Latin America, asking for news of missing relatives believed to be working in the United States. Eventually, Tepeyac identified 113 cases of missing people and 857 displaced workers connected to the September 11 disaster.[60] The organization was instrumental in documenting their cases and helping survivors obtain relief funds. Just as pressing, however, are the hundreds of petitions for assistance in locating missing family members that may have no direct relationship to the events in New York and that remain unresolved. Esperanza Chacón, the director of Urgent Affairs for Tepeyac, argues that the enforced invisibility of undocumented workers in the United States makes it impossible to clarify the status of these reports of missing persons.[61] Despite the ready availability of cellular phones and electronic communications media for sustaining communal and familial ties among migrants, it was all too clear in 2001 that migration could still threaten sending households with dissolution and loss.

The events of 9/11 foreclosed on the plans of presidents Bush and Fox for a binational agreement that would facilitate guest-worker programs and provide amnesty to hundreds of thousands of undocumented Mexicans residing in the United States. In the wake of the attacks, the term "amnesty" became political poison. In Mexico, the loss of Mexican nationals at the World Trade Center provoked renewed debate about the implications of mass migrations and economic dependency for state sovereignty and the coherence of Mexico's national community. In 2003, public pressure forced Gerónimo Gutiérrez Fernández, then subsecretary for North America in Mexico's Office of Foreign Relations (SRE), to admit openly that his office received an annual average of five thousand requests for assistance in locating persons presumed missing in the course of emigration to the United States.[62] Mexican officials consider the actual number to be far higher, since the SRE figure only reflects the fraction of incidents in which the state becomes involved. Gutiérrez Fernández reported that his office resolves 20 percent of the cases, but he did not elaborate on the specific outcomes of these investigations. The SRE has since outlined a proposal for creating an electronic database for biogenetic data that would assist the state in tracking and identifying the missing, a proposal made urgent by the complicated task of repatriating the remains of Mexicans who die abroad.

The border crossing has always threatened migrants with disappearance or death, and certainly with dislocation from kin and community. The 2001 catastrophe in New York brought the fragility of transnational ties into focus once more, during a period when migrant remittances reached their peak share of Mexican GDP.[63] Mexican settlements in New York followed patterns established by earlier labor migrations; new arrivals to Manhattan and Long Island in the 1990s were just as successful in forming mutual-aid societies and exerting economic and political force in their Puebla hometowns as their conationals in Los Angeles or Houston.[64] Many perils of recent migration are in fact not *new*, but the diffusion of migrant circuits beyond the southwestern United States does reflect significant changes in traditional forms of transnational settlement, even from older sending regions.[65] Established patterns of seasonal migration for work have given way to higher rates of permanent settlement in the United States, with greater numbers of women and children migrating to obtain work and to unify families, despite conditions of increased risk.[66] Emigration has shifted from being a rural phenomenon to encompassing industrialized towns and cities, and every Mexican state now confronts the vast scale of out-migration to the United States. These demographic shifts correspond to stalled economic and political reforms in Mexico as state failure continues to promote mass emigration. Jorge Durand and Douglas Massey comment that in Mexico "migrant networks are much stronger in rural than in urban areas because rural social networks are stronger and more dense."[67] The dispersal of emigrants thus implies a different risk for sending urban communities, given their greater social diffusion.

The new hazards and congestion of the border crossing may thus ultimately alter the social networks observed in studies of migrant communities.[68] The prolonged crises of Mexican economic restructuring and the weakness of state protections for emigrants have had profound implications for how displaced Mexicans, both internal and transnational migrants, may experience and express their nationality in the migratory circuit. Mexicans living abroad form hometown associations in order to provide resources for sending communities, a process that the government sought to coopt through a program of matching funds for migrant remittances. Federal, state, and local authorities in Mexico promised to match migrant donations on a "Three for One" ratio, with the hope of diverting private remittances to state expenditures. In Chicago, for example, a group of migrants from Indaparapeo, Michoacán, pooled resources to establish a scholarship program for the town's youth and resisted the state government's suggestion that monies be set aside for new roads and drainage.[69] Grupo Indaparapeo chose to develop the town's human capital over state-run projects as a direct rebuke to officials for their failure to meet its most basic obligations to the townspeople. Whereas the private contributions for the scholarship are always on time, Grupo Indaparapeo reported that matching funds were always in short supply. Members of the hometown association may have exercised the forms of *postnational* agency described in current studies of migration, but they did so in a concerted effort to recover and reconstitute *national* citizenship.[70] The Michoacán migrants designed the scholarship program so that townspeople would not have to leave home to seek their livelihood. After a century of out-migration, their initiative represents a purchase against loss and estrangement in the next generation.

Mexican leaders have expressed alarm at the volume of the exodus, which once more threatens the unity of the nation-state and its primary hold over its citizens. In a 2006 conference devoted to the estimated seven million Mexicans residing illegally in the United States, the Mexican Minister of Foreign Affairs, Luis Ernesto Derbez, called for U.S. forbearance on the problem of unauthorized migration. Asserting that undocumented workers contribute between $300 and $400 billion to the U.S. economy every year, Derbez argued that a new temporary-worker program would be needed for the duration while Mexico pursued the necessary economic development that could produce sufficient jobs for the emigrant population. "The word temporary means we put our house in order," Derbez stated. "I will need help to have these people who are now at the age of working have a job."[71] Jorge Santibañez, the director of the Colegio de la

Frontera Norte in Tijuana, Mexico, echoed Derbez's sense of national abjection before the economic superiority of the U.S. job market: "Migrants are actors in a national tragedy."[72] (Santibañez's remarks recall the sentiments of Mexican intellectuals during the Bracero Program of the 1950s, when immigration scholar and activist Ernesto Galarza termed migration "a failure of roots.") Even as Mexican officials defend migrants by pointing to the globalization of the labor market and the integration of both national economies, they must ultimately admit that emigration is an indicator of state failure. Such an admission leads almost immediately to a displacement of the problem onto the emigrants themselves. Santibañez voiced his demand, *while in the United States*, for Mexican policies that would act as a deterrent on emigration by imposing penalties on nationals who cross the border illegally. Given that at the time the U.S. House of Representatives and Senate were deadlocked over the most draconian proposals for immigration reform, these remarks by a Mexican official abroad convey the inordinate emotion driving economic and social policy in the two countries. *Emigrants are not so much governed in Mexico as they are mourned.*

Current anxieties about border hazards also appear in Mexican popular media, in texts that narrate significant shifts in how migration is managed both at the level of lived experience and at the level of consumer culture. In December 2003, Telemundo aired the Mexican novela *El alma herida* [The Wounded Soul], a serial melodrama devoted to a migrant family shattered at the border crossing.[73] The show earned strong ratings and became known as "una de las novelas más queridas por el público hispano" [one of the most beloved novelas of the Hispanic public].[74] The storyline followed familiar motifs for reinforcing national identity by depicting the dangers of pursuing material aspirations in the United States:

> Una familia llena de esperanzas toma la difícil decisión de cruzar la frontera en busca del sueño americano, déjandolo todo atrás sin sospechar que el destino les jugará una mala pasada separándolos trágicamente.

> [Full of hope, a family makes the difficult decision to cross the border in search of the American dream. They leave everything behind not knowing that destiny is about to play them a bad hand, separating them tragically from one another.][75]

The family does not make it across the border intact: the father and two children meet up with abusive police, while the pollero [smuggler] forces Catalina, the mother, across to the United States. The sixty-five episodes follow the daughter and mother's efforts at family reunification, allegorizing the broader process of Mexican migration since 1965. The border imposes total familial separation and threatens its annihilation: the plot turns on the family's question of whether the mother has died or abandoned them. The story ultimately ends in a bloodbath, with the daughter electing between two male partners in two countries, a choice that implies that her honor can be safeguarded only in Mexico. However contrived, *El alma herida* nevertheless departs from standard nationalist discourse by anchoring its story in a female, rather than a male, migrant. The status of the family depends on the recovery of the missing mother, not its wage-earning father, and her recuperation comes through the agency of the enterprising daughter Eugenia, who first crosses the border at age eleven. *El alma herida* thus fulfills the function of melodrama to nourish a female spectatorship; it does so through a migrant imaginary now thoroughly feminized.

As is often the case, the popular media are far more equipped than the state to engage with the complex subjective processes that emigration entails for many Mexicans. *El alma herida* captivated audiences on both sides of the border crossing, creating a transnational sphere of communication where the Mexican government has failed to do so. By affirming migrant suffering—in fact, enlarging its melodrama so that it cannot be sublimated and normalized—the telenovela also makes room for the subjectivity of those whom the state has been all too willing to disavow. As the plot moves toward the restoration of Eugenia's citizenship, it also points to where the state has refused to act.

Disappearing Migrants

The formal institutions that enshrine Mexican citizenship show the strain induced by the uncertainties of the border passage: the Office of Foreign Relations (SRE), which oversees Mexican consulates, vacillates between a discourse that interpellates emigrants as full nationals and something

approaching an official language of mourning. "Tu calidad de indocumen-
tado no te convierte en delincuente" [Your undocumented status does not
make you a criminal] reads a Web document for the Consul General of
New York, which goes on to explain the human-rights protections that
cover migrants in the United States.[76] Within this assertion is a latent recognition of the threat of loss—of personal sovereignty for the migrant, of
national sovereignty for the Mexican state—inherent in the unauthorized
border crossing. The transit from citizenship to unauthorized status in the
United States is, in fact, a process of conversion, effected *through* violence
—the sanctioned interdiction of the state, which may seize and remove
migrants by its use of force, or the extralegal, informal aggressions of nonstate actors.

The Instituto Nacional de Migración [INM, National Institute of Migra-
tion] generated controversy in the early 2000s by issuing pamphlets to
potential migrants that delineate the hazards of the border crossing. The
guides contain emergency telephone numbers, the details of consular
services and immigration documents, and information about migrants'
protections under international law. With their graphic depictions of migrant deaths, the books become an inventory of *passing* as well as passage in pages devoted to the many ways the border can kill. In a section
devoted to the Sonoran desert, the *Guía del Migrante Yucateco* [Guide for
the Yucatecan Migrant] lists the symptoms of dehydration, only to conclude, "Si tienes estos síntomas, estás en peligro de morir lentamente" [If
you have these symptoms, you are in danger of dying slowly].[77] The irony
is, of course, that the Mexican government cannot do more than forecast
this death. Mexican sovereignty does not extend to providing gainful employment to nationals at home, nor does it provide safe passage for those
leaving the country.

This point came home to me in an interview with officers from the
Grupos Beta de Protección a Migrantes [Beta Groups for the Protection
of Migrants], the Mexican border patrol in Ciudad Juárez, in 2003. C. Roberto Gaytan Saucedo, the interim director for the INM in Juárez, reported that the scale of migration makes the task of policing the desert
region impossible. Officially a humanitarian operation of the INM, Grupos
Beta claimed just seven officers for the vast Juárez metropolitan region in
2003. Like generations of border officers before him, Gaytan Saucedo admitted that every seizure of a migrant merely delays the eventual cross-

ing.[78] Grupos Beta has resorted to posting signs in the desert about the perils of migration, advising women to purchase pepper spray as a defense against male aggressors. The empty gesture makes it clear that women alone are responsible for their personal safety. The state functions of security do not extend into this denationalized border zone, nor do they cover the bodies of women moving through this space. Mexican sovereignty and state power are so compromised in the border region that the Grupos Beta does not dare to venture into the path of armed criminal groups operating in the desert; the absurdity of pepper spray here makes a cruel joke of the state's disinterest in women's suffering. In March 2005, Claudia Smith, president of the Coalition in the Defense of the Migrant, stated that one in ten women report being raped in the attempt to cross the border.[79]

In this context, the INM warning "hay caminos sin regreso" [there are paths of no return] doubles as an admonition and an admission of state complicity in migrant suffering. Neoliberal governance has only exacerbated the government's role as a broker for cheap labor. The failure of market-led development has forced individual states to compete with one another for migrant remittances. Various states now issue their own localized migrant guidebooks, which combine the national discourse on the border crossing with promotions of regional identity and loyalty. The *Guía del Migrante Yucateco* offers information on Yucatecan clubs and mutual-aid societies in California, stressing the interest of the state government in helping migrants organize abroad. "Yendo o viniendo Yucateco sigue siendo" [Going or coming, you remain Yucatecan], it reads, displaying an official regard for how local Mayan ethnicity offers a vital resource for group survival in the United States.[80] Of course, those Yucatecos who perish or vanish do not remain Yucateco. On average, five migrants from southern Mexican states die every month trying to reach the northern border, and many more disappear. The state's invocation of human rights or cultural unity as a supplement to citizenship collapses under the pressure to obtain migrant remittances at any cost. The guidebook's final assertion, "cuida tu vida" [guard your life] underlines how life, in this instance, gets reduced to a vehicle for income generation. In their ambivalent discourse of nationalism and mourning, migrant guides articulate contradictions in Mexican development: the links between nation-building and migration mark the state's intimacy with death.

The proliferating reports of migrant disappearances reflect the uncertainties of this moment for sending communities in Mexico. It is impossible to examine the ephemeral websites devoted to the missing without considering the weight of the disappearances on the fragile linkages of kin and conationals in transnational space. Family photographs, passport pictures, and identification cards posted to sites operated by the Mexican consulate adopt both the form of official immigration documents and more personal narrative to describe the disappeared. "Odilon Vera Mendez, 32," listed by height, weight, hair and eye color, complexion, and facial features, appears online in a photograph depicting the young man at a track meet. The race tag on his chest, "L959," stands in for the official imprint of the state identification number, the mug shot, passport, or perhaps the bracero registration number of past migrations. The photo caption reads,

> Lugar de Origen: Huauchinango, Puebla. Últimos datos conocidos: Salió de Tetela de Ocampo, Puebla el pasado 13 de noviembre de 2001, con destino a Estados Unidos para trabajar, pero hasta la fecha su familia no tiene noticias de él.

> [Place of birth: Huauchinango, Puebla. Last known: He departed from Tetela de Ocampo, Puebla, on 13 November 2001, on route to work in the United States, but to this date, his family has received no news of his whereabouts.][81]

Between the precision of Tetela de Ocampo, Puebla (population 25,859, 304.89 square kilometers in area, and 3,000 meters above sea level) and the uncharted route to work in the United States, the vast terrain of transnational space presents its threat to identity, to kinship, to territoriality itself.

The interrupted biographies of the disappeared represent a rupture in time and space for sending families and towns. For the bereft, not knowing whether the missing person is alive or dead disrupts the narrative of transnational community, both in its symbolic unity and in the material sense of economic survival and the futurity of family lines. One image in particular, from the Consul General website, invites analysis: Azucena Quezada Olea, of Morelos, last seen in 2002.[82] The young woman in the photograph stands in a parking lot that could be anywhere in the north-

Left: Odilon Vera Méndez, missing since November 13, 2001.
Right: Azucena Quezada Olea, missing since 2002. ("Protección
a Mexicanos," Consul General de México, online resource for
missing persons)

south circuit of migrant travels. Her shirt bears the tourist logo for Kentucky, perhaps a sign of her connection to this new outpost of Mexican
labor or perhaps a souvenir of her tourist travel. The nondescript background is nonetheless an occasion for a portrait, for memorialization of
the moment, of her being there. Azucena Quezada Olea smiles as she
gazes out at the camera, one hand shyly at her face, another hand holding
a young child. She occupies the whole of the image: the child next to her
is only partly in the picture. The child looks so much like Azucena that
the image can only imply their relatedness. And yet the border of the photograph bisects the child.

The photograph of the missing woman captures what seems ineffable
in narratives of border crossing, the sense that the migrant occupies a
place and no place at once. Disappearance implies not only the loss of the
woman herself but the destruction that her death or departure means for
the child. Familial dislocation, occurring across national boundaries, puts
children's identities and protection in crisis. Children lose their minimal
political status once separated from their parents in the migrant circuit. In
a larger sense, the photograph illuminates the profoundly unsettling ways

in which transnational migration remakes kinship and reveals how kinship cannot mitigate against loss. In this instance, the vanishing of Azucena makes a ghost of her child.

The unacknowledged costs of Mexican mobility find expression in the rumors of human traffic and bondage that circulate within migrant communities. The spectacular horror of these stories may correspond to actual incidents, but in their elaboration, rumors also project the phantasmagoric aspect of migrant imaginaries. Lists of missing persons obtain symbolic significance as an inchoate form of contestation to the way government policies continue to displace the burden of maintaining transnational labor circuits from the state onto private individuals and households. The consular lists of the disappeared that preserve accounts of the missing as parents, children, partners, and friends are a form of desperate contestation to the binational state apparatus that converts the undocumented into people without status, people without a place. And yet the disappeared are nonetheless *present*; their stories of loss remake the narratives of kinship, community, and belonging that sustain the transnational circuit.

Reports of migrant deaths and disappearances in the transnational circuit linking the United States and Mexico should disturb the fiction of the regulated border. The fate of the undocumented reveals the violence with which both states have acted over time to rationalize the boundaries of their territory and citizenship. Sharp increases in the number of undocumented migrants and the concurrent escalation of border militarization have made the journey to the United States more hazardous and the possibilities of return to Mexico more uncertain. Furthermore, as migration has increasingly extended outward from the Southwest, it has challenged the dominant frameworks for depicting or explaining the Mexican presence in the United States. As the costs of Mexican labor migrations have become more visible, state institutions and communications media in both countries have had to address the hazards, both physical and psychological, of unauthorized entry and settlement in the United States. Disappearances of various sorts are revealed in the growing rosters of missing persons kept by the Mexican Office of Foreign Relations (Secretaría de Relaciones Exteriores) and immigrant organizations; these numbers reveal the instability of those narratives of kinship, class, and nationality that have historically functioned to delimit accounts of migrations as loss for sending communities.

Given the recent developments, the melancholic aspect of the journey north has surfaced with a new urgency, putting in crisis the tale of the enterprising migrant "seeking a better life." Stories of disappearance and lonely deaths put the flesh back on the bare-bones figure of the "guest worker" at a moment when the Mexican state confers neither a living nor rights to poor citizens, and when U.S. officials and civilians alike routinely detain, abuse, and exploit migrants with little regard for international human-rights conventions. The two nations collude in producing a class of denationalized subjects whose personhood is discursively consigned to mere economic being as disposable labor or is legally reduced to the mere status of criminal trespasser.

In closing, I want to consider the significance of other vanishings. Ciudad Juárez is not only the place of arrival and departure for thousands in the migrant circuit; throughout this period of increased migration, the city has been a terminus of utter brutality for the victims of feminicidio.[83] The northern boomtown, whose principal function is to support the mobility of capital, goods, and labor, has been the site of unprecedented killings of girls and women, residents of the Juárez colonias.[84] Many more young women are missing. For more than a decade, state and federal officials have permitted the murders to continue with impunity. The nation that sends thousands of its people into the migrant labor circuit has little to offer as protection for the female citizens whose vitality and labors sustain the fragile social ecology of the border space. Images of the missing girls travel the same networks as the pictures advertising the names of disappeared migrants. Currently, El Paso and Ciudad Juárez are sites of ardent campaigns against the feminicidio and the death of migrants in the border crossing. The success of these local mobilizations will depend on effective witness to migrants' stories of bereavement and absence. The political forms that we devise in this moment of global transformation must consider the violence that brings the circuits of human mobility into traffic with death, an immovable death, a departure with no return.

Afterword

A través de la línea/
Across the Line

This book had its origin in my own initiations into the migrant imaginary. I grew up in a city without Mexicans, and I sometimes thought that my mother brought every Mexican person passing through into our Philadelphia home. Her long labors over brilliant piñatas for our birthdays figured the many pains that she took to nourish a Mexican childhood for my sister and me from the distance of the northeastern United States. I had no idea that I was living on the verge of a new exodus from Latin America, one that would reanimate our own latinidad within a broader field of solidarity and struggle. The civil wars in Central America and U.S.-sponsored repression across the region drew a new cartography of struggle for my own transnational family during the 1970s and 1980s. Alongside the intimate language of long-distance kinship, I learned the lexicon of terror and exile, and protest. I remember meeting one teenager who spoke of crossing on foot the length of Mexico and the United States for sanctuary from the Guatemalan genocide. Kanjobal Mayas and Salvadoran trade unionists who spoke out in public conferences on the Central American wars donned bandanas to cover their faces, redrawing the boundaries of safety or danger in my childhood. The map that these migrants drew was not simply of new relations of territoriality and nation but of memory from below, an assertion of presence against forgetting.

Alma López, *Santa Niña de Mochis, 1848 Series* (1998). (Reproduced with generous permission from the artist)

My Philadelphia family plotted new ordinals of belonging in the embrace of this migrant imagination as it arrived in the persons of salvadoreñas/os and guatemaltecas/os fleeing state terror, or in the new settlements of mexicana/o field workers in Kennett Square, Pennsylvania. The salvadoreños who sometimes stayed with us during their long exile, the young guatemalteca Rigoberta Menchú who teased my father for looking like El Dios Padre gringo, and the migrant trade unionists offered a familial relationship as proxy for my abuelos, tíos, and primos in Guadalajara, even as their personal histories of trauma and dislocation remained far beyond my understanding. Their joyful offerings of language, prayer, and food—of convivencia [conviviality]—taught an unmistakable lesson in the ethics of survival. De la tierra somos, no somos ilegales [We are of the earth, we are not illegal].

This is my own children's inheritance: to grow up within a migrant community far more diverse and vibrant than the Philadelphia of my childhood, or their father's Sacramento. In the spring of 2006, amid the immigrant-rights movement, Antonio and Thalia also learned the migrant vernacular of struggle: they thrilled in the chants of amnistía en general [amnesty for all]. One afternoon in May, they staged a rally on our lawn, complete with plastic microphones and attentive stuffed animals. "Let all the people be!" Thalia called, and Antonio added, "Let the Mexicans wear their sombreros! ¡Sí se puede!"

They knew that another world is possible. Sí se puede. Sí se puede. Sí se puede.

This is the dance of history in our day, Salman Rushdie tells us, the crossing of borders. During the ten years I devoted to this book, the mobility of peoples around the globe has reached levels that defy categorization in the meager language we bring to human movement: migrant, refugee, immigrant, displaced person, exile.

We are witness to emergent forms of social life that correspond to the vast scale of human displacement and change, and we see the resurgence of repressive violence by state and nonstate actors who seek dominion over border crossers. The rising index of armed conflict in the Mexico-U.S. boundary points to the fundamental debility of human-rights protections when pitted against the prerogatives of state sovereignty and global capitalism. Since 1994, the traffic in human beings has become among the most lucrative trades in the transborder region, as criminal gangs exploit the militarized border space to wage their war for profit. The border is home to migrants from throughout Latin America, who flee the immiseration of their indigenous economies under neoliberal development and the criminal violence that undoes the promises of democratization in many polities. Not only that, but the fact that the northern Mexican boundary gives way to the largest consumer market in the world has brought numerous enterprises to the region: tourism schemes but also cartels that sell workers, sex, drugs, and arms. Operations in the border are fully global, linking Eastern Europe, Asia, Latin America, and elsewhere. The new imperatives of the U.S. war on terror sanction the violent interdiction of migrants and border residents on a vaster scale, with greater penalties. All these processes entail violence that is gendered in nature, with severe implications for poor migrants and for women and children in the border cities.

At the close of the twentieth century, the border cities witnessed violence of an unprecedented scale: since 1993, as we have seen, some four hundred girls and women have been tortured and killed in Ciudad Juárez and Chihuahua. Another thousand are missing. The death rates for Mexican migrants have risen 600 percent since the passage of Operation Gatekeeper in 1994. This violence is not aberrant but central to the current regime of unregulated capitalist growth and unequal development. The Mexico-U.S. border is a critical locus for the transnational circuits that form the global political economy and its neoliberal governance.

Migrants and border people wage ardent struggles to resist their conversion into life that has no value. It is an effort that demands our solidarity and witness as comunidades de convivencia a través de la línea [communities of conviviality across the line]. The fragile social ecology of the transborder space hangs in the balance.

In 1940, Walter Benjamin looked at a painting by Paul Klee and saw the portents of the future under fascism, and he drafted a statement on the responsibilities of the scholar before history. His Angelus Novus stood as a figure of witness to the European catastrophe. Benjamin wrote,

> This is how one pictures the angel of history. His face is turned toward the past. Where we perceive a chain of events, he sees one single catastrophe which keeps piling wreckage and hurls it in front of his feet. The angel would like to stay, awaken the dead, and make whole what has been smashed. But a storm is blowing in from Paradise; it has got caught in his wings with such a violence that the angel can no longer close them. The storm irresistibly propels him into the future to which his back is turned, while the pile of debris before him grows skyward. This storm is what we call progress.[1]

The philosopher imagined his angel in an age when the grand narratives of modernity anchored history in the power of the nation-state and its privileged subjects and anchored cultural value in the emanations of art and thought from Europe. It is not so today.

To me the Angelus Novus for our time appears in a digital print by the Chicana artist Alma López, entitled *Santa Niña de Mochis* (1993).[2] In the image, a young girl stands astride the U.S.-Mexican boundary, wearing a first-communion dress and costume wings, her sandaled feet perched over the patient cherub who traditionally bears the Virgen de Guadalupe, patroness of the Americas. Behind her lies the vast urban landscape of the border cities, within it a women's picket line and a patrol car. The image captures both the burdens of history and an abiding faith in its potential transformation. But today the border economies place inordinate burdens on girls like this one. The feminicidio is certainly the most extreme danger facing poor young girls and women, but it is the symptom of a deeper order of violence at work in the region. The Santa Niña would like to stay, awaken the dead, and make whole what has been smashed at this unnatural boundary.

The border space no longer exists—it is no longer periphery or margin. It is becoming a more generalized condition. The border crossing has produced its own wounded figure of witness. She is the maker of worlds. Today, the angel of history is a little Mexican girl.

NOTES

NOTES TO THE INTRODUCTION

1. Salman Rushdie, *Step across This Line: Collected Nonfiction* (New York: Random House, 2002), p. 365.

2. Cited by Gaspar Rivera-Salgado in a study sponsored by the Woodrow Wilson International Center for Scholars. See Xochitl Bada, Jonathan Fox, and Andrew Selee, eds., *Invisible No More: Mexican Migrant Civic Participation in the United States* (Washington, DC: Woodrow Wilson International Center for Scholars, 2006), p. 5.

3. Cited by Rivera-Salgado, in *Invisible No More*, p. 5. HR 4437, sponsored by the Republican congressman from Wisconsin Jim Sensenbrenner, failed to pass the Senate, and the Congress was ultimately unable to produce a compromise immigration bill in either 2006 or 2007.

4. Timoteo, in Jorge Durand, ed., *El Norte es como el mar: Entrevistas a trabajadores migrantes en Estados Unidos* (Guadalajara: Universidad de Guadalajara, 1996), p. 182.

5. Ernesto Galarza, *Merchants of Labor: The Mexican Bracero Story* (Charlotte, NC: McNally and Loftin, 1964), p. 17.

6. Arturo Islas, *Migrant Souls* (New York: Avon Books, 1991).

7. Cornelius Castoriadis, *The Imaginary Institution of Society*, translated by Kathleen Blamey (Cambridge, MA: MIT Press, 1987).

8. See also Charles Taylor, *Modern Social Imaginaries* (Durham, NC: Duke University Press, 2004).

9. Dilip Parameshwar Gaonkar, "Toward New Imaginaries: An Introduction," *Public Culture* 14.1 (2002): p. 4.

10. Taylor, *Modern Social Imaginaries*, p. 2.

11. See Benedict Anderson, *Imagined Communities: Reflections on the Origin and Spread of Nationalism* (1983; repr., London: Verso, 1991).

12. The anthropologist Arjun Appadurai has examined the contradiction between the global cultural shifts produced by mass migrations and the rise of transnational communications media and the continued primacy of localized nationalism. See *Modernity at Large: Cultural Dimensions of Globalization* (Minneapolis: University of Minnesota Press, 1996).

13. Tomás Rivera, *Y no se lo tragó la tierra/And the Earth Did Not Swallow Him* (1971), trans. Evangelina Vígil Piñon (Houston: Arte Público, 1987).

14. Juan Bruce-Novoa, *Chicano Authors: Inquiry by Interview* (Austin: University of Texas Press, 1980).

15. Antonio Gramsci, "History of the Subaltern Classes: Methodological Criteria," in *Selections from the Prison Notebooks*, ed. and trans. Quintin Hoare and Geoffrey Nowell Smith (New York: International Publishers, 1971), p. 206.

16. Ramón Saldívar, *Chicano Narrative: The Dialectics of Difference* (Madison: University of Wisconsin Press, 1990), p. 77.

17. The English translation is by Evangelina Vígil Piñon.

18. Milagritos are miniature figures placed on shrines in petition for intervention from a saint. They commonly take the shape of parts of the body afflicted by illness or of a desired object, like a house.

19. James C. Scott, *Domination and the Arts of Resistance: Hidden Transcripts* (New Haven, CT: Yale University Press, 1990), p. 108.

20. Etienne Balibar, "The Nation Form: History and Ideology," in Etienne Balibar and Immanuel Wallerstein, *Race, Nation, Class: Ambiguous Identities*, pp. 86–106 (London: Verso, 1991), 90–91.

21. Adolfo Gilly, *The Mexican Revolution*, translated by Patrick Camiller (London: Verso, 1976), p. 343.

22. David G. Gutiérrez, *Walls and Mirrors: Mexican Americans, Mexican Immigrants, and the Politics of Ethnicity* (Berkeley: University of California Press, 1995), p. 49. The quotation comes from Ralph Taylor in *House Committee on Immigration from Countries of the Western Hemisphere: Hearings*, 1930, p. 265.

23. See Bartholomew H. Sparrow, *The Insular Cases and the Emergence of American Empire* (Lawrence: University Press of Kansas, 2006); Christina Duffy-Burnett and Burke Marshall, eds., *Foreign in a Domestic Sense: Puerto Rico, American Expansion, and the Constitution* (Durham, NC: Duke University Press, 2001); and Matthew Frye Jacobson, *Barbarian Virtues: The United States Encounters Foreign Peoples at Home and Abroad, 1876–1917* (New York: Hill and Wang, 2000).

24. Balibar, "Nation Form," p. 91. See also Alicia Schmidt Camacho, "Migrant Subjects: Race, Labor and Insurgency in the Mexico-U.S. Borderlands" (Ph.D. diss., Stanford University, 2000), which centers on the efforts of migrants and tejanos to retain a transborder community within and against the U.S. nation-state.

25. Aurelio, interviewed by Enrique Martínez Curiel in Ameca, Jalisco, in 1992, in Durand, *El Norte es como el mar*, p. 29 (my translation).

26. Durand, *El Norte es como el mar*, p. 28.

27. Aurelio, in Durand, *El Norte es como el mar*, p. 30.

28. Raymond C. Ileto, "Outlines of a Nonlinear Emplotment of Philippine History," in *The Politics of Culture in the Shadow of Capital*, ed. Lisa Lloyd and David Lloyd, pp. 98–131 (Durham, NC: Duke University Press, 1997), 125–26.

NOTES TO CHAPTER 1

1. From the Spanish verb "enganchar," meaning "to hook." The term was used in common parlance for subcontracted workers hired either in Mexico or in the United States.

2. Juanita and Arnold Vasquez, "Kidnapped," in Señoras of Yesteryear, *Mexican American Harbor Lights* (Pictorial History) (Indiana, IL: Señoras of Yesteryear, 1987), p. 13.

3. See David G. Gutiérrez, *Walls and Mirrors: Mexican Americans, Mexican Immigrants, and the Politics of Ethnicity* (Berkeley: University of California Press, 1995), pp. 44–45.

4. See Devra Weber, *Dark Sweat, White Gold: California Farm Workers, Cotton, and the New Deal* (Berkeley: University of California Press, 1994), pp. 48–53.

5. Ibid., p. 50.

6. Gutiérrez, *Walls and Mirrors*, p. 45.

7. See Zaragoza Vargas, *Labor Rights Are Civil Rights: Mexican American Workers in Twentieth-Century America* (Princeton, NJ: Princeton University Press, 2005), p. 7.

8. "El Ferrocarril" [The Train], in Manuel Gamio, *Mexican Immigration to the United States: A Study of Human Migration and Adjustment* (1930; repr., New York: Dover, 1971), pp. 92–93 (my translation). Gamio collected the corrido during his 1926–1927 study of Mexican migrants in the United States.

9. Juanita and Arnold Vásquez, "Kidnapped," p. 13.

10. See Neil Foley, *The White Scourge: Mexicans, Blacks, and Poor Whites in Texas Cotton Culture* (Berkeley: University of California Press, 1998); Weber, *Dark Sweat, White Gold*; Vargas, *Labor Rights Are Civil Rights*; and Mae M. Ngai, *Impossible Subjects: Illegal Aliens and the Making of Modern America* (Princeton, NJ: Princeton University Press, 2004).

11. See Ramón Saldívar, *The Borderlands of Culture: Américo Paredes and the Transnational Imaginary* (Durham, NC: Duke University Press, 2006).

12. See Ngai, *Impossible Subjects*.

13. Carlos Vélez-Ibáñez, *Border Visions: Mexican Cultures of the Southwest United States* (Tucson: University of Arizona Press, 1996), p. 72.

14. Ngai, *Impossible Subjects*, p. 4.

15. Vargas, *Labor Rights Are Civil Rights*, p. 7.

16. Manuel Peña, *The Texas-Mexican Conjunto: History of a Working-Class Music* (Austin: University of Texas Press, 1985), p. 40. See also Steven Loza, *Barrio Rhythms: Mexican American Music in Los Angeles* (Urbana: University of Illinois Press, 1993), pp. 22–25. The two scholars give different recording dates for the

song. The version I draw from comes from Arhoolie Records, the company operated by musicologist Chris Strachwitz. Strachwitz's liner notes are also Peña's principal source for his discussion of the Bañuelos brothers. See *Texas-Mexican Border Music, Vol. 4* (Berkeley, CA: Arhoolie Records, 1975). Useful recording information for the Hermanos Bañuelos is available in Richard Spottswood, *Ethnic Music on Record: A Discography of Ethnic Recordings Produced in the United States, 1893 to 1942*, vol. 4, *Spanish, Portuguese, Philippine, Basque* (Urbana: University of Illinois Press, 1992), pp. 1662–64.

17. Peña, *Texas-Mexican Conjunto*, p. 39.

18. Loza, *Barrio Rhythms*, pp. 22–23. The English translation comes from Loza, although I have modified it slightly.

19. See Stephen J. Pitti, *The Devil in Silicon Valley: Northern California, Race and Mexican Americans* (Princeton, NJ: Princeton University Press, 2003); and José E. Limón, *Dancing with the Devil: Society and Cultural Poetics in Mexican-American South Texas* (Madison: University of Wisconsin Press, 1994).

20. Pitti writes that "ideologies of race, like the Devil, took on different forms, assumed different guises, and extracted varying costs, but the manifestations of violence, which always attend racism were its most constant feature." Pitti, *Devil in Silicon Valley*, pp. 1–2.

21. Mark Reisler, "Always the Laborer, Never the Citizen: Anglo Perceptions of the Mexican Immigrant during the 1920s," in *Between Two Worlds: Mexican Immigrants in the United States*, ed. David G. Gutiérrez (Wilmington, DE: Jaguar Books, Scholarly Resources, 1996), p. 38.

22. See Spottswood, *Ethnic Music on Record*, vol. 4, p. 1664.

23. "El Deportado" in Chris Strachwitz, comp., *Corridos and Tragedias de la Frontera 1: First Recordings of Historic Mexican-American Ballads (1928–37)* (Berkeley, CA: Arhoolie Records, 1994). I have omitted the repeated lines that start each stanza.

24. In the 1969 article "Ideology and Ideological State Apparatuses," Althusser imagined a scene in which a policeman yells "Hey you!" to a passerby. The policeman's hail represents the action of the law on the citizen-subject, as it both compels the person to accept the authority of the state and also simultaneously constitutes the person as a social subject. The Althusser essay appears in Louis Althusser, *Lenin and Philosophy and Other Essays*, trans. Ben Brewster (New York: Monthly Review Press, 1971). See Judith Butler's important reformulation of the Althusserian model in the context of her theory of gender performance, in Judith Butler, *Bodies That Matter: On the Discursive Limits of "Sex"* (London: Routledge, 1993), pp. 121–23.

25. In 2003, the Mexican American recording artist Jae-P revisited the two

corridos in the song "Ni de Aquí Ni de Allá" ("Neither from here nor there") with the lyrics "el latino hoy en día no es un simple lavaplatos" [the Latino of today is no simple dishwasher]. Jae-P acknowledges his ambivalent status in either nation but demands full rights in each. As in previous generations, his migrant status is an effect of transborder class formations, not elective choice: "México yo te quiero y allá me enterarán / pero aquí está la lana y me la tengo que chingar" [Mexico I love you, they will bury me there / but here is where the money is and I have to suck it up]. Jae-P, *Ni de Aquí, Ni de Allá* (Univisión Music Group, 2003).

26. Luisa Moreno, "Non-Citizen Americans of the South West," address delivered at the Panel on Deportation and the Rights of Asylum of the Fourth Annual Conference of the American Committee for Protection of Foreign Born, Washington, DC, March 3, 1940.

27. Etienne Balibar, "The Nation Form: History and Ideology," in Etienne Balibar and Immanuel Wallerstein, *Race, Nation, Class: Ambiguous Identities*, pp. 86–106 (London: Verso, 1991), p. 93.

28. R. Saldívar, *Borderlands of Culture*, p. 19.

29. The life and works of Américo Paredes are the subject of numerous studies, including Leticia Garza-Falcón, *Gente Decente: A Borderlands to the Rhetoric of Dominance* (Austin: University of Texas Press, 1998), pp. 156–97; José E. Limón, *Mexican Ballads, Chicano Poems* (Berkeley, : University of California Press, 1992); idem, *Dancing with the Devil* (Madison: University of Wisconsin Press, 1994); Renato Rosaldo, *Culture and Truth: The Remaking of Social Analysis* (Boston: Beacon, 1987); José David Saldívar, *Border Matters: Remapping American Cultural Studies* (Berkeley: University of California Press, 1997); Ramón Saldívar, *Chicano Narrative: The Dialectics of Difference* (Madison: University of Wisconsin Press, 1990); idem, introduction to *The Hammon and the Beans and Other Stories*, by Américo Paredes (Houston: Arte Público, 1994), pp. vii–li; and idem, *Borderlands of Culture*.

30. My biographical notes on Paredes derive from the following sources: Hector Calderón and José R. López Morín, "Interview with Américo Paredes," *Nepantla: Views from the South* 1.1 (2000): pp. 197–228; María Herrera-Sobek, "Américo Paredes: A Tribute," *Mexican Studies/Estudios Mexicanos* 6.2 (summer 2000): pp. 239–66; José R. López Morín, "The Life and Early Works of Américo Paredes," *Western Folklore* 64.1&2 (winter/spring 2005): pp. 7–28; and R. Saldívar, *Borderlands of Culture*.

31. See Benjamin Heber Johnson, *Revolution in Texas: How a Forgotten Rebellion and Its Bloody Suppression Turned Mexicans into Americans* (New Haven, CT: Yale University Press, 2003).

32. R. Saldívar, introduction to *Hammon and the Beans*, p. vii.

33. J. Saldívar, *Border Matters*, p. 37.

34. Américo Paredes, *Between Two Worlds* (Houston: Arte Público, 1991), p. ii.

35. Américo Paredes, *Folklore and Culture on the Texas-Mexican Border*, ed. Richard Bauman (Austin: University of Texas Press, 1993), p. 24.

36. J. Saldívar, *Border Matters*, pp. 53–54.

37. Paredes, *Between Two Worlds*, p. 26.

38. Ibid., p. 139.

39. R. Saldívar, *Chicano Narrative*, p. 12.

40. Paredes, *Between Two Worlds*, p. 139.

41. I examine the authoritative 1935 revision of the poem, which Paredes included in his 1991 collection, *Between Two Worlds*.

42. Ibid., p. 139.

43. Ibid., p. 26.

44. Ibid., p. 38.

45. Houston A. Baker Jr., *Blues Ideology, and Afro-American Literature: A Vernacular Theory* (Chicago: University of Chicago Press, 1984), p. 1.

46. Paredes, *Between Two Worlds*, p. 26.

47. Lisa Lowe, *Immigrant Acts: On Asian American Cultural Politics* (Durham, NC: Duke University Press, 1996), p. 25.

48. Paredes, *Between Two Worlds*, p. 26.

49. See Vargas, *Labor Rights Are Civil Rights*.

50. Quoted in Roberto R. Calderón and Emilio Zamora, "Manuela Solis Sager and Emma Tenayuca: A Tribute," in *Chicana Voices: Intersections of Class, Race, and Gender*, ed. Teresa Córdova, Norma Cantú, Gilberto Cardenas, Juan García, and Christine M. Sierra (Albuquerque: University of New Mexico Press, 1993), p. 39.

51. Vargas, *Labor Rights Are Civil Rights*, p. 125.

52. Quoted in ibid., p. 138.

53. Irene Ledesma, "Texas Newspapers and Chicana Workers' Activism, 1919–1974," *Western Historical Quarterly* 26.3 (autumn 1995): pp. 309–31. Ledesma died young, leaving a remarkable project unfinished. Her work excavated the tangled history of gender, race, and labor activism in the period.

54. La Pasionaria was the pseudonym that Dolores Ibárruri adopted in her columns for the miners' newspaper *El Minero*. She was the editor for the prominent left-wing newspaper *El Mundo Obrero* during the period of the Second Republic. Later, Ibárruri became first secretary and then president of the Communist Party of Spain. For more of her story, see her memoir, published in English as *They Shall Not Pass: The Autobiography of La Pasionaria* (New York: New World, 1976).

55. Quoted in Geoffrey Rips, "Living History: Emma Tenayuca Tells Her Story," *Texas Observer*, October 28, 1983, pp. 7–15.

56. Vargas, *Labor Rights Are Civil Rights*, p. 145.

57. Joseph Stalin, "The National Question," in *Essential Stalin: Major Theoretical Writings*, ed. and introd. Bruce Franklin (Garden City, NY: Anchor Books, 1972), p. 8.

58. Emma Tenayuca and Homer Brooks, "The Mexican Question in the Southwest," *The Communist* 18 (March 1939), p. 262.

59. For a fascinating study of similar tensions between Latin American revolutionary projects and their subjects, see María Josefina Saldaña-Portillo, *The Revolutionary Imagination in the Age of Development* (Durham, NC: Duke University Press, 2003).

60. Antonio Gramsci, "History of the Subaltern Classes: Methodological Criteria," in "Notes on Italian History" (1934–35), in *Selections from the Prison Notebooks*, ed. and trans. Quintin Hoare and Geoffrey Nowell Smith (New York: International Publishers, 1971), pp. 54–55.

61. Gabriela González, "Carolina Munguía and Emma Tenayuca: The Politics of Benevolence and Radical Reform," *Frontiers* 24.2&3 (2003): p. 217.

62. Michel Foucault, *Discipline and Punish: The Birth of the Modern Prison*, trans. Alan Sheridan (New York: Vintage, 1977).

63. Butler writes, "subjection is literally the making of a subject, the principle of regulation according to which a subject is produced. Such subjection is a kind of power that not only unilaterally *acts on* a given individual as a form of domination, but also *activates*, or forms the subject." Judith Butler, *The Psychic Life of Power: Theories in Subjection* (Palo Alto, CA: Stanford University Press, 1997), p. 18.

64. This story appears in Francisco A. Rosales, *¡Pobre Raza! Violence, Justice, and Mobilization among México Lindo Immigrants, 1900–1936* (Austin: University of Texas Press, 1999), p. 107.

65. Quoted in R. Saldívar, *Borderlands of Culture*, p. 116.

NOTES TO CHAPTER 2

1. Ernesto Galarza, *Merchants of Labor: The Mexican Bracero Story* (Charlotte, NC: McNally and Loftin, 1964), p. 16.

2. Etienne Balibar, "Class Racism," in Etienne Balibar and Immanuel Wallerstein, *Race, Nation, and Class: Ambiguous Identities*, pp. 204–16 (London: Verso, 1991), p. 211.

3. Galarza, *Merchants of Labor*, p. 17.

4. Cindy Hahamovitch, "Creating Perfect Immigrants: Guest Workers of the World in Historical Perspective," *Labor History* 44.1 (2003): 69–94. Historian Mae M. Ngai analyzes the Bracero Program under the rubric of what she terms "imported

colonialism." See Ngai, *Impossible Subjects: Illegal Aliens and the Making of Modern America* (Princeton, NJ: Princeton University Press, 2004), p. 129.

5. A 2007 survey of guest-worker programs by the Southern Poverty Law Center found systemic abuses that made the contract system resemble unfree labor. See Mary Bauer, *Close to Slavery: Guestworker Programs in the United States* (Mobile, AL: Southern Poverty Law Center, 2007), available online at http://www.splc.org.

6. Mark Reisler, "Always the Laborer, Never the Citizen: Anglo Perceptions of the Mexican Immigrant during the 1920s," in *Between Two Worlds: Mexican Immigrants in the United States,* ed. David G. Gutiérrez (Wilmington, DE: Jaguar Books, Scholarly Resources, 1996), pp. 23–44.

7. Daniel Cosío Villegas, "Mexico's Crisis" (1947), in *The Mexico Reader: History, Culture, Politics,* ed. Gilbert M. Joseph and Timothy J. Henderson (Durham, NC: Duke University press, 2002), p. 470. A collection of Cosío Villegas's essays appeared in English in 1964, with translations by Américo Paredes. See Daniel Cosío Villegas, *American Extremes [Extremos de América],* trans. Américo Paredes (Austin: University of Texas Press, 1964).

8. Cosío Villegas, "Mexico's Crisis," p. 481. For a broader discussion of Cosío Villegas, see Claire F. Fox, *The Fence and the River: Culture and Politics at the U.S.-Mexico Border* (Minneapolis: University of Minnesota Press, 1999), 97–118.

9. Cosío Villegas, "Mexico's Crisis," p. 481.

10. Pedro de Alba, *Siete artículos sobre el problema de los Braceros* [Seven Articles on the Problem of the Braceros] (Mexico DF, 1954), p. 7 (my translation).

11. Ibid., p. 24.

12. Ibid.

13. Manuel Gamio, *Mexican Immigration to the United States: A Study of Human Migration and Adjustment* (1930; repr., New York: Dover, 1971), p. 128.

14. José Lázaro Salinas, *La emigración de braceros: Visión objetiva de un problema mexicana* [The Emigration of Braceros: Objective Vision of a Mexican Problem] (Mexico DF, 1955), pp. 11–12.

15. See John Mraz and Jaime Vélez Storey, *Uprooted: Braceros in the Hermanos Mayo Lens* (Houston: Arte Público, 1996). The full depository of the Fondo Hermanos Mayo photographs and papers resides in the Archivo General de la Nación in Mexico City, Mexico.

16. See John Mraz, "Los Hermanos Mayo: Photographing the Braceros," in Mraz and Vélez Storey, *Uprooted,* pp. 11–30.

17. Ibid., p. 14.

18. Ibid., p. 28n. 8.

19. John Mraz and Jaime Vélez Storey, introduction to *Uprooted,* p. 7.

20. "Una memoria mexicana," *La Jornada,* May 2003, available online at www. jornada.unam.mx/2003/05/19/0ja73-hnsmayo.html (accessed July 17, 2006).

21. By way of contrast, refer to the 1953 film *Espaldas Mojadas* [The Wetbacks], by the prominent filmmaker Alejandro Galindo. His portrait of the Mexican emigrant offered a moral tale about the dangers of forfeiting Mexican nationality for U.S. dollars. Claire F. Fox reads the film in relation to other nationalist responses to the "bracero problem" in her book *The Fence and the River.*

22. Julio Souza Fernández, interview by John Mraz, 1988, cited in Mraz, "Los Hermanos Mayo," p. 22.

23. Jean Franco, *Plotting Women: Gender and Representation in Mexico* (New York: Columbia University Press, 1989), p. 146.

24. Ana Rosas, "Familias Flexibles (Flexible Families): Bracero Families' Lives across Cultures, Communities, and Countries" (Ph.D. diss., University of Southern California, Department of History, 2006).

25. Ernesto Galarza, *Strangers in Our Fields* (Washington, DC: Joint United States–Mexico Trade Union Committee, 1956), p. 47.

26. Ernesto Galarza, *Barrio Boy: The Story of a Boy's Acculturation* (Notre Dame, IN: University of Notre Dame Press, 1971). Galarza took this epigraph from Henry Adams.

27. For the definitive work of Ernesto Galarza, consult Stephen Pitti, "Ernesto Galarza, Mexican Immigration and Farm Labor Organizing the Postwar California," in *The Countryside in the Age of the Modern State: Political Histories of Rural America,* ed. Catherine McNicol Stock and Robert D. Johnston (Ithaca, NY: Cornell University Press, 2001), pp. 161–85. See also Stephen J. Pitti, *The Devil in Silicon Valley: Northern California, Race, and Mexican Americans* (Princeton, NJ: Princeton University Press, 2003), esp. pp. 136–47.

28. Ernesto Galarza, *The Roman Catholic Church as a Factor in the Political and Social History of Mexico* (Sacramento: Capital Press, 1928).

29. Ernesto Galarza, *La industria eléctrica en México* [The Electrical Industry in Mexico] (México DF: Fondo de Cultura Económica, 1941).

30. Pitti, "Ernesto Galarza," p. 162.

31. Galarza, *Strangers in Our Fields,* p. 17.

32. Ibid., p. 21. Galarza elaborated on the routine mistreatment of Mexican nationals in his longer study of the bracero program, *Merchants of Labor* (1964).

33. See Pitti, "Ernesto Galarza," pp. 163–66.

34. Ibid., p. 179.

35. Ibid., p. 184.

36. Ernest Greuning, preface to Galarza, *Merchants of Labor,* p. 11. Galarza himself often used Steinbeck as a frame of reference for depicting the rampant

excesses of capitalism that made the idyllic countryside of California a scene of misery for workers. He concluded *Merchants of Labor* with a description of braceros as the "millions of menials who longed to toil as managed servants for a season, however short, in East of Eden" (259). "Chanza" is the Mexican slang term for a job, implying also chance or fortune.

37. "A $10 dolares por cabeza!" (NFLU flier, 1951 or 1952), Galarza Papers, Stanford University, box 8, folder 5. The full quotation in English is, "This is not labor contracting, *it is a sale of cattle at ten dollars per head*" (emphasis in original).

38. Galarza, *Merchants of Labor*, 230.

39. Ibid., 231.

40. The verb "joder" has particular resonance in the migrant vernacular as a vulgar expression of fatalistic humor and barely controlled anger. The verb can mean "to fuck," "to mess up," or "to break." The speaker uses the adjectival form "jodido" here to convey a hopeless status of being the lowest of the low—but it describes a low status derived from having been violated, fucked up. Arte Público Press translates the passage without the slang, thus missing the expressive edginess of Rivera's prose.

41. Tomás Rivera, *Y no se lo tragó la tierra* (And the earth did not swallow him) (Houston: Piñata Books, Arte Público, 1996), p. 27 (my translation). Tomás Rivera (1935–1984) was born into a Mexican family in Crystal City that traveled the migrant labor circuit between Texas and the Midwest. He published the novel *Tierra* in 1971, for which he received the Quinto Sol Award.

42. "Esclavos Modernos: En pleno siglo de libertades los Braceros mexicanos son objetos de las mas inhumanas explotaciones" [Modern Slaves: In the Age of Liberty Mexican Braceros Are Subject to the Most Inhuman Exploitation], *El Angelino* (Los Angeles), March 4, 1949, A1; reprinted in Galarza, *Strangers in Our Fields*, p. 11.

43. See Paul Gilroy, *Against Race: Imagining Political Culture beyond the Color Line* (Cambridge, MA: Belknap, 2000).

44. Ibid., p. 83.

45. The blue card was the identification document issued to braceros.

46. Galarza, *Strangers in Our Fields*, pp. 69 and 79.

47. Galarza, *Merchants of Labor*, p. 235, quoting San Diego Farmers, Incorporated.

48. Galarza, *Strangers in Our Fields*, p. 11.

49. María Herrera-Sobek, *The Bracero Experience: Elitelore versus Folklore* (Los Angeles: UCLA Latin American Center Publications, 1979), p. 43.

50. Galarza, *Barrio Boy*, pp. 264.

51. Ibid., p. 265.

52. Ibid.

53. Américo Paredes, *The Shadow* (Houston: Arte Público, 1998), p. 2.

54. Adolfo Gilly, *The Mexican Revolution*, trans. Patrick Camiller (London: Verso, 1976), p. 11.

55. Américo Paredes, *With His Pistol in His Hand: A Border Ballad and Its Hero* (Austin: University of Texas Press, 1958). For a relevant study of revolutionary subjectivity in the Americas, see María Josefina Saldaña-Portillo, *The Revolutionary Imagination in the Americas and the Age of Development* (Durham, NC: Duke University Press, 2003).

56. Américo Paredes, interview by the author at Paredes's home in Austin, Texas, March 2, 1995. I am grateful to Ramón Saldívar both for the invitation to participate in the interview and for the use of the interview here. Saldívar published the interview in its entirety in *The Borderlands of Culture: Américo Paredes and the Transnational Imaginary* (Durham, NC: Duke University Press, 2006).

57. Oral history, in R. Saldívar, *Borderlands of Culture*, p. 140.

58. Paredes, *The Shadow*, p. 1; hereafter cited in text.

59. Juan Rulfo, the preeminent author of postrevolutionary Mexico, published his first collection of stories, *El llano en llamas*, in 1953 and *Pedro Páramo* in 1955, dates that parallel closely the years in which Paredes composed his first stories, poems, and novels.

60. José E. Limón, *Dancing with the Devil: Society and Cultural Poetics in Mexican American South Texas* (Madison: University of Wisconsin Press, 1994), p. 79.

61. Renato Rosaldo, *Culture and Truth: The Remaking of Social Analysis* (Boston: Beacon, 1987), pp. 151–52.

62. Américo Paredes, *Folklore and Culture on the Texas-Mexican Border*, ed. and introd. Richard Bauman (Austin: University of Texas Press, 1993), p. 31.

63. Ibid., p. 40.

64. Herrera-Sobek, *Bracero Experience*, p. 83.

65. Quoted in María Herrera-Sobek, *Northward Bound: The Mexican Immigrant Experience in Ballad and Song* (Bloomington: Indiana University Press, 1993), p. 152. The English translation is by Herrera-Sobek, with some minor modifications of my own.

66. See Karl Marx, "Economic and Philosophical Manuscripts of 1844," reprinted in *The Marx-Engels Reader*, 2nd ed., ed. Robert C. Tucker (New York: Norton, 1978), p. 73.

67. Kitty Calavita, *Inside the State: The Bracero Program, Immigration, and the INS* (London: Routledge, 1992).

68. Carlos Marentes, *Las Raíces del Trabajador Agrícola* [The Roots of the

Agricultural Worker] (El Paso, TX: Border Agricultural Workers Project, 1997), available online at http://ufw.org.

69. See Stephen J. Pitti, "Bracero Justice: The Legacies of Mexican Contract Labor," conference paper for "Repairing the Past: Confronting the Legacies of Slavery, Genocide and Caste," Gilder Lehrman Center for the Study of Slavery, Resistance, and Abolition, Yale University, October 27–29, 2006, www.yale.edu/glc/justice/index.htm.

NOTES TO CHAPTER 3

1. Doreen Massey, *Space, Place, and Gender* (Minneapolis: University of Minnesota Press, 1994), p. 195.

2. Luisa Moreno Bemis to Robert Kenny, March 16, 1950, San Diego, California, quoted in Carlos Larralde and Richard Griswold del Castillo, "Luisa Moreno: A Hispanic Civil Rights Leader in San Diego," *Journal of San Diego History* 41.4 (fall 1995): p. 13.

3. Judith Baca, *The Great Wall of Los Angeles* (1976–1983), on view at the website for the Los Angeles–based Social and Public Art Resource Center (SPARC), www.sparcmurals.org (accessed July 27, 2006).

4. Judith Baca, "Our People Are the Internal Exiles," an interview by Diane Neumaier, in *Cultures in Contention*, ed. Douglas Kahn and Diane Neumaier (Seattle: Real Comet, 1985), pp. 62–75.

5. See Vicki Ruiz, "Una Mujer sin Fronteras (A Woman without Borders): Luis Moreno and Latina Labor Activism," *Pacific Historical Review* 73.1 (2004): pp. 1–20.

6. Ibid, p. 2.

7. Luisa Moreno, "Non-citizen Americans of the South West," address delivered at the Panel on Deportation and the Rights of Asylum of the Fourth Annual Conference of the American Committee for the Protection of the Foreign Born, Washington, DC, March 3, 1940. See my discussion in chapter 1.

8. Larralde and del Castillo, "Luisa Moreno."

9. Luis Moreno interview, May 12, 1971, cited in Larralde and del Castillo, "Luisa Moreno," p. 9.

10. Ruiz, "Una Mujer sin Fronteras," p. 19.

11. Ibid.

12. Quoted in Larralde and del Castillo, "Luisa Moreno," p. 13.

13. Bert Corona, quoted in Mario T. García, *Memories of Chicano History: The Life and Narrative of Bert Corona* (Berkeley: University of California Press, 1994), p. 119.

14. Mae Ngai, *Impossible Subjects: Illegal Aliens and the Making of Modern America* (Princeton, NJ: Princeton University Press, 2004), pp. 237–38.

15. Jeffrey M. Garcilazo, "McCarthyism, Mexican Americans, and the Los Angeles Committee for the Protection of the Foreign-Born, 1950–1954," *Western Historical Quarterly* 32.3 (autumn 2001): pp. 273–95. I heard Jeff deliver an incisive account of his revisionist history of the Cold War and Mexican American politics at the American Studies Association Meetings in Kansas City, Missouri, November 3, 1996. His presence is greatly missed.

16. David G. Gutiérrez, *Walls and Mirrors: Mexican Americans, Mexican Immigrants, and the Politics of Ethnicity* (Berkeley: University of California Press, 1995), p. 142.

17. Larralde and del Castillo, "Luisa Moreno," p. 15.

18. See Elaine Tyler Mae, *Homeward Bound: American Families in the Cold War Era* (New York: Basic Books, 1988). For a more expansive analysis of the variety of discourses on women and domesticity during the Cold War, see Joanne Meyerowitz, ed., *Not June Cleaver: Women and Gender in Postwar America, 1945–1960* (Philadelphia: Temple University Press, 1994).

19. See Margaret Rose, "Gender and Civil Activism in Mexican American Barrios in California," in Meyerowitz, *Not June Cleaver*, pp. 177–200.

20. Jack Cargill, "Empire and Opposition: The 'Salt of the Earth' Strike," in *Labor in New Mexico: Unions, Strikes, and Social History since 1881*, ed. Robert Kern (Albuquerque: University of New Mexico Press, 1983), pp. 183–267.

21. "Empire Zinc Stalling Forces Bayard Strike," *Mine-Mill Union*, October 23, 1950, p. 3.

22. Zaragoza Vargas, *Labor Rights Are Civil Rights: Mexican American Workers in Twentieth-Century America* (Princeton, NJ: Princeton University Press, 2005), p. 223.

23. Ibid., p. 169.

24. Cargill, "Empire and Opposition," pp. 192–93; see also Ellen Baker, "'I Hate to Be Calling Her a Wife Now': Women and Men in the Salt of the Earth Strike, 1950–1952," in *Mining Women: Gender in the Development of a Global Industry, 1670–2005*, ed. Jaclyn J. Gier and Laurie Mercier (New York: Palgrave Macmillan, 2006), pp. 213–32.

25. Cargill, "Empire and Opposition," p. 195.

26. Mine-Mill officials espoused an internationalist vision:

The same companies we deal with in the United States and Canada have properties in Mexico—American Smelting & Refining Co., Phelps Dodge, and Anaconda. Just as these companies fight to keep the workers apart in one mine or plant, they fight to keep them apart at national and international levels. The higher the level of union solidarity, the greater are the benefits to the working people.

Orville Larson, Vice President, Mine-Mill Union, Mexico City address to Mexican Miners Union, May 15, 1950, cited in "Pact Will Strengthen Both Unions, Larson Tells Mexican Miners' Parley," *Mine-Mill Union*, June 5, 1950, p. 2.

27. José Fuentes, "Es el tiempo para destruir la barrera" [It Is Time to Break Down the Barrier], *Mine-Mill Union*, December 17, 1951, p. 4.

28. Morris Wright, "We Move toward Coordinated Action of All Metal Miners of the Americas," *Mine-Mill Union*, June 5, 1950, p. 1.

29. Ibid.

30. Larson, address to Mexican Miners Union.

31. Vargas, *Labor Rights Are Civil Rights*, pp. 168–70; see also Mario García, *Mexican Americans: Leadership, Ideology, and Identity, 1930–1960* (New Haven, CT: Yale University Press, 1989), pp. 180–86.

32. Vargas, *Labor Rights Are Civil Rights*, p. 169.

33. Quoted in García, *Mexican Americans*, p. 184.

34. Ibid., p. 201.

35. Richard Griswold del Castillo, *The Treaty of Guadalupe Hidalgo: A Legacy of Conflict* (Norman: University of Oklahoma Press, 1990), p. 148.

36. For more on ANMA, see García, *Mexican Americans*, pp. 199–227.

37. "Mine-Mill Members Help Found Mexican-American Association," *Mine-Mill Union*, October 22, 1950, p. 8.

38. Ibid.

39. "ANMA President Lauds Mine-Mill," *Mine Mill Union*, December 17, 1951, p. 6.

40. "ANMA Votes All Out Aid to Empire Zinc Strikers," *Mine-Mill Union*, December 17, 1951, p. 4.

41. Deborah Silverton Rosenfelt, "New Mexico—The Background," in *Salt of the Earth*, by Michael Wilson and Deborah Silverton Rosenfelt (New York: Feminist Press, 1978), p. 117.

42. "Empire Zinc Stalling Forces Bayard Strike"; Cargill, "Empire and Opposition," pp. 196–97.

43. Ellen Baker conducted extensive oral interviews with women involved in the strike. See Baker, "'I Hate to Be Calling Her a Wife Now.'"

44. See Ellen Baker, "*Salt of the Earth*: Women, The Mine, Mill, and Smelter Workers' Union, and the Hollywood Blacklist in Grant County, New Mexico, 1941–1953" (Ph.D. diss., University of Wisconsin, Department of History, 1999). Consult her invaluable book, *On Strike and on Film: Mexican American Families and*

Blacklisted Filmmakers in Cold War America (Chapel Hill: University of North Carolina Press, 2007).

45. Quoted in Cargill, "Empire and Opposition," p. 203.

46. Baker, "*Salt of the Earth*," p. 206.

47. See Cargill, "Empire and Opposition"; Baker, "*Salt of the Earth*," pp. 198–200; and Wilson and Rosenfelt, *Salt of the Earth*, p. 202.

48. Cargill, "Empire and Opposition," p. 203.

49. See Ellen Baker's excellent discussion of the gendered division of labor in the mining industries of Grant County in "*Salt of the Earth*," pp. 55–63.

50. See, for instance, June Nash's account of Bolivian beliefs in her classic study, *We Eat the Mines and the Mines Eat Us: Dependency and Exploitation in Bolivian Tin Mines*, rev. ed. (New York: Columbia University Press, 1993); see also Barbara Kingsolver, *Holding the Line: Women in the Great Arizona Mine Strike of 1983* (Ithaca, NY: ILR Press, 1996), pp. 2–3.

51. "Bayard Women Pickets Can't Be Stopped," *Mine-Mill Union*, July 1951; Cargill, "Empire and Opposition," pp. 207–9; Baker, "*Salt of the Earth*," pp. 210–12.

52. "Pay Tribute to the Bayard Women," *Mine-Mill Union*, August 13, 1951, p. 6.

53. "Meet Rachel Juárez, E-Z Strike Heroine," *Mine-Mill Union*, September 10, 1951, p. 2.

54. *Silver City Daily Press*, July 13, 1951, p. 2, cited in Baker, "*Salt of the Earth*," p. 212. On Juárez's remarkable record in the strike, see "Meet Rachel Juárez, E-Z Strike Heroine."

55. Quoted in "Tear Gas, Arrests Fail to Break Bayard Lines," *Mine-Mill Union*, July 2, 1951, p. 1.

56. "Heroic Bayard Women Hold Line," *Mine-Mill Union*, July 16, 1951, p. 2.

57. Ibid.

58. Ibid.

59. Cargill, "Empire and Opposition," p. 210.

60. "Jencks's Wife Convicted for 'Touching' Man Who Beat Her," *Mine-Mill Union*, October 8, 1951, p. 2.

61. José Fuentes, "'This Strike Will Not Be Lost,'" *Mine-Mill Union*, July 30, 1951, p. 8.

62. Ibid.

63. Ibid.

64. *Mine-Mill Union*, October 23, 1950, p. 3.

65. Cargill, "Empire and Opposition," pp. 229–39.

66. Ibid., p. 242.

67. Ibid., p. 245.

68. Quoted in Vicki Ruiz, *From Out of the Shadows: Mexican Women in Twentieth-Century America* (New York: Oxford University Press, 1999), p. 101.

69. See the following studies of the film: James J. Lorence, *The Suppression of Salt of the Earth: How Hollywood, Big Labor and Politicians Blacklisted a Movie in Cold War America* (Albuquerque: University of New Mexico Press, 1999); Wilson and Rosenfelt, *Salt of the Earth*; and Baker, "*Salt of the Earth*."

70. Paul Jarrico, quoted in Lorence, *The Suppression of Salt of the Earth*, p. 58.

71. Wilson and Rosenfelt, *Salt of the Earth*, p. 127.

72. *Newsweek* headline; Victor Reisel, 1953, quoted by Paul Jarrico, in Wilson and Rosenfelt, *Salt of the Earth*, p. 131.

73. Quoted in Tom Miller, "Class Reunion: *Salt of the Earth* Revisited," *Cineaste* 13.3 (1984): p. 34.

74. Deborah Silverton Rosenfelt, "Commentary," in Wilson and Rosenfelt, *Salt of the Earth*, p. 95.

75. Michael Wilson, "*Salt of the Earth*: Screenplay" (1953), in Wilson and Silverton Rosenfelt, *Salt of the Earth*, p. 90; hereafter cited in text.

76. Jean Franco, *Plotting Women: Gender and Representation in Mexico* (New York: Columbia University Press, 1989), p. 187.

77. Ruiz, *From Out of the Shadows*, p. 101.

78. Mariana Ramírez, quoted in Rosenfelt, "Commentary," p. 113.

79. These photographs belong to the Clinton Jencks Papers, 1950-1957, housed at Arizona State University. They are archived within the Chicano Research Collection and may be viewed online at http://aao.lib.asu.edu (accessed June 18, 2007).

80. Mariana Ramírez, quoted in Rosenfelt, "Commentary," p. 122.

81. Ibid., pp. 119–20.

82. Virginia Chacón, quoted in Tom Miller, "Class Reunion," p. 36.

83. Cargill, Rosenfelt, and Baker coincide in their conclusions on the strike, based on their oral histories of these women.

84. Wilson and Rosenfelt, *Salt of the Earth*, p. 136.

85. Ibid., p. 146.

86. Baker cites her interview with Clinton Jencks, who acknowledged his awareness of Cipriano Montoya's battery of Feliciana Montoya during the strike. Baker, "*Salt of the Earth*," p. 175.

87. Ibid., p. 169.

88. See the *Silver City Daily Press*, July 26, 1961, cited in Ellen Baker's discussion of the case in "*Salt of the Earth*," pp. 318–20.

89. Quoted in Baker, "*Salt of the Earth*," p. 286.

90. Despite the fact that their livelihood as miners depended in part on

military contracts, the Local 890 officers indicted Empire Zinc for wartime profiteering, both in Germany during World War II and in the Korean conflict.

91. See, for instance, Juan Chacón's recollections in "Union Made," in Wilson and Rosenfelt, *Salt of the Earth*, pp. 180–82.

NOTES TO CHAPTER 4

1. Lorna Dee Cervantes, *Emplumada* (Pittsburgh: University of Pittsburgh Press, 1981), p. 66.

2. Elizabeth Martínez, "An Exchange on La Raza," *New York Review of Books*, February 12, 1970, available online at www.nybooks.com/articles/11062 (accessed December 15, 2007).

3. Ibid.

4. David G. Gutiérrez, *Walls and Mirrors: Mexican Americans, Mexican Immigrants and the Politics of Ethnicity* (Berkeley: University of California Press, 1995), p. 183.

5. Chris Crass, "Towards Social Justice: Elizabeth 'Betita' Martínez and the Institute for MultiRacial Justice," Colours of Resistance website, http://colours.mahost.org/articles/crass3.html (accessed August 15, 2006).

6. Ibid.

7. Elizabeth "Betita" Martínez, "A View from New Mexico: Recollections of the Movimiento Left," *Monthly Review* 54.3 (July-August 2002): p. 79.

8. Ibid.

9. Valentina Valdés, *El Grito del Norte*, October 10, 1969.

10. Betita Martínez, "Lo que vi en Vietnam (What I Saw in Vietnam)," *El Grito del Norte*, August 29, 1970.

11. George Mariscal, *Aztlán and Vietnam: Chicano and Chicana Experiences of the War* (Berkeley: University of California Press, 1999), p. 6.

12. Elizabeth Martínez, ed., *450 Years of Chicano History in Pictures* (Albuquerque: Chicano Communications Center, 1976).

13. Martínez, "View from New Mexico," p. 7.

14. Soon after, in 1976, Martínez moved to the Bay Area, where she taught courses in ethnic and women's studies and helped build leftist institutions like the Peace and Freedom Party. In 1997, Martínez cofounded the Institute for MultiRacial Justice in the city's Mission District. In recognition for this and other projects in defense of human rights, Martínez was one of a thousand women nominated for the Nobel Peace Prize in 2005. See Melanie E. L. Bush, "Martínez, Elizabeth Sutherland 'Betita,'" in *Latinas in the United States: A Historical Encyclopedia*, ed. Vicki

Ruiz and Virginia Sánchez Korrol (Bloomington: Indiana University Press, 2006), 429–30.

15. Evangelina Márquez and Margarita Ramírez, "Women's Task Is to Gain Liberation," *Sin Fronteras* (1977), reprinted in *Essays on La Mujer,* ed. Rosaura Sánchez and Rosa Martínez, pp. 188–94 (Los Angeles: UCLA Chicano Studies Research Center, 1977), p. 194.

16. See, for instance, George Mariscal, *Brown-Eyed Children of the Sun: Lessons from the Chicano Movement* (Albuquerque: University of New Mexico Press, 2005).

17. Armando Navarro, "Chicanos: El México de Afuera," on Navarro's website, http://aztlan.net/navarro.htm. See also Armando Navarro, *La Raza Unida Party: A Chicano Challenge to the U.S. Two-Party System Dictatorship* (Philadelphia: Temple University Press, 2000).

18. *El Plan de Delano* (1966). Luis Valdez authored the text, in consultation with César Chávez. The two modeled the statement on *El Plan de Ayala*, the historic revolutionary manifesto drafted in 1911 by supporters of Emiliano Zapata in Morelos, Mexico.

19. *El Plan de Delano.*

20. Ernesto Chávez, *"Mi Raza Primero!": Nationalism, Identity and Insurgency in the Chicano Movement in Los Angeles, 1966–1978* (Berkeley: University of California Press, 2002).

21. *El Plan Espiritual de Aztlán* (1969). The preamble of the text was drafted by Alurista, a Chicano poet from San Diego. The full plan was ratified at the Youth and Liberation Conference in Denver. For full text, see Rudolfo A. Anaya and Francisco A. Lomelí, eds., *Aztlán: Essays on the Chicano Homeland* (Albuquerque: University of New Mexico Press, 1991), pp. 1–5.

22. See Elena Poniatowska, *La noche de Tlatelolco* [The Night of Tlatelolco] (1971; repr., Madrid, Spain: Girón Books, 1999). For documents linked to the Mexican "Dirty War," see Kate Doyle et al., "The Tlatelolco Massacre: U.S. Documents on Mexico and the Events of 1968" (Washington, DC: George Washington University, National Security Archive, October 19, 2003); and Kate Doyle, "Draft Report Documents 18 Years of Dirty War in Mexico" (Washington, DC: George Washington University, National Security Archive, February 26, 2006), available online at http://www.gwu.edu/~nsarchiv/index.html.

23. See Kate Doyle, "Human Rights and the Dirty War in Mexico" (Washington, DC: George Washington University, National Security Archive, May 11, 2003).

24. President Luis Echeverría, speaking through his translator, Donald F. Barnes, from the transcript of a meeting between President Luis Echeverría and Richard Milhouse Nixon, recorded on June 15, 1971, between 10:31 a.m. and 12:10

p.m. in the Oval Office of the White House by President Nixon. Also present at the meeting were Alexander M. Haig Jr. and the translator, Donald F. Barnes. Acquired and redacted by the National Security Archive through a Freedom of Information Act request. The text corresponds to Conversation No. 735-1, Cassette Nos. 2246–2248 of the Nixon Tapes. See Kate Doyle, "The Nixon Tapes: Secret Recordings from the Nixon White House on Luis Echeverría and Much Much More" (Washington, DC: George Washington University, National Security Archive, August 18, 2003).

25. President Richard Milhouse Nixon, Conversation No. 735-1, Cassette Nos. 2246–2248 of the Nixon Tapes.

26. President Luis Echeverría, speaking through the translator, Donald F. Barnes. Conversation No. 735-1, Cassette Nos. 2246–2248 of the Nixon Tapes.

27. Ibid.

28. Ibid.

29. See Lorena Oropeza, *¡Raza Sí! ¡Guerra No! Chicano Protest and Patriotism during the Viet Nam War Era* (Berkeley: University of California Press, 2005).

30. Cynthia A. Enloe, *Bananas, Beaches, and Bases: Making Feminist Sense of International Politics* (London: Pandora, 1989), p. 44.

31. Anne McClintock, *Imperial Leather: Race, Gender, and Sexuality in the Colonial Context* (London: Routledge, 1995), p. 353.

32. See, for instance, Norma Alarcón, "Chicana Feminism: In the Tracks of 'the' Native Woman," *Cultural Studies* 4.3 (1990): pp. 248–56; Angie Chabram Dernersesian, "I Throw Punches for My Race but I Don't Want to Be a Man: Writing Us-Chica-nos (Girl, Us)/Chicanas—into the Movement Script," in *Cultural Studies*, ed. Lawrence Grossberg, Cary Nelson, and Paula Treichler (New York: Routledge, 1992), pp. 81–95; Denise A. Segura and Beatríz M. Pesquera, "Beyond Indifference and Antipathy: The Chicano Movement and Chicana Feminist Discourse," *Aztlán* 19.2 (fall 1988–1990): pp. 69–92.

33. *El Plan de Santa Barbara.* Originally published as *El Plan de Santa Barbara: A Chicano Plan for Higher Education* (Oakland, CA: La Causa, 1971).

34. Enriqueta Longeaux y Vásquez, "The Woman of La Raza," in *From the Barrio: A Chicano Anthology*, ed. Luis Omar Salinas and Lillian Faderman (San Francisco: Canfield, 1973), p. 20.

35. Ibid.

36. Robin Morgan, *Sisterhood Is Powerful: An Anthology of Writings from the Women's Liberation Movement* (New York: Random House, 1970).

37. Longeaux y Vásquez, "The Woman of La Raza," pp. 20–21.

38. Ibid., p. 22.

39. Ibid., p. 23.

40. Ibid.

41. Vicki Ruiz, *From Out of the Shadows: Mexican Women in Twentieth-Century America* (New York: Oxford University Press, 1999), p. 102.

42. Dionne Espinoza, "'Revolutionary Sisters': Women's Solidarity and Collective Identification among Chicana Brown Berets in East Los Angeles, 1967–1970," *Aztlán* 26.1 (spring 2001): pp. 17–58.

43. Ibid., pp. 20–21.

44. Ibid., p. 20.

45. Paul Gilroy, *Small Acts: Thoughts on the Politics of Black Cultures* (London: Serpent's Tail, 1993), p. 11.

46. Mirta Vidal, "Women: New Voice of La Raza," in *Chicanas Speak Out!* (New York: Pathfinder, 1971), p. 8.

47. Ibid., p. 13.

48. Betty García-Bahne, "La Chicana and the Chicano Family," in Sánchez and Martínez Cruz, *Essays on La Mujer*, p. 35.

49. Ibid., p. 39.

50. Ibid., p. 37.

51. Comisión Feminil Mexicana Nacional, "CFM Resolutions" (Goleta, CA: CFMN, June 2, 1973), CFMN Collection, housed at the California Ethnic and Multicultural Archives, CFMN Administrative Records, box 1, folder 13.

52. H. Curtis Wood Jr., "Statement of Address," *Contemporary OB/GYN* (January 1973), quoted in Carlos G. Vélez-Ibañez, "The Nonconsenting Sterilization of Mexican Women in Los Angeles," in *Twice a Minority: Mexican American Women*, ed. Margarita Melville (St. Louis: C. V. Mosby, 1980), p. 239.

53. See Alexandra Minna Stern, *Eugenic Nation: Faults and Frontiers of Better Breeding in Modern America* (Berkeley: University of California Press, 2005).

54. The term "alien citizens" comes from historian Mae Ngai. See Mae Ngai, *Impossible Subjects: Illegal Aliens and the Making of Modern America* (Princeton, NJ: Princeton University Press, 2004), p. 8.

55. Quoted in Vélez-Ibañez, "Nonconsenting Sterilization," p. 244.

56. Ibid., p. 245.

57. Fredric Jameson, *Postmodernism, or, The Logic of Late Capitalism* (Durham, NC: Duke University Press, 1991), p. 51. See also Raúl Homero Villa, *Barrio-Logos: Space and Place in Urban Chicano Literature and Culture* (Austin: University of Texas Press, 2000).

58. Lorna Dee Cervantes, *Emplumada* (Pittsburgh: University of Pittsburgh Press, 1981).

59. Lorna Dee Cervantes, "Beneath the Shadow of the Freeway," in ibid., 11.

60. Lorna Dee Cervantes in *Partial Autobiographies: Interviews with Twenty Chicano Poets,* ed. Wolfgang Binder (Erlangen, Germany: Verlag, Palm & Enke, 1985), p. 44.

61. Villa, *Barrio-Logos,* p. 206.

62. Cervantes, "Beneath the Shadow of the Freeway," p. 12.

63. Cervantes, "Barco de Refugiados/Refugee Ship," in *Emplumada,* p. 41.

64. Ibid.

65. Ibid.

66. Cervantes, "Visions of Mexico While Writing at a Symposium in Port Townsend, Washington," in *Emplumada,* p. 45.

67. Ibid., p. 47.

68. Ibid.

69. Ibid., p. 46.

70. Cervantes, "Meeting Mescalito at Oak Hill Cemetery," in *Emplumada,* p. 10.

71. Ibid.

72. Ibid.

73. Cervantes, "Cannery Town in August," in *Emplumada,* p. 6.

74. See Vicki Ruiz, *Cannery Women, Cannery Lives: Mexican Women, Unionization, and the California Food Processing Industry, 1930–1950* (Albuquerque: University of New Mexico Press, 1987).

75. Cervantes, "Emplumada," in *Emplumada,* p. 66.

76. Ibid.

77. Ibid.

78. Ibid.

79. The San Francisco Bay Area Strike Support Committee, "Conditions for Women Workers," *Union Drive in the Southwest: Chicano Strike at Farah,* pp. 2–3, quoted in Laura E. Arroyo, "Industrial and Occupational Distribution of Chicana Workers," *Aztlán* 4.2 (fall 1973): pp. 343–82.

80. See Arroyo, "Industrial and Occupational Distribution"; Laurie Coyle, Gayle Hershatter, and Emily Honig, "Women at Farah: An Unfinished Story" (1980), reprinted in *Women and Power in American History: A Reader, Volume 2,* ed. Kathryn Kish Sklar and Thomas Dublin (Englewood Cliffs, NJ: Prentice Hall, 1991), pp. 248–62; Ruiz, *From Out of the Shadows,* pp. 127–32; and Emily Honig, "Women at Farah Revisited: Political Mobilization and Its Aftermath among Chicana Workers in El Paso, Texas, 1972–1992," *Feminist Studies* 22.2 (summer 1996): pp. 425–52.

81. San Francisco Bay Area Strike Support Committee, "Conditions for Women Workers," p. 15

82. Quoted in Coyle, Hershatter, and Honig, "Women at Farah," p. 258.

83. Cited in Mario T. García, "La Frontera as Symbol and Reality in Mexican American Thought," *Mexican Studies/Estudios Mexicanos* (summer 1985): p. 216.

84. Ibid.

85. Márquez and Ramírez, "Women's Task Is to Gain Liberation," p. 189.

86. Ibid., p. 192.

87. Ibid., p. 191.

88. Ibid.

89. Ibid., p. 193.

NOTES TO CHAPTER 5

1. Amitava Kumar, *Passport Photos* (Berkeley: University of California Press, 2000), p. 171.

2. Richard Rodriguez, *Days of Obligation: An Argument with My Mexican Father* (New York: Viking, 1992), p. xv.

3. I follow Rodriguez's spelling of his surname. The author drops the accent over the letter "i" that is customary in its Spanish usage. I read Rodriguez's second memoir as a response to the writings of Octavio Paz on the Mexican character. See Octavio Paz, *The Labyrinth of Solitude: Life and Thought in Mexico*, trans. Lysander Kemp (New York: Grove, 1961).

4. Richard Rodriguez, *Hunger of Memory: The Education of Richard Rodriguez* (New York: Bantam, 1982); idem, *Days of Obligation*. "Atravesado" refers to one who crosses borders and is crossed over by them. See Marcos Sánchez-Tranquilino and John Tagg, "The Pachuco's Flayed Hide: Mobility, Identity, and Buenas Garras," in *Cultural Studies*, ed. Lawrence Grossberg, Cary Nelson, and Paula Treichler (New York: Routledge, 1992), pp. 556–70.

5. During the post-civil-rights period, proponents of cultural pluralism sought new frameworks for expanding democratic participation in the United States. Latina/o anthropologists coined the term "cultural citizenship" for expressions of ethnic particularity within the public sphere, in order to argue for the compatibility between group identities and national belonging. See William Vincent Flores and Rina Benmayor, eds., *Latino Cultural Citizenship: Claiming Identity, Space, and Rights* (Boston: Beacon, 1998).

6. Kumar, *Passport Photos*, p. 171.

7. Rodriguez, *Hunger of Memory*, p. 171.

8. Ibid., p. 7.

9. Norma Alarcón, "Tropology of Hunger: The 'Miseducation' of Richard Rodriguez," in *The Ethnic Canon: Histories, Institutions, and Interventions*, ed. David

Palumbo-Liu (Minneapolis: University of Minnesota Press, 1995), pp. 140–52. See also Rosaura Sánchez, "Calculated Musings: Richard Rodriguez' Metaphysics of Difference," in Palumbo-Liu, *Ethnic Canon*, pp. 153–73; and Ramón Saldívar, *Chicano Narrative: The Dialectics of Difference* (Madison: University of Wisconsin Press, 1990).

10. Wendy Brown, *States of Injury: Power and Freedom in Late Modernity* (Princeton, NJ: Princeton University Press, 1995), p. 9.

11. Richard Rodriguez, *Brown: The Last Discovery of America* (New York: Penguin Books, 2002), p. 121.

12. See Horacio Roque Ramírez, "Claiming Queer Cultural Citizenship: Gay Latino (Im)Migrant Cultures in San Francisco," in *Queer Moves: Sexuality, International Migration, and the Contested Boundaries of U.S. Citizenship*, ed. Eithne Luibhéid and Lionel Cantú (Minneapolis: University of Minnesota Press, 2005); and "'That's My Place': Negotiating Racial, Sexual, and Gender Politics in San Francisco's Gay Latino Alliance (GALA), 1975–1983," *Journal of the History of Sexuality* 12.3 (April 2003): pp. 224–58.

13. For the political-economic history of neoliberalism, consult David Harvey, *A Brief History of Neoliberalism* (London: Oxford University Press, 2005).

14. For further information about the specific policies that defined the neoliberal turn, see Dennis Shaw, Robert N. Gwynne, and Thomas Klak, *Alternative Capitalisms* (London: Oxford University Press, 2003).

15. See John Ehrman, *The Eighties: America in the Age of Reagan* (New Haven, CT: Yale University Press, 2005).

16. See Greg Grandin, *The Last Colonial Massacre: Latin America in the Cold War* (Chicago: University of Chicago Press, 2004); idem, *Empire's Workshop: Latin America, the United States, and the Rise of the New Imperialism* (New York: Metropolitan Books, 2006).

17. On U.S. military intervention in Nicaragua, see James M. Scott, *Deciding to Intervene: The Reagan Doctrine and American Foreign Policy* (Durham, NC: Duke University Press, 1996). For a useful synthesis of the history of Central American civil wars and U.S. military intervention in the 1980s, consult James Dunkerley, *The Pacification of Central America: Political Change in the Isthmus, 1987–1993* (New York: Verso, 1994).

18. See Grandin, *Last Colonial Massacre*.

19. See Grandin, *Empire's Workshop*.

20. See Ehrman, *The Eighties*.

21. Amartya Sen, *Development as Freedom* (New York: Anchor Books, 1999).

22. Susan González Baker, "Demographic Trends in the Chicana/o Population: Policy Implications for the Twenty-First Century," in *Chicanas/Chicanos at the*

Crossroads, ed. David R. Maciel and Isidro D. Ortíz, pp. 5–24 (Tucson: University of Arizona Press, 1996), p. 22.

23. On Latin America, see Alejandro Portes and Kelley Hoffman, "Latin American Class Structures: Their Composition and Change during the Neoliberal Era," *Latin American Research Review* 38.1 (February 2003): pp. 41–82.

24. Through their sustained binational research project, Douglas S. Massey and Jorge Durand have provided an important guide to examining this new migration. The report of this work appears in Douglas S. Massey and Jorge Durand, eds., *Crossing the Border: Research from the Mexican Migration Project* (New York: Russell Sage, 2004). See also Douglas S. Massey, Jorge Durand, and Emilio Parrado, "The New Era of Mexican Migration to the United States," *Journal of American History* 86.2 (September 1999): pp. 518–636. In the same volume, see David G. Gutiérrez, "Migration, Emergent Ethnicity, and the 'Third Space': The Shifting Politics of Nationalism in Greater Mexico," *Journal of American History* (September 1999): pp. 481–517.

25. Marcelo Suárez-Orozco and Mariela M. Páez, "The Research Agenda," in *Latinos: Remaking America,* ed. Marcelo Suárez-Orozco and Mariela M. Páez (Berkeley and Cambridge, MA: University of California Press and the David Rockefeller Center for Latin American Studies at Harvard University, 2002), pp. 9–10.

26. Ibid., p. 10.

27. U.S. Bureau of the Census, 2000, available online at http://www.census.gov/; see also the Office of Immigration Statistics, available online at http://www.uscis.gov/graphics/shared/statistics/.

28. See Jeffrey S. Passell, "Estimates of the Size and Characteristics of the Undocumented Population," Pew Hispanic Center, Washington, DC, March 3, 2006.

29. González Baker, "Demographic Trends in the Chicana/o Population," p. 6.

30. See David G. Gutiérrez, *Walls and Mirrors: Mexican Americans, Mexican Immigrants, and the Politics of Ethnicity* (Berkeley: University of California Press, 1995).

31. Julie A. Phillips and Douglas S. Massey, "The New Labor Market: Immigrants and Wages after IRCA," *Demography* 36.2 (May 1999): pp. 233–46.

32. For a discussion of anti-immigrant measures contained in 1996 immigration legislation, see Michael J. Wishnie, "Introduction: Immigration and Federalism," *New York University Annual Survey of American Law* (November 12, 2002): pp. 283–93.

33. For information on deportation, see the various reports produced by the National Immigration Law Center, http://www.nilc.org/index.htm.

34. González Baker, "Demographic Trends in the Chicana/o Population," p. 22.

35. See, in particular, the case of indigenous migrants: Jonathan Fox and Gaspar Rivera-Salgado, "Building Civil Society among Indigenous Migrants," *U.S.-Mexico Policy Bulletin* 7 (July/August 2005): pp. 1–9.

36. Archdiocese of Guatemala, *Guatemala Never Again! The Recovery of Historical Memory Project: The Official Report of the Human Rights Office, Archdiocese of Guatemala* (New York: Orbis Books, 1999).

37. Jaime Cortez, "Interview with Ester Hernández" (San Francisco: Galería de la Raza, August 9, 2001), available online at http://galeriadelaraza.org (accessed October 20, 2006).

38. Richard Rodriguez, *Victim of Two Cultures* (New York: Insight Media, 1990).

39. Rodriguez, *Brown*.

40. Rodriguez, *Days of Obligation*, p. 75.

41. Richard Rodriguez, "An American Writer," in *The Invention of Ethnicity*, ed. Werner Sollors (London: Oxford University Press, 1989), p. 3.

42. For examples, see Oscar Zeta Acosta, *Autobiography of a Brown Buffalo* (1972; repr., New York: Vintage, 1989); Alurista, *nationchild plumaroja 1969–1972* (San Diego: Toltecas en Aztlán, Centro Cultural de la Raza, 1972); Rudolfo Anaya, *Bless Me, Ultima* (1972; repr., New York: Warner Books, 1994); and Miguel Méndez, *Peregrinos de Aztlán* (Tempe, AZ: Bilingual Review Press, 1992).

43. The quotation comes from R. Saldívar, *Chicano Narrative*, p. 155.

44. Rodriguez, *Days of Obligation*, p. xv.

45. Ibid., p. xvi.

46. Ibid., p. xv.

47. Michael M. J. Fischer, "Ethnicity and the Postmodern Arts of Memory," in *Writing Culture: The Poetics and Politics of Ethnography*, ed. James Clifford and George E. Marcus, pp. 194–233 (Berkeley: University of California Press, 1986), p. 195.

48. Ibid.

49. Rodriguez, *Days of Obligation*, p. xviii.

50. Ibid.

51. Renato Rosaldo, *Culture and Truth: The Remaking of Social Analysis* (Boston: Beacon, 1989), p. 69.

52. Rodriguez, *Days of Obligation*, p. xix.

53. See Emily Hicks, *Border Writing: The Multidimensional Text* (Minneapolis: University of Minnesota Press, 1991), p. xxvi.

54. Leo Chávez, *Covering Immigration: Popular Images and the Politics of the Nation* (Berkeley: University of California Press, 2001).

55. Rob Wilson, "Producing American Selves: The Form of American Biography," *Boundary* 2 (1991): p. 106.

56. Rodriguez, interview by Bill Moyers, "Richard Rodriguez: Victim of Two Cultures," Bill Moyers' World of Ideas Series, Public Broadcasting Service (Princeton, NJ: Films for the Humanities, 1994).

57. Ibid.

58. Renato Rosaldo's discussion of unmarked citizenship appears in *Culture and Truth.*

59. Stanley Millman, "California's Proposition 187 and Its Lessons," *New York Law Journal,* January 3, 1995, p. 3, col. 1.

60. For more on this subject, consult Timothy Dunn, *The Militarization of the U.S.-Mexico Border, 1978–1992: Low Intensity Conflict Doctrine Comes Home* (Austin: Center for Mexican American Studies, University of Texas, 1996).

61. U.S. English advertisement, *U.S. News and World Report,* October 2, 1995, p. 60.

62. Judge Samuel C. Kiser, quoted in Sam Howe Verhovek, "Mother Scolded by Judge for Speaking in Spanish," *New York Times,* August 30, 2005 (accessed online at NYTimes.com, October 19, 2006).

63. Ibid.

64. See James A. Ferg-Cadima, "Black, White, and Brown: Latino School Desegregation Efforts in the Pre– and Post–*Brown v. Board of Education* Era" (Washington, DC: Mexican American Legal Defense and Education Fund, May 2004), available online at http://www.maldef.org.

65. Rodriguez, *Hunger of Memory,* p. 5.

66. Rodriguez, *Days of Obligation,* p. 65–66.

67. Ibid., p. 66.

68. Richard Rodriguez, "Go North, Young Man," *Mother Jones* 20.4 (July-August 1995): p. 33.

69. Ibid.

70. Richard Rodriguez, "Illegal Immigrants: Prophets of a Borderless World," *New Perspectives Quarterly* 12.1 (winter 1995): p. 63.

71. Rodriguez, "Go North, Young Man," p. 34.

72. Richard Rodriguez, "Closed Doors," in *Arguing Immigration: The Debate over the Changing Face of America,* ed. Nicolaus Mills, pp. 143–47 (New York: Touchstone, 1994), p. 147.

73. Lora Romero, "'When Something Goes Queer': Familiarity, Formalism, and Minority Intellectuals in the 1980's," *Yale Journal of Criticism* 6.1 (1993): p. 122.

74. Gloria Anzaldúa, *Borderlands/La frontera: The New Mestiza* (San Francisco: Aunt Lute, 1987). This work was preceded by her collaboration with Cherríe Moraga on *This Bridge Called My Back: Writings by Radical Women of Color,* ed.

Gloria Anzaldúa and Cherríe Moraga (New York: Kitchen Table, 1984). This volume established the metaphor of the bridge as a figure for both the multiple affinities among women of color and the multiple oppression of women marginalized by class, race, and gender.

75. Rodriguez, *Days of Obligation*, p. 92.

76. Ibid.

77. Ibid, pp. 92–93.

78. Ibid., p. 101.

79. Thanks to Yvonne Yarbro-Bejarano for this phrase.

80. Rodriguez, *Days of Obligation*, p. 103.

81. Ibid.

82. Rodriguez, *Hunger of Memory*, p. 126.

83. Rodriguez, *Days of Obligation*, p. 105.

84. Rosaldo, *Culture and Truth*, p. 200.

85. Eve K. Sedgwick, *Epistemology of the Closet* (Berkeley: University of California Press, 1990), p. 7.

86. Rodriguez, *Days of Obligation*, p. 96.

87. Stuart Hall, "New Ethnicities" (1988), in *Stuart Hall: Critical Dialogues in Cultural Studies*, ed. David Morley and Kuan Hsing Chen, pp. 441–49 (London: Routledge, 1996), p. 446.

88. Rodriguez, *Brown*, pp. 139–40.

89. Ibid., p. 143.

90. George M. Fredrickson, *Racism: A Short History* (Princeton, NJ: Princeton University Press, 2002), p. 6.

91. Rodriguez, *Brown*, p. xv.

92. Ibid., p. 35.

93. Rafael Pérez-Torres, *Mestizaje: Critical Uses of Race in Chicano Culture* (Minneapolis: University of Minnesota Press, 2006), p. 17.

94. María Josefina Saldaña-Portillo, "Who's the Indian in Aztlán? Rewriting Mestizaje, Indianism, and Chicanismo from the Lacandon," in *The Latin American Subalterns Studies Reader*, ed. Ileana Rodríguez, pp. 402–23 (Durham, NC: Duke University Press, 2001), p. 413.

95. Ellen Barry, "Judge Orders Woman to Learn English," *Los Angeles Times*, February 14, 2005, available online at http://spanish.about.com (accessed October 20, 2006); emphasis added.

96. Southern Poverty Law Center, "Mexican Woman Fights for Custody of Her Daughter," Southern Poverty Law Center website, May 17, 2005, http://www.spl center.org (accessed October 20, 2006).

97. Natalia Mielczarek, "Judge Tells Moms in Custody Cases to Learn English," *Tennessean,* January 29, 2005, available online at http://cgi.Tennessean.com (accessed October 20, 2005).

98. Ellen Barry, "Learn English, Judge Tells Moms," *Los Angeles Times,* February 14, 2005.

99. For example, see Leon Fink, *The Maya of Morgantown: Work and Community in the Nuevo New South* (Chapel Hill: University of North Carolina Press, 2003).

100. Barry, "Learn English."

101. Wendy Brown, *States of Injury: Power and Freedom in Late Modernity* (Princeton, NJ: Princeton University Press, 1995).

102. Ibid., p. 7.

103. Kendall Thomas, "Beyond the Privacy Principle," in *After Identity: A Reader in Law and Culture,* ed. Dan Danielson (London: Routledge, 1995), pp. 277–93. The Supreme Court overruled *Bowers* in 2003, in the case of *Lawrence v. Texas,* 539 U.S. 558 (2003); the court held that sodomy laws are unconstitutional.

104. Ibid., p. 280.

105. Ibid., p. 282.

106. Ibid., p. 283.

107. Ibid.

108. Ibid., p. 281.

109. Nancy Fraser, "Rethinking the Public Sphere: A Contribution to the Critique of Actually Existing Democracy," in *Habermas and the Public Sphere,* ed. Craig Calhoun (Cambridge, MA: MIT. Press, 1991), pp. 109–42.

110. Francisco Alarcón, "Naturaleza Criminal/Natural Criminal," in *Body in Flames/Cuerpo en llamas* (San Francisco: Chronicle Books, 1990), pp. 44–45.

111. Ibid.

112. Ibid.

113. Alarcón, "Gramática/Grammar," in *Body in Flames,* pp. 22–23.

114. Ibid.

115. Ibid.

116. Ibid.

NOTES TO CHAPTER 6

1. María Guadalupe Torres, testimony presented at the Global Tribunal on Accountability for Women's Human Rights, in Huariou, China between August 30 and September 8, 1995. Her presentation formed part of a nongovernmental-organization forum convened by the Center for Women's Global Leadership. Phoebe McKinney transcribed the statement on behalf of the American Friends

Service Committee, which was a partner of the Comité Fronterizo de Obreras in Matamoros. Phoebe McKinney, "Memorandum to the National Community Relations Committee" (Philadelphia: American Friends Service Committee, 1995).

2. The term "maquiladora" or "maquila" refers to a Mexican factory that imported materials for assembly or processing without the obligation of paying duties or tariffs. Mexican factories exported completed products for sale by the parent company. Maquiladoras were originally located along the northern boundary with the United States within the designated export-processing zone, but they were subsequently expanded into the country's interior. Following Mexico's entry into the General Agreement on Tariffs and Trade, and the passage of the North American Free Trade Agreement, factories could sell goods in Mexican markets and companies could be owned entirely by foreign capital.

3. Gayatri Chakravorty Spivak, "The Political Economy of Women as Seen by a Literary Critic," in *Coming to Terms: Feminism, Theory, Politics*, ed. Elizabeth Weed (New York: Routledge, 1989), p. 229.

4. Torres, testimony, in McKinney, "Memorandum."

5. See Samir Amin, *Maldevelopment: Anatomy of a Global Failure* (London: Zed Books, 1990). On the activities of Union Carbide and the continuing situation in Bhopal, refer to the website maintained by Corporate Watch at www.corpwatch. org/.

6. International Medical Commission on Bhopal, *Bhopal: A Tragic Model of an Industrial-Induced Epidemic* (December 1996). See also the special edition of the *Journal of International Perspectives in Public Health* 11–12 (Toronto: International Institute of Concern for Public Health, 1996).

7. For more on the temporal and spatial ordering of late capitalism, see David Harvey, *The Condition of Postmodernity: An Inquiry into the Origins of Cultural Change* (Malden, MA: Blackwell, 1990).

8. Torres, testimony, in McKinney, "Memorandum," pp. 5–6.

9. Harvey, *Condition of Postmodernity*, p. 145.

10. For a comprehensive discussion of the relationship between Fordism and post-Fordism, refer to Devon G. Peña, *The Terror of the Machine: Technology, Work, Gender, and Ecology on the U.S.-Mexico Border* (Austin: Center for Mexican American Studies, University of Texas Press, 1997).

11. Peña makes this point quite forcefully in his study of Ciudad Juárez, *Terror of the Machine*; see also Jefferson Cowie, *Capital Moves: RCA's Seventy-Year Quest for Cheap Labor* (New York: New Press, 1999).

12. Cowie, *Capital Moves*, p. 2.

13. María Patricia Fernández-Kelly and June Nash, eds., *Women, Men, and the International Division of Labor* (Albany: State University of New York Press, 1983).

14. The phrase "global cities" comes from Saskia Sassen. See Saskia Sassen, *The Global City: London, New York, Tokyo,* 2nd ed. (Princeton, NJ: Princeton University Press, 2001).

15. See Saskia Sassen, *The Mobility of Labor and Capital: A Study in International Investment and Labor Flow* (Cambridge: Cambridge University Press, 1990); and idem, *Losing Control? Sovereignty in the Age of Globalization* (New York: Columbia University Press, 1996).

16. See Diane Elson and Ruth Pearson, "'Nimble Fingers Make Cheap Workers': An Analysis of Women's Employment in Third World Export Manufacturing," *Feminist Review* 7 (spring 1981): pp. 87–107.

17. For a related discussion of the colonial discourses framing the "Third World woman," see Chandra Talpade Mohanty, "Women Workers and Capitalist Scripts: Ideologies of Domination, Common Interests, and the Politics of Solidarity," in *Feminist Genealogies, Colonial Legacies, Democratic Futures,* ed. M. Jacqui Alexander and C. T. Mohanty (New York: Routledge, 1997), pp. 3–30.

18. The classic example is Ester Boserup, *Women's Role in Economic Development* (New York: St. Martin's, 1970).

19. "World Program of Action for the Implementation of the Objectives of the UN Decade for Women," Report of the UN World Conference of the UN Decade for Women, A/Conf. 94/35 (New York: United Nations, 1980), available online at www.un.org; see also Irene Tinker and Jane Jaquette, "The UN Decade for Women: Its Impact and Legacy," *World Development* 15.3 (1987): pp. 419–27.

20. Boserup, *Women's Role in Economic Development.* Lourdes Benería and Gita Sen reassessed Boserup's work in their article "Accumulation, Reproduction, and Women's Roles in Economic Development: Boserup Revisited," *Signs* 7.2 (1991): pp. 279–98.

21. See, for instance, Diane Elson, *Male Bias in Development* (Manchester: Manchester University Press, 1991).

22. Arturo Escobar, *Encountering Development: The Making and Unmaking of the Third World* (Princeton, NJ: Princeton University Press, 1995), pp. 6, 9.

23. James Ferguson, *The Anti-Politics Machine: Development, Depoliticization, and Bureaucratic Power in Lesotho* (Minneapolis: University of Minnesota Press, 1994).

24. Chandra Talpade Mohanty, "Under Western Eyes: Feminist Scholarship and Colonialist Discourses," in *Third World Women and the Politics of Feminism,* ed. C. T. Mohanty, Ann Russo, and Lourdes Torres (Bloomington: Indiana University Press, 1987), p. 53.

25. Barbara Crossette, "The Second Sex in the Third World," *New York Times,* September 10, 1995, sec. 4, p. 1.

26. Elson and Pearson, "'Nimble Fingers Make Cheap Workers.'"

27. See María Patricia Fernández-Kelly, *For We Are Sold, I and My People* (Albany: State University of New York Press, 1983); Norma Iglesias Prieto, *La flor más bella de la maquiladora: Historias de vida de la mujer obrera en Tijuana, B.C.N.* (México DF: Consejo Nacional de Fomento Educativo, Collección Frontera, 1985); Aihwa Ong, *Spirits of Resistance and Capitalist Discipline: Factory Women in Malaysia* (Albany: State University of New York Press, 1987); Peña, *Terror of the Machine*; Leslie Salzinger, *Genders in Production: Making Workers in Mexico's Border Factories* (Berkeley: University of California Press, 2003); Susan Tiano, *Patriarchy on the Line: Labor, Gender, and Ideology in the Mexican Maquila Industry* (Philadelphia: Temple University Press, 1994); and Melissa W. Wright, *Disposable Women and Other Myths of Global Capitalism* (London: Routledge, 2006).

28. Elson and Pearson, "'Nimble Fingers Make Cheap Workers.'"

29. Iglesias Prieto, *La flor mas bella de la maquiladora*. For a more updated discussion of the maquiladora system, see Wright, *Disposable Women*.

30. Lorraine Gray, *The Global Assembly Line* (New York: New Day Films, 1983).

31. See Wright, *Disposable Women*.

32. Peña, *Terror of the Machine*, p. 80.

33. Keller Easterling, *Enduring Innocence: Global Architecture and Its Political Masquerades* (Cambridge, MA: MIT Press, 2005), p. 1.

34. This social geography is made vivid in the documentary film *Maquilapolis* (City of Factories), a project made in collaboration between Grupo Factor X, a feminist labor-advocacy organization in Tijuana, and filmmakers Vicky Funari and Sergio de la Torre. Grupo Factor X founded La Casa de la Mujer (The House for Women) in Tijuana in 1989, which operated as one of the first feminist organizations in Baja California. See Vicky Funari and Sergio de la Torre, *Maquilapolis* (ITVS, 2006).

35. Manuel Pastor and Carolyn Wise, "State Policy, Distribution, and Neoliberal Reform in Mexico," *Journal of Latin American Studies* 29 (1997): pp. 419–56.

36. Miguel de la Madrid Hurtado, *Primer informe de gobierno 1983: Que rinde ante an H. congreso de la Unión* (México DF: Presidencia de la República, 1983).

37. On the debt crisis and women's economic burdens, see Lourdes Arizpe, *Mujer y crisis: Respuestas ante la recesión* (México DF: Editorial Nueva Sociedad, 1990).

38. See the *Jornada sin Fronteras* website, http://www.jornadasinfronteras.com/ligder/maquilatitlan.htm.

39. Armando Bartra, "Los derechos del que migra y el derecho de no migrar," *La Jornada sin Fronteras*, December 3, 2002, www.jornadasinfronteras.com (accessed November 6, 2006).

40. Jesús Ramírez Cuevas, "Las hijas de maquitatitlán," *La Jornada sin Fronteras,* May 29, 2005, www.jornadasinfronteras.com (accessed November 6, 2006).

41. Sandra Arenal, *Sangre joven: Las maquiladoras por dentro* (México DF: Editorial Nuestro Tiempo, 1986); all translations are mine.

42. Fernando Carmona, preface to Arenal, *Sangre joven,* p. 10.

43. Arenal, *Sangre joven,* p. 11.

44. In the context of performance, Coco Fusco has explored a similarly disembodied subjectivity, that of black subjects in artistic production. See her collection *The Bodies That Were Not Ours and Other Writings* (New York: Routledge, 2001); Fusco refers to artistic appropriations of black bodies.

45. Michel Foucault, *Discipline and Punish: The Birth of the Prison* (New York: Vintage Books, 1995), p. 26. Foucault refers to a process of subjection that corresponds not only to operations of direct violence or ideology but to more diffuse effects of a network of "apparatuses and institutions" that produce relations of domination.

46. Arenal, *Sangre joven,* p. 66.

47. Ibid., pp. 31–32.

48. Ibid., p. 33.

49. See Peña, *Terror of the Machine,* chap. 1.

50. Henry Ford, *My Life and Work* (1922), quoted in ibid., p. 3.

51. Elaine Scarry, *The Body in Pain: The Making and Unmaking of the World* (New York: Oxford University Press, 1987), p. 11.

52. Donna Haraway, "A Manifesto for Cyborgs: Science, Technology, and Socialist Feminism in the 1980's," in *Feminism/Postmodernism,* ed. Linda J. Nicholson (New York: Routledge, 1990), p. 222.

53. Ibid., p. 216. The version I am working from is a revision of her 1983 essay. The text has generated considerable scholarship and debate, which lies beyond the scope of this chapter. Chela Sandoval adopted the figure of the cyborg in her own theoretical analysis of emancipatory politics and the subjectivity of the Third World/woman of color. See her influential essay "U.S. Third World Feminism: The Theory and Method of Oppositional Consciousness in the Postmodern Worlds," *Genders* 10 (spring 1991): pp. 1–24.

54. Sandoval, "U.S. Third World Feminism."

55. See my discussion in Alicia Schmidt Camacho, "Migrant Subjects: Race, Labor, and Insurgency in the Mexico-U.S. Borderlands" (Ph.D. diss., Stanford University, 2000).

56. Haraway, "Manifesto for Cyborgs," pp. 216 and 203.

57. Ibid., p. 200.

58. Gloria Anzaldúa, *Borderlands/La Frontera: The New Mestiza* (San Francisco: Aunt Lute, 1987).

59. Norma Alarcón offers this modest recollection of founding the press: "there weren't enough other women of color or Latinas for me to have a conversation with." See "Third Woman Press," California Feminist Presses Collection website, http://www.lib.berkeley.edu/doemoff/womstu/fempress/thirdwoman.html.

60. Sonia Saldívar-Hull, "Feminism on the Border: From Gender Politics to Geopolitics," in *Criticism in the Borderlands: Studies in Chicano Literature*, ed. Hector Calderón and José David Saldívar (Durham, NC: Duke University Press, 1991), p. 208.

61. Norma Alarcón, "Chicana Feminism: In the Tracks of 'the' Native Woman," *Cultural Studies* 4.3 (1990): p. 250.

62. Anzaldúa, *Borderlands/La frontera*, p. 194.

63. Yvonne Yarbro-Bejarano, "Deconstructing the Lesbian Body: Cherríe Moraga's *Loving in the War Years*," in *Chicana Lesbians: The Girls Our Mothers Warned Us About*, ed. Carla Trujillo (Berkeley: Third Woman, 1991), p. 143.

64. Anzaldúa, *Borderlands/La frontera*, p. 194.

65. The key texts of feminist and queer critiques by scholars of color include the following anthologies: Gloria T. Hull, Patricia Bell Scott, and Barbara Smith, eds., *All the Women Are White, All the Blacks Are Men, but Some of Us Are Brave: Black Women's Studies* (New York: Feminist Press, 1981); Gloria Anzaldúa and Cherríe Moraga, *This Bridge Called My Back: Writing by Radical Women of Color* (New York: Kitchen Table, 1983); Barbara Smith, *Home Girls: A Black Feminist Anthology* (New York: Kitchen Table, 1983); and Mohanty, Russo, and Torres, *Third World Women and the Politics of Feminism*.

66. Norma Alarcón, "Cognitive Desires: An Allegory of/for Chicana Critics," in *Listening to Silences: New Essays in Feminist Criticism*, ed. Elaine Hedges and Shelley Fisher Fishkin (New York: Oxford University Press, 1994), p. 261.

67. Ibid., p. 270.

68. See my discussion in Alicia Schmidt Camacho, "Ciudadana X: Gender Violence and the Denationalization of Women's Rights in Ciudad Juárez, Mexico," *New Centennial Review: Interdisciplinary Perspectives on the Americas* 6.1 (2005): pp. 255–92.

69. See Wayne A. Cornelius, "Death at the Border: Efficacy and Unintended Consequences of US Immigration Control Policy," *Population and Development Review* 27.4 (2001): pp. 661–85.

70. Julia Monárrez Fregoso, a scholar at the Colegio de la Frontera Norte in Ciudad Juárez, has been the leading scholar on the Chihuahuan feminicide. See

her essay, "Feminicidio sexual serial en Ciudad Juárez, 1993–2001," *Debate feminista* 13.25 (April 2002). Statistical information on the feminicidio comes from Justicia Para Nuestras Hijas, available online at www.espanol.geocities.com/justhijas/.

71. The term "necropolitical" comes from Achille Mbembe and references a state of social polarization and antagonism in which "the political, under the guise of war, or resistance, or of the fight against terror, makes the murder of the enemy its primary and absolute objective." Achille Mbembe, "Necropolitics," *Public Culture* 15.1 (2003): p. 24, quoted in Rosa Linda Fregoso, "'We Want them Alive!': The Politics and Culture of Human Rights," *Social Identities* 12.2 (March 2006): pp. 109–38. See also Lisa Lowe, "The Gender of Sovereignty," forthcoming in *The Scholar and the Feminist* (www.barnard.edu/sfonline/).

72. Anzaldúa, *Borderlands/La frontera*, p. 25.

73. Marisela Norte, "Act of the Faithless," *Norte/Word* (Lawndale, CA: New Alliance Record Company, 1991). I have transcribed the piece from the compact-disc recording, so the line breaks and form reflect my own experience of the piece. All subsequent quotations from the poem are from my transcriptions of the CD.

74. Norte, *Norte/Word*. Michelle Habell-Pallán discusses Norte's performances in her marvelous book, *Loca Motion: The Travels of Chicana and Latina Popular Culture* (New York: NYU Press, 2005).

75. Rosario Sanmiguel, "Las hilanderas," in *Callejón Sucre y otros relatos* (Chihuahua, Mexico: Ediciones del Azar, 1994), pp. 41–46. I am indebted to the author, as well as to Dra. María Soccorro Tabuenca Córdoba, in my discussion of the story. For more on Sanmiguel, consult Debra Castillo and María Soccorro Tabuenca Córdoba, *Border Women: Writing from La Frontera* (Minneapolis: University of Minnesota Press, 2002); see also María Soccorro Tabuenca Córdoba, "The Rearticulation of the Border Territory in the Stories of Rosario Sanmiguel," in *Ethnography at the Border*, ed. Pablo Vila (Minneapolis: University of Minnesota Press, 2003), pp. 279–305.

76. Castillo and Tabuenca Córdoba, *Border Women*, p. 39.

77. Asked to describe her use of poetic form, Norte has answered that the length of her poem reflects the duration of her route on the Number 18 bus through her neighborhood. She both writes for, and writes among, her fellow travelers. See Marisela Norte, "Best MTA Bus Line: The Number 18, Yes, Let's Take a Trip down Whittier Boulevard," in *Los Angeles and the Future of Urban Cultures*, ed. Raúl Homero Villa and George J. Sánchez, special issue of the *American Quarterly* 56.3 (September 2004): pp. 507–10.

78. "Con safos" is a slang expression used in graffiti. Its literal meaning is "with safety," and it functions as an admonition that the author's writing is pro-

tected and demands respect. See José Antonio Burciaga, *Drink Cultura: Chican-ismo* (Santa Barbara, CA: Joshua Odell Editions, 1993).

79. Ramón Saldívar, *Chicano Narrative: The Dialectics of Difference* (Madison: University of Wisconsin Press, 1990), p. 190.

80. This concept of the border appears in Gloria Anzaldúa, *Borderlands/La frontera*, and Sonia Saldívar-Hull, *Feminism on the Border: Chicana Gender Politics and Literature* (Berkeley: University of California Press, 2000). See also Norma Alarcón, "The Theoretical Subject(s) of *This Bridge Called My Back* and Anglo-American Feminism," in Calderón and Saldívar, *Criticism in the Borderlands*, pp. 28–39.

81. Emma Pérez, "Sexuality and Discourse: Notes from a Chicana Survivor," in Trujillo, *Chicana Lesbians*, pp. 159–84. Pérez's phrase "sitio y lengua" means "place and language/tongue."

82. Michelle Habell-Pallán, "No Cultural Icon: Marisela Norte," in *Women Transforming Politics: An Alternative Reader*, ed. Cathy J. Cohen, Kathleen B. Jones, and Joan C. Tronto (New York: NYU Press, 1997), p. 263.

83. The phrase comes from Castillo and Tabuenca Córdoba, *Border Women*, p. 64.

84. See Tabuenca Córdoba, "Rearticulation of the Border Territory."

85. Ibid., p. 284; emphasis in original.

86. Sanmiguel, "Las hilanderas," pp. 41–46.

87. Ibid., p. 41; all translations of the story are mine.

88. Ibid., p. 42.

89. Ibid.

90. Ibid., p. 43.

91. Yolanda López, "Grandmother: Victoria F. Franco," in *Yolanda López: Three Generations* (San Diego: Mandeville Center for the Arts, San Diego State University, 1978).

92. Sanmiguel, "Las hilanderas," p. 43.

93. Ibid., p. 44.

94. Ibid.

95. Ibid., p. 45.

96. Ibid.

97. Jacques Lacan, "The Mirror Stage" (1949), in *Identity: A Reader*, ed. Paul du Gay, Jessica Evans, and Peter Redman (London: Sage, 2000), pp. 44–50.

98. Sanmiguel, "Las hilanderas," p. 45.

99. Ibid., p. 46.

100. Rolando Romero, "Postdeconstructive Spaces," *Siglo XX/Twentieth Century II* (1993): pp. 225–33, quoted in Castillo and Tabuenca Córdoba, *Border Women*, p. 15.

NOTES TO CHAPTER 7

1. Michael Hardt and Antonio Negri, *Empire* (Cambridge, MA: Harvard University Press, 2000), p. 210.

2. Padre Ademar Barilli, quoted in the United States Conference of Catholic Bishops, Migration and Refugee Services, "Central American Church Leaders Want Humane Immigration Policies," Catholic News Services, 2006, www.catholicnews.com (accessed October 28, 2006).

3. *Retablo of Concepción Zapata*, in Jorge Durand and Douglas S. Massey, *Miracles on the Border: Retablos of Mexican Migrants to the United States* (Tucson: University of Arizona Press, 1995), pp. 138–39.

4. Ibid.

5. Ibid., 138.

6. Refer to Sylvanna M. Falcón, "Rape as a Weapon of War: Advancing Human Rights for Women at the U.S.-Mexico Border," *Social Justice* 28.2 (2001): pp. 31–50.

7. On this loss, see also Jean Franco, *Decline and Fall of the Lettered City: Latin America in the Cold War* (Cambridge, MA: Harvard University Press, 2002).

8. Douglas S. Massey, "When Less Is More: Border Enforcement and Undocumented Migration," *Testimony Before the Subcommittee on Immigration, Citizenship, Refugees, Border Security, and International Law*, Committee on the Judiciary, U.S. House of Representatives (Washington, DC, April 20, 2007).

9. Barilli, quoted in U.S. Conference of Catholic Bishops, "Central American Church Leaders."

10. See Daniel D. Arreola and James R. Curtis, "Cultural Landscapes of the Mexican Border Cities," *Aztlán* 21.1–2 (1992–1996): pp. 1–48.

11. In fact, many of those stranded or deported are children. María Eugenia Hernández Sánchez, "Deported Children in Ciudad Juárez," paper presented at the Center for Latin American and Iberian Studies, Yale University, New Haven, Connecticut, October 12, 2005.

12. Douglas S. Massey, Jorge Durand, and Emilio Parrado, "The New Era of Mexican Migration to the United States," *Journal of American History* 86.2 (September 1999): pp. 518–636.

13. See, for instance, Jorge Durand and Patricia Arias, *Experiencia migrante: Iconografía de la migración México-Estados Unidos* (Mexico DF: Altexto, 2000); and María Herrera Sobek, *Northward Bound: The Mexican Immigrant Experience in Ballad and Song* (Bloomington: Indiana University Press, 1993).

14. Matthew Jacobson elaborates on the concept of migrant sorrows in *Special Sorrows: The Diasporic Imagination of Irish, Polish, and Jewish Immigrants in*

the United States (Berkeley: University of California Press, 2002). His work offers a vital reminder that the repudiation of "new migrants" (and their languages) has been a prominent feature of U.S. national formation in every phase of mass immigration.

15. "Preamble," North American Free Trade Agreement, October 7, 1992.

16. For a view of NAFTA through the lens of U.S.-Mexican relations, see Jorge I. Domínguez and Rafael Fernández de Castro, *United States and Mexico: Between Partnership and Conflict* (London: Routledge, 2001). On the broader corporate, union, and government forces shaping the trade agreement, see Michael Dreiling, *Solidarity and Contention: The Politics of Security and Sustainability in the NAFTA Conflict* (New York: Taylor and Francis, 2000).

17. For essays on the general effects of neoliberal policies on labor in Latin America, see Sebastian Edwards and Nora Lustig, eds., *Labor Markets in Latin America: Combining Social Protection with Market Flexibility* (Washington, DC: Brookings Institution Press, 1997). A far more vivid picture of the suppression of labor power in the era of NAFTA appears in the works of David Bacon. See *The Children of NAFTA: Labor Wars on the U.S./Mexico Border* (Berkeley: University of California Press, 2004); and *Communities without Borders: Images and Voices from the World of Migration* (Ithaca, NY: ILR Press/Cornell University Press, 2006).

18. Joseph Nevins, *Operation Gatekeeper: The Rise of the "Illegal Alien" and the Making of the U.S.-Mexico Boundary* (London: Routledge, 2002), p. 2.

19. See Leo R. Chavez, *Covering Immigration: Popular Images and the Politics of the Nation* (Berkeley: University of California Press, 2001).

20. Office of the Inspector General, "Operation Gatekeeper: An Investigation into Allegations of Fraud and Misconduct" (July 1998), available online at www.usdoj.gov/oig/special/9807/gkp01.htm (accessed October 28, 2006).

21. Jeffrey S. Passel, "Estimates of the Size and Characteristics of the Undocumented Population," Pew Hispanic Center, Washington, DC, March 3, 2006.

22. Luis Alberto Urrea, *The Devil's Highway: A True Story* (New York: Little, Brown, 2004).

23. This figure comes from Amnesty International, "United States of America: Human Rights Concerns in the Border Region with Mexico," May 20, 1998. Further details are available in statistics compiled by the Mexican Foreign Relations Office for the past decade. The figure is corroborated by various nongovernmental agencies, including the California Rural Legal Assistance Foundation of El Centro, California, crla.org.

24. Roberto Martínez, "Tenth Anniversary of Operation Gatekeeper: Ni Una Muerte Más," address delivered at the University of San Diego Forum on Operation Gatekeeper, October 2, 2004.

25. Miguel Escobar Valdez, Consul for Mexico at Douglas, Arizona, interview by the author, Tempe, Arizona, April 9, 2004. For an illustration of consular functions related to the disappearance of Mexican migrants, see the website for the Mexican Consulate of New York, www.consulmexny.org/esp/proteccion_tabla_desaparecidos.htm (accessed November 20, 2005).

26. Documentation of this shift in migration and settlement patterns appears in Douglas S. Massey and Jorge Durand, eds., *Crossing the Border: Research from the Mexican Migration Project* (New York: Russell Sage, 2004). On the forms of transnational community in this period, see Robert Courtney Smith, *Mexican New York: Transnational Lives of New Immigrants* (Berkeley: University of California Press, 2006).

27. See Massey and Durand, *Crossing the Border*.

28. Office of the Inspector General, "Operation Gatekeeper: An Investigation into Allegations of Fraud and Misconduct," July 1998, available online at www.usdoj.gov/oig/special/9807/gkp01.htm (accessed October 28, 2006).

29. Martínez, "Tenth Anniversary of Operation Gatekeeper."

30. Nevins, *Operation Gatekeeper*, p. 2.

31. Abel Valenzuela Jr., Nik Theodore, Edwin Meléndez, and Ana Luz González, "On the Corner: Day Labor in the United States," UCLA Center for the Study of Urban Poverty, January 2006, p. i.

32. Ibid., p. ii.

33. Jeffrey Passell, Randolph Capps, and Michael E. Fix, "Undocumented Immigrants: Facts and Figures," Urban Institute, May 12, 2004, available online at http://www.urban.org/url.cfm?ID=1000587.

34. Catherine L. Fisk and Michael J. Wishnie, "The Story of Hoffman Plastic Compounds, Inc. v. NLRB: Labor Rights without Remedies for Undocumented Immigrants," in *Labor Law Stories*, ed. Laura J. Cooper and Catherine L. Fisk (New York: Foundation, 2005).

35. Michael J. Wishnie, "Immigrants and the Right to Petition," *New York University Law Review* 78.2 (2003): p. 669.

36. For a representative treatment of Cunningham's vigilante activism, see Pamela Colloff, "The Battle for the Border," *Texas Monthly* (April 2001), available online at www.texasmonthly.com (accessed December 15, 2007). Here the metaphors of war depict the armed ranchers and unarmed migrants as equal combatants squared off the in the border space.

37. John González, "Rancher Convicted in Immigrant's Death," *Houston Chronicle*, August 25, 2001, A33.

38. Statement by George W. Bush recorded on October 29, 2001, at a White House press event to announce "Increasing Immigration Safeguard." Transcript

available online at www.whitehouse.gov/news/releases/2001/10/20011029-15.html, "Remarks by the President in Photo Opportunity with Homeland Security Council." See Mark Danner, *The Secret War: The Downing Street Memo and the Iraq's War Buried History* (New York: New York Review of Books, 2006).

39. Oliver North, "America's Back Door to Terror," *www.TownHall.com*, October 23, 2006, www.townhall.com/columnists/OliverNorth/2006/10/20/back_door_to_terror.

40. Susan Carroll and Daniel González, "Napolitano Taps Disaster Funds for Southern Counties," *Arizona Republic*, August 15, 2005, www.azcentral.com/arizona republic/news/articles/0816borderemergency16.html.

41. Peter Baker, "Bush Set to Send Guard to Border," *Washington Post*, May 15, 2006, A1.

42. Budget shortfalls have hampered the implementation of this program.

43. Americas Watch, "Frontier Injustice: Human Rights Abuses along the Border with Mexico Persist amid Climate of Impunity," May 1993, available online at http://www.hrw.org. See also Jorge A. Vargas, "U.S. Border Patrol Abuses, Undocumented Mexican Workers, and International Human Rights," *San Diego International Law Journal* 2 (2001): 1.

44. See, for example, the case *Leiva v. Ranch Rescue*, filed June 26, 2003. The plaintiffs, Fatima del Socorro Leiva Medina and Edwin Alfredo Mancia González, were awarded a settlement of close to $1.5 million in damages from the Ranch Rescue of Texas. They were part of a group of undocumented Salvadorans illegally detained by the ranchers on March 18, 2003. The case was successfully prosecuted by the Mexican American Legal Defense and Education Fund (MALDEF) and the Southern Poverty Law Center. See http://www.splcenter.org/.

45. Richard L. Skinner, Semiannual Report to the Congress, April 1–September 30, 2006, Department of Homeland Security, Office of the Inspector General, October 31, 2006, available online at http://dgs.gov.

46. Greg Grandin, "Empire's Workshop: Latin America, the United States, and the Rise of the New Imperialism," an interview with Amy Goodman and Juan González, *Democracy Now*, Pacifica Radio, May 11, 2006.

47. Ibid.

48. Instituto Nacional de Inmigración, "Estadísticas Migratorias," www.inami.org (accessed October 28, 2006).

49. Manuel Orozco, "Transnacionalismo y Desarrollo en Centroamérica," Inter-American Development Bank, October 2006, available online at www.iadb.org (accessed October 28, 2006).

50. Barilli, quoted in U.S. Conference of Catholic Bishops, "Central American Church Leaders."

51. For data on the migrants' use of coyotes or polleros, see Jorge Durand and Douglas S. Massey, "What We Learned from the Mexican Migration Project," in Durand and Massey, *Crossing the Border*, 1–14. On human traffic, see Peter Andreas, "The Transformation of Migrant Smuggling across the U.S.-Mexican Border," in *Global Human Smuggling: Comparative Perspectives*, ed. David Kyle and Rey Koslowski (Baltimore: Johns Hopkins University Press, 2001), pp. 107–28. See also John Bailey and Jorge Chabat, eds., *Transnational Crime and Public Security: Challenges to Mexico and the United States* (La Jolla, CA: Center for US-Mexican Studies, University of California at San Diego, 2002).

52. Quoted in U.S. Conference of Catholic Bishops, "Central American Church Leaders."

53. See related works by the anthropologist Jonathan Xavier Inda: "Biopower, Reproduction, and the Migrant Woman's Body," in *Decolonial Voices: Chicana and Chicano Cultural Studies in the 21st Century*, ed. Arturo J. Aldama and Naomi Quiñonez (Bloomington: Indiana University Press, 2002), pp. 98–112; and "Foreign Bodies: Migrants, Parasites, and the Pathological Nation," *Discourse: Journal for Theoretical Studies in Media and Culture* 22.3 (2000): pp. 46–62.

54. Durand and Massey, "What We Learned," p. 13.

55. Ibid., p. 12.

56. Sigmund Freud, "Mourning and Melancholia" (1917), in *The Freud Reader*, ed. Peter Gay (New York: Norton, 1989), pp. 584–88.

57. See Judith Butler, *The Psychic Life of Power: Theories in Subjection* (Palo Alto, CA: Stanford University Press, 1997); David Eng and David Kazanjian, eds., *Loss: The Politics of Mourning* (Berkeley: University of California Press, 2002); and Ann Anlin Cheng, *The Melancholy of Race: Psychoanalysis, Assimilation, and Hidden Grief* (New York: Oxford University Press, 2001).

58. Ari Luis Palos, *Beyond the Border/Más Allá de la Frontera* (Kentucky: Dos Vatos Productions, 2001). Quotations are my translations and transcriptions.

59. Details of the case appear in Mary E. O'Leary, "Scam Cost Illegal Aliens $150G," *New Haven Register*, January 6, 2006, pp. A1, A4.

60. El Asociación Tepeyac de Nueva York, "Missing but Not Counted," November 2002, compiled in September 11 digital archive, http://911digitalarchive.org/collections/asntepeyac (accessed November 15, 2002).

61. Ibid.

62. See press communications of the Secretaría de Relaciones Exteriores—México, http://sre.gob.mx (accessed January 5, 2006).

63. See Roberto Suro, "Remittance Senders and Receivers: Tracking the Transnational Channels," Pew Hispanic Center report, written in partnership with the Multilateral Investment Fund, Washington DC, November 24, 2003, available

online at http://www.pewhispanic.org/page.jsp?page=reports (accessed November 15, 2005).

64. Smith, *Mexican New York*.

65. Durand and Massey, *Crossing the Border*.

66. Jeffrey S. Passel, "Unauthorized Migrants: Numbers and Characteristics," Pew Hispanic Center Project report, Washington, DC, June 14, 2005, available online at www.pewhispanic.org (accessed November 2, 2005).

67. Durand and Massey, "What We Learned," p. 10.

68. See especially Smith, *Mexican New York*; Roger Rouse, "Mexican Migration to the U.S.: Family Relations in a Transnational Migrant Circuit" (Ph.D. diss., Stanford University, 1989); and Luin Goldring, "Diversity and Community in Transnational Migration: A Comparative Study of Two Mexican U.S. Migrant Communities" (Ph.D. diss., Cornell University, 1992).

69. Carrie Kahn and Lourdes García Navarro, "Immigrants Run Scholarship Program for Mexicans," *Morning Edition*, National Public Radio, January 6, 2006; see npr.org.

70. The term "postnational" describes the exercise of political agency outside the migrant's country of origin. The term also references a range of loyalties, social networks, or political claims that extend beyond the boundaries of national citizenship. See Linda Basch, Nina Glick Schiller, and Cristina Szanton Blanc, *Nations Unbound: Transnational Projects, Postcolonial Predicaments, and Deterritorialized Nation-States* (Langhorne, UK: Gordon and Breach, 1994); Linda Bosniak, "The State of Citizenship: Citizenship Denationalized," *Indiana Journal of Legal Studies* 7.2 (2000): pp. 447–510; Saskia Sassen, "The Repositioning of Citizenship: Emergent Subjects and Spaces for Politics," *CR: The New Centennial Review* 3.2 (summer 2003): pp. 41–66; and Yasemin Nuhoólu Soysal, *Limits of Citizenship: Migrants and Postnational Membership in Europe* (Chicago: University of Chicago Press, 1994).

71. Luis Ernesto Derbez, Minister of Foreign Affairs for Mexico, "Managing Global Migrations: A Mexican Perspective," keynote address delivered at the conference "Rethinking Global Migration: New Realities, New Opportunities, New Challenges," New York University, May 25, 2005, audio available online at http://steinhardt.nyu.edu/igems/CONFERENCE/program.html.

72. Jorge Santibañez, remarks at "Rethinking Global Migration" conference, New York University, May 25, 2005, audio available online at http://steinhardt.nyu/edu/igems/CONFERENCE/program.html.

73. *El alma herida* [The Wounded Soul] was a co-production of Telemundo and Argos in Mexico. The program completed shooting in 2003 and aired in the United States throughout 2004.

74. Organic Broadcast Project, http://broadcast.organicframework.com (accessed November 18, 2005).

75. My translation. Story synopsis and cast information available at http://tdmnovelas.tripod.com/elalmaherida/ (accessed November 18, 2005).

76. "Protección a Mexicanos," Consulado General de México, www.consulmexny.org/esp/proteccion_migratorios.htm (accessed November 12, 2005).

77. Gobierno del Estado de Yucatán, *Guia del Migrante Yucateco* (Yucatán, 2004), p. 32.

78. The United States instituted an official Border Patrol unit in 1924. C. Roberto Gaytan Saucedo, interview by author, Ciudad Juárez, November 13, 2003.

79. Claudia Smith, quoted in "Rapes on the US-Mexico Border Up," United Press International, March 18, 2005. Smith argues that given the low rates of reporting crime, the actual number of rapes may be much higher.

80. Gobierno del Estado Yucatán, *Guía del Migrante Yucateco,* p. 79.

81. "Protección a Mexicanos."

82. Ibid.

83. See chapter 6.

84. See my discussion of the feminicidio in Alicia Schmidt Camacho, "Body Counts on the Mexico-US Border: Feminicidio, Reification, and the Theft of Mexicana Subjectivity," *Chicana/Latina Studies* 4.1 (2004): pp. 22–60; and idem, "Ciudadana X: Gender Violence and the Denationalization of Women's Rights in Ciudad Juárez, Mexico," in *New Centennial Review: Interdisciplinary Perspectives on the Americas* 6.1 (2005): pp. 255–92.

NOTES TO THE AFTERWORD

1. Walter Benjamin, "Theses on the Philosophy of History" (1950), in *Illuminations*, ed. and introd. Hannah Arendt (New York: Schocken Books, 1968), pp. 257–58.

2. Alma López, *Santa Niña de Mochis* (1998), on view at www.almalopez.net.

INDEX

ABOUT THE AUTHOR

Alicia Schmidt Camacho is the Sarai Ribicoff Associate Professor of American Studies and Ethnicity, Race and Migration at Yale University. Her scholarship addresses migration, labor, gender violence, and culture in the Mexico-U.S. border region and the broader Americas. She is a contributor to Connecticut and binational initiatives devoted to immigrant and human rights.